Microsoft Sentinel in Action

Second Edition

Architect, design, implement, and operate Microsoft Sentinel as the core of your security solutions

Richard Diver

Gary Bushey

John Perkins

BIRMINGHAM—MUMBAI

Microsoft Sentinel in Action
Second Edition
Copyright © 2022 Packt Publishing

All rights reserved. No part of this book may be reproduced, stored in a retrieval system, or transmitted in any form or by any means, without the prior written permission of the publisher, except in the case of brief quotations embedded in critical articles or reviews.

Every effort has been made in the preparation of this book to ensure the accuracy of the information presented. However, the information contained in this book is sold without warranty, either express or implied. Neither the authors, nor Packt Publishing or its dealers and distributors, will be held liable for any damages caused or alleged to have been caused directly or indirectly by this book.

Packt Publishing has endeavored to provide trademark information about all the companies and products mentioned in this book by the appropriate use of capitals. However, Packt Publishing cannot guarantee the accuracy of this information.

Group Product Manager: Vijin Boricha
Publishing Product Manager: Meeta Rajani
Senior Editor: Arun Nadar
Content Development Editor: Sulagna Mohanty
Technical Editor: Arjun Varma
Copy Editor: Safis Editing
Project Coordinator: Shagun Saini
Proofreader: Safis Editing
Indexer: Vinayak Purushotham
Production Designer: Vijay Kamble

First published: May 2020

Second edition: January 2022

Production reference: 1021221

Published by Packt Publishing Ltd.
Livery Place
35 Livery Street
Birmingham
B3 2PB, UK.

ISBN 978-1-80181-553-6

www.packt.com

Contributors

About the authors

Richard Diver is a senior technical business strategy manager for the Microsoft Security Solutions group, focused on developing security partners. Based in Chicago, Richard works with advanced security and compliance partners to help them build solutions across the entire Microsoft platform, including Microsoft Sentinel, Microsoft Defender, Microsoft 365 security solutions, and many more. Prior to Microsoft, Richard worked in multiple industries and for several Microsoft partners to architect and implement cloud security solutions for a wide variety of customers around the world. Any spare time he gets is usually spent with his family.

Gary Bushey is an Azure security expert with over 25 years of IT experience. He got his start early on when he helped his fifth-grade math teacher with their programming homework and worked all one summer to be able to afford his first computer, a Commodore 64. When he sold his first program, an apartment management system, at 14 he was hooked. During his career, he has worked as a developer, consultant, trainer, and architect. When not spending time in front of a computer, you can find him hiking in the woods, taking pictures, or just picking a direction and finding out what is around the next corner.

John Perkins is the founder and principal of Threat Angler, a cybersecurity service provider that specializes in managed services, professional services, and training with a focus on delivering cybersecurity outcomes to customers of all shapes and sizes. John has over 20 years of experience in cybersecurity and has contributed to nearly all cybersecurity disciplines during his career. He has experience with numerous applications, including Microsoft Sentinel, and has designed, built, and led managed security services for several large service providers. In his free time, John enjoys spending time with his family, traveling, and staying active.

About the reviewers

Ashwin Patil currently works as a senior program manager for **Microsoft Threat Intelligence Center (MSTIC)** and has over 10 years' experience entirely focused on security monitoring and incident response, defending enterprise networks. In his current role, he primarily works on threat hunting, detection research in **Kusto Query Language (KQL)** for Microsoft Sentinel, and developing Jupyter notebooks written in Python/R to do threat hunting and investigation across a variety of cloud and on-premises security event log data sources. He has a bachelor's degree in computer engineering and possesses various SANS certifications, including GCIA, GCFE, and GCIH in the field of **Digital Forensics and Incident Response (DFIR)**.

Dennis Pike is the original sales engineer at Island, a stealth mode security startup. He would tell you more, but they may put him on an island with nothing but a volleyball. Born in Kentucky, he surprisingly can't stand bourbon and ended up a nationally ranked beer judge instead. He holds a BSc in systems engineering from the University of Virginia and has spent the last 25 years working in IT, including as a Global Black Belt – Advanced Security Analytics at Microsoft where he focused on Microsoft Sentinel.

> *I want to thank my wife, Heather, for her patience, love, and support.*

Rod Trent is a senior cloud security advocate for Microsoft and an Microsoft Sentinel global SME helping customers migrate from existing SIEMs to Microsoft Sentinel to achieve the promise of better security through improved efficiency without compromise. He is a husband, dad, and first-time grandfather (so speak slowly and loudly). He spends his spare time (if such a thing does truly exist) simultaneously watching Six Million Dollar Man episodes and writing KQL queries.

Table of Contents

Preface

Section 1: Design and Implementation

1
Getting Started with Microsoft Sentinel

The current cloud security landscape	4	Private infrastructure integrations	20
The cloud security reference framework	5	Service pricing for Microsoft Sentinel	20
SOC platform components	8	Scenario mapping	24
Mapping the SOC architecture	10	Step 1 – defining the new scenarios	24
Log management and data sources	10	Step 2 – explaining the purpose	25
Operations platforms	11	Step 3 – the kill chain stage	25
Threat intelligence and threat hunting	14	Step 4 – which solution will perform detection?	26
SOC mapping summary	14	Step 5 – what actions will occur instantly?	27
Security solution integrations	15	Step 6 – severity and output	27
Cloud platform integrations	16	Step 7 – what action should the analyst take?	27
Integrating with Amazon Web Services (AWS)	17	Summary	29
Integrating with Google Cloud Platform (GCP)	17	Questions	29
Integrating with Microsoft Azure	18	Further reading	30

2

Azure Monitor – Introduction to Log Analytics

Technical requirements	32	The summary bar	53
Introduction to Azure		The Events and alerts over time section	53
Monitor Log Analytics	32	The Recent incidents section	53
Planning a workspace	36	The Data source anomalies section	53
		The Potential malicious events section	53
Creating a workspace using the portal	37	The Democratize ML for your SecOps section	53
Creating a workspace using PowerShell or the CLI	39	Connecting your first data source	54
Creating an Azure Resource Management template	39	Obtaining information from Azure virtual machines	54
Using PowerShell	42		
Using the CLI	43	Advanced settings for Log Analytics	58
Exploring the Overview page	46	Agents management	59
Managing permissions for the workspace	47	The Agents configuration options	60
		Computer Groups	61
Enabling Microsoft Sentinel	49		
Exploring the Microsoft		Summary	65
Sentinel Overview page	52	Questions	65
The header bar	52	Further reading	66

Section 2: Data Connectors, Management, and Queries

3

Managing and Collecting Data

Choosing data that matters	70	Configuring Microsoft Sentinel connectors	77
Understanding connectors	73		
Native connections – service to service	74	Configuring Log Analytics storage options	83
Direct connections – service to service	74		
API connections	75	Calculating the cost of data ingestion and retention	85
Agent-based	75		

Reviewing alternative storage options	87	Questions	89
Summary	89	Further reading	89

4
Integrating Threat Intelligence with Microsoft Sentinel

Introduction to TI	92	Configuring the MineMeld TI feed	104
Understanding STIX and TAXII	94	Confirming the data is being ingested for use by Microsoft Sentinel	113
Choosing the right intel feeds for your needs	95	Summary	116
Implementing TI connectors	96	Questions	116
Enabling the data connector	96	Further reading	116
Registering an app in Azure AD	98		

5
Using the Kusto Query Language (KQL)

Running KQL queries	118	The ago() function	140
Introduction to KQL commands	120	String operators	140
Tabular operators	122	Summary	142
Query statements	139	Questions	142
The let statement	139	Further reading	142
Scalar functions	140		

6
Microsoft Sentinel Logs and Writing Queries

An introduction to the Microsoft Sentinel Logs page	144	The Queries pane	159
		The Functions pane	159
Navigating through the Logs page	144	The Filter pane	160
		The KQL code window	164
The page header	145	Running a query	168
The Tables pane	155	The Results window	168
		Learn more	176

Table of Contents

Writing a query	176	Summary	180
The billable data ingested	177	Questions	181
Map view of logins	178	Further reading	181
Other useful tables	179		

Section 3: Security Threat Hunting

7
Creating Analytic Rules

An introduction to Microsoft Sentinel Analytics	185	Creating a new rule using the wizard	198
Types of analytic rules	186	Managing analytic rules	218
Navigating through the Analytics home page	188	Summary	219
		Questions	220
Creating an analytic rule	197	Further reading	220
Creating a rule from a rule template	197		

8
Creating and Using Workbooks

An overview of the Workbooks page	222	Managing workbooks	239
		Workbook step types	241
The workbook header	223	Text	242
The Templates view	224	Query	243
Workbook detail view	225	Metric	247
Missing required data types	225	Parameters	248
Saved template buttons	226	Links/tabs	254
Walking through an existing workbook	228	Groups	258
		Advanced Settings	260
		Style	264
Creating workbooks	230		
Creating a workbook using a template	231	Summary	265
Creating a new workbook from scratch	232	Questions	265
		Further reading	266
Editing a workbook	234		
Advanced editing	237		

9
Incident Management

Using the Microsoft Sentinel Incidents page	**268**	The Entities tab	285
		The Comments tab	286
The header bar	268	**Investigating an incident**	**287**
The summary bar	269	Showing related alerts	288
The search and filtering section	269	The Timeline button	291
Incident listing	271	The Info button	292
Incident details pane	273	The Entities button	292
Using the Actions button	279	The Insights button	293
Exploring the full details page	**281**	The Help button	293
The Timeline tab	282	**Summary**	**294**
The Alerts tab	283	**Questions**	**294**
The Bookmarks tab	284	**Further reading**	**294**

10
Configuring and Using Entity Behavior

Introduction to Microsoft Sentinel Entity behavior	**298**	Insights	307
Enabling Entity behavior	**298**	**Creating Entity behavior queries**	**307**
Overview of the Entity behavior page	**300**	Header bar	308
		Activities list	309
The header bar	301	Activity details pane	310
The search section	301	Adding a new activity	311
Entities with alerts	302	**Summary**	**317**
Overview of the Entity behavior details page	**303**	**Questions**	**317**
		Further reading	**317**
Identifying information	303		
Notable events	304		

11
Threat Hunting in Microsoft Sentinel

Introducing the Microsoft Sentinel Hunting page	**320**	Associating a bookmark with an incident	339
The header bar	321	**Using Microsoft Sentinel notebooks**	**342**
The summary bar	323	The header bar	342
The hunting queries list	323	The summary bar	343
Hunting query details pane	324	The notebook list	343
Working with Microsoft Sentinel hunting queries	**327**	The notebook details pane	344
Adding a new query	328	**Creating a workspace**	**348**
Editing a query	329	**Performing a hunt**	**349**
Cloning a query	329	Developing a premise	350
Deleting a query	330	Determining data	350
Adding to Livestream	330	Planning a hunt	351
Creating an analytics rule	330	Executing an investigation	352
Working with livestream	**330**	Responding	352
Working with bookmarks	**332**	Monitoring	352
Creating a bookmark	333	Improving	353
Viewing bookmarks	335	**Summary**	**353**
		Questions	**354**
		Further reading	**354**

Section 4: Integration and Automation

12
Creating Playbooks and Automation

Introduction to Microsoft Sentinel playbooks	**360**	The header bar	362
		The summary bar	363
Introduction to Microsoft Sentinel Automation	**361**	Automation rules listing	363
		Adding a new automation rule	**364**

Playbook pricing	369	Creating a new playbook	377
Types of playbooks	370	Using the Logic Apps Designer page	378
Overview of the Microsoft Sentinel connector	370	The Logic Apps Designer header bar	380
Exploring the Playbooks tab	372	The Logic Apps Designer workflow editor section	382
Logic app listing	373		
Logic app settings page	373	Creating a simple Microsoft Sentinel playbook	382
The menu bar	374	Summary	390
The header bar	374	Questions	390
The essentials section	375	Further reading	390
The Runs history section	376		

13

ServiceNow Integration for Alert and Case Management

A brief history of Microsoft Sentinel and ServiceNow integration	394	Steps to integrate Microsoft Sentinel with ServiceNow	396
Integrating Microsoft Sentinel with ServiceNow ITSM using Microsoft Sentinel Logic Apps	394	Configuring the Microsoft Azure portal	397
		Installing the Microsoft Sentinel integration plugin in ServiceNow	404
Integrating Azure security alert sources (not just Sentinel) with ServiceNow Security Incident Response via the Microsoft Graph Security API	395	Configuring the ServiceNow Sentinel plugin to authenticate to Microsoft Sentinel	404
		Creating profiles in the ServiceNow Sentinel integration plugin	405
Integrating Microsoft Sentinel with ServiceNow Security Incident Response via an API directly to Microsoft Sentinel	396	Summary	415

Section 5: Operational Guidance

14
Operational Tasks for Microsoft Sentinel

Dividing SOC duties	420	**Operational tasks for SOC analysts**	424
SOC engineers	420	Daily tasks	424
SOC analysts	421	Weekly tasks	424
Operational tasks for SOC engineers	421	Monthly tasks	425
Daily tasks	421	Ad hoc tasks	425
Weekly tasks	422	**Summary**	425
Monthly tasks	423	**Questions**	426
Ad hoc tasks	423		

15
Constant Learning and Community Contribution

Official resources from Microsoft	428	**Using GitHub**	433
Official documentation	428	GitHub for Microsoft Sentinel	433
Tech community – blogs	428	GitHub for community contribution	434
Tech community – forums	429	**Specific components and supporting technologies**	434
Feature requests	430	Kusto Query Language	434
LinkedIn groups	431	Jupyter Notebook	435
Other resources	431	Machine learning with Fusion	435
Resources for SOC operations	432	Azure Logic Apps	436
MITRE ATT&CK® framework	432	**Summary**	437
National Institute of Standards for Technology (NIST)	432		

Assessments

Other Books You May Enjoy

Index

Preface

Microsoft Sentinel is an intelligent security service developed by Microsoft with a focus on integrating and bringing together cloud security and artificial intelligence. *Microsoft Sentinel in Action* will help you to gain enough understanding to make the most of Azure services to secure your environment against modern cybersecurity threats.

During Ignite 2021, Microsoft announced that Azure Sentinel will be renamed to Microsoft Sentinel. However, changing the name everywhere is a very time consuming task and, as of when this book was finished, the process was not yet completed. Due to this, some images shown still show Azure Sentinel rather than Microsoft Sentinel as the name change were yet to be completed in the Azure portal, however, the functionality is still the same.

Who this book is for

If you are an IT professional with prior experience in other Microsoft security products and Azure and are now looking to expand your knowledge to incorporate Microsoft Sentinel, then this book is for you. Security experts using an alternative SIEM tool who want to adopt Microsoft Sentinel as an additional service or as a replacement will also find this book useful.

What this book covers

Chapter 1, *Getting Started with Microsoft Sentinel*, includes an overview of the cloud security architecture as we see it today. This information lays a foundation for understanding what a modern **Security Operations Center** (**SOC**) is and why Microsoft Sentinel plays a key role. We will focus on the specific components needed to create a SOC platform and how Microsoft Sentinel brings all the data together to provide a central analysis and action capability.

Chapter 2, *Azure Monitor – Introduction to Log Analytics* , focuses on the creation of the Azure Log Analytics workspace, which is where we store all the log data for Microsoft Sentinel to analyze. This is an important first step in configuring Microsoft Sentinel.

Chapter 3, *Managing and Collecting Data*, teaches you how to collect data, manage the data to prevent overspend, and query the data for useful information as part of your threat hunting and other security activities.

Chapter 4, *Integrating Threat Intelligence with Microsoft Sentinel*, explains the options available for adding threat intelligence feeds to Microsoft Sentinel to enable the security team to have a greater understanding of the potential threats against their environment. Threat intelligence feeds add contextual information to the data gathered from logs across the organization.

Chapter 5, *Using the Kusto Query Language*, provides an introduction to the **Kusto Query Language (KQL)** and has some sample queries for you to work out for yourself.

Chapter 6, *Microsoft Sentinel Logs and Writing Queries*, expands on the skills learned in *Chapter 5*, *Using the Kusto Query Language*, to create useful Microsoft Sentinel queries to discover anomalous behaviors and patterns of activity.

Chapter 7, *Creating Analytic Rules*, teaches you how to take KQL queries and use them to create Microsoft Sentinel analytic rules to create incidents.

Chapter 8, *Creating and Using Workbooks*, explains the concept of workbooks, how to use workbook templates, how to edit an existing workbook, and how to create your own workbook.

Chapter 9, *Incident Management*, discusses Microsoft Sentinel incidents, what they are, how to manage them, and how to investigate them.

Chapter 10, *Configuring and Using Entity Behavior*, teaches you another way of obtaining more information about your incident by using Entity behavior.

Chapter 11, *Threat Hunting in Microsoft Sentinel*, discusses Microsoft Sentinel hunting queries and how to use them and touches upon Jupyter notebooks.

Chapter 12, *Creating Playbooks and Automation*, provides an overview of Microsoft Sentinel playbooks and will discuss using the Microsoft Sentinel trigger and actions to perform automations.

Chapter 13, *ServiceNow Integration for Alerts and Case Management*, expands upon what was learned in *Chapter 12*, *Creating Playbooks and Automation*, to provide a step-by-step guide on how to create a workflow that creates a ServiceNow ticket from an Microsoft Sentinel alert. These same steps could be modified to work with any ticketing agent.

Chapter 14, *Operational Tasks for Microsoft Sentinel*, will provide some operational guidance on various tasks that should be performed daily, weekly, monthly, and as needed.

Chapter 15, *Constant Learning and Community Contribution*, will finish the book by offering guidance on where to get the latest information and how to contribute to the community that is growing to support the development and sharing of security-related information and techniques.

To get the most out of this book

We recommend that you have access to an Azure environment where you have the proper rights to create your Micosoft Sentinel environment. Prior usage of the Azure portal would also be beneficial.

Software/hardware covered in the book	OS requirements
Active Azure subscription	Windows, Mac OS, or Linux (any)

Download the color images

We also provide a PDF file that has color images of the screenshots/diagrams used in this book. You can download it here: https://static.packt-cdn.com/downloads/9781801815536_ColorImages.pdf.

Conventions used

There are a number of text conventions used throughout this book.

`Code in text`: Indicates code words in text, database table names, folder names, filenames, file extensions, pathnames, dummy URLs, user input, and Twitter handles. Here is an example: "In the following example, when looking at the rows where the state is `NORTH CAROLINA`, all the columns other than `State` and `duration` will be empty since the `NCEvents` table only has the `State` and `duration` columns."

A block of code is set as follows:

```
let FLEvents = StormEvents
| where State == "FLORIDA";
let NCEvents = StormEvents
| where State == "NORTH CAROLINA"
| project State, duration = EndTime - StartTime;
NCEvents | union FLEvents
```

Bold: Indicates a new term, an important word, or words that you see onscreen. For example, words in menus or dialog boxes appear in the text like this. Here is an example: "To run the samples for this chapter, you will need to expand the **Samples** logs on the left-hand side of the screen and then select **StormEvents**."

Any command line input or output is written as follows:

```
StormEvents
| distinct State
| order by State asc
```

> **Tips or Important Notes**
> Appear like this.

Get in touch

Feedback from our readers is always welcome.

General feedback: If you have questions about any aspect of this book, mention the book title in the subject of your message and email us at customercare@packtpub.com.

Errata: Although we have taken every care to ensure the accuracy of our content, mistakes do happen. If you have found a mistake in this book, we would be grateful if you would report this to us. Please visit www.packtpub.com/support/errata, selecting your book, clicking on the Errata Submission Form link, and entering the details.

Piracy: If you come across any illegal copies of our works in any form on the Internet, we would be grateful if you would provide us with the location address or website name. Please contact us at copyright@packt.com with a link to the material.

If you are interested in becoming an author: If there is a topic that you have expertise in and you are interested in either writing or contributing to a book, please visit authors.packtpub.com.

Preface   xvii

Share Your Thoughts

Once you've read *Microsoft Sentinel in Action*, we'd love to hear your thoughts! Scan the QR code below to go straight to the Amazon review page for this book and share your feedback.

https://packt.link/r/1801815534

Your review is important to us and the tech community and will help us make sure we're delivering excellent quality content.

Section 1: Design and Implementation

In this section, you will get an overview of Microsoft Sentinel, including the current cloud landscape, the cloud security reference framework, **Security Operations Center** (**SOC**) platform components, and how to map the architecture. You will also learn about the Azure Monitor Log Analytics resource, including planning your Log Analytics instance, how to create a new instance, and attaching it to Microsoft Sentinel.

This section contains the following chapters:

- *Chapter 1, Getting Started with Microsoft Sentinel*
- *Chapter 2, Azure Monitor – Introduction to Log Analytics*

1
Getting Started with Microsoft Sentinel

Welcome to the first chapter in this book about Microsoft Sentinel. To understand why this solution was developed and how best to use it in your organization, we need to explore the cloud security landscape and understand each of the components that may feed data into, or extract insights from, this system. We also need to gain a baseline understanding of what a strong **Security Operations Center** (**SOC**) architecture looks like, and how Microsoft Sentinel is going to help build the foundations for a cost-effective and highly automated cloud security platform.

In this chapter, we will cover the following topics:

- The current cloud security landscape
- The cloud security reference framework
- SOC platform components
- Mapping the SOC architecture
- Security solution integrations
- Cloud platform integrations
- Private infrastructure integrations

- Service pricing for Microsoft Sentinel
- Scenario mapping

The current cloud security landscape

To understand your security architecture requirements, you must first ensure that you have a solid understanding of the IT environment that you are trying to protect. Before deploying any new security solution, there is a need to map out the solutions that are currently deployed and how they protect each area of the IT environment. The following list provides the major components of any modern IT environment:

- End user habits that are counter-productive to security endeavors
- Identity for the authentication and authorization of access to systems
- Networks to gain access to internal resources and the internet
- Storage and compute in the data center for internal applications and sensitive information
- End user devices and the applications they use to interact with data
- And in some environments, you can include **Industrial Control Systems** (**ICS**) and the **Internet of Things** (**IoT**)

When we start to look at the threats and vulnerabilities for these components, we quickly find ourselves deep in the alphabet soup of problems and solutions.

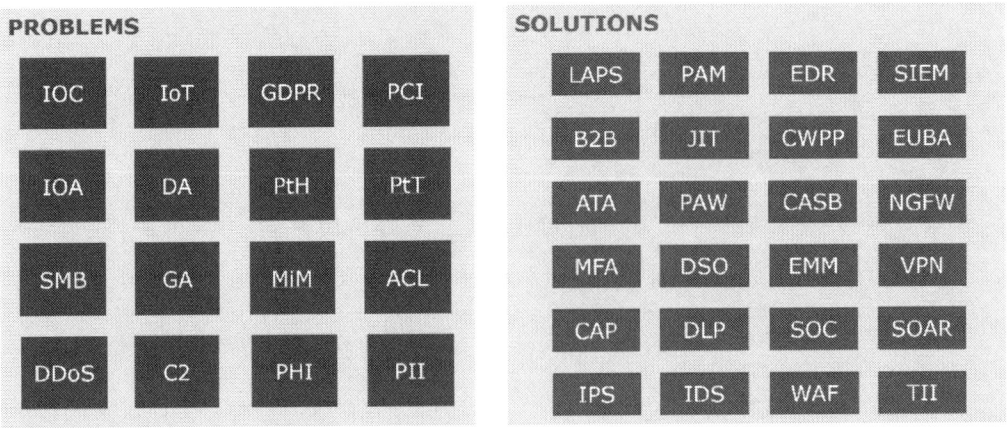

Figure 1.1 – The alphabet soup of cybersecurity

This is by no means an exhaustive list of the potential acronyms available. Understanding these acronyms is the first hurdle; matching them to the appropriate solutions and ensuring they are well deployed is another challenge altogether (a table of these acronyms can be found in the appendix of this book).

The cloud security reference framework

To assist with the discovery and mapping of current security solutions, we developed the cloud security reference framework. The following diagram is a section of this framework that provides the technical mapping components, and you can use this to carry out a mapping of your own environment:

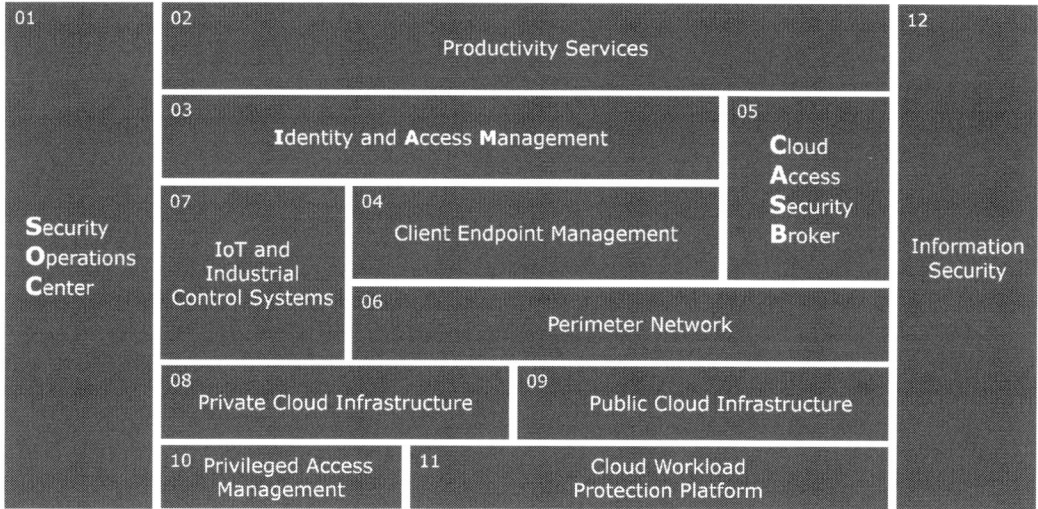

Figure 1.2 – Technical mapping components; the cloud security reference framework

Each of these 12 components is described in the following list, along with some examples of the types of solutions to consider as they relate to integration with Microsoft Sentinel and the rest of your security architecture:

1. **Security Operations Center**: At a high level, this includes the following technologies and procedures: log management and **Security Incident and Event Monitoring (SIEM)**, **Security Orchestration and Automated Response (SOAR)**, vulnerability management, threat intelligence, incident response, and intrusion prevention/detection. This component is explored further in the *Mapping the SOC architecture* section later in this chapter.

2. **Productivity Services**: This component covers any solution currently in use to protect the business productivity services that your end users rely on for their day-to-day work. This may include email protection, SharePoint Online, OneDrive for Business, Box, Dropbox, Google apps, and Salesforce. Many more will appear in the future, and most of these should be managed through a **Cloud Access Security Broker (CASB)** solution.

3. **Identity and Access Management**: Identities are among the most important entities to track. Once an attacker gains access to your environment, their main priority is to find the most sensitive accounts and use them to exploit systems further. In fact, identity is usually one of the first footholds in your IT environment, usually through a successful phishing attack. A simple resolution is to implement multi-factor authentication, ensuring that even if a password is stolen (or guessed), the attacker would need multiple attempts to access the system.

4. **Client Endpoint Management**: This component covers a wide range of endpoints, from desktops and laptops to mobile devices and kiosk systems, all of which should be protected by specialized solutions such as **Endpoint Detection and Response (EDR)**, **Mobile Device Management (MDM)**, and **Mobile Application Management (MAM)** solutions to ensure protection from advanced and persistent threats against the operating systems and applications. This component also includes secure printing, managing peripherals, and any other device that an end user may interact with, such as the future of virtual reality/augmentation devices.

5. **Cloud Access Security Broker (CASB)**: This component has been around for several years and is finally becoming a mainstay of modern cloud security infrastructure due to the increased adoption of cloud services. The CASB is run as a cloud solution that can ingest log data from **Software as a Service (SaaS)** applications and firewalls and will apply its own threat detection and prevention solutions. Information coming from the CASB will be consumed by the SIEM solution to add to the overall picture of what is happening across your diverse IT environment.

6. **Perimeter Network**: One of the most advanced components, when it comes to cybersecurity, must be the perimeter network. This used to be the first line of defense and for some companies still is the only line of defense. That is changing now, and we need to be aware of the multitude of options available; from external-facing advanced firewalls, web proxy servers, and application gateways to virtual private networking solutions and secure DNS, this component will also include protection services such as **Distributed Denial of Service (DDoS)**, **Web Application Firewall (WAF)**, and intrusion protection/detection services.

7. **IoT and Industrial Control Systems**: **ICS** are usually operated and maintained in isolation from the corporate environment, known as the **Information Technology/Operational Technology (IT/OT)** divide. These are highly bespoke systems that may have existed for decades and are not easily updated or replaced. The networks and devices may be highly sensitive to any latency or attempts to scan; instead, the recommended approach is passive monitoring of network traffic.

   The reference to IoT is different, yet similar; in these systems, there will be a lot of small devices that collect data and control critical business functions without working on the same network. Some of these devices can be smart to enable automation; others are single-use (vibration or temperature sensors). The volume and velocity of data that can be collected from these systems can be very high. If useful information can be gained from the data, then consider filtering the information before ingesting it into Microsoft Sentinel for analysis and short- or long-term retention.

8. **Private Cloud Infrastructure**: This may be hosted in local server rooms, a specially designed data center, or hosted with a third-party provider. The technologies involved in this component will include storage, networks, internal firewalls, and physical and virtual servers. The data center has been the mainstay of many companies for the last 2-3 decades, but most are now transforming into hybrid solutions, combining the best of cloud (public) and on-premises (private) solutions. The key consideration here is how much of the log data you can collect and transfer to the cloud for Microsoft Sentinel ingestion. We will cover data connectors more in *Chapter 3, Managing and Collecting Data*.

   Active Directory is a key solution that should also be included in this component. It will be extended to public cloud infrastructure (component **09**) and addressed in the *Privileged Access Management* section (component **10**). The best defense for Azure Active Directory is to deploy the Microsoft Defender for Identity solution, which Microsoft developed to specifically protect Active Directory domain controllers.

9. **Public Cloud Infrastructure**: These solutions are now a mainstay of most modern IT environments, beginning either as an expansion of existing on-premises virtualized server workloads, a disaster recovery solution, or an isolated environment created and maintained by the developers. A mature public cloud deployment will have many layers of governance and security embedded into the full life cycle of creation and operations. This component may include **Infrastructure as a Service (IaaS)**, **Platform as a Service (PaaS)**, and **Software as a Service (SaaS)** services; each public cloud service provider offers its own security protections that can be integrated into Microsoft Sentinel.

10. **Privileged Access Management**: This is a critical component, not to be overlooked, especially in terms of gaining access to the SOC platform and associated tools. The **Privileged Access Management (PAM)** capability ensures all system-level access is highly governed, removing permissions when not required, and making a record of every request for elevated access. Advanced solutions will ensure password rotation for service accounts, management of shared system accounts (including SaaS services such as Twitter and Facebook), and the rotation of passwords for the local administrator accounts on all computers and servers. For the SOC platform, consider implementing password vaults and session recording for evidence gathering.

11. **Cloud Workload Protection Platform**: This component may also be known as **Cloud Security Posture Management (CSPM)**, depending on the view of the solution developed. This is a relatively new area for cloud security and is still maturing.

    Whatever they are labeled as, these solutions address the same problems: how do you know that your workloads are configured correctly across a hybrid environment and protect the resources within each of those environments? This component will also include any DevOps tools implemented to orchestrate the deployment and ongoing configuration management of solutions deployed to private and public cloud platforms. This solution should be capable of continuously scanning for, and potentially enforcing, configuration compliance with multiple regulatory and industry-standard frameworks.

12. **Information Security**: This component is critical to securing data at rest and in transit, regardless of the storage: endpoint, portable, or cloud storage. This component is important to cover secure collaboration, digital rights management, securing email (in conjunction with component **02**, (**Productivity Services**), scanning for regulated data, and other sensitive information.

The cloud security reference framework is meant to be a guide to what services are needed to secure your cloud implementation. In the next section, we will look at the SOC in more detail.

SOC platform components

As described earlier, the SOC platform includes a range of technologies to assist with the proactive and reactive procedures carried out by various teams. Each of these solutions should help the SOC analysts to perform their duties at the most efficient level to ensure a high degree of protection, detection, and remediation.

The core components of the SOC include log management and SIEM, SOAR, vulnerability management, threat intelligence, and incident response. All these components are addressed by the deployment of Microsoft Sentinel. Additional solutions will be required, and integrated, for other SOC platform capabilities such as intrusion prevention/detection, file integrity monitoring, and disaster recovery.

An SOC deployment using Microsoft Sentinel comprises the following components:

- **Azure Monitor** Log Analytics workspaces are created for data collection and analysis. These were originally created to ensure a cloud-scale log management solution for both cloud-based and physical data center-based workloads. Once the data is collected, a range of solutions can then be applied to analyze the data for health, performance, and security considerations. Some solutions were created by Microsoft, and others were created by partners.

- **Microsoft Sentinel** was developed to address the need for a cloud-native solution as an alternative to existing server-based SIEM solutions that have become a mainstay of security and compliance over the last decade. Microsoft Sentinel is built upon the existing services of Azure Monitor and Log Analytics. It is also integrated with other services such as Logic Apps and Azure Data Explorer.

    The popularity of cloud services provides some key advantages, including reduced storage costs, rapid scale compute, automated service maintenance, and continuous improvement as Microsoft creates new capabilities based on customer and partner feedback.

    One of the immediate benefits of deploying Microsoft Sentinel is rapid enablement without the need for costly investment in the supporting infrastructure, such as servers, storage, and complex licensing. The Microsoft Sentinel service is charged based on data consumption, per gigabyte per month. This allows the initial deployment to start small and grow as needed until full-scale deployment and maturity can be achieved.

    Ongoing maintenance is also simplified as there are no servers to maintain or licenses to renew. You will want to ensure regular optimization of the solution by reviewing the data ingestion and retention for relevance and suitability. This will keep costs reasonable and improve the quality of data used for threat hunting.

- **Logic Apps** provides integration with a vast array of enterprise solutions, ensuring workflows are connected across the multiple cloud platforms and to existing on-premises solutions. This is a core part of the integration and automation (SOAR) capabilities of the platform.

Logic Apps is a standards-based solution that provides a robust set of capabilities. You can also use third-party SOAR solutions if you have already invested in one of those platforms.

The SOC platform components are a starting point, but there may be several other services you will want to deploy in your SOC implementation. In the next section, we will look at an approach to mapping the SOC architecture's current state and requirements.

Mapping the SOC architecture

To implement a cohesive technical solution for your SOC platform, you will need to ensure that the following components are reviewed and thoroughly implemented. This is best done on a routine basis and incorporates regularly testing for the strength of each capability using penetration testing experts that will provide feedback and guidance to help improve any weaknesses.

Log management and data sources

The first component of an SOC platform is the gathering and storing of log data from a diverse range of systems and services across your IT environment. This is where you need careful planning to ensure that you are collecting and retaining the most appropriate data. Some key considerations we can borrow from other well-documented big data guidance are listed here:

- **Variety**: You need to ensure you have data feeds from multiple sources to gain visibility across the spectrum of hardware and software solutions across your organization.
- **Volume**: Too large a volume and you could face some hefty ingestion and storage fees; too small and you could miss some important events that may lead to preventing you from fully analyzing a breach.
- **Velocity**: Collecting real-time data is critical to reducing response times, but it is also important that the data is processed and analyzed in real time too.
- **Value/veracity**: The quality of data is important to understand the meaning; too much noise will hamper investigations.
- **Validity**: The accuracy and integrity must be verified to ensure that the right decisions can be made.
- **Volatility**: How long is the data useful for? Not all data needs to be retained long term; once analyzed, some data can be dropped quickly.

- **Vulnerability**: Some data is more sensitive than other data, and when collected and correlated together in one place, can become an extremely valuable data source to a would-be attacker.

- **Visualization**: Human interpretation of data requires some level of visualization. Understanding how you will show this information to the relevant audience is a key requirement for reporting.

Microsoft Sentinel provides a range of data connectors to ensure that all types of data can be ingested and analyzed. Securing Azure Monitor will be covered in *Chapter 2, Azure Monitor – Introduction to Log Analytics*, and connector details will be available in *Chapter 3, Managing and Collecting Data*.

Operations platforms

Traditionally, a SIEM was used to look at all log data and reason over it, looking for any potential threats across a diverse range of technologies. Today, there are multiple platforms available that carry out self-monitoring and alerting functionality, like the way a SIEM would work, except they are designed with a specific focus on a particular area of expertise. Each platform may carry out its own log collection and analysis, provide specific threat intelligence and vulnerability scanning, and make use of machine learning algorithms to detect changes in user and system behavior patterns. If they are advanced systems, they will also provide a level of automated response in reaction to the threats detected.

The following solutions each have a range of capabilities built in to collect and analyze logs, carry out immediate remediations, and report their findings to the SIEM solution for further investigation and cross-analysis:

- **Identity and Access Management (IAM)**: The IAM solution may be made up of multiple solutions, combined to ensure the full life cycle management of identities from creation to destruction. The IAM system should include governance actions, such as approvals, attestation, and the automated cleanup of group membership and permissions management. IAM also covers the capability of implementing multi-factor authentication: a method of challenging the sign-in process to provide more than a simple combination of user ID and password. All actions carried out by administrators and user-driven activities should be recorded and reported to the SIEM for context and end user behavior analytics.

Modern IAM solutions will also include built-in user behavior analytics to detect changes in baseline patterns, suspicious activities, and the potential of insider-threat risks. These systems should also be integrated with a CASB solution to provide session-based authentication controls, which is the ability to apply further restrictions if the intent changes or access to higher-sensitivity actions is required. Finally, every organization should implement privileged access management solutions to control access to sensitive systems and services.

- **Endpoint Detection and Response (EDR)**: Going beyond anti-virus and anti-malware, a modern endpoint protection solution will include the ability to detect and respond to advanced threats as they occur. Detection will be based not only on signature-based known threats but also on patterns of behavior and integrated threat intelligence. Detection expands from a single machine to complete visibility across all endpoints in the organization, both on the network and roaming across the internet.

  Response capabilities will include the ability to isolate the machine from the network, to prevent the further spread of malicious activities, while retaining evidence for forensic analysis and providing remote access for investigators. The response may also trigger other actions across integrated systems, such as mailbox actions to remove threats that are executed via email or removing access to specific files on the network to prevent further execution of malicious code.

  Many companies have already invested in an EDR solution due to their effectiveness in reducing the risk of intrusion via advanced attacks. The trend now is to mature this implementation and focus on **Extended Detection and Response (XDR)** platforms: an XDR solution will include EDR, IAM, CASB, and several other solutions integrated to ensure complete attack chain detection and response capabilities.

- **CASB**: A CASB is now a critical component in any cloud-based security architecture. With the ability to ingest logs from network firewalls and proxy servers, as well as connecting to multiple cloud services via their APIs, the CASB has become the first point of collation for many user activities across the network, both on-premises and when directly connected to the internet. This also prevents the need to ingest these logs directly into the SIEM (saving on costs) unless there is a need to directly query these logs rather than pivoting from the SIEM to the CASB portal to carry out an investigation.

A CASB will come with many connectors for deep integration into cloud services, as well as connection to the IAM system to help govern access to other cloud services (via **Single Sign-On** (**SSO**)), acting as a reverse proxy and enforcing session-based controls. The CASB will also provide many detection rule templates to deploy immediately, as well as offering the ability to define custom rules for an almost infinite set of use cases unique to your organization. The response capabilities of the CASB are dependent on your specific integrations with the relevant cloud services; these can include the ability to restrict or revoke access to cloud services, prevent the upload or download of documents, or hide specific documents from the view of others.

- **Cloud Workload Protection Platform** (**CWPP**): The CWPP may also be known as a **Cloud Security Posture Management** (**CSPM**) solution. Either of these will provide the unique capability of scanning and continuously monitoring systems to ensure that they meet compliance and governance requirements. This solution provides a centralized method for vulnerability scanning and for carrying out continuous audits across multiple cloud services (such as **Amazon Web Services** (**AWS**) and **Microsoft Azure**), while also centralizing policies and remediation actions. Resources within these services can be protected by implementing policies and technologies including **Just In Time** (**JIT**) access and **Attack Surface Reduction** (**ASR**).

    When these solutions are deployed, it is one less capability that we need the SIEM to provide; instead, it can take a feed from the service to understand the potential risk and provide an integration point for remediation actions.

- **Next-Generation Firewall** (**NGFW**): Firewalls have been the backbone of network security since the 1980s and remain a core component of the segmentation and isolation of internal networks, as well as acting as the front door for many internet-facing services. With NGFW, not only do you get all the benefits of previous firewall technologies, but now you can carry out deep packet inspection for the application layer security and integrated intrusion detection/prevention systems. The deployment of NGFW solutions will also assist with the detection and remediation of malware and advanced threats on the network, preventing the spread to more hosts and network-based systems.

As you can see from these examples, the need to deploy a SIEM to do all the work of centrally collecting and analyzing logs is in the past. With each of these advanced solutions deployed to manage their specific area of expertise, the focus of SIEM changes to look for common patterns across the solutions as well as monitoring those systems that are not covered by these individual solutions. With Microsoft Sentinel as the SIEM, it will also act as the SOAR, enabling a coordinated response to threats across each of these individual solutions, preventing the need to re-engineer them all each time there is a change in requirements for alerting, reporting, and responding.

Threat intelligence and threat hunting

Threat intelligence adds additional context to the log data collected. Knowing what to look for in the logs and how to identify serious events requires a combination of threat hunting skills and the ongoing intelligence feed from a range of experts that are deep in the field of cybercrime research. Much of this work is augmented by **Artificial Intelligence** (**AI**) platforms; however, a human touch is always required to add that gut-feeling element that many detectives and police officers will tell you they get from working their own investigations in law enforcement.

SOC mapping summary

The following diagram provides a summary of the multiple components that come together to help to make up the SOC architecture, with some additional thoughts when implementing each one:

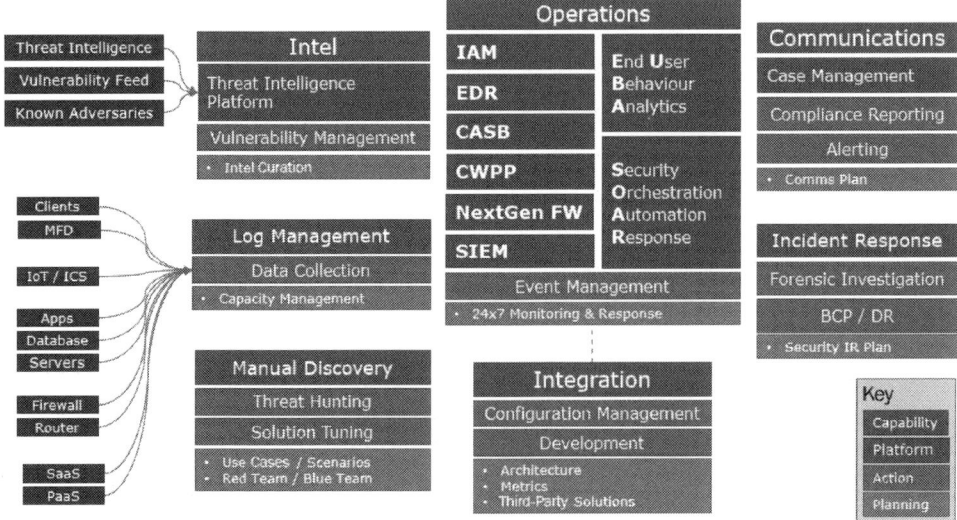

Figure 1.3 – The SOC mapping summary

This solution works best when there is a rich source of log data streaming into the log management solution, tied in with data feeds coming from threat intel and vulnerability scans and databases. This information is used for discovery and threat hunting and may indicate any issues with configuration drift. The core solutions of the SOC operations include the SIEM, CASB, and EDR, among others, each with its own **End User Behavior Analytics (EUBA)** and SOAR capabilities. Integrating these solutions is a critical step in minimizing the noise and working toward improving the speed of response. The outcome should be the ability to report accurately on the current risk profile, compliance status, and clearly communicate in situations that require an immediate response and accurate data.

Security solution integrations

Microsoft Sentinel is designed to work with multiple security solutions, not just those that are developed by Microsoft.

At the most basic level, log collection and analysis are possible from any system that can transmit its logs via the Syslog collectors. More detailed logs are available from those that support CEF-encoded Syslog endpoints that share Windows event logs. The preferred method, however, is to have direct integration via APIs to enable two-way communication and help to manage the integrated solutions. More details relating to these options are included in *Chapter 3, Managing and Collecting Data*.

> **Common Event Format (CEF)**
>
> CEF is an industry-standard format applied to Syslog messages, used by most security vendors to ensure commonality between platforms. Microsoft Sentinel provides integrations to easily run analytics and queries across CEF data. For a full list of Microsoft Sentinel CEF source configurations, review the article at `https://aka.ms/SentinelGrandlist`.

Microsoft is continually developing integration options. At the time of writing, the list of integrated third-party solution providers includes the following:

Agari	Akamai	Alcide
Alsid	Amazon AWS	Apache
Aruba Networks	Barracuda	BETTER Mobile
Beyond Security	Blackberry	Broadcom (Symantec)
Check Point	Cisco	Citrix Systems Inc.
CyberArk	Darktrace	ESET
ExtraHop Networks	F5 Networks	Forcepoint
ForgeRock Inc.	Fortinet	Google
Illusive	Imperva	Juniper
Morphisec	Netskope	NXLog
Okta	Onapsis	One Identity LLC.
Orca Security	Palo Alto Networks	Perimeter 81
Proofpoint	Pulse Secure	Qualys
Salesforce	SonicWall	Sophos
Squadra Technologies	Squid	Thycotic, Inc
Trend Micro	Vectra AI	VMware
WireX Systems	Zimperium	Zscaler

Table 1.1 – Data connector list of companies

As you can see from this list, many of the top security vendors are available directly in the portal. Microsoft Sentinel provides the ability to connect to a range of security data sources with built-in connectors, ingest the log data, and display dashboards using pre-defined workbooks.

Cloud platform integrations

One of the key reasons you might be planning to deploy Microsoft Sentinel is to manage the security of your cloud platform deployments. Instead of sending logs from the cloud provider to an on-premises SIEM solution, you will likely want to keep that data off your local network, to save on bandwidth usage and storage costs.

Let's now look at how some of these platforms can be integrated with Microsoft Sentinel.

Integrating with Amazon Web Services (AWS)

AWS provides API access to most features across the platform, which enables Microsoft Sentinel to be a rich integration solution. The following list provides some of the common resources that should be integrated with Microsoft Sentinel if enabled in an AWS account(s):

- AWS CloudTrail logs provide insights into AWS user activities, including failed sign-in attempts, IP addresses, regions, user agents, and identity types, as well as potentially malicious user activities with assumed roles.

- AWS CloudTrail logs also provide network-related resource activities, including the creation, update, and deletion of security groups, network **access control lists** (**ACLs**) and routes, gateways, elastic load balancers, **Virtual Private Cloud** (**VPC**), subnets, and network interfaces.

Some resources deployed within an AWS account(s) can be configured to send logs directly to Microsoft Sentinel (such as Windows event logs). You may also deploy a log collector (Syslog, CEF, or Logstash) within an AWS account(s) to centralize the log collection, the same as you would for a private data center.

Integrating with Google Cloud Platform (GCP)

Google provides API access to most features of both **GCP** and the G Suite solution. G Suite Connector is currently in development. If you are managing either a G Suite or a **GCP** instance and want to use Microsoft Sentinel to secure them, you should consider the following options (until a fully supported connector is available):

- REST API—this feature is still in development; when released, it will allow you to create your own investigation queries.

- Deploy a CASB solution that can interact with GCP logs, control session access, and forward relevant information to Microsoft Sentinel.

- Deploy a log collector such as Syslog, CEF, or Logstash. Ensure that all deployed resources can forward their logs via the log collector to Microsoft Sentinel.

Integrating with Microsoft Azure

The **Microsoft Azure** platform provides direct integration with many Microsoft security solutions, and more are being added every month:

- Azure Active Directory, for collecting audit and sign-in logs to gather insights about app usage, Conditional Access policies, legacy authentication, self-service password reset usage, and the management of users, groups, roles, and apps.
- Azure Active Directory Identity Protection, which provides user and sign-in risk events and vulnerabilities, with the ability to remediate these risks immediately.
- Azure Activity, for insights into subscription-level events such as Azure Resource Manager, service health, write operations on resources, and the status of activities performed in Azure.
- Azure DDoS Protection, for the protection of web services that could be susceptible to attack through **DDoS**.
- Microsoft Defender, the integrated CWPP for security management across Azure, AWS, GCP, and hybrid deployments.
- Microsoft Defender for IoT, for insights into the IoT and OT networks with recommendations based on the severity of the risk.
- Azure Firewall, the managed, cloud-based network security service to protect Azure Virtual Networks.
- Microsoft Information Protection, to classify and optionally protect sensitive information.
- Azure Key Vault, for securely storing and accessing secrets including API keys, passwords, certificates, or cryptographic keys.
- **Azure Kubernetes Service (AKS)**, an open source, fully managed container orchestration service to manage and deploy Docker containers.
- Azure SQL Database, a fully managed PaaS database engine. This connector lets you stream the audit and diagnostic logs into Microsoft Sentinel.
- An Azure storage account, a cloud solution for modern data storage scenarios.
- DNS, to improve investigations for clients that try to resolve malicious domain names, talkative DNS clients, and other DNS health-related events.
- Dynamics 365, for insights into admin, user, and support activities on this platform.

- Microsoft 365 Defender, a consolidation of multiple connectors (Endpoint, Identity, Office 365, and Microsoft Cloud App Security (MCAS)).
- Microsoft Defender for Cloud Apps, to gain visibility into connected cloud apps (SaaS), cloud services (IaaS and PaaS), and an analysis of firewall and proxy logs.
- Microsoft Defender for Endpoint, a security platform designed to prevent, detect, investigate, and respond to advanced threats across all client devices.
- Microsoft Defender for Identity, to gain visibility of the events and user analytics on Active Directory domain controllers.
- Microsoft Defender for Office 365, to provide insights into ongoing user activities, such as file downloads, access requests, changes to group events, and mailbox activity. This solution also protects advanced attacks in emails (such as phishing and whaling), Teams, SharePoint Online, and OneDrive for Business.
- Threat intelligence – TAXII, a service to ingest TAXII v2.0- and v2.1-compatible data sources to enable monitoring, alerting, and hunting using threat intelligence.
- Microsoft threat intelligence platforms, for integration with the Microsoft Graph Security API data sources: This connector is used to send threat indicators from Microsoft and third-party threat intelligence platforms.
- Windows Firewall, if enabled on your servers and clients (recommended).
- Azure **WAF**, to protect applications from common web vulnerabilities such as SQL injection and cross-site scripting.

Microsoft makes many of these log sources available to Microsoft Sentinel for no additional log storage charges, which could provide a significant cost saving when considering other SIEM tool options.

Other cloud platforms will provide similar capabilities, so review the options as part of your ongoing due diligence across your infrastructure and security landscape.

Whichever cloud platforms you choose to deploy, we encourage you to consider deploying suitable CWPP and CSPM solutions to provide additional protections against misconfiguration and compliance violations. These solutions can then forward events to Microsoft Sentinel for central reporting, alerting, and remediation.

In the next section, we will look at how you can integrate with private or on-premises infrastructure to ensure full coverage of your IT estate.

Private infrastructure integrations

The primary method of integration with your private infrastructure (such as an on-premises data center) is the deployment of native connectors, where supported. The next logical step is to deploy the new **Azure Monitor Agent (AMA)** for those services that can support it. Otherwise, the remaining on-premises services can forward their logs' Syslog servers, which act as data collectors. While endpoints can be configured to send their data to Microsoft Sentinel directly, you will likely want to centralize the management of this data flow. The key consideration for this deployment is the management of log data volume; if you are generating a large volume of data for security analytics, you will need to transmit that data over your internet connections (or private connections such as ExpressRoute).

The Syslog data collectors can be configured to reduce the load by filtering the data, but a balance must be found between the volume and velocity of data collected to have sufficient available bandwidth to send the data to Microsoft Sentinel. Investment in increased bandwidth should be considered to ensure adequate capacity based on your specific needs.

A second method of integration involves investigation and automation to carry out actions required to understand and remediate any issues found. Automation may include the deployment of Azure Automation to run scripts, or through third-party solution integration, such as a **SOAR** platform, depending on the resources being managed.

Keep in mind that should your private infrastructure lose connectivity to the internet, your systems will not be able to communicate with Microsoft Sentinel during the outage. Investments in redundancy and fault tolerance should be considered.

In the next section, we will discuss the pricing options for Microsoft Sentinel.

Service pricing for Microsoft Sentinel

There are several components to consider when pricing Microsoft Sentinel:

- A charge for ingesting data into Log Analytics
- A charge for running the data through Microsoft Sentinel
- Retention of data, past the initial 90-day default retention allowance
- Charges for running Logic Apps for Automation (optional)
- Charges for running your own machine learning models (optional)
- The cost of running any VMs for data collectors (optional)

The cost of Azure Monitor and Microsoft Sentinel is calculated by how much data is consumed, which is directly impacted by the connectors: which type of information you connect to and the volume of data each node generates. This may vary each day throughout the month as changes in activity occur across your infrastructure and cloud services. Some customers notice a change based on their customer sales fluctuations, or when they come under a **DDoS** attack.

The pricing is also influenced by how long the data is retained within Microsoft Sentinel. The default is 90 days but can be extended to up to 2 years. Most security operations require between 6 and 12 months of hot data retention. After the set retention period, use **Azure Data Explorer** (**ADX**) to retain data for as long as required (up to 99 years).

The initial pricing option is to use **Pay as You Go** (**PAYG**). With this option, you pay a fixed price per **Gigabyte** (**GB**) ingested, charged on a per-day basis. Microsoft has provided the option to commit to varying volume tiers and receive discounts in return based on larger volumes of data.

It is worth noting that Microsoft has made available some connectors that do not incur a data ingestion cost. The data from these connectors could account for 10-20% of your total data ingestion, which reduces your overall costs. Currently, the following data connectors are not charged for ingestion (generally the free ingestion is for alerts only; some connectors do provide the full data ingestion). The details are here: `https://azure.microsoft.com/en-us/pricing/details/azure-sentinel/#faq`.

- Azure Activity (activity logs for Azure operations)
- Azure Active Directory Identity Protection (for tenants with Azure Active Directory P2 licenses)
- Microsoft Information Protection
- Microsoft Defender
- Azure Security Center
- Microsoft 365 Defender
- Microsoft Defender for Cloud Apps
- Microsoft Defender for Endpoint
- Microsoft Defender for Office 365
- Microsoft Defender for Identity
- Office 365 audit logs (all Teams, Exchange admin, and SharePoint activity logs)

The pricing works by charging on a PAYG basis for each day, based on actual data consumption. There are capacity commitment tiers available to provide discount pricing when the volume of data ingested regularly reaches the reservation limits:

- 100 GB
- 200 GB
- 300 GB
- 400 GB
- 500 GB
- 1,000 GB (1 TB)
- 2,000 GB (2 TB)
- 5,000 GB (5 TB)

With capacity reservation, a fixed price is paid for the data each day at that tier, then charges are incurred at a PAYG price for each GB over that tier amount. The PAYG pricing is set to the same amount as the committed tier discount price. When you work out the calculations for the pricing tiers, it makes financial sense to increase to the next tier when you reach the point where the reservation is cheaper than paying PAYG pricing, which is between 50 and 80%.

For example, if you are ingesting an average of 130 GB per day, you will pay for the first 100 GB at a fixed price per GB, and then pay a PAYG price per GB for the additional 30 GB (example per day = $296). Now, if you increase your daily usage to 185 GB, you will save money by increasing your plan to the 200 GB option (example per day = $276) and paying for the extra capacity, instead of paying for the 100 GB (fixed) + 85 GB (PAYG) (total per day = $384.80).

When you look at the amount of data you are using, you may see a trend toward more data being consumed each month as you expand the solution to cover more of your security landscape. As you approach the next tier, you should consider changing the pricing model; you have the option to change once every 30 days.

The next area of cost management to consider is retention and long-term storage of the Microsoft Sentinel data. By default, the preceding pricing includes 90 days of retention. For some companies, this is enough to ensure visibility over the last 3 months of activity across their environment; for others, there will be a need to retain this data for longer, sometimes between 2 and 7 years depending on regulatory requirements in your country or industry. There are two primary ways of maintaining data long term, and both should be considered and chosen based on price and technical requirements:

- **Azure Monitor**: This is the native storage for Microsoft Sentinel and provides a default hot storage option of 90 days, which can be upgraded to store the hot data for up to 2 years.

    Pros: The data is available online and in Azure Monitor, enabling direct queries using KQL searches, and the data can be filtered to only retain essential information.

    Cons: This is likely the most expensive option per GB compared to the other options.

- **Azure Data Explorer (ADX)**: This solution can maintain data indefinitely; pricing is based on a combination of the volume of data and the amount of compute required to carry out searching. Generally, this will be one-tenth of the cost of Microsoft Sentinel for long-term storage.

    Pros: The data is available online and in Azure, enabling direct queries using KQL searches. The data can be filtered to only retain essential information.

    Cons: This is a separate service and requires some initial configuration and integration effort for unsupported tables.

- **Other storage options**: Cloud-based or physical-based storage solutions can be used to store the data indefinitely, usually enabled by sending data via *Event Hubs* or *Azure Storage*.

    Pros: Cheaper options are available from a variety of partners.

    Cons: Additional charges will be made if data is sent outside of Azure, and the data cannot be queried by Microsoft Sentinel. Using this data requires another solution to be implemented to query the data when required.

Each of these components is highly variable across deployments, so you will need to carry out this research as part of your design. Also, research the latest region availability and ascertain whether Microsoft Sentinel is supported in the various government clouds, such as in China.

Scenario mapping

For the final section of this chapter, we are going to look at an important part of SOC development: scenario mapping. This process is carried out on a regular basis to ensure that tools and procedures are tuned for effective analysis and have the right data flow and that responses are well defined to ensure appropriate actions are taken upon detection of potential and actual threats. To make this an effective exercise, we recommend involving a range of different people with diverse skill sets and viewpoints, both technical and non-technical. You can also involve external consultants with specific skills and experience in threat hunting, defense, and attack techniques.

The following process is provided as a starting point. We encourage you to define your own approach to scenario mapping and improve it each time the exercise is carried out.

Step 1 – defining the new scenarios

In this first step, we articulate one scenario at a time; you may want to use a spreadsheet or other documentation methods to ensure information is gathered, reviewed, and updated as required:

- **Impact analysis**: This will be the summary of the complete analysis, based on the next components. You may want to provide a scoring system to ensure that the implementation of security controls is handled in priority order, based on the severity of the potential impact.

- **Risk versus likelihood**: While some scenarios would have a high risk of catastrophe if they were to occur, we must also balance that risk with the potential of them occurring. Risk calculations help to justify the budget and controls required to mitigate the risk but keep in mind that you are unlikely to achieve complete mitigation, and there is always a need to prioritize the resources you have, to implement the controls.

- **Cost and value estimate**: Estimate the value of the resource to your organization and the cost to protect it. This may be a monetary value or percentage of the IT security budget, or it could be some other definable metric such as time and effort. If the cost outweighs the value, you may need to find a more affordable way to protect the resource.

- **Systems impacted**: Create a list of the systems that are most likely to be targeted to get to the resources and information in one or many scenarios (primary systems) and a list of the other systems that could be used or impacted when attacking the primary systems (these are secondary systems). By understanding the potential attack vectors, we can make a map of the targets and ensure they are being monitored and protected.
- **People impacted**: For each scenario, list the relevant business groups, stakeholders, and support personnel that would be involved or impacted by a successful attack. Ensure that all business groups can contribute to this process and articulate their specific scenarios. Work with stakeholders and support personnel to ensure clear documentation for escalation and resolution.
- **Customers impacted**: For some scenarios, we must also consider the customer impact as regards the loss or compromising of their data or an outage caused to services provided to them. Make notes about the severity of the customer impact, and any mitigations that should be considered.

Step 2 – explaining the purpose

For each scenario, we recommend providing a high-level category to help group similar scenarios together. Some categories that may be used include the following:

- **System health**: This is the scenario focused on ensuring the operational health of a system or service required to keep the business running.
- **Compliance**: This is the consideration due to compliance requirements specific to your business, industry, or geographical region.
- **Vulnerability**: Is this a known system or process vulnerability that needs mitigation to protect systems or processes?
- **Threat**: This is any scenario that articulates a potential threat but may not have a specific vulnerability associated with it.
- **Breach**: These are scenarios that explore the impact of a successful breach.

Step 3 – the kill chain stage

The **kill chain** is a well-known construct that originated in the military and was later developed as a framework by Lockheed Martin (see here for more details: `https://en.wikipedia.org/wiki/Kill_chain`). Other frameworks are available, or you can develop your own.

Use the following list as headers to articulate the potential ways in which resources can become compromised in each scenario and at each stage of the kill chain:

- Reconnaissance
- Weaponization
- Delivery
- Exploitation
- Installation
- Command and control
- Actions on objectives

Step 4 – which solution will perform detection?

Review the information from earlier in this chapter to map which component of your security solutions architecture will be able to detect the threats for each scenario:

- SIEM
- CASB
- DLP
- IAM
- EDR
- NGFW
- WAF
- CWPP
- CSPM
- Many others

Step 5 – what actions will occur instantly?

As we aim to maximize the automation of detection and response, consider what actions should be carried out immediately, and then focus on enabling the automation of these actions.

Actions may include the following:

- Logging and alerting
- Notifying/warning the end user
- Blocking the action
- Offering alternative options/actions
- Triggering a workflow

Step 6 – severity and output

In this step, you should be able to assign a number to associate with the severity level, based on the impact analysis in the previous steps. For each severity level, define the appropriate output required:

- **Level 0** – Logs and reports
- **Level 1** – Dashboard notifications
- **Level 2** – Generate events in the ticketing system
- **Level 3** – Alerts sent to groups/individuals
- **Level 4** – Automatic escalation to the senior management team (sirens and flashing lights are optional!)

Step 7 – what action should the analyst take?

Whereas the *Step 5 – what actions will occur instantly?* section was an automated action, this step is a definition of what the security analysts should do. For each scenario, define what actions should be taken to ensure an appropriate response, remediation, and recovery.

The following diagram is a simple reference chart that can be used during the scenario-mapping exercise:

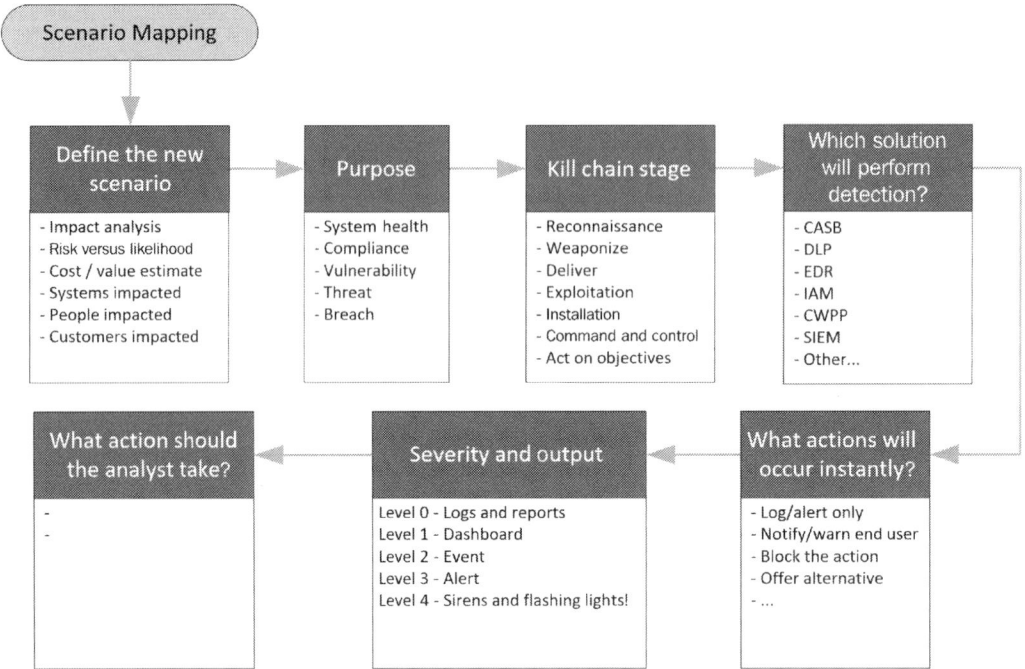

Figure 1.4 – The scenario-mapping process

By following this seven-step process, your team can better prepare for any eventuality. By following a repeatable process, and improving that process each time, your team can share knowledge with each other, and carry out testing to ensure that protection and detection are efficient and effective as well as identifying new gaps in solutions that must be prioritized.

You should commit to taking time away from the computer and start to develop this type of tabletop exercise on a regular basis. Some organizations only do this once per year, while others will do it on a weekly basis or as needed based on the demands they see in their own systems and company culture.

Summary

In this chapter, we introduced Microsoft Sentinel and how it fits into the cloud security landscape. We explored some of the widely used acronyms for both problems and solutions and then provided a useful method of mapping these technical controls to the wide array of options available from many security platform providers today. We also looked at the future state of SOC architecture to ensure you can gain visibility and control across your entire infrastructure: physical, virtual, and cloud-hosted.

Finally, we looked at the potential cost of running Microsoft Sentinel as a core component of your security architecture and how to carry out the scenario-mapping exercise to ensure you are constantly reviewing the detections, the usefulness of the data, and your ability to detect and respond to current threats.

In the next chapter, we will take the first steps toward deploying Microsoft Sentinel by configuring an Azure Monitor Log Analytics workspace. Azure Monitor is the bedrock of Microsoft Sentinel for storing and searching log data. By understanding this data collection and analysis engine, you will gain a deeper understanding of the potential benefits of deploying Microsoft Sentinel in your environment.

Questions

1. What is the purpose of the cloud security reference framework?
2. What are the three main components when deploying an SOC based on Microsoft Sentinel?
3. What are some of the main operation platforms that integrate with a SIEM?
4. Can you name five of the third-party (non-Microsoft) solutions that can be connected to Microsoft Sentinel?
5. How many steps are involved in the scenario-mapping exercise?

Further reading

You can refer to the following URLs for more information on topics covered in this chapter:

- Lessons learned from the Microsoft SOC – Part 1: Organization, at `https://www.microsoft.com/security/blog/2019/02/21/lessons-learned-from-the-microsoft-soc-part-1-organization/`

- Lessons learned from the Microsoft SOC – Part 2a: Organizing People, at `https://www.microsoft.com/security/blog/2019/04/23/lessons-learned-microsoft-soc-part-2-organizing-people/`

- Lessons learned from the Microsoft SOC – Part 2b: Career paths and readiness, at `https://www.microsoft.com/security/blog/2019/06/06/lessons-learned-from-the-microsoft-soc-part-2b-career-paths-and-readiness/`

- The Microsoft Security blog, at `https://www.microsoft.com/security/blog`

2
Azure Monitor – Introduction to Log Analytics

In this chapter, we will explore the Azure Monitor Log Analytics platform, which is used to store all the log data that will be analyzed by Microsoft Sentinel. This is the first component that needs to be designed and configured when implementing Microsoft Sentinel and will require some ongoing maintenance to configure the data storage options and control the costs associated with the solution.

This chapter will also explain how to create a new Log Analytics Workspace using the Azure portal, PowerShell, and the CLI. Once a workspace has been created, we will learn how to attach various resources to it so that information can be gathered, and we will explore the other navigation menu options.

We will cover the following topics in this chapter:

- Introduction to Azure Monitor Log Analytics
- Creating a workspace using the portal
- Creating a workspace using PowerShell or the CLI

- Managing permissions for the workspace
- Enabling Microsoft Sentinel
- Exploring the Microsoft Sentinel Overview page
- Connecting your first data source
- Advanced settings for Log Analytics

Technical requirements

Before you start creating Log Analytics workspaces and using Microsoft Sentinel, you will need to set up an **Azure tenant** and subscription. It does not matter what type of Azure tenant you have, if you have one that you can use. If you do not have access to an Azure tenant, you can set up a free trial by following the instructions at `https://azure.microsoft.com/en-us/free/`.

Once you have a tenant, you will need a subscription as well, if there is not one that you can use already. Depending on the type of Azure tenant you have access to, you may need to contact someone else to create the subscription. If you need help creating a new subscription, go to `https://docs.microsoft.com/en-us/azure/cost-management-billing/manage/create-subscription`.

Introduction to Azure Monitor Log Analytics

Azure Monitor is the name of a suite of solutions built within the Azure platform to collect logs and metrics, with that information then being used to create insights, visualizations, and automated responses. Log Analytics is one of the main services created to analyze the logs gathered. The platform supports near real-time scenarios, is automatically scaled, and is available to multiple services across Azure (including Microsoft Sentinel). The **Kusto Query Language** (**KQL**) is used to obtain information from logs, allows complex information to be queried quickly, and the queries can be saved for future use. In this book, we will refer to this service simply as Log Analytics.

To create a Log Analytics workspace, you must first have an Azure subscription. Each subscription is based on a specific geographic location that ties the data storage to that region. The region selection is decided based on where you want your data to be stored; consider the distance between the source data and the Azure data center (region), alongside any legal requirements for data sovereignty and the requirements for your organization. The selection of the region will also impact the costs associated with both Log Analytics and Microsoft Sentinel.

Each workspace has its own separate data repository, and each can be configured uniquely to meet the business and technical requirements for security, governance, and cost management. Microsoft Sentinel is enabled on individual Log Analytics workspaces; we therefore recommend that you centralize all your security logs in a dedicated central workspace where you enable Microsoft Sentinel and have all other log data types stored in a separate workspace (such as performance logs). If your organization requires you to create more than one location for your data to meet the legal or technical requirements, then you will need to run multiple instances of Microsoft Sentinel (one per Log Analytics workspace), and each instance would need to be monitored and managed individually, in which case you should consider the deployment of **Azure Lighthouse**.

> **Azure Lighthouse**
>
> Microsoft has addressed the need to manage multiple Azure subscriptions, within and across tenants, in a centralized console. This is usually deployed by managed service providers who have multiple customers, although it may also be used by organizations who have deployed multiple Azure subscriptions due to complex requirements. Microsoft Sentinel is now a supported resource for this portal, and more features are expected to be added in time to ensure strong compatibility for interacting directly with Microsoft Sentinel.

34   Azure Monitor – Introduction to Log Analytics

The following diagram shows how Log Analytics workspaces relate to the rest of Azure. Each workspace resides in a single resource group, although there can be multiple workspaces in a single resource group and most likely other Azure resources. Each resource group belongs to a single subscription, and each subscription belongs to a single Azure tenant. There can be, and usually are, multiple resource groups in a subscription, and many companies will have multiple subscriptions in a tenant, as shown in the following figure:

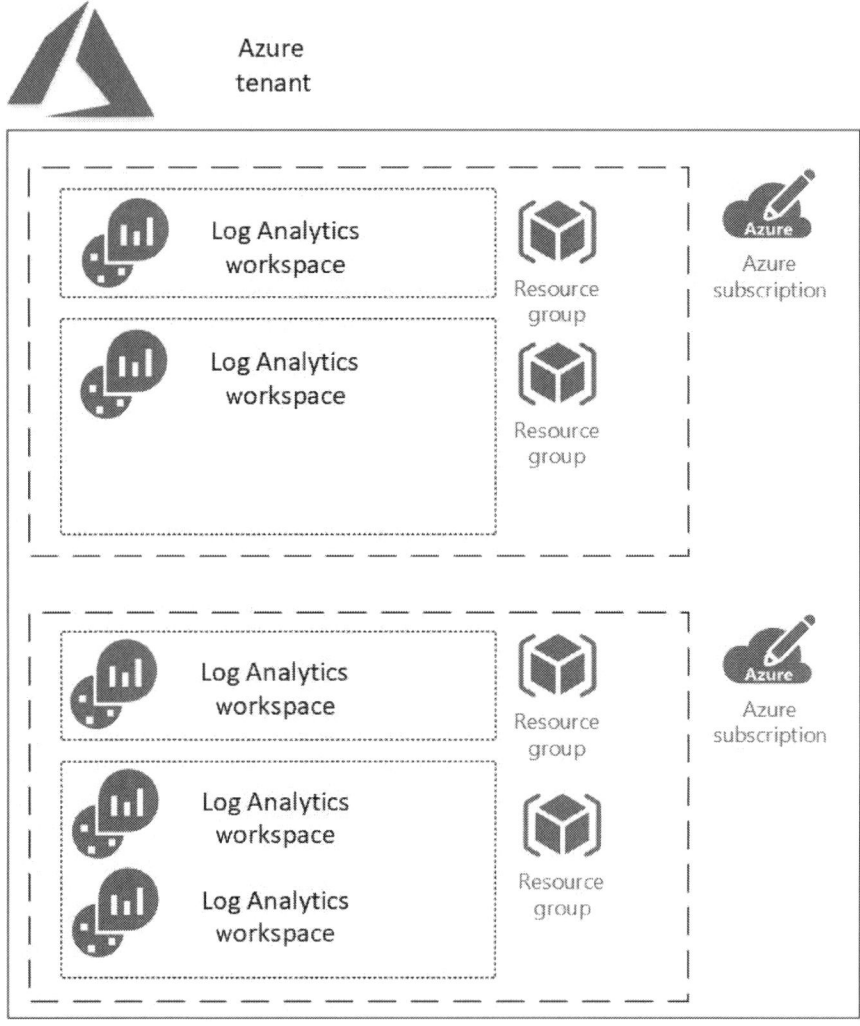

Figure 2.1 – Azure tenant for Log Analytics

Once created, a workspace can be used to gather information from many different sources, including the following:

- Azure resources in the same subscription
- Azure resources in different subscriptions
- Data from other cloud services (such as **Amazon Web Services** and **Google Cloud Platform**)
- Data from your private data center (on-premises or third-party hosted)
- Data from on-premises resources (via secure internet connections)
- Data from IoT and industrial control systems

To protect the collected data, security and governance controls are built into this solution; the Log Analytics service manages your data in a secure cloud data repository and ensures that the data is secured with multiple layers of protection, including the following:

- Data segregation and isolation, with geographic sovereignty
- Data retention and deletion policies, per data source type
- Internationally certified standards for physical security, inherited from the Azure subscription (commercial and government)
- Microsoft-managed incident management processes
- Certified conformity to multiple compliance and regulatory standards
- Secure channels for sending data to Log Analytics; SSL encrypted with certificate-based authentication via port 443
- Workspace and role-based access permissions, managed by the customer; more details are provided later in this chapter

For more information on the way data is secured, we recommend reading the official Microsoft documentation: `https://docs.microsoft.com/en-us/azure/azure-monitor/logs/data-security`.

Planning a workspace

While it is easy to just go and create a workspace, it is better to plan out the workspace configuration beforehand to avoid having to perform reworking later. Some of the aspects to consider include the following:

- **The name of the workspace**: This must be unique across all of Azure. It should be descriptive enough to show what service this workspace provides just by looking at the name. It is recommended that your company name and the word `Sentinel` are used in the name.

  If this raises concerns that the name will make it a bigger target for bad actors, use whatever naming convention that makes sense and meets corporate standards. For detailed information on Azure naming best practices, use this link: `https://docs.microsoft.com/en-us/azure/cloud-adoption-framework/ready/azure-best-practices/naming-and-tagging`.

- **The subscription the workspace belongs to**: It is recommended that a separate subscription is created just for Microsoft Sentinel use to limit access to it. If this is not feasible, choose an appropriate subscription to use.

- **The location of the workspace**: The workspace should reside in the same location as the resources feeding it to prevent egress charges that would occur if you sent the data from one location to another. Large companies will most likely have resources in many different locations, in which case it would make sense to use the location that has the most resources and has the lowest price for the workspace. Keep in mind that there may be laws in place that denote where the data must reside.

  For more information on Log Analytics pricing, see `https://azure.microsoft.com/en-us/pricing/details/monitor`.

- **Which resource group will the workspace reside in**: It is recommended that all the Microsoft Sentinel resources reside in the same resource group, although that is not a hard and fast rule. If it makes more sense to have all your workspaces in one resource group, Microsoft Sentinel in another, and the workbooks in a third resource group, then do that. This will not affect the performance of Microsoft Sentinel at all.

- **Which pricing tier to use**: If the subscription being used to house the workspace has had a workspace created in it before April 2, 2018, or if the subscription is part of a Microsoft Enterprise Agreement that was in place prior to February 1, 2019, you will continue to have access to the legacy pricing tiers. Otherwise, only **Per GB (2018)** is shown, and data is charged for ingestion and retention per GB. The legacy options are as follows:

- **Free**: There is no charge for the data being ingested, although there is a 500 MB daily limit, and the data is retained for only 7 days. This can only be used for lab and research purposes.
- **Standalone (Per GB)**: This is the same as **Per GB (2018)**.
- **Per Node (OMS)**: Use this one if **OMS E1 Suite**, **OMS E2 Suite**, or **OMS Add-On for System Center** have been purchased to use the authorization that came from those purchases.

Planning your workspace before you create it is very important. Make sure to select a unique and meaningful name, the proper location to avoid egress charges, the correct resource group, and other decisions prior to deployment will save you from frustration or complete reworking later. A very good article on this topic was written by Tiander Turpijn: `https://techcommunity.microsoft.com/t5/azure-sentinel/best-practices-for-designing-an-azure-sentinel-or-azure-security/ba-p/832574`.

Creating a workspace using the portal

This section will describe how to create the Log Analytics workspace using the Azure portal. This is a graphical representation of the PowerShell and CLI commands discussed later and, as such, may be the easiest way to start working with workspaces:

1. In the Azure portal, enter `Log Analytics workspaces` in the search bar at the top of the screen. This will show a list of services that are related to the search term entered. Locate and click on the **Log Analytics workspaces** link.
2. Click the **Add** button to create a new workspace:

Figure 2.2 – Creating a new Log Analytics workspace

3. Enter the required values in the new blade:

    A. Enter the name for the workspace.

    B. Select a **Subscription** where this will reside.

    C. Choose the **Resource group** for this workspace.

    D. Select the **Location** where this workspace will reside.

    E. For the **Pricing tier** option, **Per GB (2018)** will automatically be selected.

    The blade will look something like this:

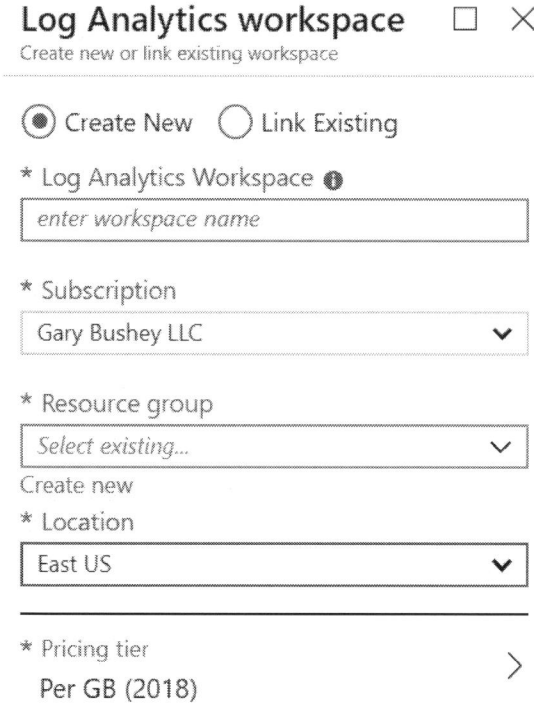

Figure 2.3 – Log Analytics workspace options

4. When all the values have been filled in, click the **OK** button at the bottom of the screen to continue. Even though the button will change to say **Validating**, it is also creating the workspace in the background.

5. Once the workspace has been created, you will be taken back to the listing of all the workspaces. You may need to refresh this listing to see your new workspace.

That is all there is to creating a workspace using the Azure portal. While this is very easy to do, there may be times when you will want to perform these same actions using command-line actions, and that will be described next.

Creating a workspace using PowerShell or the CLI

There are times when you need to be able to consistently recreate an Microsoft Sentinel environment. Perhaps you are just testing all the various configuration options, creating environments for many different subscriptions for an international company, or creating instances for customers. No matter the reason, if you need to create many Microsoft Sentinel environments that are all the same, using PowerShell or the **Command-Line Interface** (**CLI**) is a better option than doing it in the Azure portal.

Creating an Azure Resource Management template

When creating a new Log Analytics workspace using PowerShell in this lab, you will use an **Azure Resource Management** (**ARM**) template to perform the actual configuration. While you can create the workspace directly using either of the technologies, using an ARM template provides additional benefits, including being able to easily recreate the workspace, use the ARM template in a DevOps workflow, or use it in Azure Blueprints.

> **Note**
> A complete discussion of ARM templates is beyond the scope of this lab, but briefly, an ARM template is a JSON file that describes what needs to be created in Azure. It contains parameters, which are the values that a user will provide to determine items such as name, location, and pricing tier. It can also have variables, which are internal values that can be used to determine other values. It will also have a list of one or more resources, which are the Azure resources to create.

Go to `https://docs.microsoft.com/en-us/azure/azure-monitor/platform/template-workspace-configuration` and copy the JSON text. You will be pasting this into a file that you create later.

In this example, you will be prompted for the workspace name and the location, but the pricing tier will default to `pergb2018` due to the presence of a `defaultValue` entry. If you do not wish to have those defaults, you can either change the values shown or remove the entire `defaultValue` line, including the comma at the end, in which case you will be prompted for the values when executing the command.

JSON is just text, so while you can use a program such as Notepad to view it, it is recommended that you use something like *Visual Studio* or *Visual Studio Code*, which provide options including color coding and showing available commands. We will be using a version of Visual Studio Code in the Azure portal for this lab.

In your Azure portal, click on the **Cloud Shell** icon in the top right-hand corner of the screen:

Figure 2.4 – Launching Cloud Shell

If prompted, select the subscription you are currently using for Microsoft Sentinel and then click **Create Storage**. This will only have to be done once, so if you have used Cloud Shell previously you will not be prompted for this.

At the bottom of the screen will be Cloud Shell, which should look like the following screenshot. The text may not match exactly what is shown here:

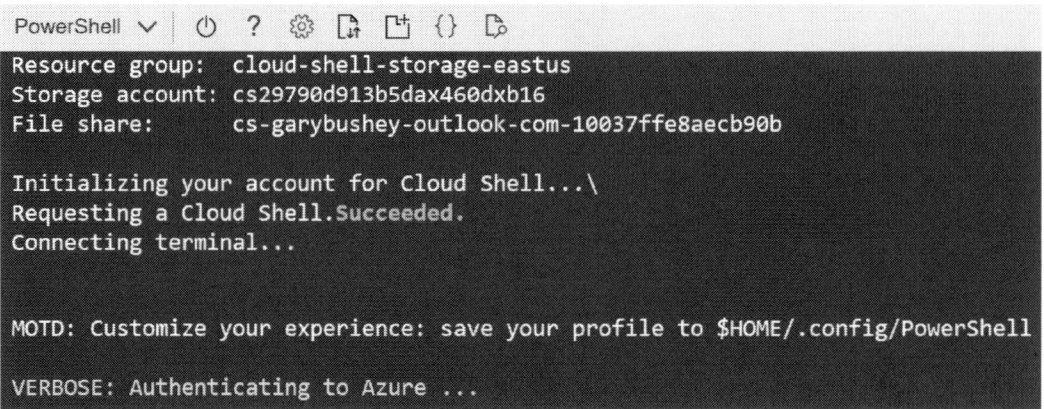

Figure 2.5 – Cloud Shell setup

If, in the top left-hand corner, it says **Bash** rather than **PowerShell**, use the dropdown to change it to **PowerShell**, as that will have the command we need for this lab.

Creating a workspace using PowerShell or the CLI   41

> **Note**
> If you want to run this on your own computer rather than via the Azure portal, go to `https://docs.microsoft.com/en-us/powershell/azure/install-az-ps` to learn how to install the Azure PowerShell module, or `https://docs.microsoft.com/en-us/cli/azure/install-azure-cli?view=azure-cli-latest` to install the Azure CLI module.

Once Cloud Shell has finished loading, enter the following:

```
code deployworkspacetemplate.json
```

This will start a version of Visual Studio Code that you can use in Cloud Shell. Type the code from the preceding snippet. On the right side of the screen, click on the context menu and click **Save**. You can then either click the **X** to close the editor or click on the context menu and click on **Close Editor**:

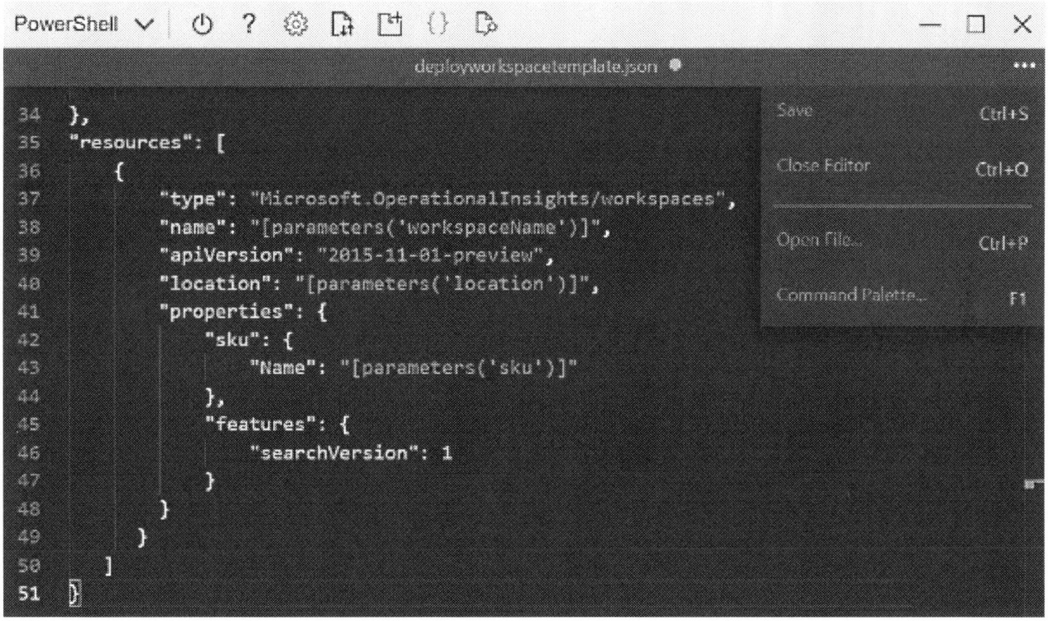

Figure 2.6 – PowerShell deployment using a JSON template

That is how you can use the CLI to create a new Log Analytics ARM template. This is the external file that we will be using in the following sections to create the new workspace.

Using PowerShell

PowerShell is a scripting language that can be used across various machines, including Windows and Linux computers, and was built on top of **.NET**. Because of this, it can accept .NET objects, making it incredibly powerful. PowerShell has many different commands, including some which are specifically created for working with Azure, which we will use here.

Follow these steps to create a new workspace using PowerShell:

1. Determine in which resource group the workspace will reside. If you have one already created, skip to *step 3*.

2. To create a new resource group, run this command:

   ```
   New-AzResourceGroup -Name <resource-group-name> -Location <location>
   ```

   Replace `<resource-group-name>` with the name of the new resource group and `<location>` with the location where the resource group will reside, such as `EastUS` or `WestUS`. If you do not know what to use for your location, run this command:

   ```
   Get-AzLocation
   ```

   Find the location you want and use the value listed under `Location`.

3. Enter the following command:

   ```
   New-AzResourceGroupDeployment -Name <deployment-name> -ResourceGroupName <resource-group-name> -TemplateFile $HOME/deployworkspacetemplate.json
   ```

   Replace `<deployment-name>` with the name of this deployment. You can use something like `<labworkspace>`. It is not important what you enter, as this is just a placeholder name so that when you look at the resource group, you can distinguish the various deployments. Replace `<resource-group-name>` with the name of the resource group where the workspace will reside.

4. You will be prompted for the Log Analytics workspace name as well. Enter a valid name and press *Enter* to continue.

5. Once the command has finished running, it will show a success screen with a summary of the values used as follows:

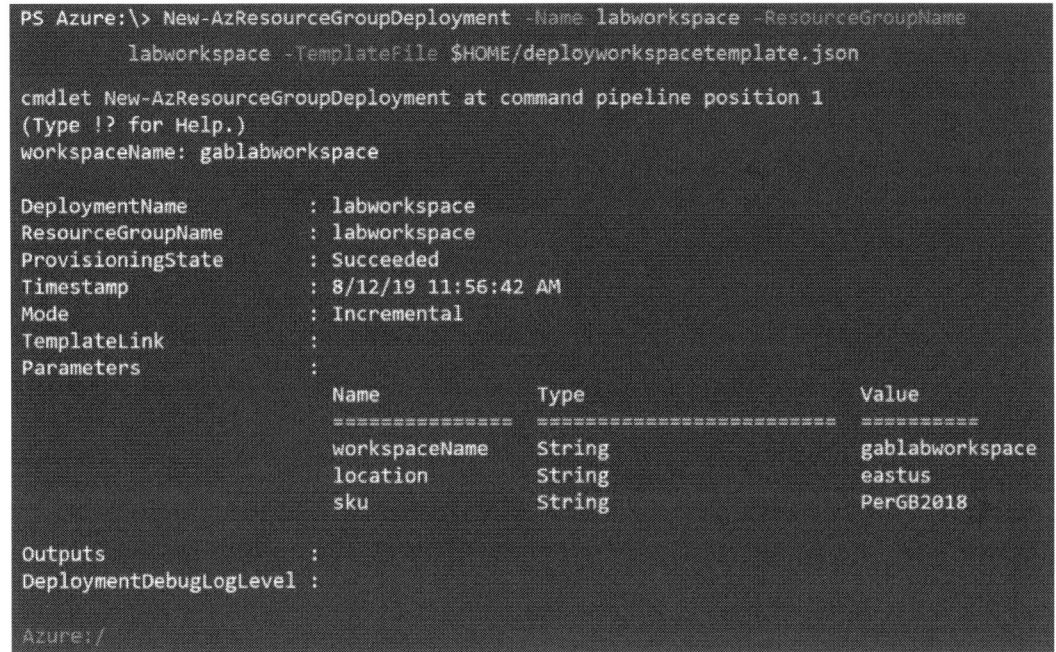

Figure 2.7 – Running New-AzResourceGroupDeployment in PowerShell

If you get an error screen, make sure to read the message, as the messages are usually quite specific as to what caused the error.

6. Close the Cloud Shell session.

That is how you can create a new Log Analytics workspace using an ARM template and PowerShell. This can be preferable to using the Azure portal as it is repeatable. Next, we will look at using the Azure CLI and see how to create a new workspace without using the ARM template.

Using the CLI

The Azure CLI is also a cross-platform scripting tool developed by Microsoft. Initially, it was the only tool that was cross-platform, so if you were working on a computer that was not running Windows, it was your only option. PowerShell is now cross-platform as well, so the main difference between the two is that the Azure CLI can create Azure resources directly without using an ARM template.

The following steps describe how to run the CLI from the Azure portal. If you want to run this on your local computer, you will need to make sure you have the CLI installed. Go to `https://docs.microsoft.com/en-us/cli/azure/install-azure-cli` for instructions on how to perform the installation:

1. Determine which resource group the workspace will reside in. If you have already created one, skip to *step 3*.

2. To create a new resource group, run this command:

   ```
   az group create --name <resource-group-name> --location <location>
   ```

3. Replace `<resource-group-name>` with the name of the new resource group and `<location>` with the location where the resource group will reside, such as `EastUS` or `WestUS`. If you do not know what to use for your location, run this command:

   ```
   az account list-locations
   ```

4. Find the location you want and use the value listed under `name`.

5. Enter the following command:

   ```
   az group deployment create --resource-group <my-resource-group> --name <my-deployment-name> --template-file deploylaworkspacetemplate.json
   ```

   Replace `<deployment-name>` with the name of this deployment. You can use something like `<labworkspace>`. It is not important what you enter, as this is just a placeholder name so that when you look at the resource group, you can distinguish the various deployments. Replace `<resource-group-name>` with the name of the resource group where the workspace will reside.

Creating a workspace using PowerShell or the CLI   45

You will be prompted for the Log Analytics workspace name as well. Enter a valid name and press *Enter* to continue.

Once the command has finished running, it will show either the JSON values for this workspace, as shown in the following screenshot, or an error message. Note that not all the JSON is shown for brevity:

```
PS /home/gary> az group deployment create --resource-group labworkspace --name labworkspace --template-file deployworkspacetemplate.json
This command is implicitly deprecated because command group 'group deployment' is deprecated and will be removed in a future release. Use 'deployment group' instead.
Please provide string value for 'workspaceName' (? for help): labworkspace
{
    "id": "/subscriptions/                              /resourceGroups/labworkspace/providers/Microsoft.Resources/deployments/labworkspace",
    "location": null,
    "name": "labworkspace",
    "properties": {
        "correlationId": "28456301-6114-4739-8285-38765d8e0f5b",
        "debugSetting": null,
        "dependencies": [
            {
                "dependsOn": [
                    {
                        "id": "/subscriptions/                              /resourceGroups/labworkspace/providers/Microsoft.OperationalInsights/workspaces/labworkspace",
                        "resourceGroup": "labworkspace",
                        "resourceName": "labworkspace",
                        "resourceType": "Microsoft.OperationalInsights/workspaces"
                    }
                ],
                "id": "/subscriptions/                              /resourceGroups/labworkspace/providers/Microsoft.OperationsManagement/solutions/SecurityInsights(labworkspace)",
                "resourceGroup": "labworkspace",
                "resourceName": "SecurityInsights(labworkspace)",
                "resourceType": "Microsoft.OperationsManagement/solutions"
            },
            {
                "dependsOn": [
                    {
                        "id": "/subscriptions/                              /resourceGroups/labworkspace/providers/Microsoft.OperationsManagement/solutions/SecurityInsights(labworkspace)",
                        "resourceGroup": "labworkspace",
                        "resourceName": "SecurityInsights(labworkspace)",
                        "resourceType": "Microsoft.OperationsManagement/solutions"
                    }
                ],
                "id": "/subscriptions/                              /resourceGroups/labworkspace/providers/Microsoft.Resources/deployments/enableDataConnectorsKind",
                "resourceGroup": "labworkspace",
                "resourceName": "enableDataConnectorsKind",
                "resourceType": "Microsoft.Resources/deployments"
            }
        ],
```

Figure 2.8 – Running az group deployment create in the CLI

Note that as stated earlier, you can use the Azure CLI to create the Log Analytics workspace directly using the `az monitor log-analytics workspace create` command. Go to https://docs.microsoft.com/en-us/azure/azure-monitor/logs/quick-create-workspace for more information on this command.

6. Close the Cloud Shell session.

Now we can explore the overview page of Log Analytics.

Exploring the Overview page

No matter how you created your Log Analytics workspace, the rest of the work in this lab will be done using the Azure portal:

1. Open the portal and go to the Log Analytics solution page.
2. Find your new Log Analytics workspace for Microsoft Sentinel and click on it. This will take you to the **Overview** screen, as shown in the following screenshot:

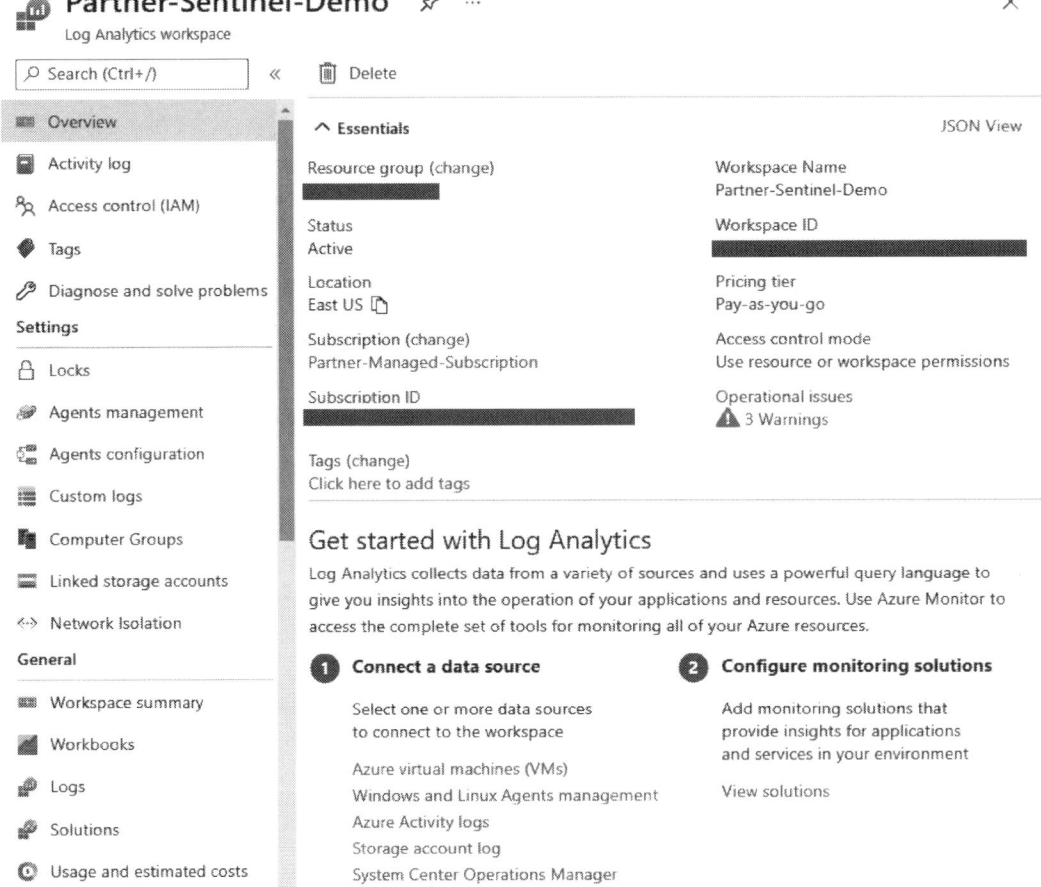

Figure 2.9 – Overview page for Log Analytics

Note that only part of the screen is shown due to the amount of information on this page.

3. Starting with the **Essentials** listing at the top of the page, we can review the following items:

   A. **Resource group**: The resource group where the workspace resides. Selecting [**change**] will allow you to move to another resource group.

   B. **Status**: The status of the workspace should show **Active**.

   C. **Location**: The Azure location where the workspace resides.

   D. **Subscription name**: The subscription this resource is associated with. Selecting [**change**] will allow you to move to another subscription.

   E. **Subscription ID**: The unique GUID for the preceding subscription, which is useful when calling Microsoft for technical support.

   F. **Workspace name**: The name of the Log Analytics workspace.

   G. **Workspace ID**: The GUID for the workspace, which is also useful when calling Microsoft for technical support.

   H. **Pricing tier**: The pricing tier for the workspace.

   I. **Management services**: View the activity log for the workspace.

   J. **Access control mode**: This determines how users are granted permission to access the information in this workspace. Refer to the following section for more information.

The previous sections described the various ways that you can create a new Log Analytics workspace to use with Microsoft Sentinel. This can be done either through the Azure portal or programmatically using either PowerShell or CLI commands. Once the workspace has been created, we next need to ensure that access is restricted to only those users who need to access it.

Managing permissions for the workspace

Before we connect and store data in the workspace and enable Microsoft Sentinel to carry out analytics on the data, let's review the options to secure access to this new resource. Azure provides three main levels of access to resources:

- **Owner**: Has the highest level of access to resources
- **Contributor**: Can create and modify resources, but cannot grant or revoke access
- **Reader**: Can view all resources

These permissions can be granted at four different levels:

- **Subscription**: The highest level of access, applies to all resources within the subscription
- **Resource group**: Applies to a specific resource group, which may contain multiple workspaces
- **Workspace**: Applies only to a specific workspace
- **Table-level RBAC**: Applies to individual tables within the Log Analytics workspace

> **Table-level RBAC**
> While there is no user interface available to set permissions on individual tables within the log, you can create Azure custom roles to set these permissions. See `https://docs.microsoft.com/en-us/azure/azure-monitor/logs/manage-access#table-level-rbac` for more information on how to do this.

Permissions can be applied using built-in roles, or you can make a custom role for specific access if you need to be more granular. To make this simpler, there are several built-in user roles we recommend using to manage access to Log Analytics for the purpose of using Microsoft Sentinel, and we recommend you apply these to the specific resource group used for Microsoft Sentinel:

- Engineers developing new queries and data connectors:

    A. Microsoft Sentinel Contributor: Provides the ability to create and edit dashboards, analytics rules, and other Microsoft Sentinel resources

    B. Microsoft Sentinel Reader: Provides read-only visibility to all Azure resources and Microsoft Sentinel logs

- Analysts running daily operations:

    A. Microsoft Sentinel Responder: Provides the ability to manage incidents, and view data, workbooks, and other Microsoft Sentinel resources

    B. Microsoft Sentinel Reader: Provides read-only visibility to all Azure resources and Microsoft Sentinel logs

More details can be found here: `https://docs.microsoft.com/en-us/azure/sentinel/roles`.

If additional permissions are required, keep to the idea of providing minimal permissions and applying only the specific resources required. It may take some trial and error to get the right outcome, but it is a safer option than providing broad and excessive permissions. For further information, please look at the following article:

`https://docs.microsoft.com/en-us/azure/azure-monitor/logs/manage-access`

Now that we have learned about managing permissions, let's move on to enabling Microsoft Sentinel.

Enabling Microsoft Sentinel

Once you have created a Log Analytics workspace that you want to use with Microsoft Sentinel, it is very easy to attach it to Microsoft Sentinel:

1. If you do not have Microsoft Sentinel enabled for your tenant, sign in to the Azure portal, enter `Microsoft Sentinel` in the search box, and select the **Microsoft Sentinel** option, as shown here:

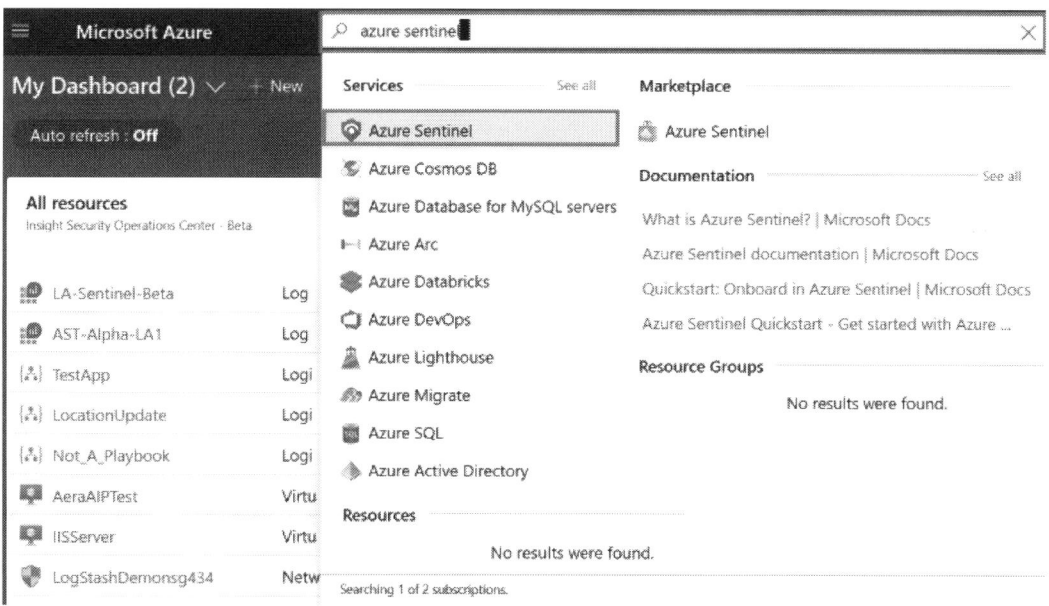

Figure 2.10 – Launching Microsoft Sentinel

2. Click the **Add** button to add a workspace to Microsoft Sentinel:

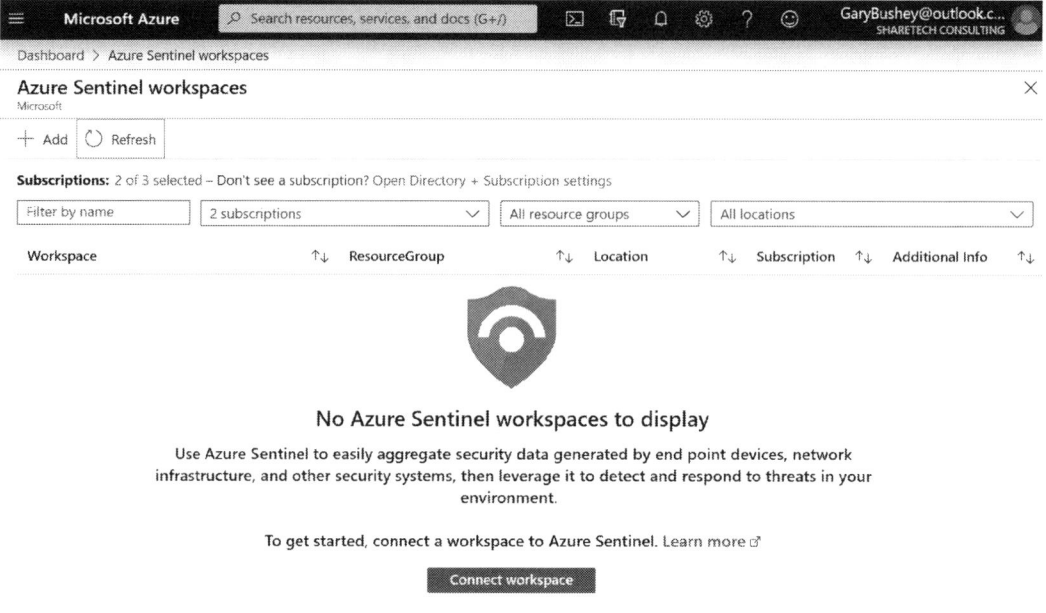

Figure 2.11 – Adding a workspace to Microsoft Sentinel

3. Select the workspace from the list provided or click **Create a new workspace** to add a new workspace using the instructions listed in *Creating a workspace using the portal* section, and then select it. Then, click the **Add Microsoft Sentinel** button at the bottom of the screen to continue:

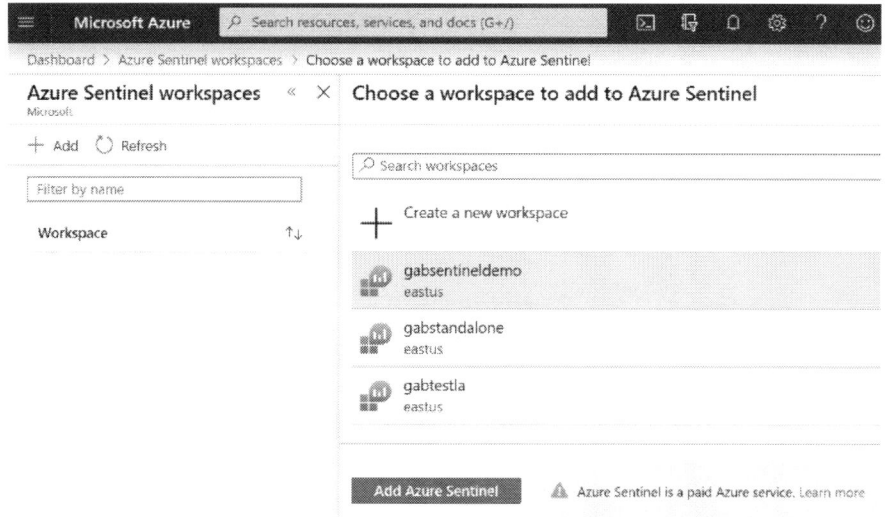

Figure 2.12 – Choosing a workspace

4. Once the workspace has been created, you will be taken to the **Overview** page of Microsoft Sentinel. This page will show a summary of the events, alerts, and incidents. Refer to the following screenshot for more information:

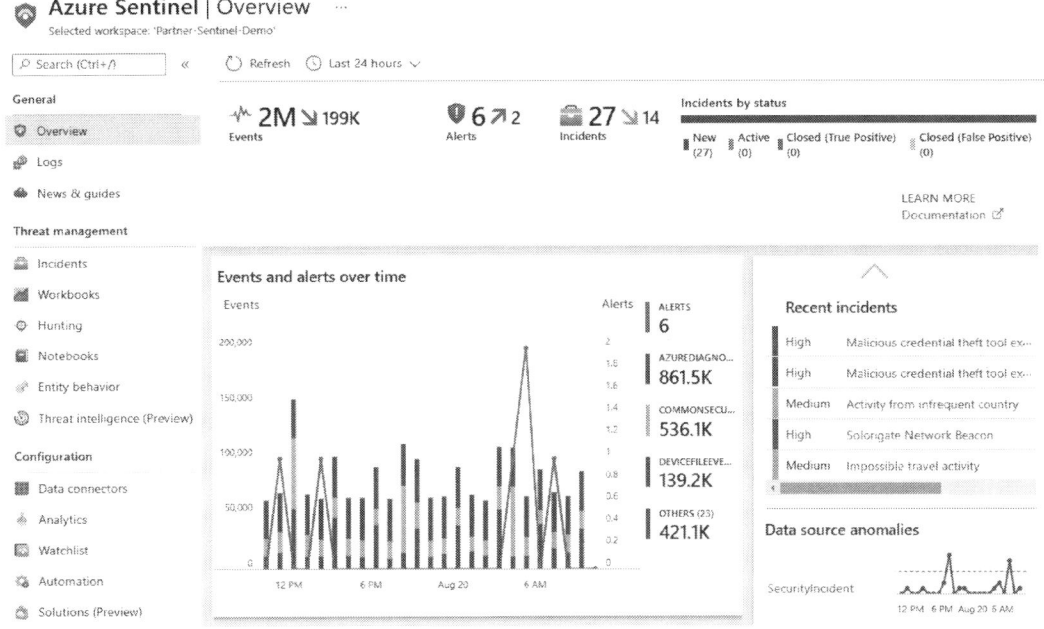

Figure 2.13 – Microsoft Sentinel Overview page

Congratulations! You now have your Microsoft Sentinel environment created and are ready to go. The **News & guides** page is where you will go automatically after attaching a Log Analytics workspace to Microsoft Sentinel. If you leave Microsoft Sentinel and go back to it, you will automatically go to the Microsoft Sentinel **Overview** page, which is described next.

Exploring the Microsoft Sentinel Overview page

The Microsoft Sentinel **Overview** page is the page that you will automatically go to when entering Microsoft Sentinel after you have associated the Log Analytics workspace with it. This page provides a general overview of the information in your Microsoft Sentinel environment and will look like the following screenshot. The actual numbers and data being shown will vary depending on your environment, of course:

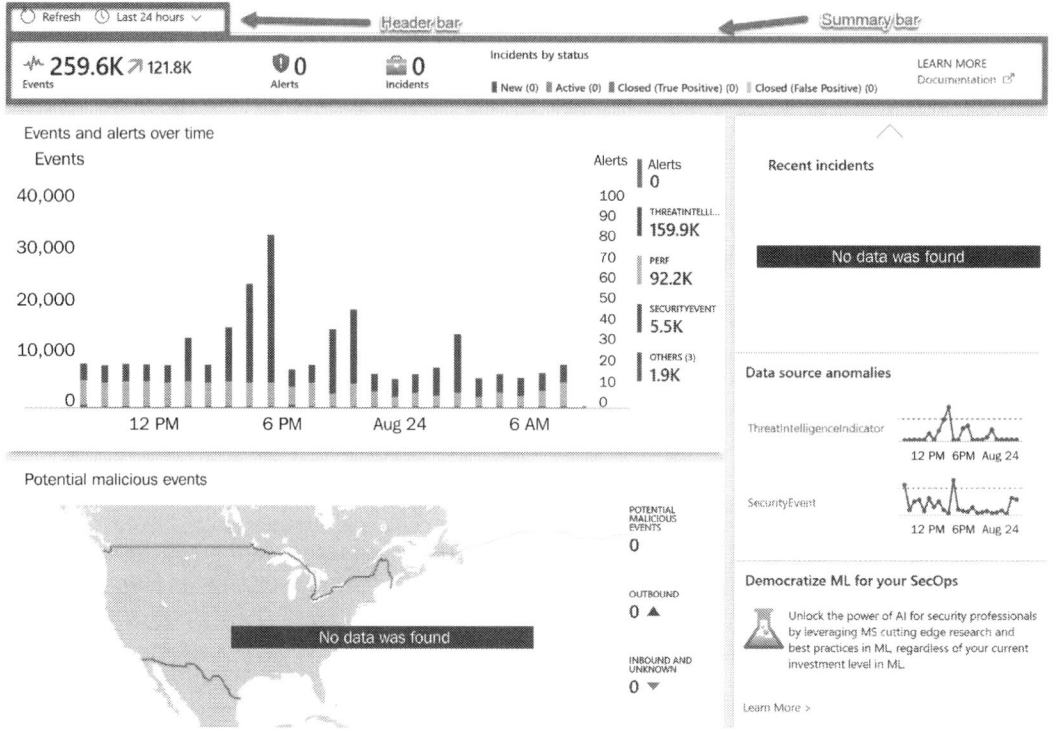

Figure 2.14 – Microsoft Sentinel Overview page

The page shown in the preceding screenshot can be broken up into various parts and each of these is described in the following sections.

The header bar

The header bar allows you to refresh the screen to see any updates, as well as to select how far back in time to look for the data. You can select the icon that looks like a clock to change how far back you want to look.

The summary bar

The summary bar will show you how much data has been ingested in the selected time, as well as how many alerts were raised, and the number of incidents those alerts created. In addition, the incidents are broken down by their status.

The Events and alerts over time section

This section will show the logs that have ingested the most data and the number of incidents created in the selected time frame. This is an interactive chart, so when you mouse over a specific time, the information will be filtered to show what happened at that time.

The Recent incidents section

This section will show up to the last five created incidents as well as the number of alerts that have generated the incident. You can click on the incident name to get more information about the incident.

The Data source anomalies section

This section will show up to two different data sources that Microsoft Sentinel's Machine Learning has determined that contain anomalies. You can click on the log name to get more information about the anomaly.

The Potential malicious events section

This section, not shown, will show an interactive map where any potential malicious events will be highlighted. You can zoom in to the map to get a very precise indication of where the event occurred.

The Democratize ML for your SecOps section

This section, not shown, provides some general information on Microsoft Sentinel's use of machine learning and provides a link where you can obtain more information.

That is the Microsoft Sentinel **Overview** page. It is a great place to go to get an overview of what is going on in your Microsoft Sentinel environment and is the landing page of Microsoft Sentinel. While *Figure 2.14* shows lots of data, when you first create a Log Analytics workspace, it will be empty. The next section will explain how to start getting data into your workspace.

Connecting your first data source

Before we dig into the details of the Microsoft Sentinel data connectors (see *Chapter 3, Managing and Collecting Data*), we will review how Log Analytics enables connectivity to a range of different sources to receive data to store and analyze. Some of the data source options include the following:

- Application and OS diagnostics
- Virtual machine log data
- Azure storage account logs
- Azure Activity log
- Other Azure resources

In this section, we will show you how you can enable log collection from Azure virtual machines.

Obtaining information from Azure virtual machines

To have the **virtual machines** (**VMs**) populate a Log Analytics workspace, they need to be connected to it. This is done from the Log Analytics workspace **Overview** page.

There are two different ways to get to this page. First, you can select **Log Analytics** in the Azure portal navigation menu and then select the appropriate workspace. The second, and perhaps easier, way is to select **Settings** from the Microsoft Sentinel navigation menu and then select **Workspace settings** from the options at the top of the page, as shown in the following screenshot:

Connecting your first data source 55

Home > Azure Sentinel

Azure Sentinel | Settings
Selected workspace:

| Search (Ctrl+/) | « Pricing Settings **Workspace settings >** |

General

- Overview
- Logs
- News & guides

Threat management

- Incidents
- Workbooks
- Hunting
- Notebooks
- Entity behavior
- Threat intelligence (Preview)

Configuration

- Data connectors
- Analytics
- Watchlist (Preview)
- Automation
- Community
- **Settings**

Azure Sentinel pricing

Azure Sentinel is billed based on the volume of data ingested for analysis in Azure Sentinel. Azure Sentinel offers a flexible and predictable pricing model.
There are two ways to pay for the Azure Sentinel service: Capacity Reservations and Pay-As-You-Go. The cost for Azure Sentinel depends on the pricing tier selected. Learn more about Azure Sentinel pricing.

> This does not include the Azure Log Analytics price for ingesting data. Learn more about Log Analytics pricing.

∨ **100 GB/day**
50% discount over Pay-as-you-go

∨ **200 GB/day**
55% discount over Pay-as-you-go

∨ **300 GB/day**
57% discount over Pay-as-you-go

∨ **400 GB/day**
58% discount over Pay-as-you-go

∨ **500+ GB/day**
60% discount over Pay-as-you-go

∨ **Pay-as-you-go**   Current tier
Per GB

> You can increase your workspace data retention to **90 days for free** because you are an Azure Sentinel customer. Configure retention

Figure 2.15 – Microsoft Sentinel workspace settings

56　Azure Monitor – Introduction to Log Analytics

No matter which method you use to get to the page, it will look like the following screenshot:

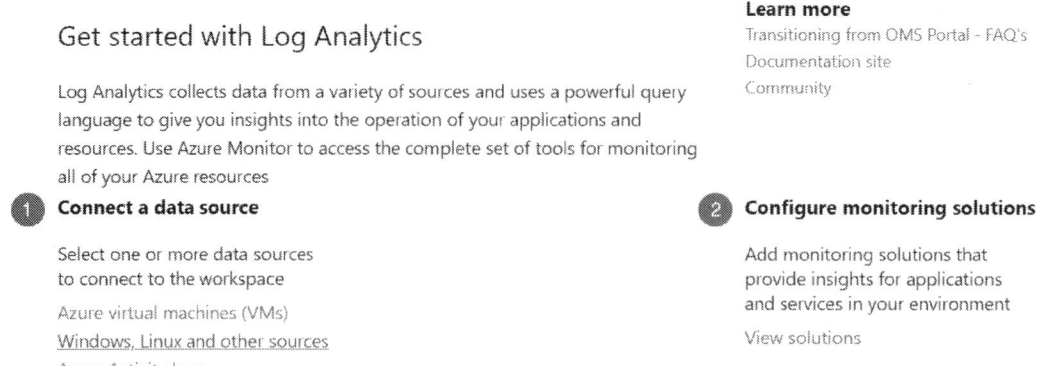

Figure 2.16 – Log Analytics overview page

Under **Workspace Data Sources**, select **Virtual machines**. This will take you to the **Virtual machines** page, which lists each VM and shows whether it is connected, as well as the OS, subscription GUID, the resource group, and the location it belongs to. The following screenshot is an example of what this page looks like:

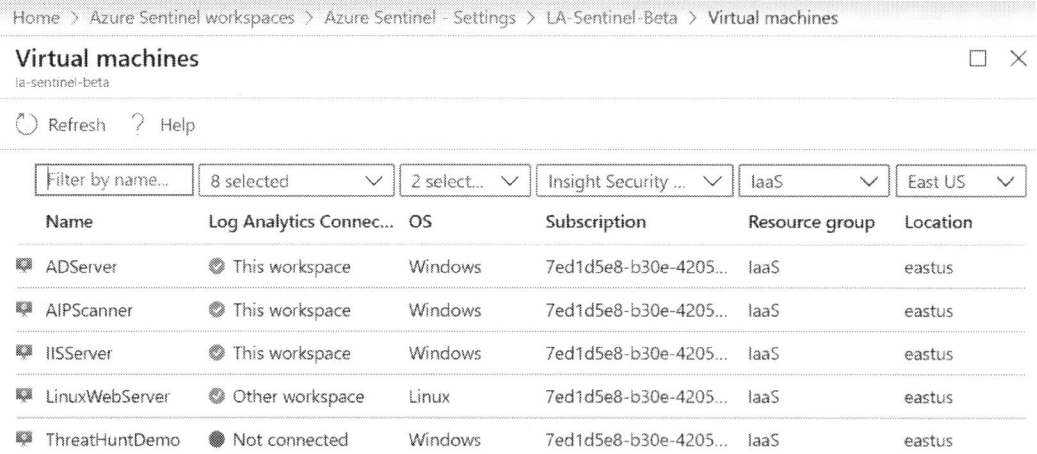

Figure 2.17 – Log Analytics – Azure Virtual machines page

You can see that the first three VMs are connected to this workspace, the fourth one, called **LinuxWebServer**, is connected to another workspace, and the final one, **ThreatHuntDemo**, is not connected to any workspace.

To change the connection status of any of the VMs, click on the row containing it. This will open a new blade, where you can either connect or disconnect the VM:

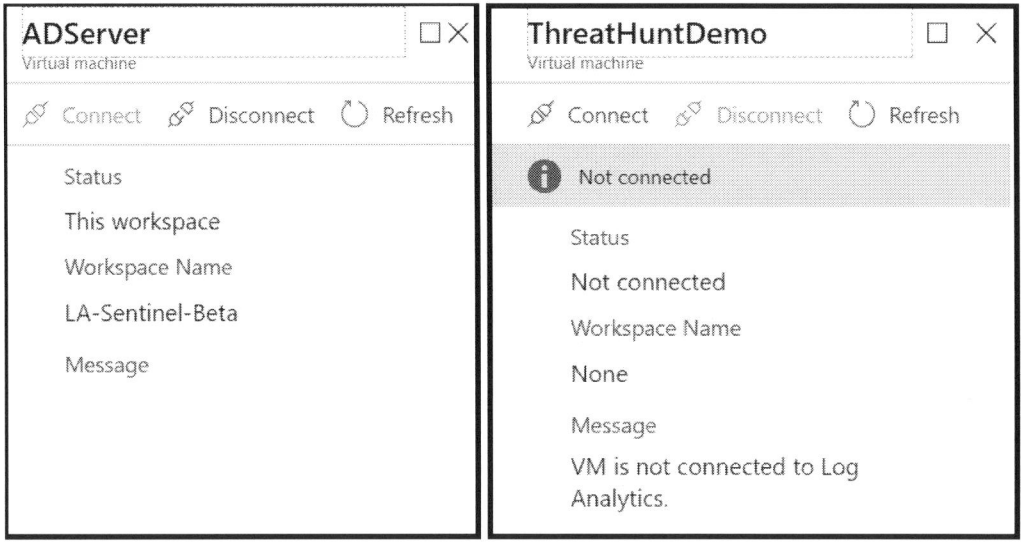

Figure 2.18 – Azure VM log data connection

Select either the **Disconnect** or **Connect** buttons to perform the action you desire.

Connecting a VM to a Log Analytics workspace downloads and installs the Microsoft Monitoring Agent to the VM, so this step can be performed automatically when provisioning the VM using tools such as *PowerShell Desired State Configuration*. However, the actual steps to perform this task are beyond the scope of this book.

In a large-scale deployment, especially with VMs that are not hosted in Azure, you may not want each individual server directly sending their logs to the Log Analytics workspace. Instead, you may consider deploying the Syslog/CEF connector to centralize log collection and data ingestion. Each VM would then point toward the CEF connector server instead of Log Analytics.

Next, we will look at the advanced settings for Log Analytics.

Advanced settings for Log Analytics

The advanced settings for Log Analytics allow you to perform actions such as connecting on-premises and other non-Azure Windows and Linux servers, Azure Storage, and System Center Management groups. You can also set what information to import from Windows and Linux servers, import IIS logs and Syslog events, and add custom logs and fields. Finally, you can create groups of computers, or use groups already created in Active Directory, **Windows Server Update Service** (**WSUS**), and SCCM, which can be used in your queries.

To get to the **Advanced settings** page, follow the instructions to get to the Log Analytics overview page in the previous section, but instead of selecting **Azure virtual machines** (**VMs**), select **Agents management**. This will open a new page, as shown in the following screenshot:

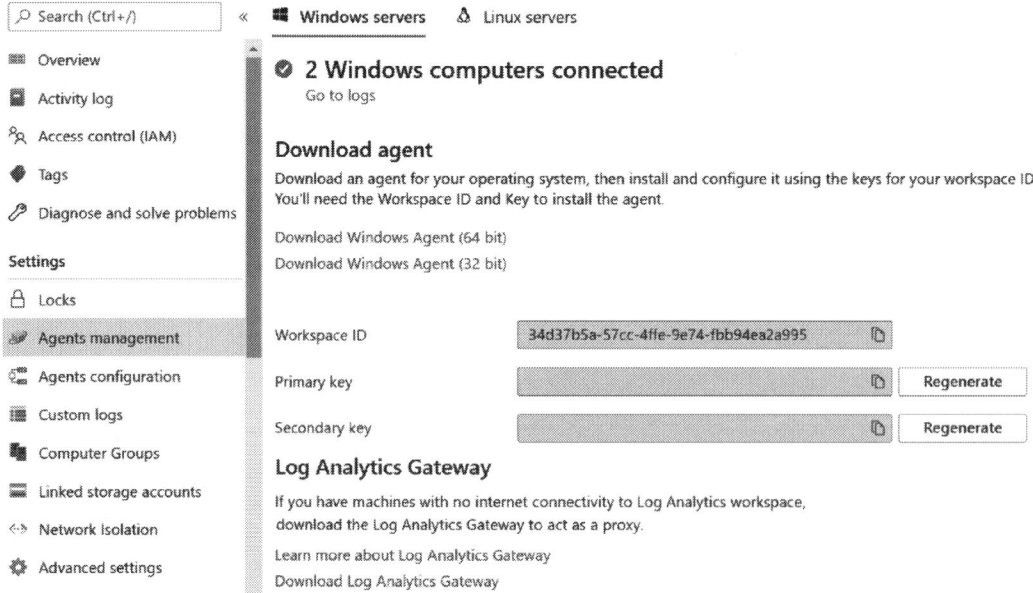

Figure 2.19 – Microsoft Sentinel Agents management

As you can see, there are two tabs for connecting to Windows and Linux servers respectively to ingest data. Each one will be discussed in the next section.

Agents management

This area allows you to attach non-Azure Windows and Linux servers:

- **Windows servers**: You can attach a non-Azure Windows-based VM to the workspace to collect Windows event logs and performance counters. Click on either **Download Windows Agent (64bit)** or **Download Windows Agent (32bit)** to match the Windows version you are using and run the program on the server. Copy the **Workspace ID** and either the **Primary key** or **Secondary key** details and fill them in when asked.

- **Linux servers**: This works the same as for Windows servers – click on the **Download Linux Agent** link and read the documentation for installation instructions.

> **Note**
> While this can be used to connect Azure VMs, it is far easier to use the steps in the previous section to do so.

Next, we will look at the **Agents configuration** page, which provides options for ingesting data from the agents.

The Agents configuration options

This area allows you to determine which data from connected servers will be imported. Selecting the **Agents configuration** page will bring you to the following page:

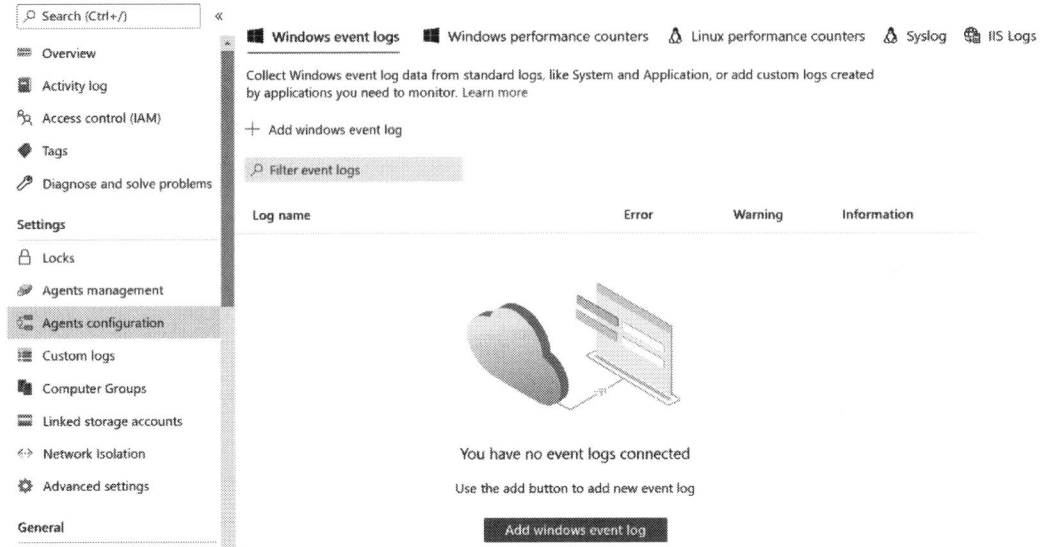

Figure 2.20 – Microsoft Sentinel Agents configuration page

Let's look at the different tabs under the **Agents configuration** option:

- **Windows event logs**: This allows you to search for all the various logs that show up in the Windows Event Viewer, including items such as the **Application**, **Setup**, and **System** logs, to have them included in the Log Analytics workspace. While having all this data can be handy, if there are a lot of Windows servers connected, it can lead to a large amount of data being imported. Note that the Windows Security log is not available since it will always be imported from any connected Windows server.

- **Windows performance counters**: This will show a listing of all the performance counters that will be included by default and their polling intervals. From here, you can change the interval or remove the counter completely. You can also add other counters to monitor.
- **Linux performance counters**: This will show a listing of all the Linux performance counters that will be included by default and the polling interval for those counters that use a polling interval. From here, you can change the interview or remove the counter completely. You can also add other counters to monitor.
- **Syslog**: This section enables the collection of data from Syslog servers. Select the severity for each facility to ensure messages are collected, and all others will be excluded. For more details review this page: `https://docs.microsoft.com/en-us/azure/azure-monitor/agents/data-sources-syslog`.
- **IIS Logs**: This determines whether W3C-format IIS log files will be ingested from Windows web servers. An example of this is the web logs from a Linux-based web server.

As you can see, there are a lot of ways in which you can configure the data to import. There will always be a trade-off between what data you need or want and the cost of ingesting and storing the data. In the next section, we will look at **Computer Groups**, which can help you with your queries.

Computer Groups

This section will show all the custom computer groups that have been created and provide a way to create your own. These groups can then be used in queries. You can use these groups to create queries that reference a specific set of servers that can then easily be changed without having to change the query itself.

Under the Log Analytics **Setting** menu, selecting the **Computer Groups** option will present you with the following screen:

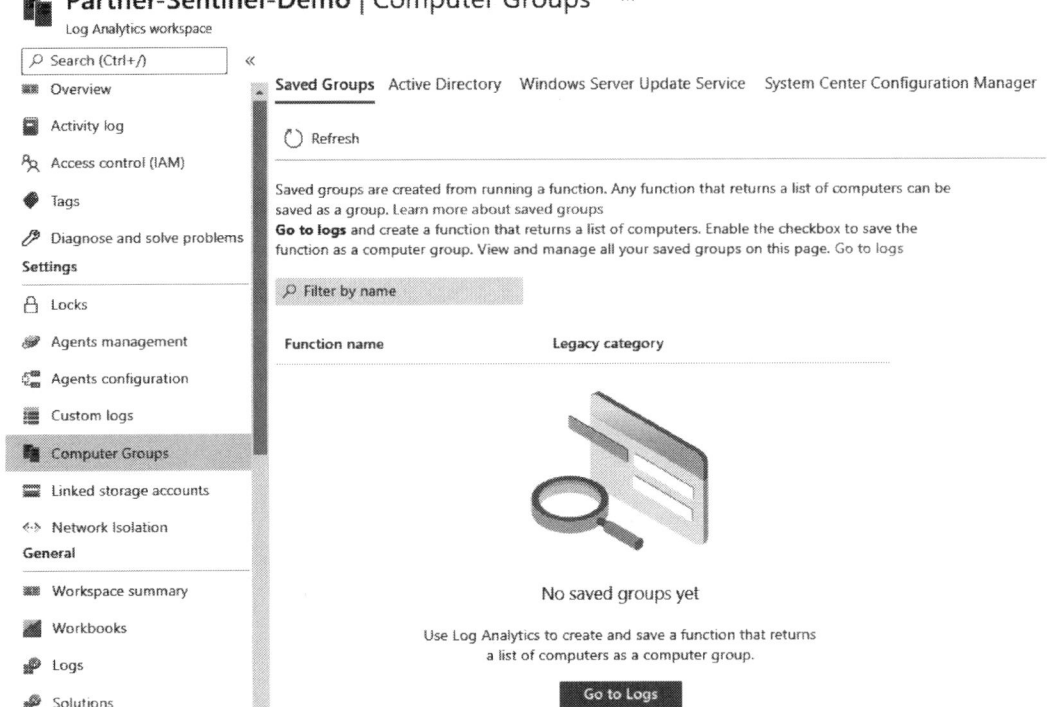

Figure 2.21 – Microsoft Sentinel Settings | Computer Groups

Let's discuss the different fields under **Computer Groups**:

- **Saved Groups**: This page will show all the custom groups that have been added. It also provides instructions on creating a computer group from a query. An example of how to do this will be provided at the end of this section.

- **Active Directory**: Select the **Import Active Directory group memberships from computers** checkbox to allow groups from Active Directory to be imported. After this is enabled, it may take a few minutes before any groups show up.

- **Windows Server Update Service**: Select the **Import WSUS group memberships** checkbox to allow groups from the Windows Server Update Service to be imported. After this is enabled, it may take a few minutes before any groups show up.

- **System Center Configuration Manager**: Select the **Import Configuration Manager collection memberships** checkbox to allow groups from SCCM to be imported. After this is enabled, it may take a few minutes before any groups show up.

Advanced settings for Log Analytics   63

There are various ways to create computer groups to help you with your queries. Each of these will be discussed in more detail in the following sections.

Adding a computer group from a query

Adding a computer group using a query involves running a query that will return a list of computers and then save that information as a computer group:

1. In the **Saved Groups** section under **Computer Groups**, click on the **Go to Logs** link to go to the **Logs** page. Enter any query that will generate a listing of computers. Here's an example:

   ```
   Heartbeat
   | where TimeGenerated > ago(30m)
   | distinct Computer
   ```

   Don't worry about what the query means, it will be explained in *Chapter 5, Using the Kusto Query Language*. For now, this will return a listing of all those computers that have sent a heartbeat to the workspace in the last 30 minutes. Note that you will need to have a server connected to Azure (see the *Obtaining information from Azure virtual machines and Connected sources* sections) to get any information from this query.

2. Click on the **Run** button to get a list of computers. If no computers are returned, change 30 to a larger value until some are returned.

3. Once you have a list, click on the **Save** button to save this query:

Figure 2.22 – Computer heartbeat query

4. Choose the **Save as function** option, then provide a name for the function.

5. Make sure to check the **Save this query as a computer group** option, otherwise it will just save as a query that can be the same as the **Name**.

6. Finally, add a **Legacy category**, which is just used to group the computer groups together.

7. Click the **Save** button, as shown in the following screenshot:

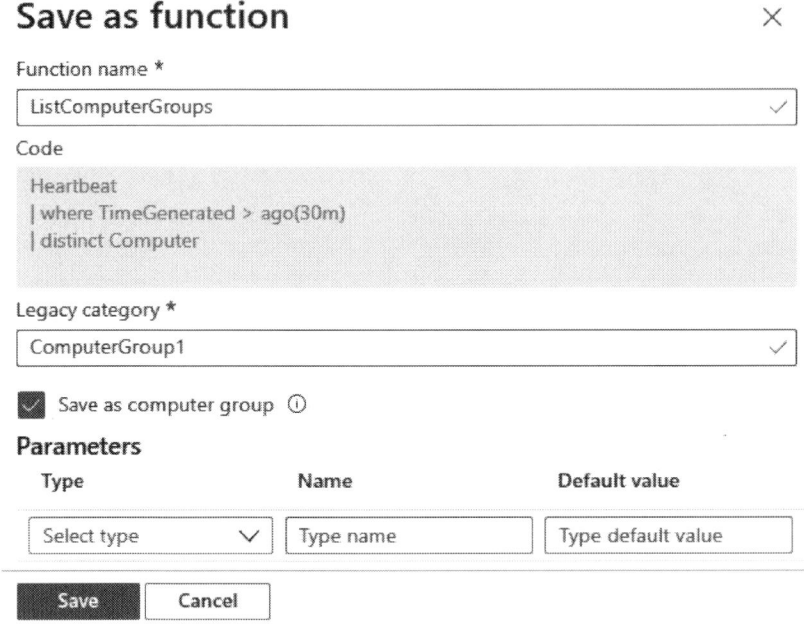

Figure 2.23 – Save query options

When you go back to the **Saved Groups** page, you will see your saved group, which will look like what is shown in the following screenshot:

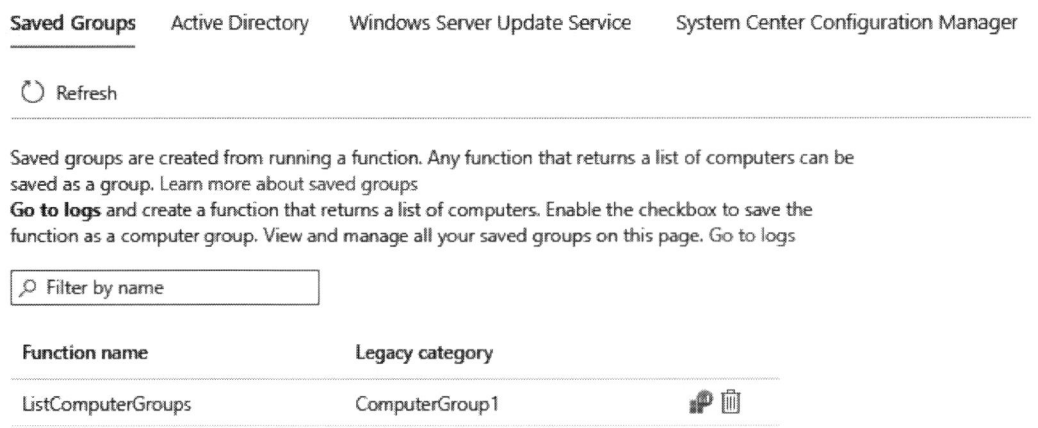

Figure 2.24 – Saved Groups

To use a saved group, enter a query like this:

```
Perf
| where Computer in (ListComputerGroups)
```

Substitute `ListComputerGroups` for the name of the query you just created. Again, do not worry about what this query means; it is just an example of how to use a saved group. It will make more sense after reading *Chapter 5, Using the Kusto Query Language*.

Summary

In this chapter, we explored the Azure Monitor Log Analytics solution, including how to create a new workspace using the Azure portal, PowerShell, or CLI, and how to configure the security options to ensure each user has the appropriate level of access. We also looked at how to connect a data source and configure some of the advanced settings. This information is very useful when you need to first configure Microsoft Sentinel, and for the future should you need to make any changes to the Log Analytics platform supporting your operational and business needs.

In the next chapter, we will look at how to select data that is most useful for security threat hunting, which connectors to use to gather the data from any system, and the options available to enable long-term data retention while keeping costs under control.

Questions

Answer these questions to test your knowledge of this chapter:

1. What is the name of the query language used in Azure Monitor Log Analytics?
2. What is the purpose of Azure Lighthouse?
3. Can you list three ways in which data is protected in Log Analytics?
4. What are the three ways to create a new Log Analytics workspace?
5. What are the recommended permissions for an engineer role?

Further reading

- *Agent data sources in Azure Monitor*: https://docs.microsoft.com/en-us/azure/azure-monitor/agents/agent-data-sources
- *Managing access to log data and workspaces in Azure Monitor*: https://docs.microsoft.com/en-us/azure/azure-monitor/logs/manage-access
- *Log Analytics agent overview*: https://docs.microsoft.com/en-us/azure/azure-monitor/agents/log-analytics-agent

Section 2: Data Connectors, Management, and Queries

In this section, you will learn how to collect data, manage data to prevent overspend, and query data for useful information as part of your threat hunting and other security activities.

This section contains the following chapters:

- *Chapter 3, Managing and Collecting Data*
- *Chapter 4, Integrating Threat Intelligence with Microsoft Sentinel*
- *Chapter 5, Using the Kusto Query Language*
- *Chapter 6, Microsoft Sentinel Logs and Writing Queries*

3
Managing and Collecting Data

One of the primary purposes of a **Security Information and Event Management** (**SIEM**) solution is to centralize the storage and analysis of security events across a diverse range of products that provide protection across your organization's IT infrastructure. To do this, the solution needs to connect to those data sources, pull the data into a central store, and manage the life cycle of that data to ensure it is available for analysis and ongoing investigations.

In this chapter, we will review the types of data that are most interesting and useful for security operations, and then explore the functionality available to connect to multiple data sources and ingest that data into Microsoft Sentinel by storing it in the Log Analytics workspace. Once the data is ingested, we need to ensure the appropriate configuration for data retention to maximize the ability to hunt for events and other security information, while also ensuring the cost of the solution is maintained at a reasonable level.

We will cover the following areas specific to data collection:

- Choosing data that matters
- Understanding connectors
- Configuring Microsoft Sentinel connectors

Then, we will cover these areas to ensure appropriate data management:

- Configuring Log Analytics storage options
- Calculating the cost of data ingestion and retention
- Reviewing alternative storage options

Choosing data that matters

Quality data management is critical to the success of big data analytics and forms the basis of how an SIEM solution works. Gathering large volumes of data for analysis is required to find security threats and unusual behavior across a vast array of infrastructure and applications. However, there needs to be a balance between capturing too little and too much data. Too little data will mean not having enough to find correlating activities, but too much data will increase the signal noise associated with alert fatigue and will increase the cost of the security solution to store and analyze the information. In this case, the security solution is Azure Log Analytics and Microsoft Sentinel, but this principle also applies to other SIEM solutions.

A recent shift in the data security landscape is the introduction of multiple platforms that carry out log analysis locally and only forward relevant events to the SIEM solution. Instead of duplicating the logs, hoping to fish relevant information from it by using a single security analysis tool (such as an SIEM solution), new security products are focused on gathering specific data and resolving threats within their own boundaries. Some examples include the following:

- **Identity and Access Management** (**IAM**) for continuous analysis and condition-based access, per session
- **Endpoint Detection and Response** (**EDR**) for detailed analysis on every host, with centralized analytics across devices for threat mapping and remediation
- A **Cloud access Security Broker** (**CASB**) for user behavior analytics across firewalls and external cloud-based solutions
- A **Next-Generation Firewall** (**NGFW**) for monitoring and responding to dynamic changes in behavior across internal- and external-facing networks

> Note
> Refer to *Chapter 1, Getting Started with Microsoft Sentinel*, for further details about each of these solutions.

Each of these solutions already gathers large volumes of data from their respective data sources; there may be certain cases where you may want to collect raw logs from these products into the SIEM for correlation across multiple data sources. However, you should consider this on a case-by-case basis to justify the cost. As an alternative, instead of collecting the raw data, these solutions can be configured to only send alerts or specific events that are actionable information. This can enable the SIEM to act as the central point of communication for analysis, alerting, and ticketing. The net result is a reduction in duplication and overall solution cost. This idea is summarized in the following diagram:

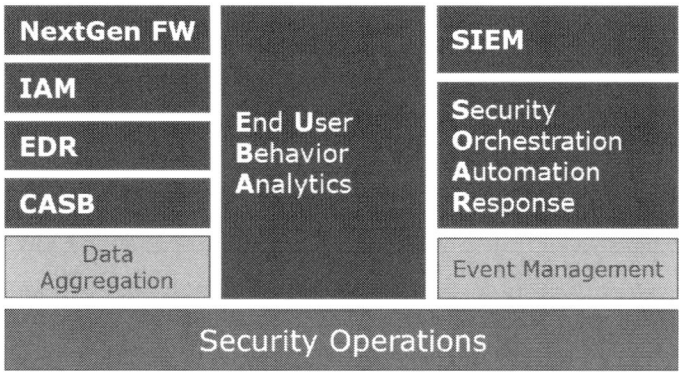

Figure 3.1 – Data for security operations

When dealing with large data volumes, we can use the seven Vs of big data to guide our decisions on what is the right data to collect, based on the priorities assigned:

- **Volume**: This directly impacts the cost of moving and storing the data.
- **Velocity**: This impacts the time to respond to an event.
- **Variety**: Are we including every aspect of apps and infrastructure?
- **Variability**: Is the information easy to understand and act upon?
- **Veracity**: Do we trust the source and accuracy of the data?
- **Visualization**: Can we use this data to create visualizations and comparisons?
- **Value**: Consistently review the value of the data, reduce waste, and retain value.

Here is an example of how to use each of these values to prioritize the data and provide some justification for the ingestion. Instead of focusing on total volume, consider the need for the quality and variety of the data to provide accurate and actionable information across multiple systems.

A summary of this topic is shown in the following figure:

7 Vs of Big Data	
Volume	How much is enough, or too much?
Velocity	How fast can we gather and analyze?
Variety	Can we see all points of view?
Variability	Standardized or requires formatting?
Veracity	How accurate and verified is the data?
Visualization	Can the data show trend analysis?
Value	Is there value in retaining old data?

Figure 3.2 – The seven Vs of big data

You can use this chart to guide your initial assessment of the types of data you need to ingest into Microsoft Sentinel and those that can be excluded. As an example: if you have implemented an EDR solution that will ingest, analyze, and alert on many client data sources, do you really need to ingest the full telemetry data into the SIEM, or can you just use the alerts? The EDR telemetry does need to be retained for longer periods, but the SIEM may not be the right place to put it. Instead, consider using a data lake such as **Azure Data Explorer**.

One area for immediate improvement is to remove any data that is not for security purposes, such as performance metrics and statistical data from applications. These can be redirected to store in another Log Analytics workspace that does not have Microsoft Sentinel enabled. We recommend you review the data pipeline periodically to ensure you are maintaining a healthy dataset, either by adding more data sources, or by tuning out some of the data that no longer meets the requirements but has costs to store and process.

In the next section, we will look at the different types of connectors available in Microsoft Sentinel.

Understanding connectors

Microsoft Sentinel relies on Log Analytics to store data for all ingested security sources, process that data, and find useful information about potential risks and security threats. The data required may be generated by many different types of resources across many different platforms, which is why we need many different options for connecting to those data sources. Understanding the options available, and how to configure them, is key to developing a strong data architecture to support the Microsoft Sentinel solution.

A summary of the connectors is shown in the following diagram:

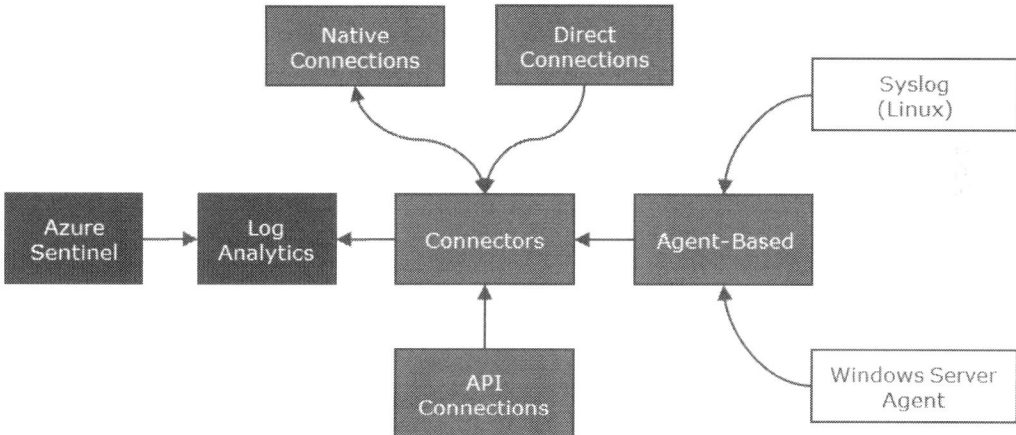

Figure 3.3 – Microsoft Sentinel connector flow

Connectors can be categorized based on the method used to ingest data from the source. Currently, there are four main types:

- Native connections
- Direct connections
- API connections
- Agent-based (Windows Server Agent and Syslog)

Let's explore each of these types in more detail.

Native connections – service to service

Microsoft Sentinel has been developed to integrate directly with several resources across Microsoft solutions, including (but not limited to) the following:

- **Azure Active Directory** (**Azure AD**), including the Azure AD Advanced Identity Protection solution
- **Office 365**, including Exchange Online, Teams, SharePoint Online, and OneDrive for Business
- **Microsoft Defender 365**, including Microsoft Defender for Endpoint, Microsoft Defender for Identity, Microsoft Defender for Office 365, and Microsoft Cloud App Security
- **Azure Security Center**, including Azure Defender
- **Microsoft Defender for Identity**

This is the preferred method for connecting to resources if the option is available. Let's look at direct connections.

Direct connections – service to service

Some connectors available in Microsoft Sentinel need to be configured from the source location. The connector will usually provide the information required and a link to the appropriate location. The data may be sent via an event hub or could be sent directly to the Log Analytics workspace. Examples of these connectors include the following:

- **Amazon Web Services** (**AWS**), for AWS CloudTrail
- Azure Firewall
- Azure Front Door
- Azure **Network Security Groups** (**NSGs**); flow logs and rule activations
- Microsoft Intune; audit logs and operational logs

Now, let's look at API connections.

API connections

Several security providers have API options that allow connections to be made to their solutions to extract the logs and bring the data into Microsoft Sentinel. This is the preferred method for connecting to third-party solutions that support it, and you have the option to create your own connectors. For further information on creating API-based connectors, see this article: `https://techcommunity.microsoft.com/t5/azure-sentinel/azure-sentinel-creating-custom-connectors/ba-p/864060`.

Examples of API-based data connectors include the following:

- Barracuda Web Application Firewall
- Symantec **Integrated Cyber Defense Exchange (ICDx)**

The next type of connection is required for services that do not support any of the preceding options, usually for virtual or physical servers, firewalls, proxy, and other network-based devices.

Agent-based

This connector type will allow for the widest range of data connections and is an industry-standard method of shipping logs between resources and SIEM solutions. There are three types of connectors to consider; you may deploy one or more depending on your needs, and you may deploy multiple instances of the same type too. Let's discuss them in detail.

Azure Monitor agent

Any server running Microsoft Windows or Linux can use the new Azure Monitor agent to collect specific data from each server and send it to Microsoft Sentinel. Read more about this highly flexible and scalable solution here: `https://docs.microsoft.com/en-us/azure/azure-monitor/agents/azure-monitor-agent-overview`.

If you are using Azure Security Center and Azure Defender to monitor and protect your servers, use this to onboard data collection instead of using the Azure Monitor agent. This can apply to servers running on-premises, in Azure, or in other cloud services such as AWS.

Syslog server

This is a transport mechanism implemented by deploying an agent on a Linux host that can act as a concentrator for many sources to send logs to, which are then forwarded on to Log Analytics for central storage. For detailed guidance on implementing a Syslog connector, please see this article: `https://docs.microsoft.com/en-us/azure/sentinel/connect-syslog`. Examples of third-party solutions that support this method include (but are not limited to) the following:

- Carbon Black
- Cisco (IronPort web security, Meraki, and others)
- Citrix
- F5 BIG-IP
- NetApp
- Palo Alto Cortex
- Trend Micro

While these options provide a wide range of options for data sources to gather, there is another method that, if available from the service provider, will give a richer dataset. Let's look at the **Common Event Format** (**CEF**) option next.

Syslog server with CEF

This is very similar to the Syslog server deployment mentioned previously. For more detailed information, see this article: `https://docs.microsoft.com/en-us/learn/modules/connect-common-event-format-logs-to-azure-sentinel/`. The CEF log format is extensible and adopted by multiple product vendors that want to provide greater detail in the logs generated. Examples of solutions that support this method include the following:

- Cisco (Umbrella, cloud security gateway, and others)
- CyberArk
- F5 Firewall
- McAfee Web Gateway
- Palo Alto Networks firewall
- Varonis
- Zscaler

With this range of connectors available, it is possible to connect to and gather information from multiple resources across all your operating environments, including on-premises, a hosted service, the public cloud, and even industrial operations environments or the **Internet of Things** (**IoT**).

Next, we will walk through the configuration of connectors in Microsoft Sentinel.

Configuring Microsoft Sentinel connectors

The **Microsoft Sentinel Data connectors** page shows the total number of connectors, how many are currently connected, and how many are in development (identified by the **Preview** status). An example of the **Data connectors** page is shown in the following screenshot:

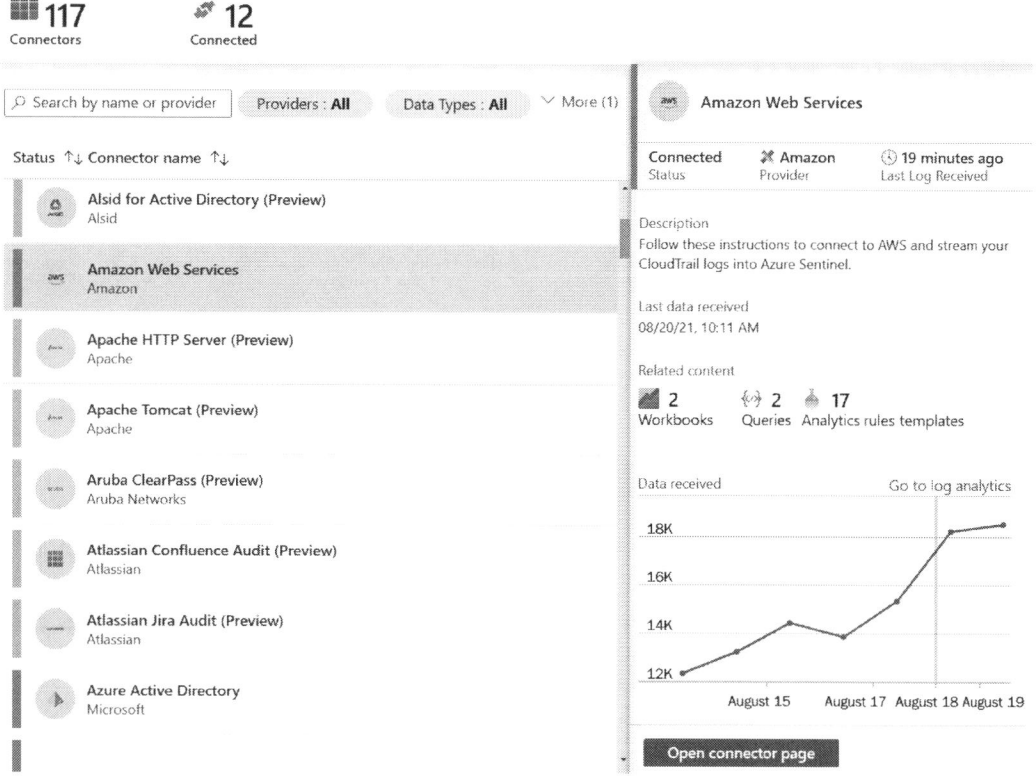

Figure 3.4 – Microsoft Sentinel Data connectors page

As you can see in the preceding screenshot, there are over 100 connectors available to implement in this Microsoft Sentinel instance. The list will continue to grow over time as more solutions become natively integrated, which is why you can see there is an ability to filter the list and search for specific data connectors. By selecting the connector on the left-hand side, we can view the connector details on the right-hand side. For this example, we will use the data connector for AWS, as shown in the following screenshot:

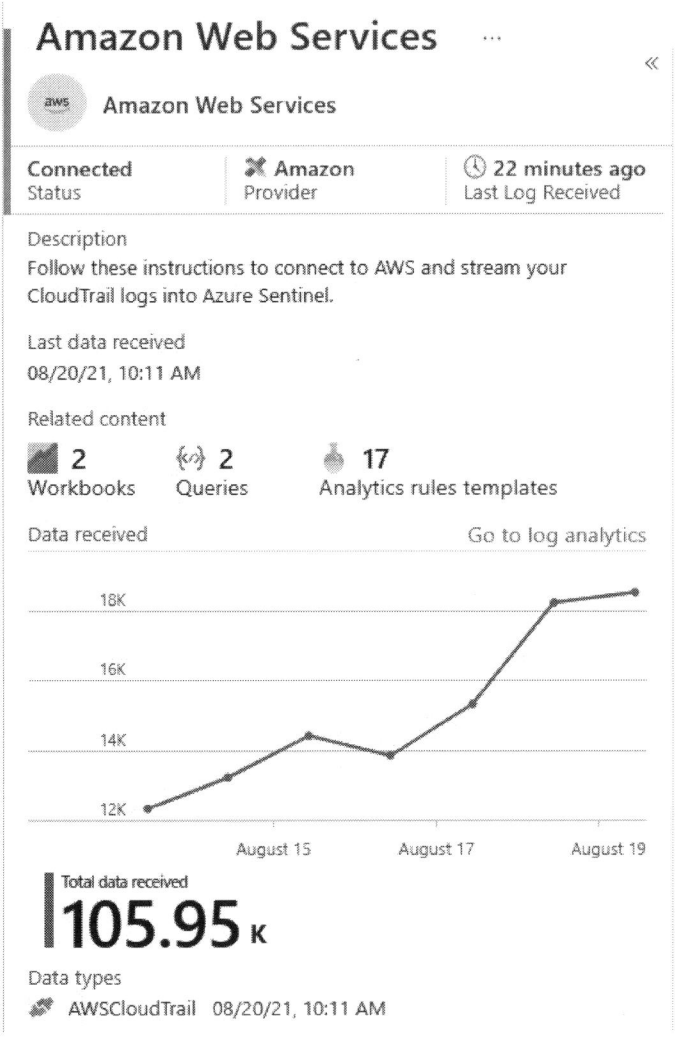

Figure 3.5 – Data connector details

At the top of the page in the preceding screenshot, we can see the status of the connector (**Connected**), the provider (**Amazon**), and the **Last Log Received** date/timestamp (should be within 1 hour).

The next section provides a description and further details about the connector, including a graph that will show the last 7 days of active log ingestion rate (when connected).

At the bottom of the page, we can see the data types that are included in this connector. In this example, we are expecting to retrieve the AWS CloudTrail logs, when enabled.

Click on the **Open connector page** button to go to the next screen and start the configuration process, as shown in the following screenshot:

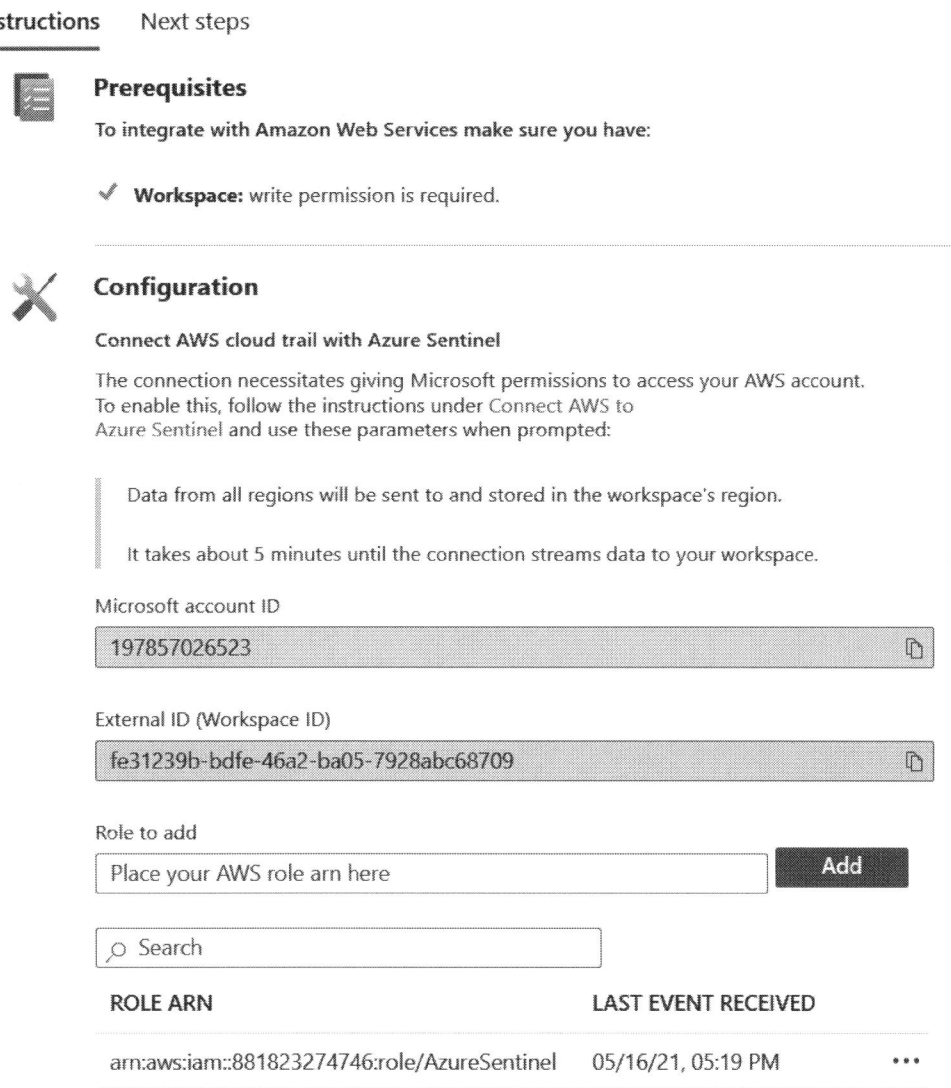

Figure 3.6 – Data connector configuration instructions

Each connector will show a slightly different screen, depending on the type of connector (native, direct, API, or agent) and the steps required to complete the configuration.

In this example, the AWS connector is an API-based connector, and instructions are provided on how to set up the required permissions for Microsoft Sentinel to access the AWS account via the API. Once completed and all steps show checkboxes rather than red Xs, you can select the **Next steps** tab to view the available workbooks and other resources available for this data connector, as shown in the following screenshot:

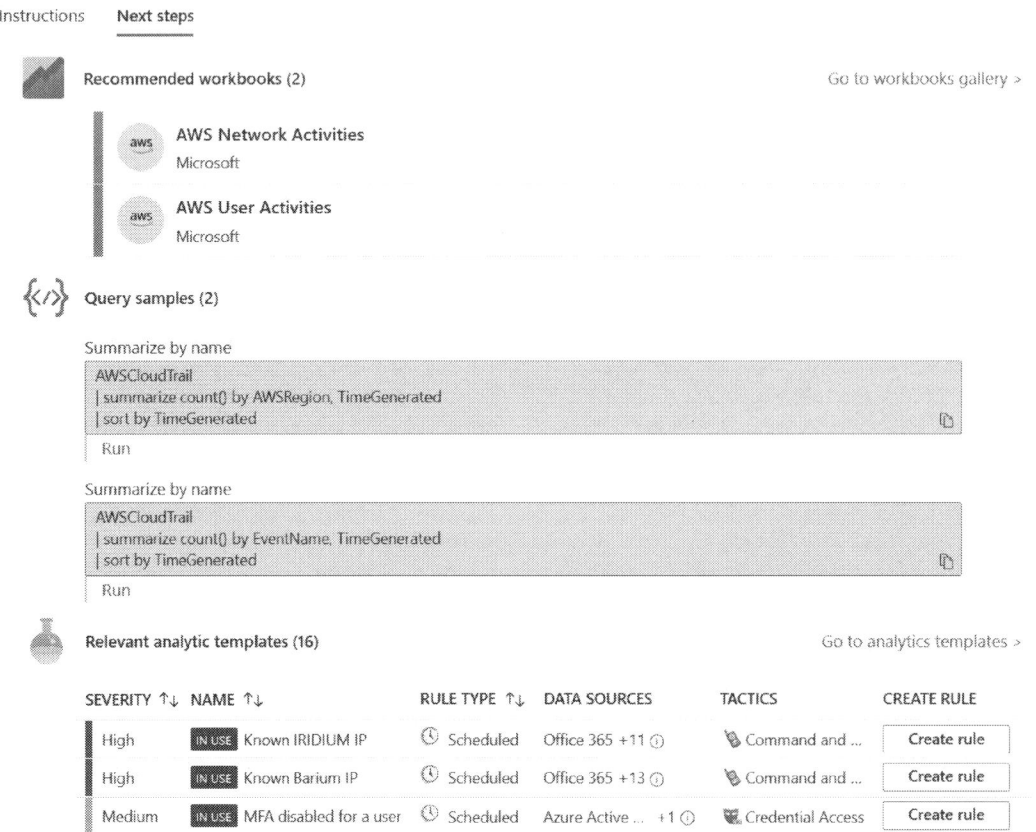

Figure 3.7 – Data connector next steps instructions

As we can see in the preceding screenshot, the AWS connector has the following two workbooks associated with it:

- **AWS Network Activities**
- **AWS User Activities**

Each of these workbooks is configured based on the information available in the AWS CloudTrail logs. The page also provides example queries you can use to get started with interrogating the logs for your own requirements. Further information about how to use workbooks can be found in *Chapter 8, Creating and Using Workbooks*.

Finally, each connector may provide one or more analytic templates that you should enable to ensure the ingested data is being analyzed. You can see an example of these rules in the following screenshot:

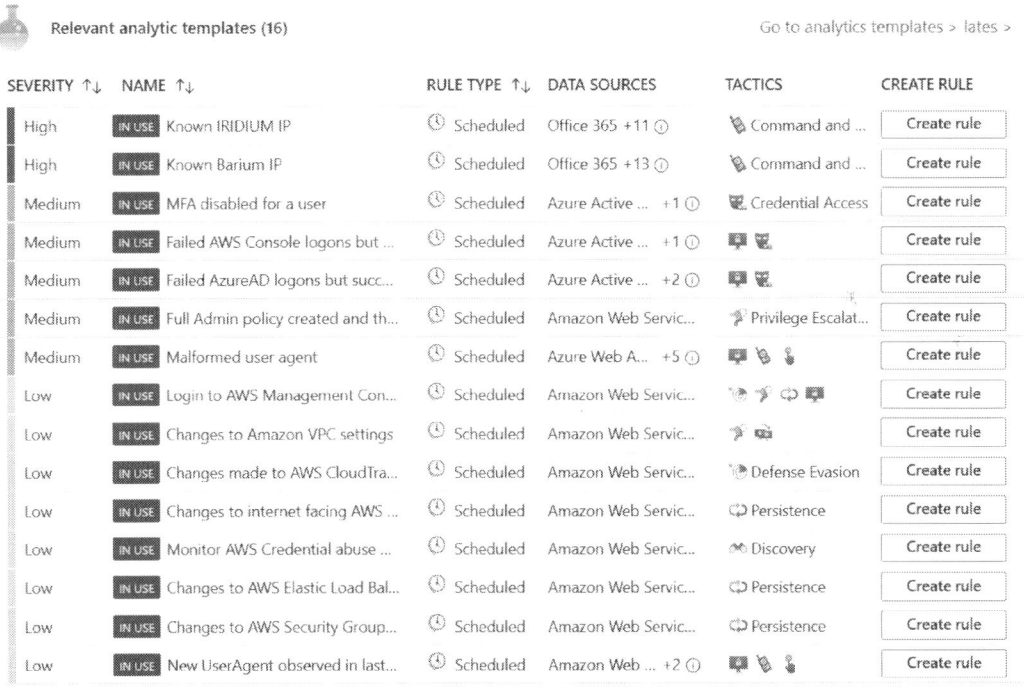

Figure 3.8 – AWS analytic templates

82 Managing and Collecting Data

We can see in the **Relevant analytic templates** section there are currently 16 templates available. Each template needs to be enabled to ensure the data is being analyzed. Select the first analytics template, and then walk through the configuration steps, as shown in the following screenshot:

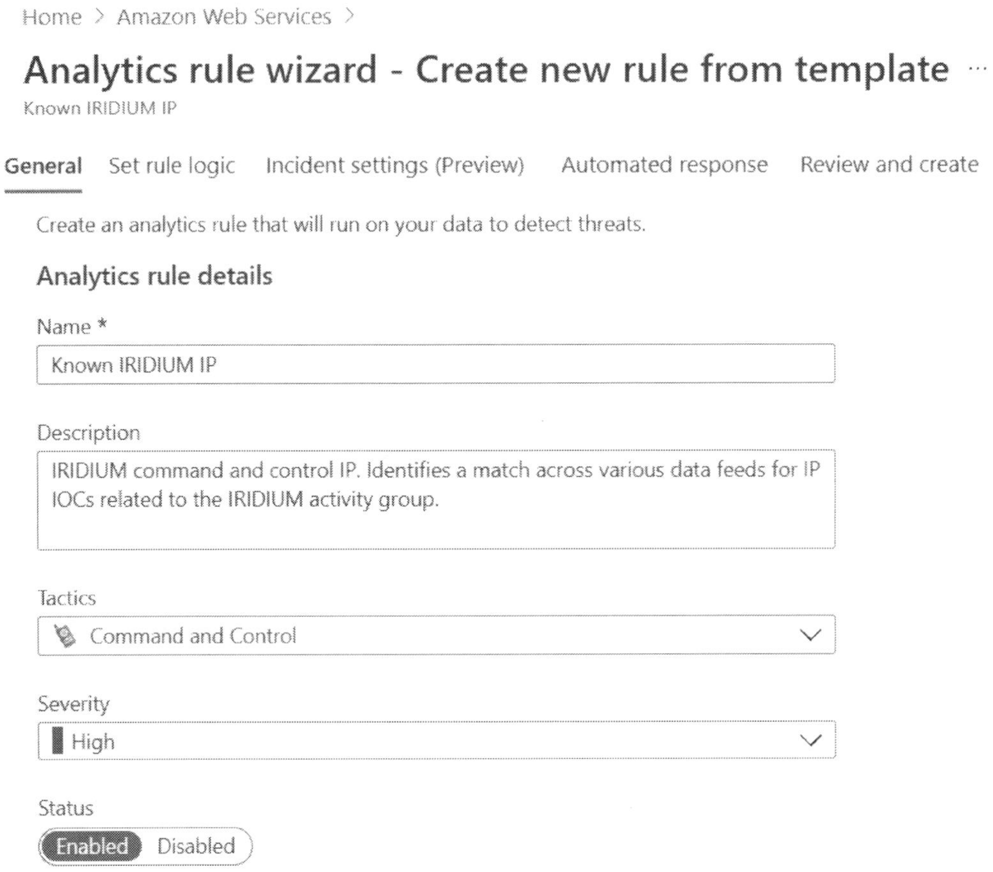

Home > Amazon Web Services >

Analytics rule wizard - Create new rule from template
Known IRIDIUM IP

General | Set rule logic | Incident settings (Preview) | Automated response | Review and create

Create an analytics rule that will run on your data to detect threats.

Analytics rule details

Name *

| Known IRIDIUM IP |

Description

| IRIDIUM command and control IP. Identifies a match across various data feeds for IP IOCs related to the IRIDIUM activity group. |

Tactics

| Command and Control ∨ |

Severity

| High ∨ |

Status

(**Enabled** Disabled)

Figure 3.9 – AWS analytics rule for Known IRIDIUM IP

Configure each page of the wizard with your desired configuration requirements, then finish the wizard and watch for the resulting impact in the number of incidents raised. If the volume is too high, reconfigure the rule to reduce how often an alert is generated, or enable the ability to group alerts into a single instance. Be careful not to over-tune the alerts to the degree where no incidents are created, as this could hide legitimate alerts that require investigation.

In the next section, we will configure the storage options available for Log Analytics.

Configuring Log Analytics storage options

Once you have completed the configuration of a few data connectors, you will begin to see how much data you will ingest and store in Log Analytics daily. The amount of data you store and retain directly impacts its associated costs (see *Chapter 1*, *Getting Started with Microsoft Sentinel*, for further details). You can view the current usage and costs by navigating to the Log Analytics workspace, then selecting **Usage and estimated costs** from the **General** menu, as shown in the following screenshot:

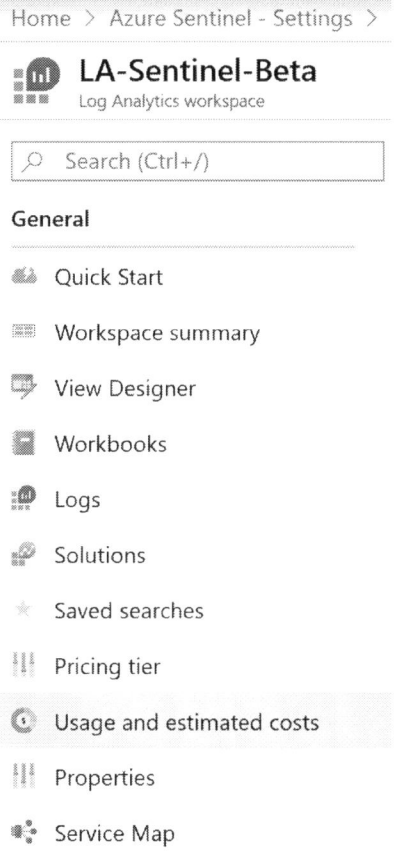

Figure 3.10 – Log Analytics navigation menu

Once it's selected, you are then presented with a dashboard of information that will show the pricing tier and current costs on the left-hand side, and graphs on the right-hand side to show the variation in daily consumption for the last 31 days. A second graph shows the total size of retained data per solution. An example of the dashboard is shown in the following screenshot:

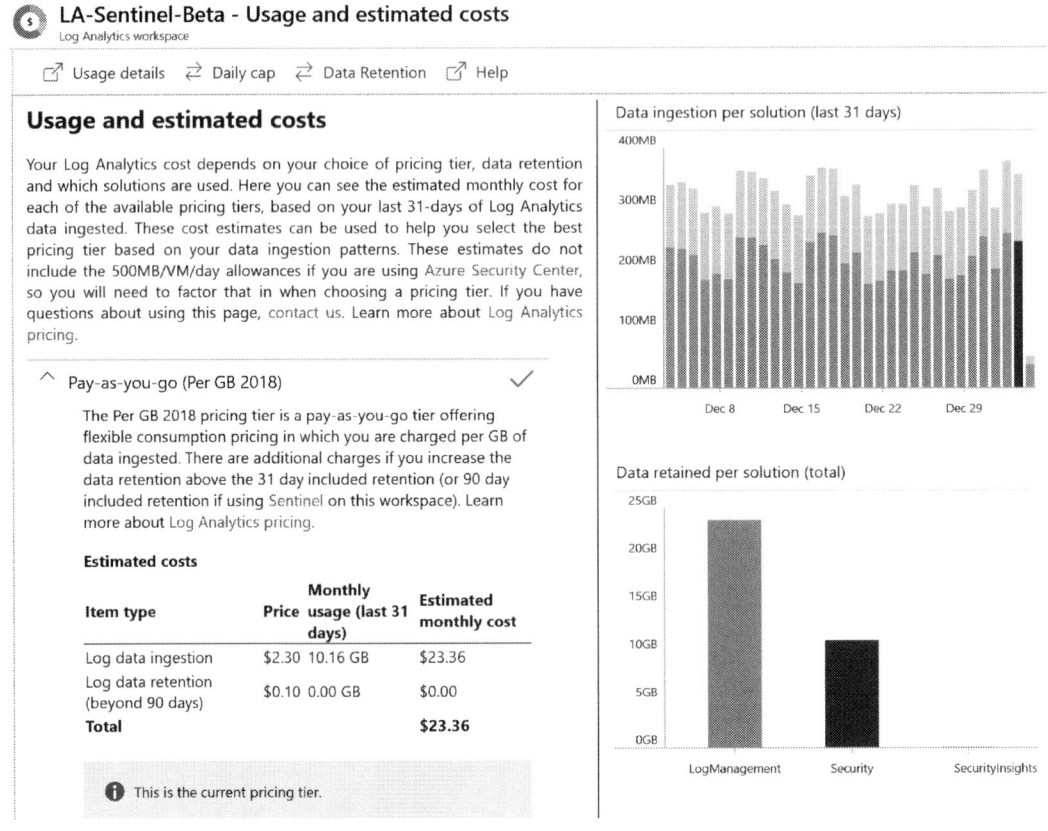

Figure 3.11 – Log Analytics usage and cost dashboard

From this page, explore two of the options available along the top menu bar:

- **Daily cap**: With this option, you can enable or disable the ability to limit how much data is ingested into the Log Analytics workspace on a per-day basis. While this is a useful control to have to limit costs, there is a risk that the capped data will result in a loss of security information that's valuable for detecting threats across your environment. We recommend only using this for non-production environments.

- **Data Retention**: This option allows you to configure the number of days data should be retained in the Log Analytics workspace. The default number for Log Analytics is 31 days; however, when Microsoft Sentinel is also enabled on the Log Analytics workspace, the default free amount is 90 days. If you choose to increase beyond 90 days, you will be charged a set fee per **gigabyte (GB)** per month.

In the next section, we will look at how we calculate the costs involved in data ingestion and retention for Microsoft Sentinel and Log Analytics.

Calculating the cost of data ingestion and retention

Many organizations need to retain security log data for longer than 90 days, and budget for it to ensure they have enough capacity based on business needs. For example, if we consider the need to keep data for 2 years, with an average daily ingestion rate of 10 GB, then we can calculate the cost of the initial ingestion and analysis, then compare this to the cost of retention. This will provide an annual cost estimate for both aspects.

The following table shows the cost for ingesting data into Log Analytics and analyzing that data in Microsoft Sentinel. This price includes 90 days of free retention:

	Per day	Per month	Per year total	2 year total
Azure Sentinel	$20	$600	$7,200	$14,600
Log Analytics	$23	$690	$8,280	$16,790
Total	$43	$1,290	$15,480	$30,960

Figure 3.12 – Example pricing table for Microsoft Sentinel

The following table shows the amount of data being retained past the free 90 days included in the preceding pricing, based on ingesting 10 GB per day:

	Day 91	Day 120	Day 270	Day 330	Day 365	Day 730
Total Data Size (GB)	910	1,200	2,700	3,300	3,650	7,300
Retention Costs (per month)	$91	$120	$270	$330	$365	$730

Figure 3.13 – Example pricing table for retention costs

Now, if we add these together, we can see the total cost of the solution over a 12-month period, shown in the following table:

	Data Size (GB)	Log Analytics	Azure Sentinel	Data Retention	Total Cost (per month)
Month 1	300	$690	$600	$0	$1,290
Month 2	600	$690	$600	$0	$1,290
Month 3	900	$690	$600	$0	$1,290
Month 4	1,200	$690	$600	$120	$1,410
Month 5	1,500	$690	$600	$150	$1,440
Month 6	1,800	$690	$600	$180	$1,470
Month 7	2,100	$690	$600	$210	$1,500
Month 8	2,400	$690	$600	$240	$1,530
Month 9	2,700	$690	$600	$270	$1,560
Month 10	3,000	$690	$600	$300	$1,590
Month 11	3,300	$690	$600	$330	$1,620
Month 12	3,600	$690	$600	$360	$1,650
Annual Totals	3.6 TB	$8,280	$7,200	$2,160	$17,645
2 Year Total	7.2 TB	$16,560	$14,400	$8,820	$39,780

Figure 3.14 – Example pricing table to compare sizing options

Based on these examples, the total cost of running Microsoft Sentinel, ingesting 10 GB per day, and retaining data for 2 years would be $39,780. Data retention accounts for 22% of the cost.

> **Note**
> These prices are based on the current rates applicable to the US East Azure region, and figures are rounded for simplicity. Actual data usage may fluctuate each month.

You can carry out your own calculations using the **Azure pricing calculator**, which will account for the commit tiers, retention, and provide a combined cost for both Log Analytics and Microsoft Sentinel. Go to this URL and modify the settings to see the different pricing: `https://azure.microsoft.com/en-us/pricing/calculator/`.

Because the charges are based on the volume of data (in GB), one way of maintaining reasonable costs is to carefully select which data is initially gathered and which data is kept long term. If you plan to investigate events that occurred more than 90 days ago, then you should plan to retain that data. Useful log types for long-term retention include the following:

- IAM events such as authentication requests, password changes, new and modified accounts, group membership changes, and more
- Configuration and change management to core platforms, networks, and access controls across cloud boundaries
- Creation, modification, and deletion of resources such as virtual machines, databases, cloud applications, **Platform-as-a-Service (PaaS)**, and **Software-as-a-Service (SaaS)** resources
- Network logs from services such as DNS, web proxy, and firewalls

Other data types can be extremely useful for initial analysis and investigation; however, they do not hold as much value when the relevance of their data reduces. They include the following:

- Information from industrial control solutions
- Events streamed from IoT devices

Also, consider that some platforms sending data to Microsoft Sentinel may also be configured to retain the original copies of the log data for longer periods of time, potentially without additional excessive costs. An example would be your firewall and CASB solutions. In the next section, we will review some of the alternative storage options you should consider for any security data that does not need to be ingested into Microsoft Sentinel for immediate analysis but is required for long-term retention and extended threat hunting activities.

Reviewing alternative storage options

The benefit of retaining data within Log Analytics is the speed of access to search the data when needed, without having to write new queries. However, many organizations require specific log data to be retained for long periods of time, usually to meet internal governance controls, external compliance requirements, or local laws. Currently, there is a limitation to retaining data within Log Analytics, as it only supports storage for up to 2 years.

The following solutions may be considered as an alternative for long-term storage, outside of Log Analytics:

- **Azure Blob Storage**: You can create a query in Azure Monitor to select the data you want to move from the Log Analytics workspace and point it to the appropriate Azure storage account. This allows for filtering of the information by type (or select everything), and only moving data that is about to come to the end of its life, which is the limit you have set for data retention in the Log Analytics workspace. Once you have the query defined, you can use **Azure Automation** to run PowerShell and load the results as a CSV file, then copy to **Azure Blob Storage**. With this solution, data can be stored for up to 400 years! For further information, see this article: `https://docs.microsoft.com/en-us/azure/azure-monitor//powershell-samples`.

- **Azure Data Explorer** (**ADX**): The most common method of using extended storage and archive of additional security data is Azure Data Explorer, which enables up to 100 years of extended storage. With this solution, you can gain great optimization of both the storage and compute required to ingest, catalog, analyze, and present the information, all using the same **Kusto Query Language** (**KQL**) queries you are using in Microsoft Sentinel. When configuring this service, you can choose between storage-optimized and compute-optimized implementation depending on the need of the security team that will carry out the investigations. During quiet times, you can optimize for storage retention, then when you need to carry out in-depth investigations you can increase the compute capacity on demand to ensure responsive search queries. There is an average cost saving of one-tenth of the price to store this data in Microsoft Sentinel. You can use the online calculator for your own value calculations: `https://dataexplorer.azure.com/AzureDataExplorerCostEstimator.html`.

As you can see, there are several options available to store the data in alternative locations, both for extended archive/retention and for additional analysis with alternative tools. We expect Microsoft will increase the number of options available.

Summary

In this chapter, we reviewed the importance of data quality and using the seven Vs of big data as a guide to selecting the right data. We also looked at the various data connectors available to retrieve logs from a wide variety of sources, and the importance of constantly reviewing the connectors for updates and additional resources, such as workbooks. You now have the skills required to set up data connectors to begin ingesting data for later use in analysis and threat hunting.

Ongoing data management plays a key part in this solution, ensuring you maintain the cost efficiency of the solution without losing valuable information that can help identify risk and mitigate potential loss. Use the information in this chapter to apply to your own environment, and review regularly.

In the next chapter, you will learn how to integrate threat intelligence feeds into Microsoft Sentinel, to enrich your data with insights from security experts and make your investigations more effective.

Questions

Use these questions to test your knowledge of this chapter:

1. Can you list the seven Vs of big data?
2. What are the four different types of data connectors?
3. What is the purpose of a Syslog server?
4. How long is data stored in Microsoft Sentinel without extra cost?
5. What are the alternative storage options for log retention?

Further reading

The following resources can be used to further explore some of the topics covered in this chapter:

- *Microsoft Sentinel: Creating Custom Connectors*: https://techcommunity.microsoft.com/t5/azure-sentinel/ azure-sentinel-creating-custom-connectors/ba-p/864060
- *Connect your external solution using Syslog*: https://docs.microsoft.com/en-us/azure/sentinel/connect-syslog

- *Connect your external solution using CEF*: https://docs.microsoft.com/en-us/azure/sentinel/connect-cef-agent?tabs=rsyslog

- *Azure Monitor PowerShell quick start samples*: https://docs.microsoft.com/en-us/azure/azure-monitor/platform/powershell-quickstart-samples

- *Tutorial: Create a pipeline with Copy Activity using Data Factory Copy Wizard*: https://azure.microsoft.com/en-us/documentation/articles/data-factory-copy-data-wizard-tutorial/

- *Introduction to Azure Data Lake Storage Gen2*: https://docs.microsoft.com/en-us/azure/storage/blobs/data-lake-storage-introduction

4
Integrating Threat Intelligence with Microsoft Sentinel

This chapter will explore the options available for adding **Threat Intelligence** (**TI**) feeds to Microsoft Sentinel to enable the security team to have a greater understanding of the potential threats against their environment. We will explore the available TI feeds from Microsoft and other trusted industry sources, and then learn how to choose the most appropriate feeds for your organization based on geography, industry, and other risk factors.

This chapter will also introduce several new topics you may not be familiar with, but we encourage you to further research to add to your **Security Operations Centre** (**SOC**) capabilities, including the collaborative efforts of **STIX** and **TAXII**, a TI framework and set of standards that will help organizations to contribute and benefit from the knowledge of others.

By the end of this chapter, you will know how to implement several TI feeds.

This chapter will cover the following topics:

- Introduction to TI
- Understanding STIX and TAXII
- Choosing the right intel feeds for your needs
- Implementing TI connectors

Introduction to TI

Due to the complex nature of cybersecurity and the sophistication of modern attacks, it is difficult for any organization to keep track of vulnerabilities and the multiple ways that an attacker may compromise a system, especially if cybersecurity is not the focus of the organization. Understanding what to look for and deciding what to do when you see a system anomaly, or another potential threat, is complex and time-consuming. This is where TI comes in handy.

TI is critical in the fight against adversaries and is now integrated with most security products; it provides the ability to set a list of indicators for detection and blocking malicious activities. You can subscribe to TI feeds to gain knowledge from other security professionals in the industry and create your own indicators that are specific to the environment you are operating in.

If you are new to this topic, there are some new keywords and abbreviations to learn:

- **Threat indicators**: This is a list of suspicious or known malicious entities, such as IP addresses, URLs, and files. They are used to alert when suspicious usage of internal files or addresses is discovered in your environment.
- **Indicators of Compromise (IoCs)**: This indicates uniquely known behaviors and activities that show signs of potential malicious intent or an actual breach. These are available as open source and some as paid-for services.
- **Alert definitions**: By combining multiple threat indicators and IoCs, you can build an alert definition that only triggers in the right context. This will reduce alert fatigue from overloading the SOC with too many false positives.
- **Malware Information Sharing Project (MISP)**: This is an open source **Threat Intelligence Platform (TIP)** and a set of open standards for threat information sharing. MISP covers malware indicators, fraud, and vulnerability information. Read more here: `https://www.misp-project.org/`.

- **Adversarial Tactics, Techniques, and Common Knowledge (ATT&CK)**: This is a knowledge base providing a list of known adversary tactics and techniques, collated from real-world observations. Microsoft has integrated this framework into the Microsoft Sentinel platform. Read more here: `https://attack.mitre.org/`.
- **Structured Threat Information eXpression (STIX)**: STIX is a standardized XML-based language, developed for the purpose of conveying cybersecurity threat data in a standard format.
- **Trusted Automated eXchange of Indicator Information (TAXII)**: TAXII is an application layer protocol for the communication of cybersecurity TI over HTTP.
- **MineMeld TI sharing**: MineMeld is an open source TI processing tool that extracts indicators from various sources and compiles them into compatible formats for ingestion into Microsoft Sentinel.
- **ThreatConnect**: This is a third-party solution that has built-in integration with Microsoft Graph Security threat indicators. This is one example of a **Threat Intelligence Platform (TIP)** that can provide a comprehensive offering, for an additional cost.

> **Note**
> ATT&CK™, TAXII™, and STIX™ are trademarks of The MITRE Corporation. MineMeld™ is a trademark of Palo Alto Networks.

Microsoft provides access to its own TI feeds via the Microsoft Graph Security **tiIndicator** API and has built connectors for integration with solutions such as **Anomali ThreatStream**, **ThreatConnect**, **Palo Alto Networks MineMeld**, **MISP**, and **TAXII**. You can also build your own integration to submit custom threat indicators to Microsoft Sentinel and Microsoft Defender. For further details, review this information: `https://docs.microsoft.com/en-us/azure/sentinel/threat-intelligence-integration`.

Once your TI sources are connected, you can use built-in TI rule templates or create new rules to generate alerts and incidents when events match threat indicators or use built-in analytics, enriched with TI. You can also correlate TI with event data via hunting queries to add contextual insights to investigations.

In the next section, we will look at the specifics of two of these recommended approaches, STIX and TAXII, which are important to understand and consider implementing within your SOC as part of designing Microsoft Sentinel.

Understanding STIX and TAXII

The MITRE Corporation is a not-for-profit company that provides guidance in the form of frameworks and standards to assist with the development of stronger cybersecurity controls; the STIX language and TAXII protocol are some examples of this development effort.

These two standards were developed by an open community effort, sponsored by the US **Department of Homeland Security (DHS)**, in partnership with The MITRE Corporation. These are not software products, but standards that products can use to enable automation and compatibility when sharing TI information with your security community and business partners.

As per the description provided by MITRE: *STIX is a collaborative community-driven effort to define and develop a standardized language to represent structured cyber threat information*. The STIX language was developed to ensure threat information can be shared, stored, and used in a consistent manner to facilitate automation and human-assisted analysis. You can read more about the STIX standard here: https://stixproject.github.io/.

The TAXII protocol was developed to provide support for TI feeds from **OpenSource Intelligence (OSINT)** and TIP supporting this standard protocol and STIX data format. You can read more details about the TAXII protocol here: https://www.mitre.org/sites/default/files/publications/taxii.pdf.

Microsoft has developed a connector to enable integration with services using the TAXII protocol, enabling the ingestion of STIX 2.0 threat indicators for use in Microsoft Sentinel.

> **Public previews**
>
> Due to the nature of agile development and an evergreen cloud environment, Microsoft makes new features available first through private previews to a select few reviewers and then releases the feature to public preview to allow wider audience participation for feedback. Your organization needs to determine whether it is acceptable to use preview features in your production tenants or restrict access to only a development/testing environment. At the time of writing, the TAXII data connector is in public preview. You can check the list of available data connectors in your Microsoft Sentinel tenant to see whether it is currently available.

In the next chapter, we will review the options for intel feeds and choose which ones are right for your organization's needs.

Choosing the right intel feeds for your needs

With Microsoft Sentinel, you can import TI from multiple sources to improve the ability of a security analyst to identify and prioritize known threats and IoCs. When configured, several optional features become available within the following Microsoft Sentinel tools:

- **Analytics**: Provides the ability to include the `ThreatIntelligenceIndicator` field to ensure the analytics rule can match log events to identified domains, email accounts, file hashes, IP addresses, or URLs.
- **Workbooks**: There is a new workbook created to show the volume, type, and confidence level of the TI that is ingested into Microsoft Sentinel and how many alerts were generated from analytics rules that match your threat indicators.
- **Hunting**: Like analytics rules, enabling TI provides the hunting queries the capability of comparing log events to TI information, allowing security investigators greater ability in their hunting scenarios.
- **Notebooks**: Notebooks are enabled for guided hunting with integrated TI, which enables analysts and security investigators to look for anomalies and hunt for malicious behavior.

There are several options available to gain access to TI feeds, and you may choose to generate your own indicators based on specific information gathered through internal IT investigations; this allows you to develop a unique list of indicators that are known to be specific to your organization. Depending on your industry and region, you may choose to share these with partner organizations and communities to gain specific information related to healthcare, government, energy, and so on.

You can choose to leverage direct integration with the **Microsoft Graph Security tiIndicator** API, which contains Microsoft's own TI, gathered across their vast internet services landscape (such as Azure, Office 365, Xbox, and Outlook).

To achieve the broadest range of intelligence, it is recommended that you also obtain TI feeds from opensource platforms, such as the following:

- The MISP opensource TIP
- MineMeld by Palo Alto Networks
- Any that are based on the MITRE STIX/TAXII standards

Optionally, you can also choose to purchase additional TI feeds from solution providers. Microsoft Sentinel currently offers the capability to integrate with the ThreatConnect platform, which is a TIP you can purchase separately. Other platforms are expected to be integrated soon; review the data connector for TIPs for any updates.

Implementing TI connectors

Microsoft Sentinel provides a data connector specifically for integration with TIP solutions (both commercial and open source). This section will provide walk-through guidance for the steps required to ingest TI data into Microsoft Sentinel, using MineMeld as an example:

1. Enabling the data connector for TIPs
2. Registering app permission in Azure **Active Directory** (**AD**)
3. Configuring the TI feed (MineMeld)
4. Confirming that the TI feed data is visible

> **Note**
> At the time of writing, this feature is still in public preview. You can enable this solution in your Microsoft Sentinel workspace to gain access to these features; however, you should expect it to change as it is developed.

Let's discuss each of these steps in detail in the following sections.

Enabling the data connector

Use the following steps to enable the data connector for TIPs within Microsoft Sentinel:

1. Navigate to the Microsoft Sentinel portal and go to the **Data connectors** page, as shown in the following screenshot:

Implementing TI connectors   97

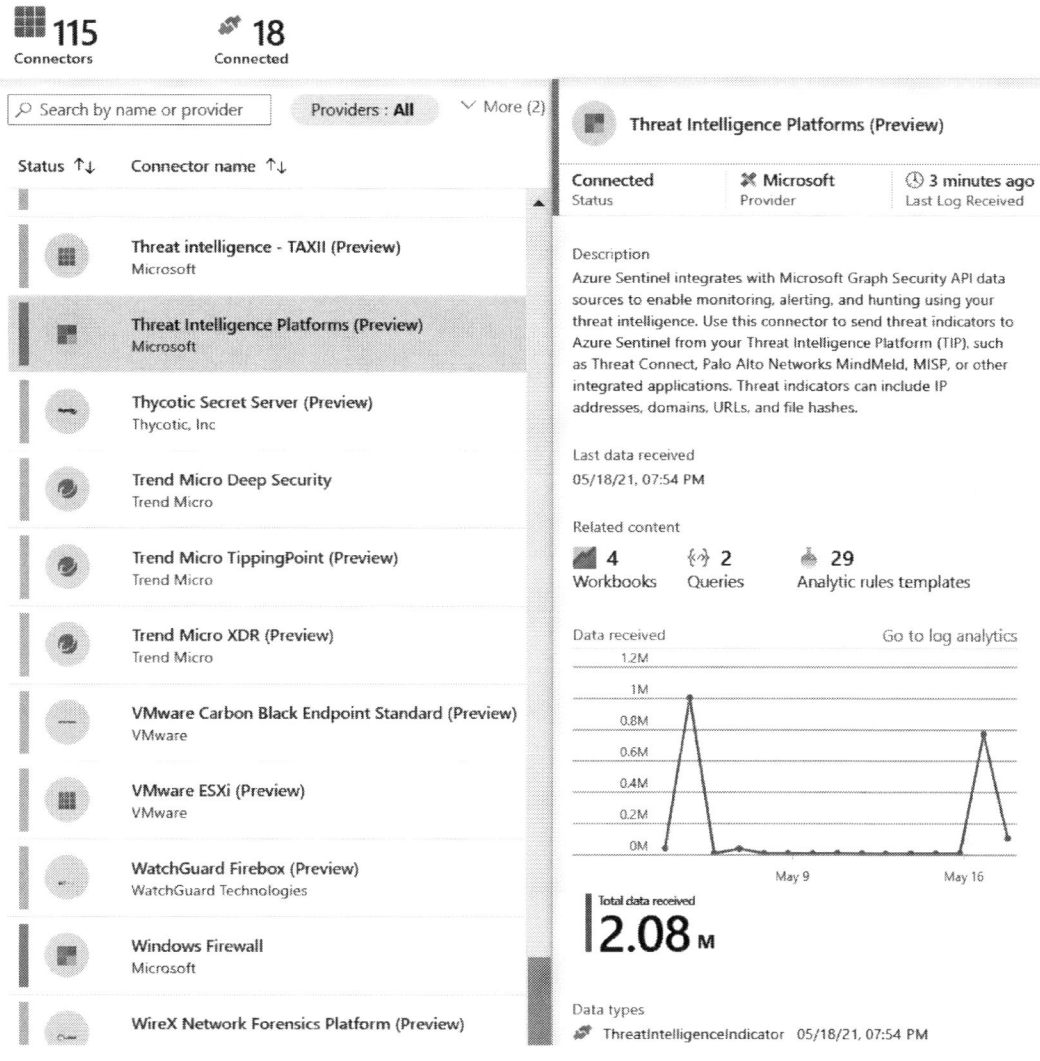

Figure 4.1 – Data connector for Threat Intelligence Platforms (Preview)

2. Select the data connector for **Threat Intelligence Platforms (Preview)**.
3. Click on the **Open connector page** button.

4. At the top of the page, you will see the prerequisites for the data connector. Review them to ensure you have properly configured the workspace and tenant permissions, as shown in the following screenshot:

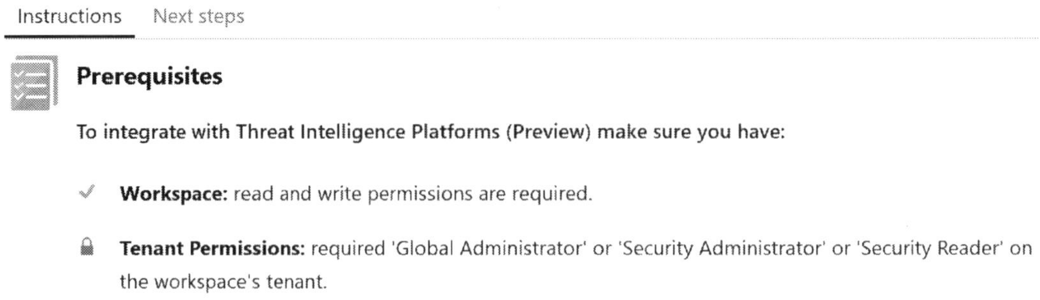

Figure 4.2 – Data connector prerequisites

5. Next, you will see the configuration steps required to ensure the data connector will function correctly. Click on the **Connect** button at the bottom of the page.

You should now have a working connector waiting for the TI feed data to flow in. Next, we will configure the app registration in Azure AD, which is necessary before setting up the MineMeld server.

Registering an app in Azure AD

In this section, we will create an app registration in Azure AD. This will be used by the TI server/service to run and send information to Microsoft Sentinel.

Use the following steps to create an app registration in Azure AD:

1. Navigate to Azure AD and select the **App registrations** option, as shown in the following screenshot:

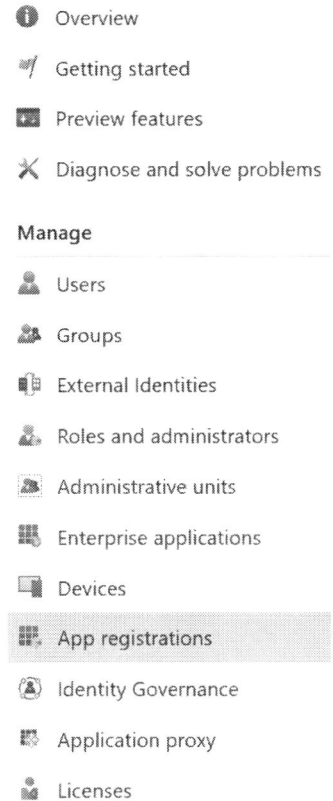

Figure 4.3 – Azure AD App registrations

2. In the toolbar, select **+ New registration**, as shown in the following screenshot:

$+$ New registration   Endpoints   Troubleshooting $\downarrow$ Download   Preview features   ...

Figure 4.4 – Creating a new app registration

3. On the next screen, provide a unique name for the specific TI connector. In this example, we are creating one for the MineMeld server, so we'll name it as shown in the following screenshot. Choose the default option for **Who can use this application or access this API?**, then select **Register**, as shown in the following screenshot:

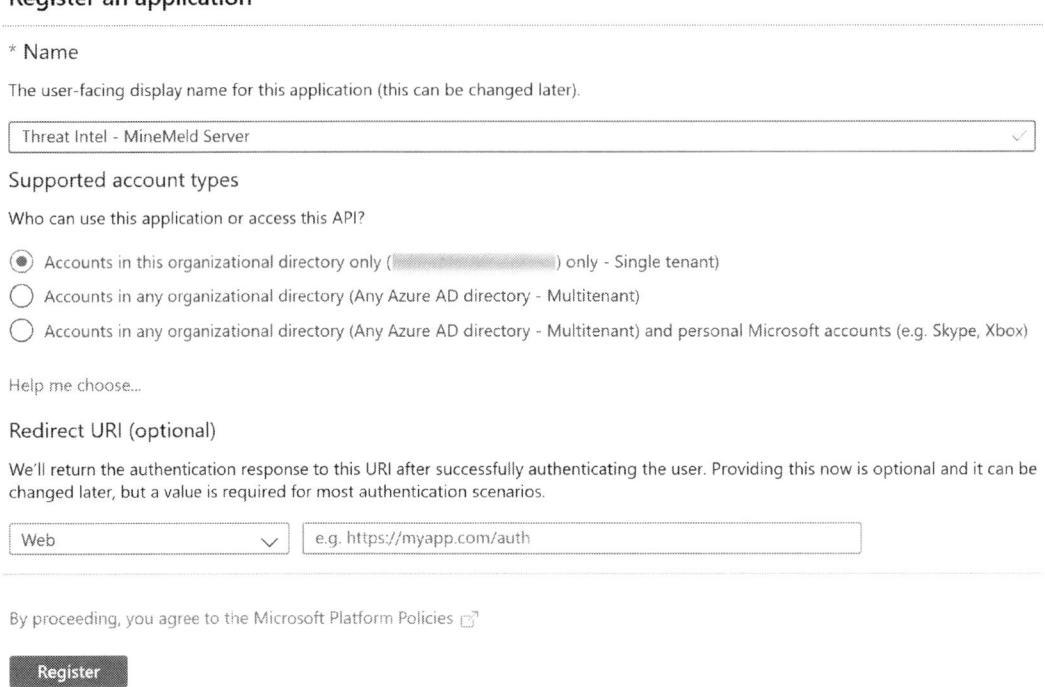

Figure 4.5 – Creating a new app registration

4. When registration is complete, you will be presented with the **Overview** page, as shown in the following screenshot:

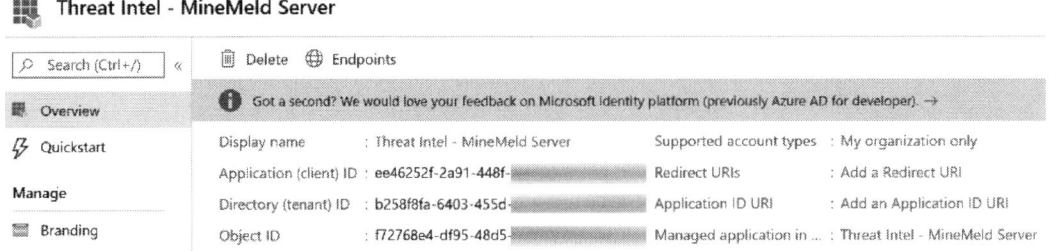

Figure 4.6 – New app registration details

When you configure your integrated TIP product, you will need to refer to these ID values.

5. Next, we will configure API permissions for the application that we registered. To do this, go to the menu on the left and select **API permissions**, as shown in the following screenshot:

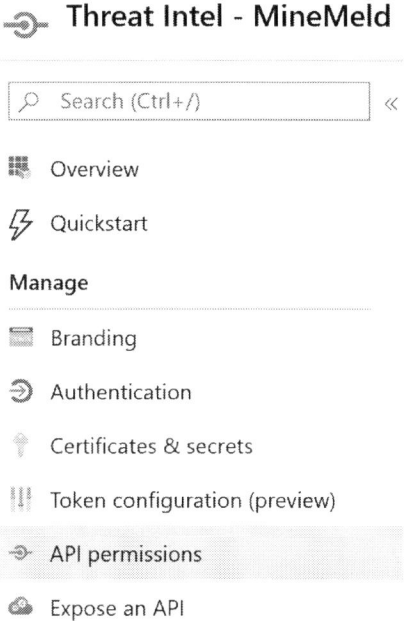

Figure 4.7 – API permissions menu option

6. When first created, there will be the default permission of **User.Read**. Select **+ Add a permission**.

7. On the next screen, select the **Microsoft Graph** API, as shown in the following screenshot:

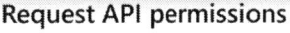

Figure 4.8 – Selecting an API

8. Then, select **Application permissions**, as shown in the following screenshot:

Figure 4.9 – Application permissions

9. In the search bar, enter `ThreatIndicators`, then select the **ThreatIndicators.ReadWrite.OwnedBy** option, as shown in the following screenshot:

Implementing TI connectors   103

Select permissions   expand all

ThreatIndicators

Permission	Admin Consent Required
∨ **ThreatIndicators (1)**	
☐ ThreatIndicators.Read.All Read all threat indicators ⓘ	Yes
☑ ThreatIndicators.ReadWrite.OwnedBy Manage threat indicators this app creates or owns ⓘ	Yes

Figure 4.10 – Searching for permissions

10. Click on **Add permissions**. On the next screen, select the **Grant admin consent for <tenant name>** button.

> **Note**
> You can also get to this screen from the Azure portal: navigate to **Azure Active Directory | App registrations | <app name> | View API Permissions | Grant admin consent for <tenant name>**.

11. You will be prompted with a screen requesting permissions consent, on which you will need to click the **Accept** button.

12. You will now be able to confirm the permissions are successfully granted by viewing the permissions and looking for the green checkmark, as in the following screenshot:

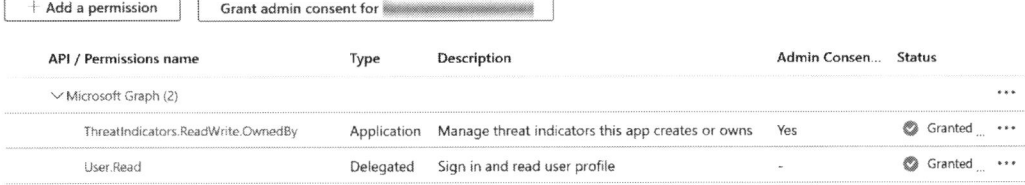

Figure 4.11 – Confirming permissions have been granted

Now that the app is registered in Azure AD, we can use this in the registration process for the TI server/service to run and send information to Microsoft Sentinel.

Next, we can start to configure the MineMeld server, which involves setting up a new **virtual machine** (**VM**) to collect and forward the TI feed.

Configuring the MineMeld TI feed

With the previous steps complete, you are ready to configure the services that will send TI data to Microsoft Sentinel. This section will walk you through the configuration of the MineMeld TI sharing solution.

> **Note**
> If the MineMeld TI server is not already running in your environment, you will need to configure the product; this guidance is only for the Microsoft Sentinel connectors.

There are three steps to this process:

1. Building the VM and installing MineMeld
2. Installing the Microsoft Graph Security API extension in MineMeld
3. Configuring the extension to connect to Microsoft Graph via the Security API

To carry out this procedure, you will need administrative access to the Azure tenant and the MineMeld service.

Building the VM and installing MineMeld

> **Note**
> At the time of testing, it was necessary to ensure only Ubuntu version 16.04 was used; other versions may not be compatible.

Ideally, you will already have the MineMeld VM configured and running in your environment; however, if you do not, you can find configuration instructions online via the official Palo Alto Networks website: `https://live.paloaltonetworks.com/t5/MineMeld-Articles/Manually-Install-MineMeld-on- Ubuntu-16-04/ta-p/253336`.

Installing the Microsoft Graph Security API extension in MineMeld

The following are the steps to install the API extension:

1. Log in to the MineMeld web portal and go to **SYSTEM** then **EXTENTIONS**.
2. Click on the Git icon and enter the following address: `https://github.com/PaloAltoNetworks/minemeld-msgraph-secapi.git`.
3. Click **RETRIEVE**, then choose **master** from the drop-down list and click **INSTALL**, as shown in the following screenshot:

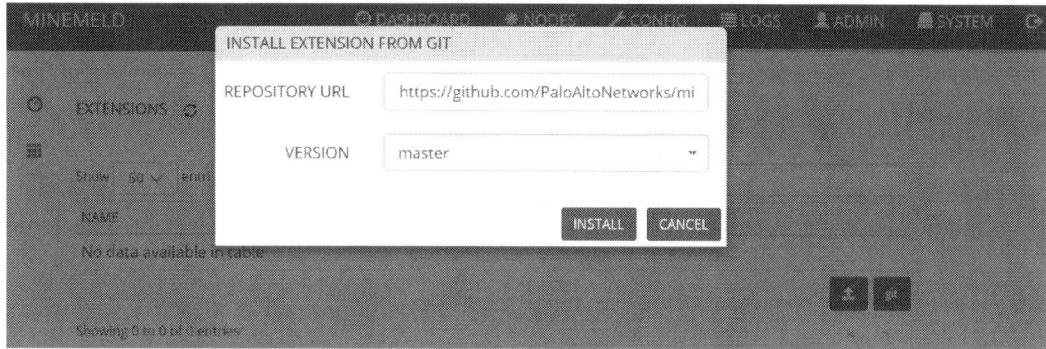

Figure 4.12 – Installing the extension from Git

4. Confirm the installation has completed, then select the **Activate** button beside the cross. To confirm activation, the API extension should show a white background instead of a gray-hashed background, as shown in the following screenshot:

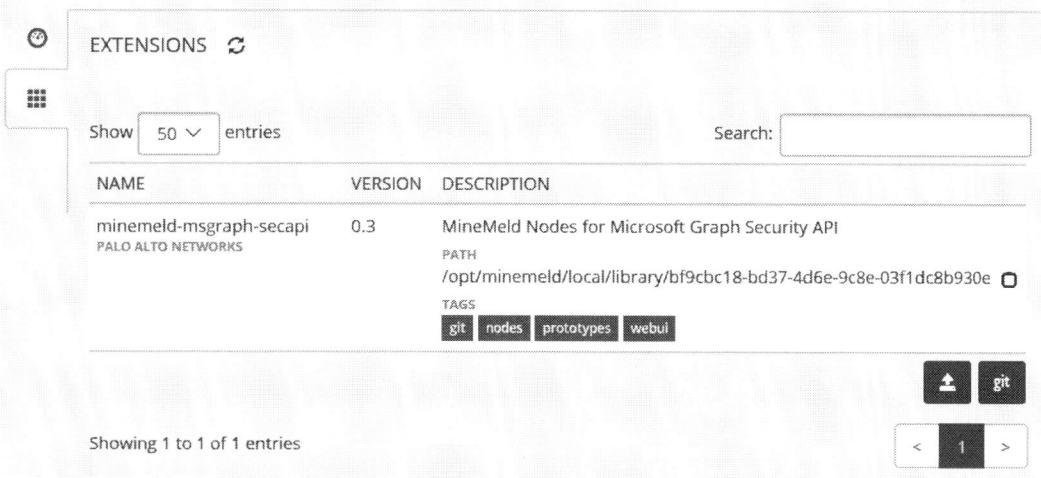

Figure 4.13 – Confirming installation of the API extension

Now that the Microsoft Graph Security API extension has been set up on the MineMeld server, we can configure the Microsoft Sentinel connector.

Configuring the Microsoft Sentinel connector

The following are the steps to configure the API extension:

1. Log in to the MineMeld web portal. Go to **CONFIG**, then select the prototypes icon at the bottom of the page with three horizontal lines (that is, the **hamburger** menu), as shown in the following screenshot:

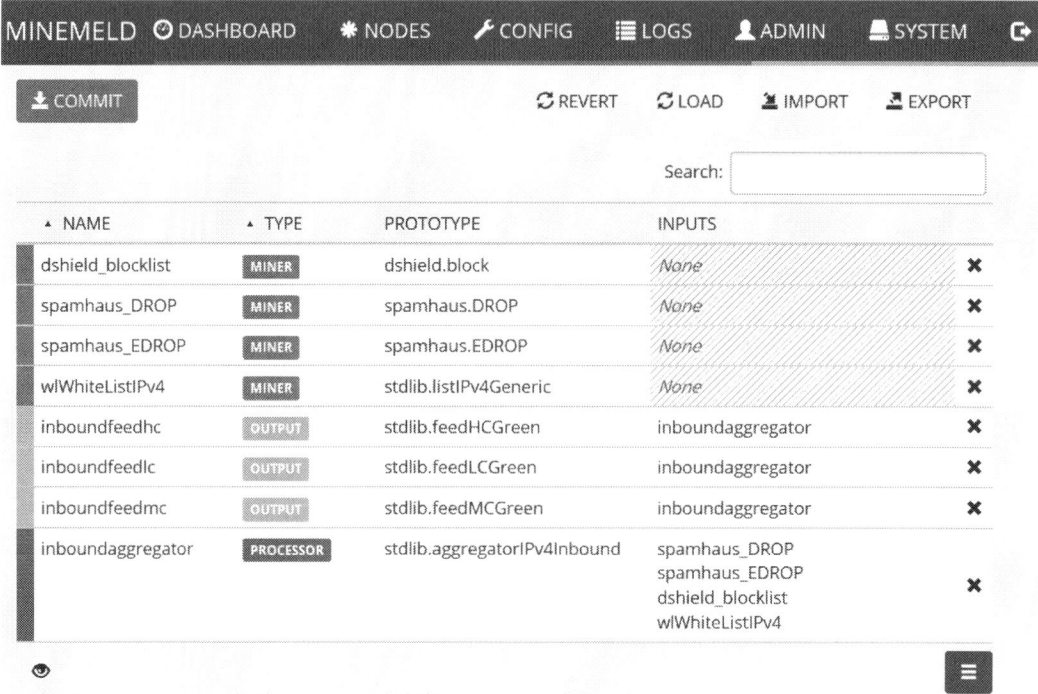

Figure 4.14 – MineMeld config page

Implementing TI connectors   107

2. As you will see, there are many options to choose from. Review the list for additional TI feeds you may want to implement, then search for Microsoft and review the results. Select the prototype named **microsoft_graph_secapi.output**:

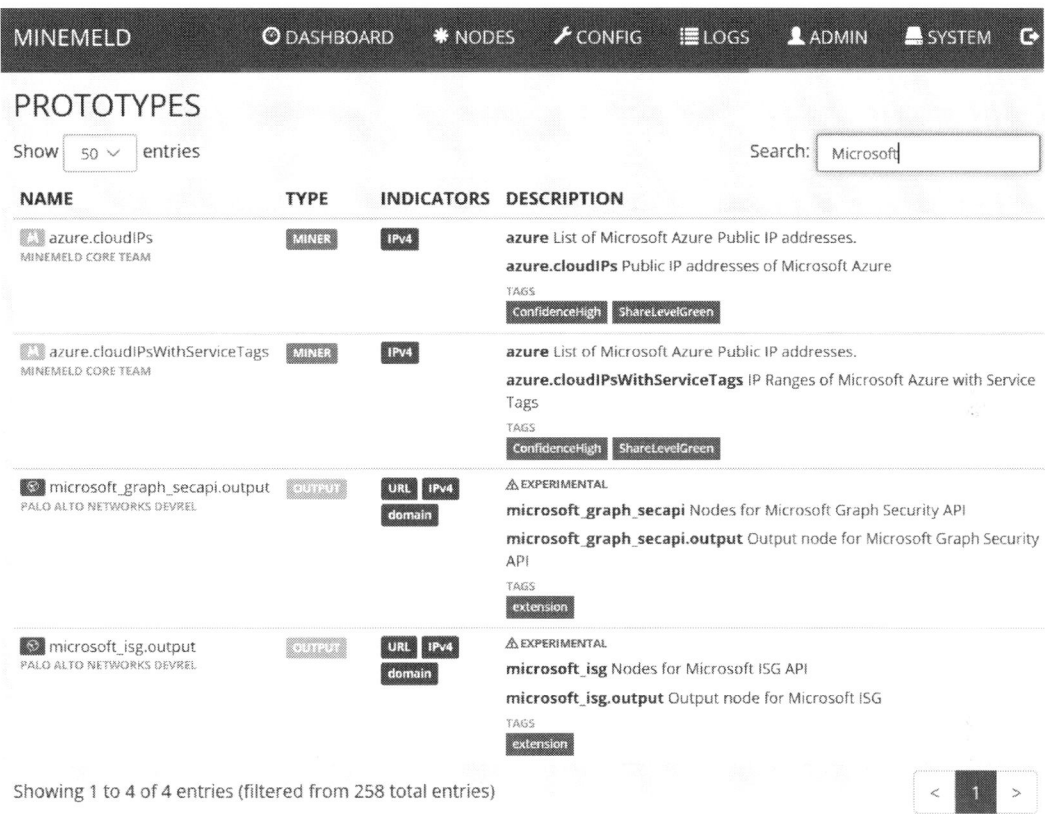

Figure 4.15 – Microsoft prototypes

3. On the next page, select **CLONE** in the top-right corner:

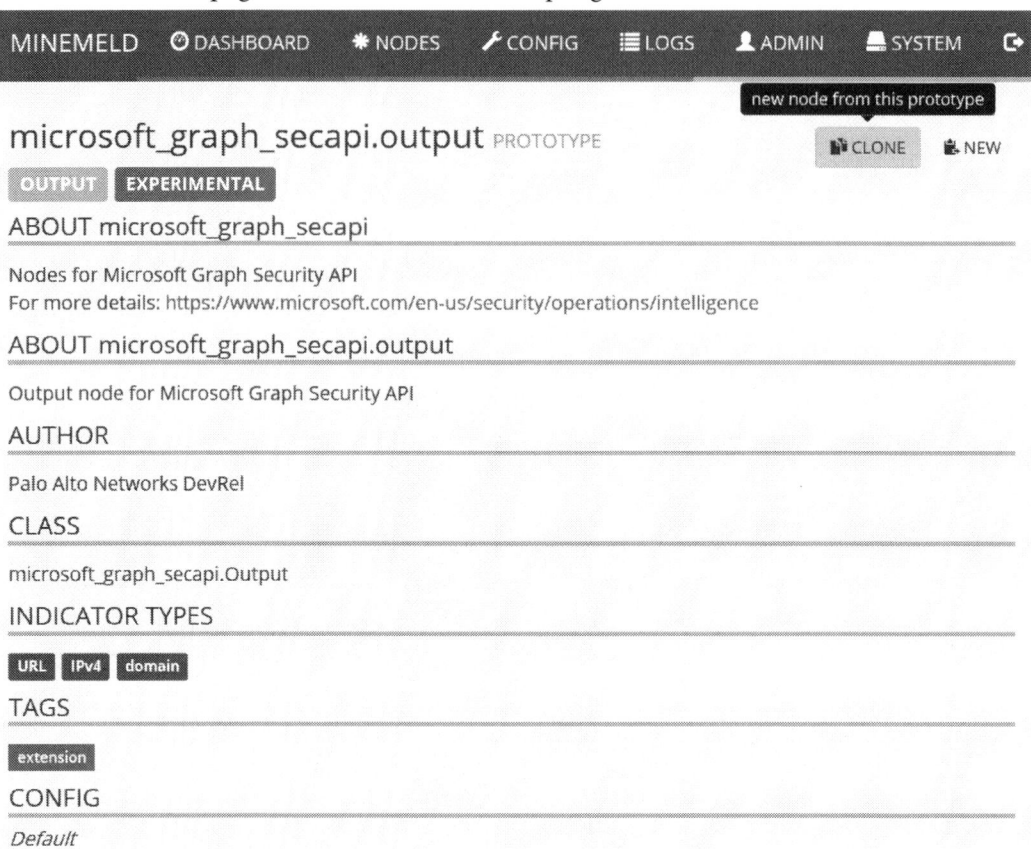

Figure 4.16 – Creating a new node from a prototype

4. On the next page, provide a name for the node, then select **inboundaggregator** for the **INPUTS** field:

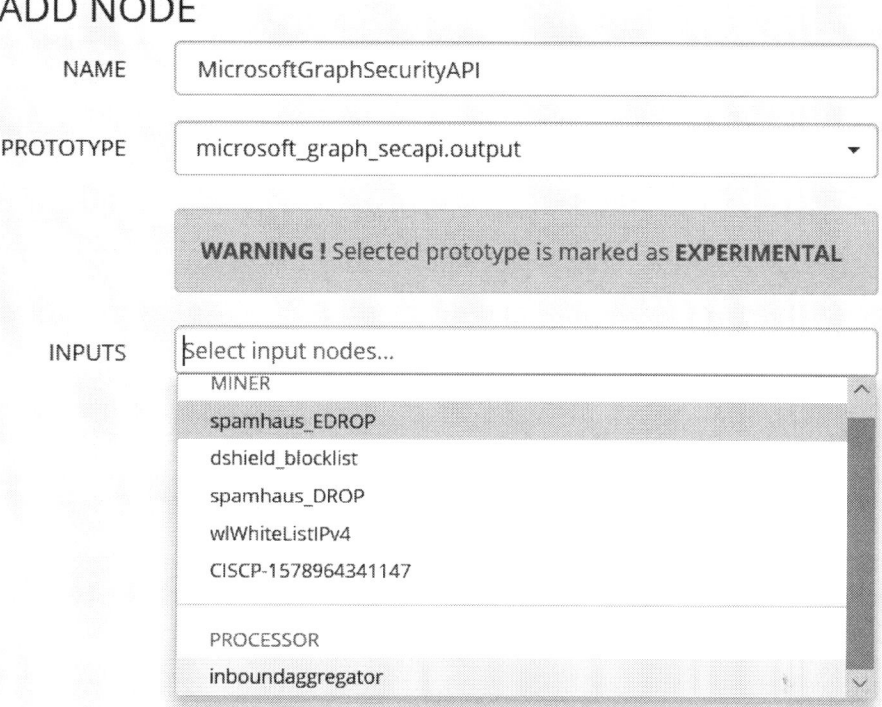

Figure 4.17 – Configuring a new node

5. Confirm the new node is active by viewing the list of nodes, as shown in the following screenshot. Select the **COMMIT** button at the top of the page. This will save the changes and restart the process to enable the new functionality:

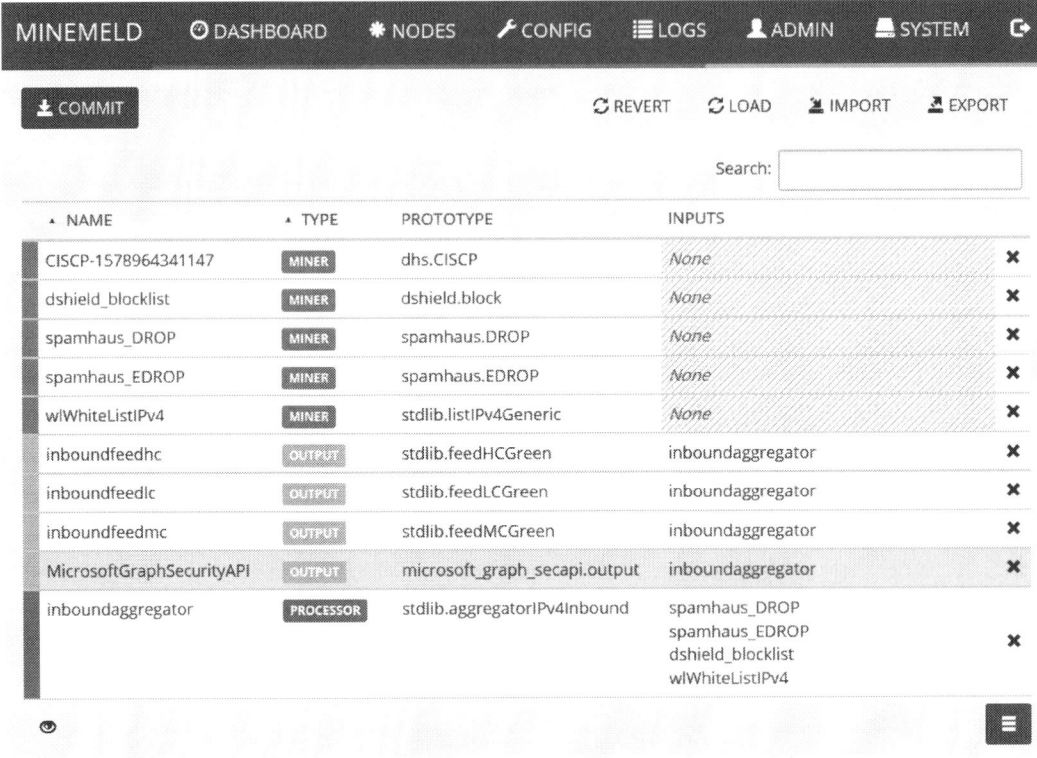

Figure 4.18 – Confirming the new node is added

6. Now go to the **NODES** tab and select the new API extension, then enter the relevant details from the previously registered app in Azure AD (see *Figure 4.6*):

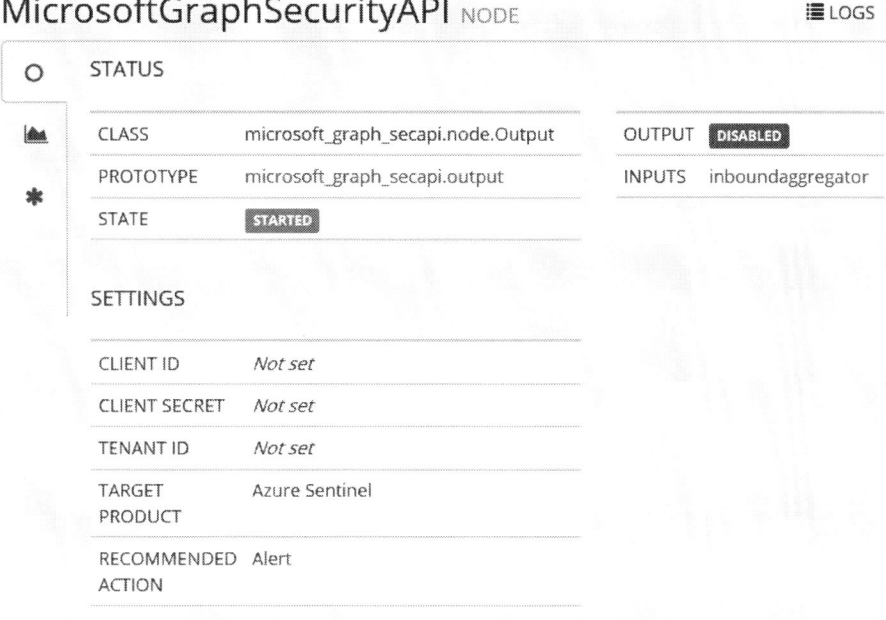

Figure 4.19 – Configuring the API extension for Microsoft Sentinel

7. For the **CLIENT SECRET** field, you need to generate a new secret in the Azure AD app. Go to the Azure AD app created earlier and select **Certificates & secrets**, and then select **+ New client secret** and follow the steps that will appear to create a new secret (ensure you copy the details because you only get one chance; otherwise, you will need to generate a new client secret again):

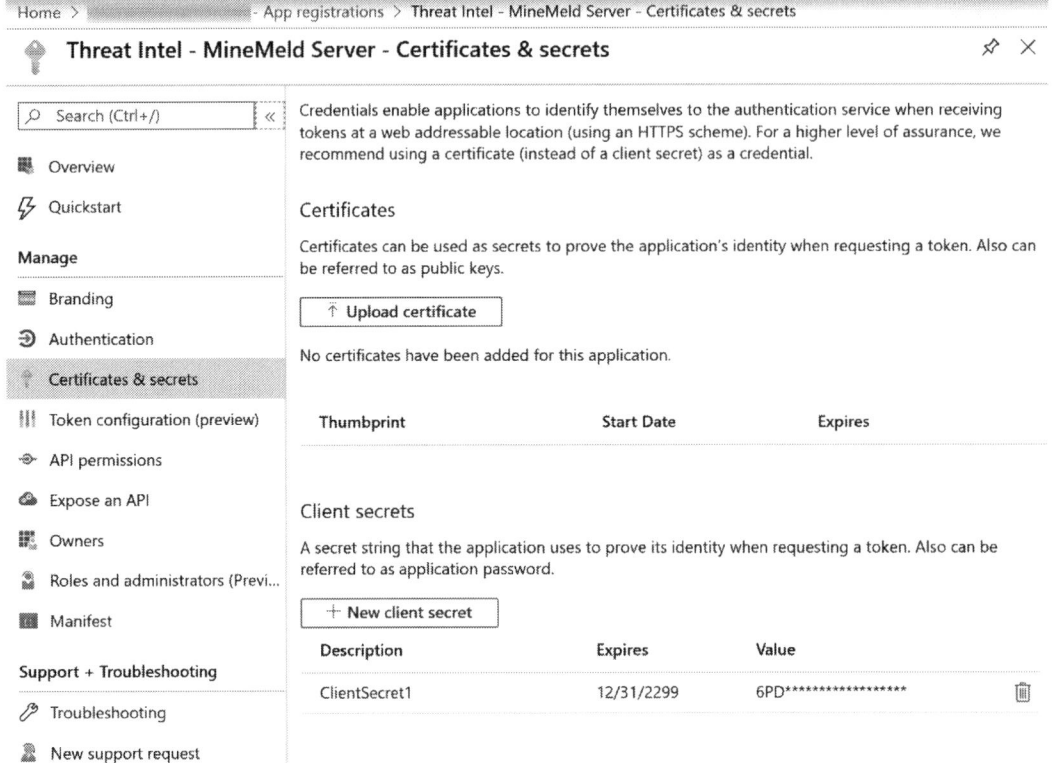

Figure 4.20 – Creating a new client secret

8. With this new secret added to the settings, you should see the following completed screen:

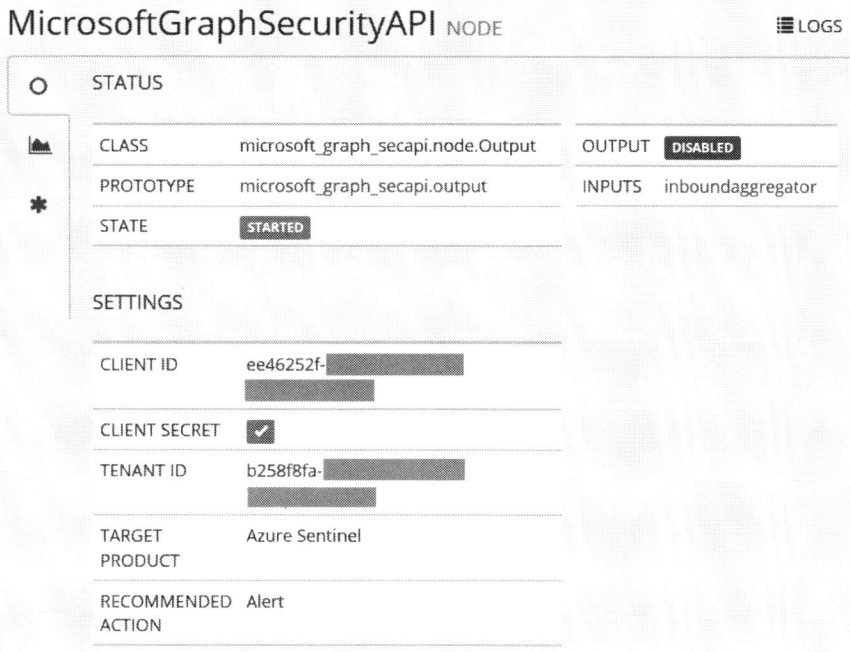

Figure 4.21 – Completed configuration

This concludes the configuration requirements for the MineMeld service. TI feeds should now be sent to your Microsoft Sentinel instance.

Confirming the data is being ingested for use by Microsoft Sentinel

To confirm the data is being sent to Microsoft Sentinel, follow these steps:

1. Go to the Azure portal, then Microsoft Sentinel.
2. Select **Logs**.
3. Type the following command into the command window and select **Run**:

```
ThreatIntelligenceIndicator
| take 100
```

4. You should see the following screen with the results:

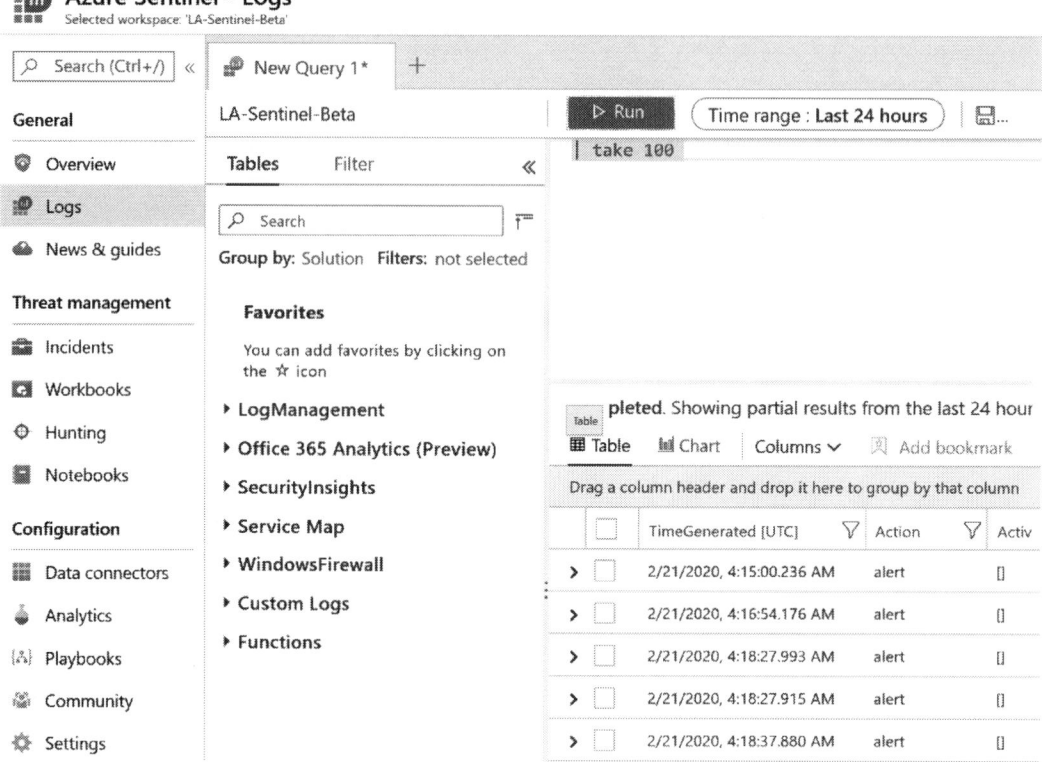

Figure 4.22 – Checking for TI feed activity

5. The following screenshot shows an example of the details for one of the events:

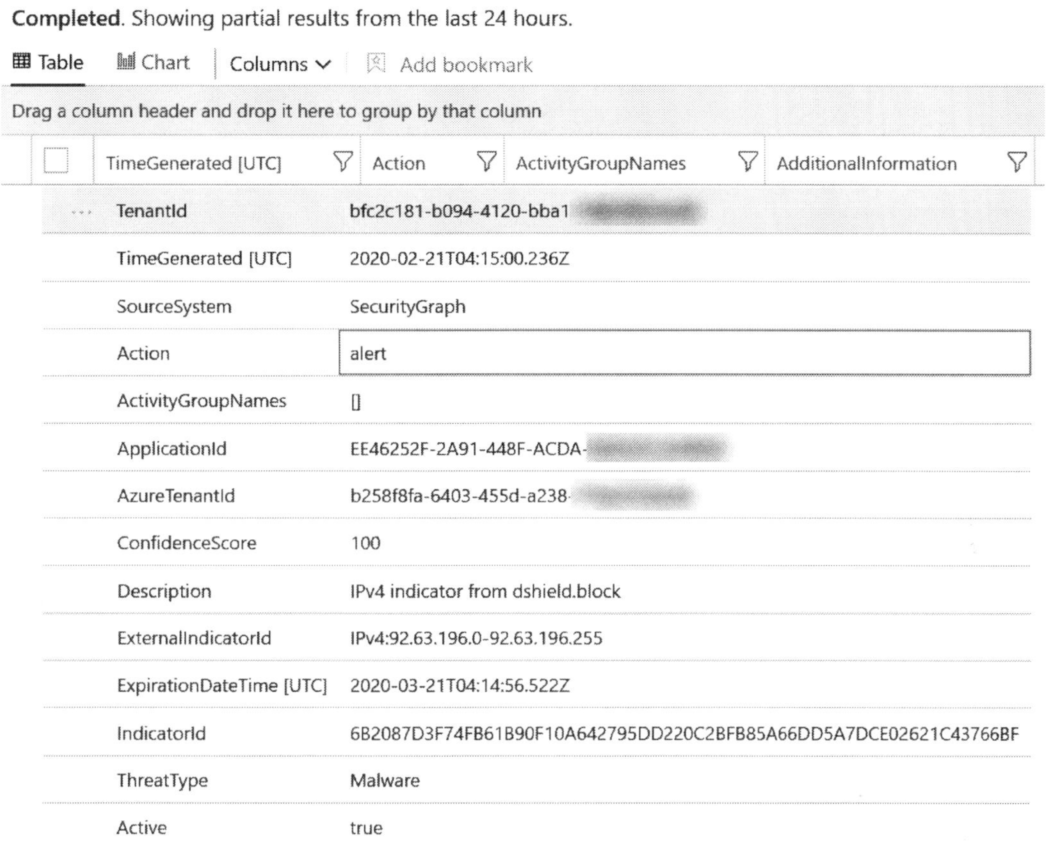
Completed. Showing partial results from the last 24 hours.
Table
Chart
Columns
Add bookmark
Drag a column header and drop it here to group by that column
TimeGenerated [UTC]
Action
ActivityGroupNames
AdditionalInformation
TenantId
bfc2c181-b094-4120-bba1
TimeGenerated [UTC]
2020-02-21T04:15:00.236Z
SourceSystem
SecurityGraph
Action
alert
ActivityGroupNames
[]
ApplicationId
EE46252F-2A91-448F-ACDA-
AzureTenantId
b258f8fa-6403-455d-a238-
ConfidenceScore
100
Description
IPv4 indicator from dshield.block
ExternalIndicatorId
IPv4:92.63.196.0-92.63.196.255
ExpirationDateTime [UTC]
2020-03-21T04:14:56.522Z
IndicatorId
6B2087D3F74FB61B90F10A642795DD220C2BFB85A66DD5A7DCE02621C43766BF
ThreatType
Malware
Active
true

Figure 4.23 – TI data feed details

You have now configured and connected the MineMeld server to your Microsoft Sentinel workspace and can see the TI data feeds appearing in the logs. You can now use this information to help to create new analytics and hunting queries, notebooks, and workbooks in Microsoft Sentinel.

We recommend regular reviews to ensure this information is both relevant and updated frequently. New TI feeds become available regularly, and you don't want to miss out on that useful information if it can help you to find new and advanced threats.

Summary

In this chapter, we explored the concept of TI, the new terminology and solution options, and the concept of creating and sharing TI feeds as a community effort. There are several options available for adding TI feeds to Microsoft Sentinel, and we know Microsoft is working to develop this even further. TI feeds will assist with the analysis and detection of unwanted behavior and potentially malicious activities. With many options to choose from, selecting the right feeds for your organization is an important part of configuring Microsoft Sentinel.

The next chapter introduces the **Kusto Query Language** (**KQL**), which is a powerful means to search all data collected for Microsoft Sentinel, including the TI data we just added.

Questions

1. Name three examples of threat indicator types.
2. What is the full name of the ATT&CK framework?
3. Which Microsoft Sentinel components can utilize TI feeds?
4. Who developed the STIX language and the TAXII protocol?

Further reading

The following resources can be used to further explore some of the topics covered in this chapter:

- Malware Information Sharing Project: https://www.misp-project.org/
- Mitre ATT&CK framework: https://attack.mitre.org/
- Microsoft Security Graph API: https://github.com/microsoftgraph/security-api-solutions/tree/master/QuickStarts
- STIX standard: https://stixproject.github.io/
- TAXII protocol: https://www.mitre.org/sites/default/files/publications/taxii.pdf
- Build a MineMeld server: https://live.paloaltonetworks.com/t5/general-articles/manually-install-minemeld-on-ubuntu-16-04/ta-p/253336
- The Microsoft Graph Security API extension in MineMeld: https://github.com/PaloAltoNetworks/minemeld-msgraph-secapi

5
Using the Kusto Query Language (KQL)

The **Kusto Query Language** (**KQL**) is a plain-text, read-only language that is used to query data stored in Azure Log Analytics workspaces. Much like SQL, it utilizes a hierarchy of entities that starts with databases, then tables, and finally columns. In this chapter, we will only concern ourselves with the table and column levels.

In this chapter, you will learn about a few of the many KQL commands that you can use to query your logs.

In this chapter, you will learn the following:

- How to test your KQL queries
- How to query a table
- How to limit how many rows are returned
- How to limit how many columns are returned
- How to perform a query across multiple tables
- How to graphically view the results

The chapter covers the following main topics:

- Running KQL queries
- Introduction to KQL commands
- Query statements
- Scalar functions

Running KQL queries

For this chapter, we will be using the sample data available in the **Azure Data Explorer** (**ADX**). This is a very useful tool for trying simple KQL commands. Feel free to use it to try the various commands in this chapter. All the information used in the queries comes from the sample data provided at `https://dataexplorer.azure.com/clusters/help/databases/Samples`.

If prompted, use the login credentials you would use to log in to the Azure portal. When you log in for the first time, you will see the following screen. Note that your login name may show up on the right-hand side of the header:

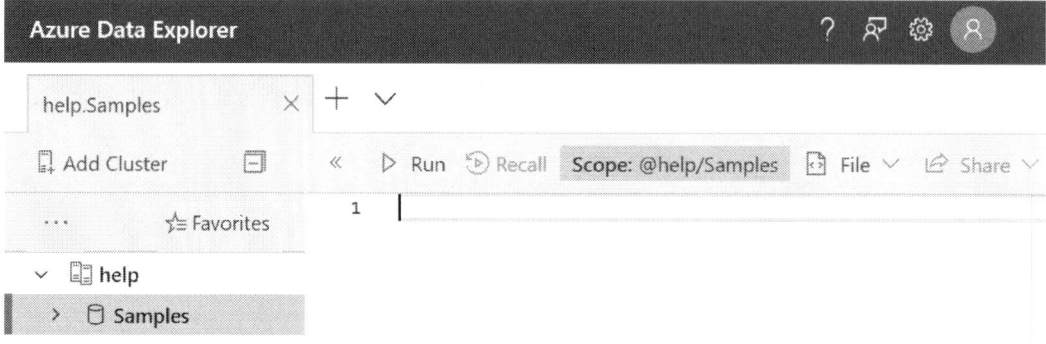

Figure 5.1 – Azure Data Explorer

To run the samples for this chapter, you will need to expand the **Samples** logs on the left-hand side of the screen and then select **StormEvents**. You can expand **StormEvents** to see a listing of fields if you want to. If you do so, your screen should look like the following:

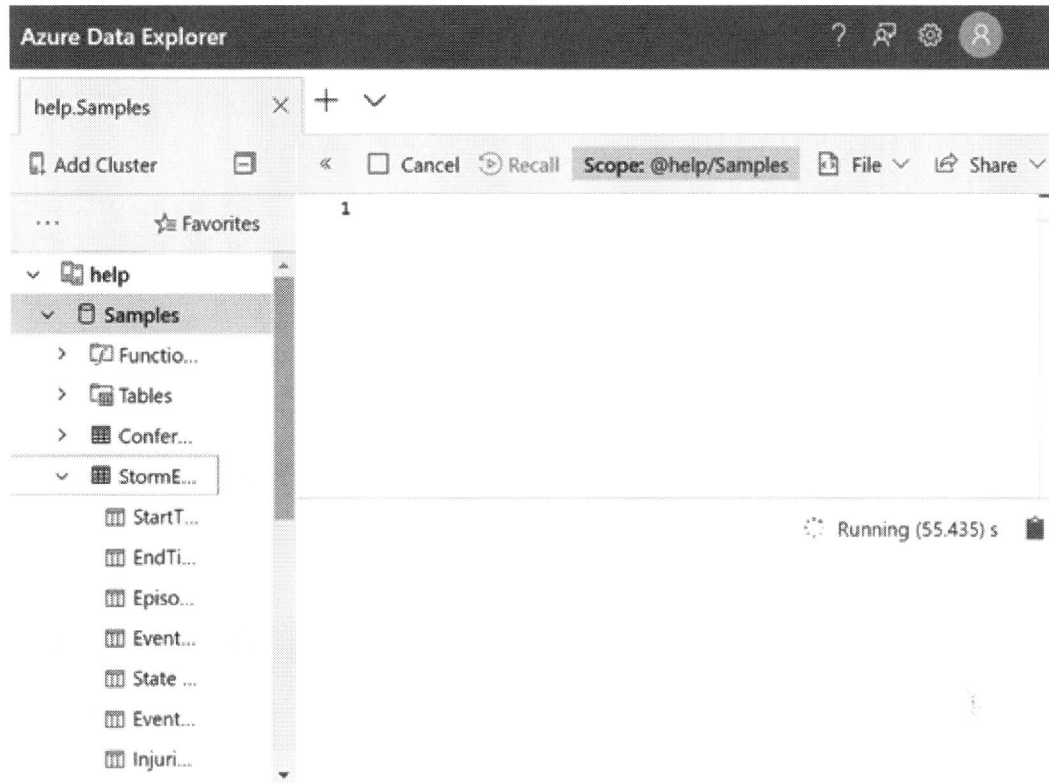

Figure 5.2 – StormEvents

To run a query, either type or paste the command into the query window at the top of the page, just to the right of the line numbered **1** in the preceding screenshot. Once the query has been entered, click on the **Run** button to run the query. The output will be shown in the results window at the bottom of the page.

In the following screenshot, a simple query was entered and run. The query was entered in the query window, and you can see that the results are shown below it:

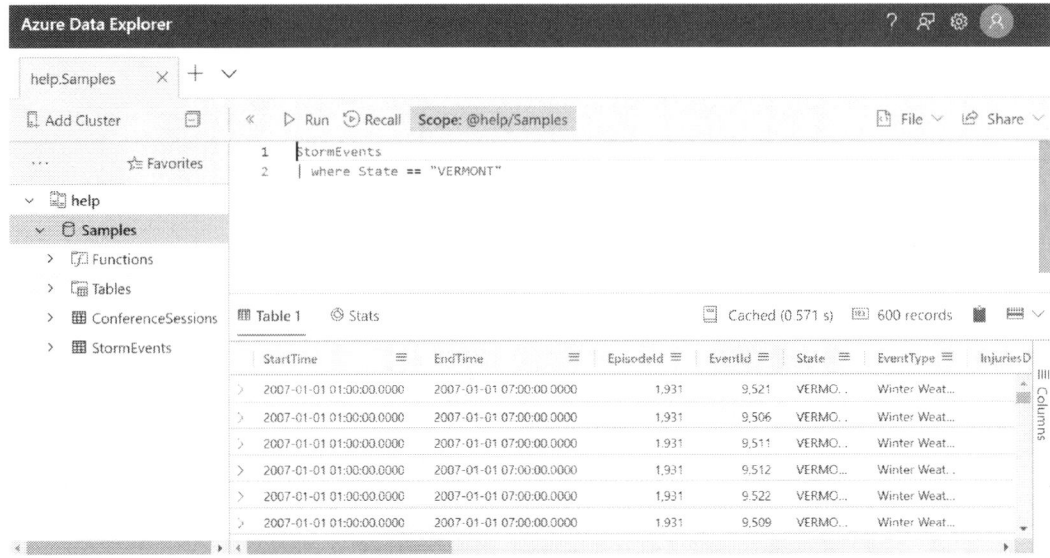

Figure 5.3 – Executed query

There is a lot more you can do with the ADX, so feel free to play around with it. Now that you understand how we are going to run the queries and view the results, let's look at some of the various commands KQL has to offer.

Introduction to KQL commands

Unlike SQL, the query starts with the data source, which can be either a table or an operator that produces a table, followed by commands that transform the data into what is needed. Each command's output can be passed into the next command by using the pipe (|) delimiter.

What does this mean? If you are familiar with SQL, you would write a statement such as `Select * from table` to get the values from the table. The same query in KQL would just be `table`, where `table` refers to the name of the log. It is implied that you want all the columns and rows. Later, we will discuss how to minimize what information is returned.

We will only be scratching the surface of what KQL can do here, but it will be enough to get you started writing your own queries so that you can develop queries for Microsoft Sentinel.

The following table provides an overview of the commands, functions, and operators we will be covering in the rest of this chapter:

Type	Name	Description
Tabular Operators	print	Prints the results of a query
	search	Searches for specific data throughout the logs
	where	Filters a table to the subset of rows that satisfy a comparison
	take/limit	Returns up to the specified number of rows
	count()	Returns the number of records in the input record set
	summarize	Produces a table that summarizes the content of the selected columns
	extend	Creates calculated columns and appends them to the result set
	project	Selects the columns to include
	distinct	Produces a table with the distinct combination of the provided columns of the input table
	sort/order	Sorts the rows of the input table into order by one or more columns
	join	Merges the rows of two tables to form a new table by matching the values of the specified column(s) from each table
	union	Takes two or more tables and returns the rows of all of them
	render	Displays the output in a chart, including pie, bar, and line charts, among others
Query Statements	let	Creates variables
Scalar Functions	ago()	Subtracts the given timespan from the current UTC clock time
String Operators	operators	Not a command but a discussion of operators to use with the where command

Table 5.1

Again, this is just a brief overview of the commands available to you when using KQL. There are a lot more commands you can use, including some that add machine learning capabilities to your queries.

> **Note**
> For a complete list of all the KQL commands and more examples, go to https://docs.microsoft.com/en-us/azure/kusto/query/index.

Let's start looking at the various commands in more detail in the following sections.

Tabular operators

A tabular operator in KQL is one that can produce data in a mixture of tables and rows. Each tabular operator can pass its results from one command to another using the pipe delimiter. You will see many examples of this throughout this chapter.

The print command

The `print` command will print the results of a simple query. You will not be using this in your KQL queries, but it is useful for trying to figure out how commands work and what output to expect.

A simple `print` command such as `print "test"` will return a single row with the text **test** on it.

The search command

As we stated earlier, to search using KQL, you just need enter the table name in the editor, rather than in SQL where you use the `select` command. This will return all the columns and all the rows of the table, up to the maximum your application will return.

So, in the ADX, if you enter `StormEvents` in the search window and click **Run**, you will see a window like the one shown in the following screenshot. Note that there are a lot more rows available; the following screenshot just shows a small sample:

Introduction to KQL commands   123

![StormEvents table screenshot]

Figure 5.4 – Sampling the rows of StormEvents

If you need to search for a specific term in all the columns in all the logs in your workspace, the `search` command will do that for you.

If you need to find all the occurrences of `York`, you can use the following command:

```
search "York"
```

This will return results like what is shown in the following screenshot. Note that I have hidden some of the columns to make it easier to see that `York` is shown in more columns than just `State`:

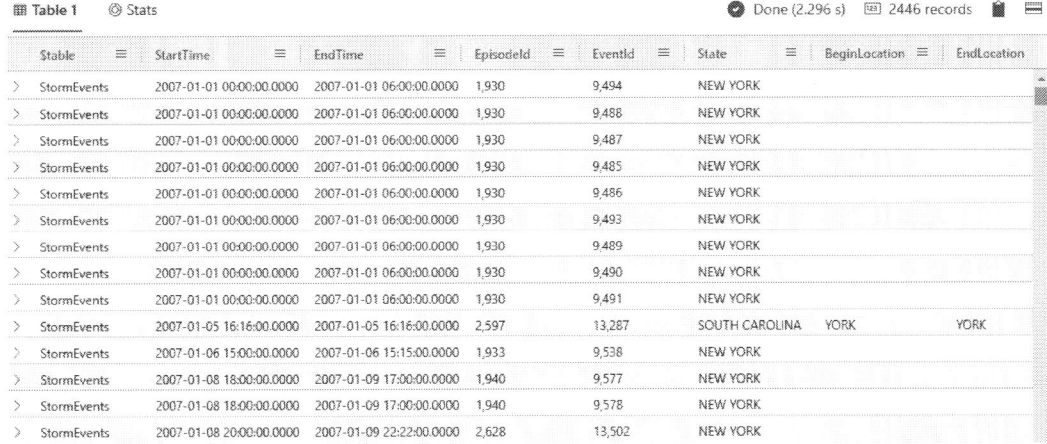

Figure 5.5 – The search command

Be warned that using the `search` command can take a significant amount of time to perform the query.

The where command

Recall from the screenshot in the *The search command* section that you get all the rows in the table when you enter the table name, up to the maximum number of rows allowed to be returned. However, 99% of the time, this is not what you want to do. You will only want a subset of the rows in the table. That is when the `where` operator is useful. This allows you to filter the rows that are returned based on a condition.

If you want to see just those storm events that happened in North Carolina, you can enter the following:

```
StormEvents
| where State == "NORTH CAROLINA"
```

This will return all the rows where the column called `State` exactly equals `NORTH CAROLINA`. Note that `==` is case-sensitive, so if there was a row that had `North Carolina` in the `State` column, it would not be returned. Later, in the *String operators* section, we will go into more depth about case-sensitive and case-insensitive commands.

The take/limit command

There may be times when you just need a random sample of the data to be returned. This is usually so you can get an idea of what the data will look like before running a larger data query.

The `take` command does just that. It will return a specified number of rows; however, there is no guarantee which rows will be returned so that you can get a better sampling.

The following command will return five random rows from the `StormEvents` table:

```
StormEvents
| take 5
```

Note that `limit` is just an alias for `take` so that the following command is the same as the preceding command. However, it's likely that different rows will be returned since the sampling is random:

```
StormEvents
| limit 5
```

While you may not use the `limit` or `take` commands much in your actual queries, these commands are very useful when you're working to define your queries. You can use them to get a sense of the data that each table contains.

The count command

There may be times when you just need to know how many rows your query will return. A lot of times, this is done to get an idea of the data size you will be working with or just to see whether your query returns any data without seeing the return values.

The `count` command will return the number of rows in the query. So, if we want to see the number of rows in the `StormEvents` table, we can enter the following:

```
StormEvents
| count
```

This will return just one column with `59,066` as the answer. Note how much faster this was than just showing all the rows in `StormEvents` using a basic `search` command and looking at the information bar to get the total. It can take around 12 seconds to process and show all the rows, compared to around 0.2 seconds to get the answer when using `count`. The time it takes to perform the query may vary, but in all cases, it will be significantly faster to just get a count of the number of rows than to look at all the rows.

The summarize command

There will be times when you just need to know the total values for a specific grouping of rows. Suppose you just need to know how many storm events occurred for each location. The following command will show that:

```
StormEvents
| summarize count() by BeginLocation
```

This will return values like the ones shown in the following screenshot:

BeginLocation	count_
MELBOURNE BEACH	1
ORMOND BEACH	1
EUSTIS	12
LOTTS	1
CRANFIELD	1
SERVICE	1
BROOKHAVEN	3
FRENCH CAMP	2
PAGO PAGO	6
VANCEBURG	3
COLDWATER	11
WAPAKONETA	6
LOCKINGTON	1
DE GRAFF	1
EASTON	8
HOMEWOOD	3

Figure 5.6 – Summarize by BeginLocation

Note that this screenshot is only showing a partial listing of the results.

You may have noticed that `count`, in this case, has parentheses after it. That is because `count`, as used here, is a function rather than an operator and, as a function, requires parentheses after the name. For a complete list of aggregate functions that can be used, go to https://docs.microsoft.com/en-us/azure/kusto/query/summarizeoperator#list-of-aggregation-functions.

The `by` keyword is telling the command that everything that follows are the columns that are being used in the query to perform the summary.

You can also list multiple columns if you want to have more detailed information. For instance, the following command will summarize `StormEvents` by `State` and then `BeginLocation`:

```
StormEvents
| summarize count() by State, BeginLocation
```

If there is more than one `BeginLocation` in a state, the state will be listed multiple times, as shown in the following screenshot:

State	BeginLocation	count_
ATLANTIC SOUTH	MELBOURNE BEACH	1
FLORIDA	ORMOND BEACH	1
FLORIDA	EUSTIS	1
GEORGIA	LOTTS	1
MISSISSIPPI	CRANFIELD	1
MISSISSIPPI	SERVICE	1
MISSISSIPPI	BROOKHAVEN	3
MISSISSIPPI	FRENCH CAMP	2
AMERICAN SAMOA	PAGO PAGO	6
KENTUCKY	VANCEBURG	3
OHIO	COLDWATER	2
OHIO	WAPAKONETA	6
OHIO	LOCKINGTON	1
OHIO	DE GRAFF	1
KANSAS	EASTON	2
MISSISSIPPI	HOMEWOOD	3

Figure 5.7 – Summarize by State and BeginLocation

Again, this screenshot is only showing a partial list of the results.

The extend command

There may be times when you need information that the table does not provide but can be generated from the data that has been provided. For example, the `StormEvents` table provides a start time and an end time for the event but does not provide the actual duration of the event. We know we can get the duration by subtracting the start time from the end time, but how can we tell KQL to do this?

The `extend` command does this. It allows you to create new columns from existing columns, or other data, such as hardcoded values. The following command will create a new column called `Duration` that will then be populated by the difference between the `EndTime` and the `StartTime` in each row of the `StormEvents` table:

```
StormEvents
| extend Duration = EndTime - StartTime
```

The following screenshot shows a sample of the output. It may not be obvious from this screenshot, but it should be noted that any column that's created using `extend` will always be shown as the last column in the list, unless specifically told otherwise (more on that later):

EventNarrative	StormSummary	Duration
At the Petersburg river gage, th...	{"TotalDamages":0,"StartTime":"...	26.14:00:00
At the Hazleton river gage, the ...	{"TotalDamages":0,"StartTime":"...	27.14:00:00
The Wabash River in Vermillion ...	{"TotalDamages":10000,"StartTi...	27.21:00:00
The Wabash in Sullivan County ...	{"TotalDamages":10000,"StartTi...	30.23:59:00
The Wabash River at Vincennes...	{"TotalDamages":10000,"StartTi...	29.10:34:00
At New Harmony, moderate flo...	{"TotalDamages":0,"StartTime":"...	30.19:00:00
Moderate flooding occurred al...	{"TotalDamages":0,"StartTime":"...	30.10:00:00
At Mount Carmel, moderate flo...	{"TotalDamages":0,"StartTime":"...	29.18:00:00
Save for brief drops below floo...	{"TotalDamages":10000,"StartTi...	19.10:24:00
The White River in Daviess Cou...	{"TotalDamages":10000,"StartTi...	23.18:47:00
The White River in Knox Count...	{"TotalDamages":10000,"StartTi...	26.10:27:00
At Mount Carmel, moderate flo...	{"TotalDamages":0,"StartTime":"...	29.19:00:00
The White River in Greene Cou...	{"TotalDamages":10000,"StartTi...	21.18:49:00

Figure 5.8 – The extend command

As we stated previously, the `extend` command does not need to use other columns as it can use hardcoded values as well, so the following command is perfectly valid:

```
StormEvents
| extend Test = strcat("KQL"," rocks")
```

Note that the `strcat` function concatenates two or more strings into one. The output will look like the following screenshot. Since we are not taking any values from the rows via a column reference, the value will always be the same, in this case, **KQL rocks**:

EventNarrative	StormSummary	Test
At the Petersburg river gage, th...	{"TotalDamages":0,"StartTime":"...	KQL rocks
At the Hazleton river gage, the ...	{"TotalDamages":0,"StartTime":"...	KQL rocks
The Wabash River in Vermillion ...	{"TotalDamages":10000,"StartTi...	KQL rocks
The Wabash in Sullivan County ...	{"TotalDamages":10000,"StartTi...	KQL rocks
The Wabash River at Vincennes...	{"TotalDamages":10000,"StartTi...	KQL rocks
At New Harmony, moderate flo...	{"TotalDamages":0,"StartTime":"...	KQL rocks
Moderate flooding occurred al...	{"TotalDamages":0,"StartTime":"...	KQL rocks
At Mount Carmel, moderate flo...	{"TotalDamages":0,"StartTime":"...	KQL rocks
Save for brief drops below floo...	{"TotalDamages":10000,"StartTi...	KQL rocks
The White River in Daviess Cou...	{"TotalDamages":10000,"StartTi...	KQL rocks
The White River in Knox Count...	{"TotalDamages":10000,"StartTi...	KQL rocks

Figure 5.9 – The extend command with hardcoded values

This command will be very useful when outputting information that may exist in multiple columns, but you want it to be shown in a single column.

The project command

If you don't need to see all the columns that a query would normally show, `project` is used to determine what columns to show. In the following query, only `StartTime`, `EndTime`, and `EventId` will be shown:

```
StormEvents
| project StartTime, EndTime, EventId
```

130　Using the Kusto Query Language (KQL)

The output is shown in the following screenshot. One item of interest is that the query took significantly less time to run than when showing all the columns:

StartTime	EndTime	EventId
2007-01-01 00:00:00.0000	2007-01-27 14:00:00.0000	7,580
2007-01-01 00:00:00.0000	2007-01-28 14:00:00.0000	7,586
2007-01-01 00:00:00.0000	2007-01-28 21:00:00.0000	11,920
2007-01-01 00:00:00.0000	2007-01-31 23:59:00.0000	11,923
2007-01-01 00:00:00.0000	2007-01-30 10:34:00.0000	11,924
2007-01-01 00:00:00.0000	2007-01-31 19:00:00.0000	7,499
2007-01-01 00:00:00.0000	2007-01-31 10:00:00.0000	7,506
2007-01-01 00:00:00.0000	2007-01-30 18:00:00.0000	7,505
2007-01-01 00:00:00.0000	2007-01-20 10:24:00.0000	11,914
2007-01-01 00:00:00.0000	2007-01-24 18:47:00.0000	11,930
2007-01-01 00:00:00.0000	2007-01-27 10:27:00.0000	11,931
2007-01-01 00:00:00.0000	2007-01-30 19:00:00.0000	7,498
2007-01-01 00:00:00.0000	2007-01-22 18:49:00.0000	11,929

Figure 5.10 – The project command

The `project` command is like `extend` in that they can both create new columns. The main difference is that the `extend` command creates a new column at the end of the result set, while the `project` command creates the column wherever it is in the list of variables. It's good practice to use the `extend` command for anything other than the simplest of computations to make it easier to read the query. There are two commands that produce the same results. The first command is as follows:

```
StormEvents
| extend Duration = EndTime - StartTime
| project StartTime, EndTime, EventId, Duration
```

The other command is as follows:

```
StormEvents
| project StartTime, EndTime, EventId, Duration = EndTime - StartTime
```

Here, you can see that the `project` command is quite useful for cleaning up the results by removing those columns you don't care about.

The distinct command

There may be times where you get multiple instances of the same value returned but you only need to see one of them. That is where `distinct` comes in. It will return only the first instance of a collection of the specified column(s) and ignore all the rest.

If I run the following command, I will get a value back for all 59,066 rows and it will include many duplicates:

The output is shown in the following screenshot. Note the multiple occurrences of **FLORIDA**, **MISSISSIPPI**, and **OHIO**:

Figure 5.11 – Rows with multiple states

If we need to see just one instance of each state, we can use the following command and only get 67 rows returned to us:

This still returns the states but only one instance of each state will be returned, as shown here:

Figure 5.12 – The distinct command

By using the `distinct` command, you can easily see which values are in a column. This can be quite useful when building up your query. In the preceding example, you can see which states are represented in the dataset without having to scroll through all the rows as you would if you didn't use `distinct`.

The sort/order command

When you run a query, by default, the rows will be returned in whatever order they were saved into the table you are querying. If we look at the results from running the last command in the *The distinct command* section, the states are returned in the order the first occurrence of the state was found in the table.

Building on the command we used in the previous section, please refer to the preceding screenshot to see the output and note that the states are returned in a random order.

Most of the time, this is not what you are looking for. You will want to see the values in a specific order, such as alphabetical or based on a time value. The `sort` command will allow you to sort the output into any order you wish.

The following command will sort the output by the `State` column:

```
StormEvents
| distinct State
| sort by State
```

A sample of the output is as follows:

Figure 5.13 – The sort command showing states listed in descending alphabetical order

Note that the output is in alphabetical order, but it is in the default descending order. While this may be what you want, if you wanted to see the states that start with A first, you will need to specify that you want the sort to be done in ascending order. The following command shows how to do that:

```
StormEvents
| distinct State
| sort by State asc
```

In the following output, you can see that those states that start with A are now shown first:

State
ALABAMA
ALASKA
AMERICAN SAMOA
ARIZONA
ARKANSAS
ATLANTIC NORTH
ATLANTIC SOUTH
CALIFORNIA
COLORADO
CONNECTICUT
DELAWARE
DISTRICT OF COLUMBIA
E PACIFIC
FLORIDA
GEORGIA
GUAM

Figure 5.14 – The sort command showing states listed in ascending alphabetical order

Note that `order` can also be used in place of `sort`, so the following command will do the same thing that we just saw:

```
StormEvents
| distinct State
| order by State asc
```

As you can see, the `sort` command is extremely useful when you need to see your output in a specific order, which will probably be most of the time.

The join command

The `join` operator will merge the rows of two tables to form a new table by matching values of the specified columns from each table. In the following contrived example, all the rows from `StormEvents` where `State` equals `North Carolina` will be combined with the rows from `FLEvents` where they have a matching `EventType` column:

```
let FLEvents = StormEvents
| where State == "FLORIDA";
FLEvents
```

```
| join (StormEvents
| where State == "NORTH CAROLINA")
on EventType
```

The `let` command will create the `FLEvents` variable around for later use. See the *let statement* section for more information.

You will use the `join` command quite a bit when writing your queries to get information from multiple tables or the same table using different parameters. Next, we will examine the `union` command and how it differs from the `join` command.

You will be using the `join` command quite often in your queries, either to combine different tables or to look at the same table in different ways.

The union command

The `union` command combines two or more tables into one. While `join` will show all the columns of the matching rows in one row, `union` will have one row for each row in each of the tables. So, if table 1 has 10 rows and table 2 has 12 rows, the new table that's created from the union will have 22 rows.

If the tables do not have the same columns, all the columns from both tables will be shown, but for the table that does not have the column, the values will be empty. This is important to remember when performing tests against the columns. If table 1 has a column called `KQLRocks` and table 2 does not, then, when looking at the new table that's created by the union, there will be a value for `KQLRocks` for the rows in table 1, but it will be empty for the rows in table 2. See the following code:

```
let FLEvents = StormEvents
| where State == "FLORIDA";
let NCEvents = StormEvents
| where State == "NORTH CAROLINA"
| project State, duration = EndTime - StartTime;
NCEvents | union FLEvents
```

In the following example, when looking at the rows where the state is NORTH CAROLINA, all the columns other than `State` and `duration` will be empty since the `NCEvents` table only has the `State` and `duration` columns. When looking at the rows where `State` is FLORIDA, the `duration` column will be empty since the `FLEvents` table does not have that column in it, but all the other columns will be filled out. The `let` command will create the `FLEvents` and `NCEvents` variables for later use. See the *let statement* section for more information.

If we run the preceding code and scroll down a bit, we will see the output shown in the following screenshot. As you can see, most of the fields where `State` equals `North Carolina` are empty since the table that we created with the `let` command only contains the `State` and `duration` fields:

State	duration	StartTime	EndTime	EpisodeId	EventId	EventType	InjuriesDirect	InjuriesIndirect	DeathsDirect	DeathsIndirect
NORTH CAROLINA	07:00:00									
NORTH CAROLINA	29.23:59:00									
NORTH CAROLINA	29.23:59:00									
NORTH CAROLINA	00:30:00									
FLORIDA		2007-01-03...	2007-01-0...	2,256	11,031	Rip Current	0	0	1	0
FLORIDA		2007-01-05...	2007-01-0...	1,829	9,014	Funnel Cloud	0	0	0	0
FLORIDA		2007-01-05...	2007-01-0...	846	3,728	Thunderstor...	0	0	0	0
FLORIDA		2007-01-05...	2007-01-0...	846	3,737	Thunderstor...	0	0	0	0
FLORIDA		2007-01-05...	2007-01-0...	846	3,738	Thunderstor...	0	0	0	0
FLORIDA		2007-01-29...	2007-01-2...	2,482	12,569	Frost/Freeze	0	0	0	0

Figure 5.15 – Output of the union command

Use the `union` command when you need to see all the columns from the selected tables, even if some of those columns are empty in one of those tables.

The render command

The `render` operator is different from all the other commands and functions we have discussed in that it does not manipulate the data in any way, only how it is presented. The `render` command is used to show the output in a graphical, rather than tabular, format.

There are times when it is much easier to determine whether something is being asked by looking at a time chart or a bar chart rather than looking at a list of strings and numbers. By using `render`, you can display your data in a graphical format to make it easier to view the results.

If we run the following command, we'll get a tabular view of the data. While this is useful, it doesn't show any outliers:

```
StormEvents
| project State, EndTime, DamageProperty
| where State =="CALIFORNIA"
```

The partial output is as follows:

State	EndTime	DamageProperty
CALIFORNIA	2007-01-01 04:35:00.0000	0
CALIFORNIA	2007-01-01 04:37:00.0000	0
CALIFORNIA	2007-01-01 11:35:00.0000	0
CALIFORNIA	2007-01-02 03:36:00.0000	0
CALIFORNIA	2007-01-02 06:30:00.0000	0
CALIFORNIA	2007-01-02 11:00:00.0000	0
CALIFORNIA	2007-01-02 11:00:00.0000	0
CALIFORNIA	2007-01-02 11:00:00.0000	0
CALIFORNIA	2007-01-02 11:00:00.0000	0
CALIFORNIA	2007-01-04 19:14:00.0000	0
CALIFORNIA	2007-01-05 03:36:00.0000	0
CALIFORNIA	2007-01-05 04:36:00.0000	0
CALIFORNIA	2007-01-05 04:57:00.0000	350,000

Figure 5.16 – Results shown in tabular format

While it does show that there was an instance of a storm event on January 5, 2007, which caused a lot of damage, was it the one that caused the most damage? We could look through the rows and look at the **DamageProperty** column for each row to find this out, but there is an easier way to do this.

If we run the following command, a line chart will be generated that shows the same data but in a graphical view:

```
StormEvents
| project State, EndTime, DamageProperty
| where State =="CALIFORNIA"
| render linechart
```

The output from this command is shown in the following screenshot. It is instantly recognizable that, while the storm we saw in January caused a lot of damage, it is nowhere near the damage caused by the storm on June 30:

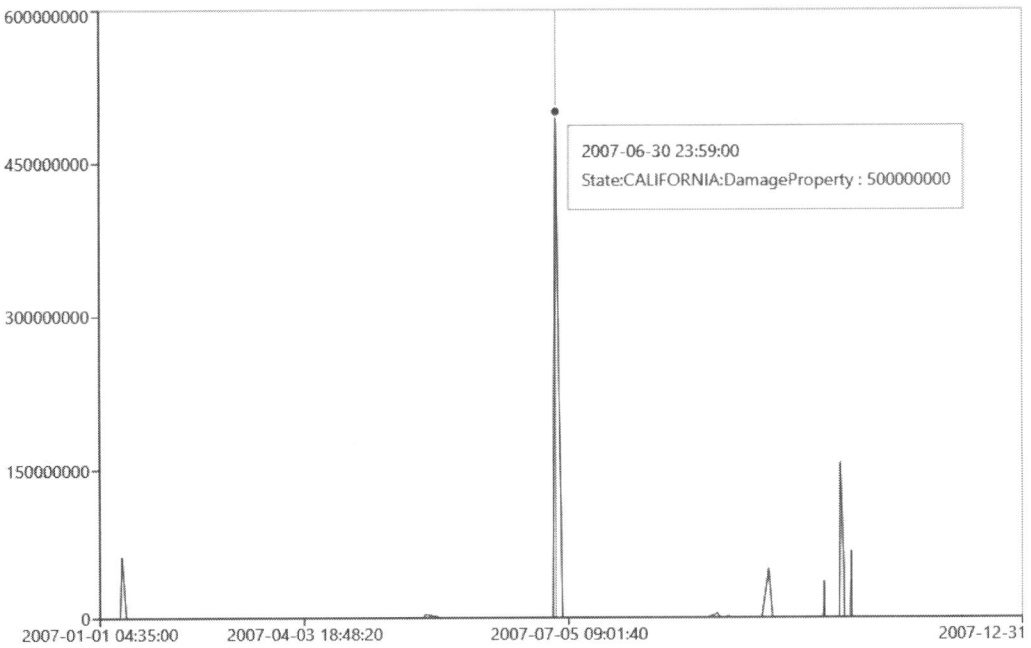

Figure 5.17 – Viewing storm damage as a graph

As shown in the preceding graph, there are times when a graphical representation of the data is more valuable than just looking at the textual output.

> **Note**
> The *x* axis is a bit misleading here with the labeling but, as you can see, when you hover your mouse over the data, the storm did occur on June 30.

Some of the other charts that can be rendered include a pie chart, an area chart, and a time chart, and each may require a different number of columns to present the data.

Query statements

Query statements in KQL produce tables that can be used in other parts of the query and must end with a semicolon (;). These commands, of which we will only discuss the `let` command here, will return entire tables that are all returned by the query. Keep in mind that a table can consist of a single row and a single column, in which case it acts as a constant in other languages.

The let statement

The `let` statement allows you to create a new variable that can be used in later computations. It is different than `extend` or `project` in that it can create more than just a column – it can create another table if desired.

So, if I want to create a table that contains all the `StormEvents` for only NORTH CAROLINA, I can use the following commands. Note the ; at the end of the `let` statement since it is indeed a separate statement:

```
let NCEvents = StormEvents
| where State == "NORTH CAROLINA";
NCEvents
```

The `let` statement can also be used to define constants. The following command will work exactly like the one earlier. Note that the second `let` references the first `let` variable:

```
let filterstate = "NORTH CAROLINA";
let NCEvents = StormEvents
| where State == filterstate;
NCEvents
```

The `let` statement is very powerful and one that you will use quite a bit when writing your queries.

Scalar functions

Scalar functions take a value and perform some sort of manipulation on it to return a different value. They are useful for performing conversions between data types, looking at only part of the variable, and performing mathematical computations.

The ago() function

The `ago()` function is used to subtract a specific timespan from the current UTC time. Remember that all times stored in the Log Analytics log are based on UTC time, unless they are times in a custom log that are specifically designed not to be. Generally, it is safe to assume that the times stored are based on UTC time.

If I wanted to look for events in `StormEvents` that ended less than an hour ago, I would use the following command. Note that this command doesn't return any values as the times stored are from 2007:

```
StormEvents
| where EndTime > ago(1h)
```

In addition to using h for hours, you can also use d for days, among others.

String operators

String and numeric operators are used in the comparisons of a `where` clause. We have already seen ==, which is a string equals operator. As we stated earlier, this is a case-sensitive operator, meaning that ABC == ABC is true but ABC == abc is false.

> **Note**
> You may need to carry out a case-insensitive comparison using =~. In this case, ABC =~ abc returns true. While there are commands to change text to uppercase or lowercase, it is good practice to not do that just for a comparison but rather do a case-insensitive comparison.

Some other string operators that can be used are as follows:

String operators

Operator	Description	Case Sensitive	Example (returns True)	Example (returns False)
`==`	Equal	Yes	`"One" == "One"`	`"One" == "ONE"`
`=~`	Equals	No	`"one" =~ "ONE"`	`"one" =~ "two"`
`contains_cs`	Right-hand string is in left-hand string	Yes	`"ONEtwo" contains_cs "ONE"`	`"ONEtwo" contains_cs "one"`
`contains`	Right-hand string is in left-hand string	No	`"ONEtwo" contains "one"`	`"ONEtwo" contains "three"`
`startswith_cs`	Right-hand string is at the beginning of the left-hand string	Yes	`"ONEtwo" startswith_cs "ONE"`	`"ONEtwo" startswith_cs "one"`
`startswith`	Right-hand string is at the beginning of the left-hand string	No	`"ONEtwo" startswith "one"`	`"ONEtwo" startswith "two"`
`endswith_cs`	Right-hand string is at the end of the left-hand string	Yes	`"oneTWO" endswith_cs "TWO"`	`"oneTWO" endswith_cs "two"`
`endswith`	Right-hand string is at the end of the left-hand string	No	`"oneTWO" endswith "two"`	`"oneTWO" endswith "one"`
`in`	Left-hand string is in one of the right-hand list of strings	Yes	`"one" in ("alpha","beta","one")`	`"ONE" in ("alpha","beta","one")`
`in~`	Left-hand string is in one of the right-hand list of strings	No	`"ONE" in ("alpha","beta","one")`	`"TWO" in ("alpha","beta","one")`

Table 5.2

In addition, by placing `!` in front of any command, that command is negated. For example, `!contains` means *does not contain* and `!in` means *not in*.

For a complete list of operators, go to `https://docs.microsoft.com/en-us/azure/data-explorer/kusto/query/datatypes-string-operators`.

Summary

In this chapter, you were introduced to the Kusto Query Language, which you will use to query the tables in your logs. You learned about some of the tabular operators, query statements, scalar functions, and string operators. In the *Questions* section, we will provide some quick questions to help you understand how to use these commands to perform your queries.

This is just the tip of the iceberg. It is highly recommended that you look at the complete KQL documentation, as listed in the *Further reading* section of the chapter, to learn about all the various commands you can use.

In the next chapter, you will learn how to take what you learned here and use it to query logs that are stored in Microsoft Sentinel using the **Logs** page.

Questions

1. How many storms occurred in California?
2. Provide a list that shows only one occurrence of each different state.
3. Provide a list of storms that caused at least $10,000 but less than $15,000 worth of damage.
4. Provide a list of storms that show the state, the amount of property damage, the amount of crop damage, and the total of the property and crop damage only.

Further reading

For more information on KQL, see the following links:

- Performing queries across resources: `https://docs.microsoft.com/en-us/azure/azure-monitor/log-query/cross-workspace-query#performing-a-query-across-multiple-resources`
- Complete KQL command documentation: `https://docs.microsoft.com/en-us/azure/data-explorer/kusto/query/`
- Running your KQL queries with sample data: `https://portal.azure.com/#blade/Microsoft_Azure_Monitoring_Logs/DemoLogsBlade`
- Additional graphical formats for queries: `https://docs.microsoft.com/en-us/azure/azure-monitor/log-query/charts`
- Date/time formats in KQL: `https://docs.microsoft.com/en-us/azure/azure-monitor/log-query/datetime-operations#date-time-basics`

6
Microsoft Sentinel Logs and Writing Queries

In the previous chapter, we looked at the **Kusto Query Language** (**KQL**) and gave a brief introduction to how to use it. In this chapter, we will learn about the **Microsoft Sentinel Logs** page. The Microsoft Sentinel Logs page is where you can see the various logs in your workspace, determine the type of data that makes up the logs, create the queries that will be used in the Analytics rules and threat hunting, as well as save these queries for later use. This will help you in creating rules and is an integral part of investigating incidents.

As part of this chapter, we will provide an overview of the Microsoft Sentinel Logs page, learn about the various sections, and look at how to use KQL to write queries. We will review the Logs screen in Microsoft Sentinel and show how to look at columns that make up the table, using both the UI and KQL. We will also look at the steps you can take to help develop your queries.

In a nutshell, the following topics will be covered:

- An introduction to the Microsoft Sentinel Logs page
- Navigating through the Logs page
- Writing a query

An introduction to the Microsoft Sentinel Logs page

The **Log Analytics** workspace follows a hierarchical pattern regarding how it organizes its information. At the top is the Log Analytics workspace. This is the container for all the individual tables for your instance of Microsoft Sentinel. This is equivalent to a database in **SQL**.

Within each workspace are individual tables. These are equivalent to a table in SQL and are the entities that hold data. They have a set of columns and zero or more rows of data.

Within each of those tables are the columns that hold the data. The columns can hold different data types including text, date/time, integers, and others.

> **Note**
> A lot of the documentation you will read will use the terms *table* and *log* interchangeably. We are choosing to use the term *table*, as that is the term **Microsoft** uses inside the Logs page and most documentation, even though the page itself is called **Logs**.

Navigating through the Logs page

The **Logs** page is where you can see a listing of all the tables that belong to your workspace, view some existing queries, write your own queries, view the results, and much more. Let's explore this page.

To get to the **Logs** page, select **Logs** from the Microsoft Sentinel navigation section. This will open the following page:

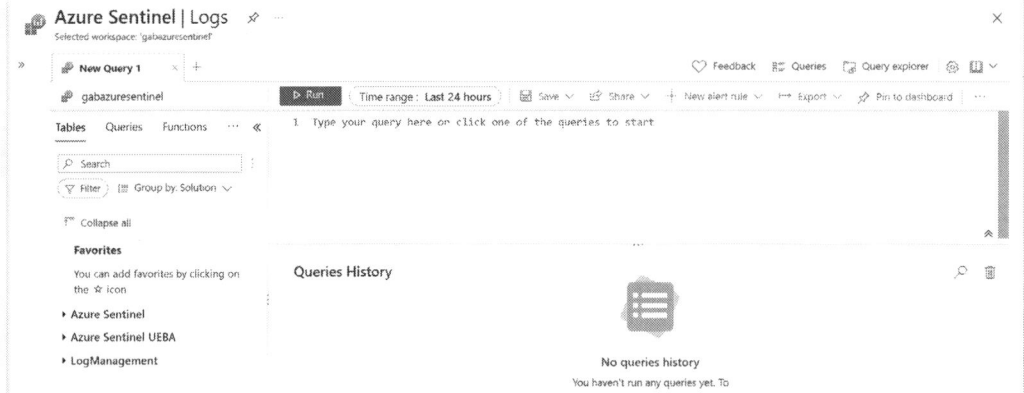

Figure 6.1 – Microsoft Sentinel Logs page

- The page header
- The Tables/Queries/Functions/More Tools panes
- The KQL code window
- The sample queries/results window

These sections can be seen in the following screenshot:

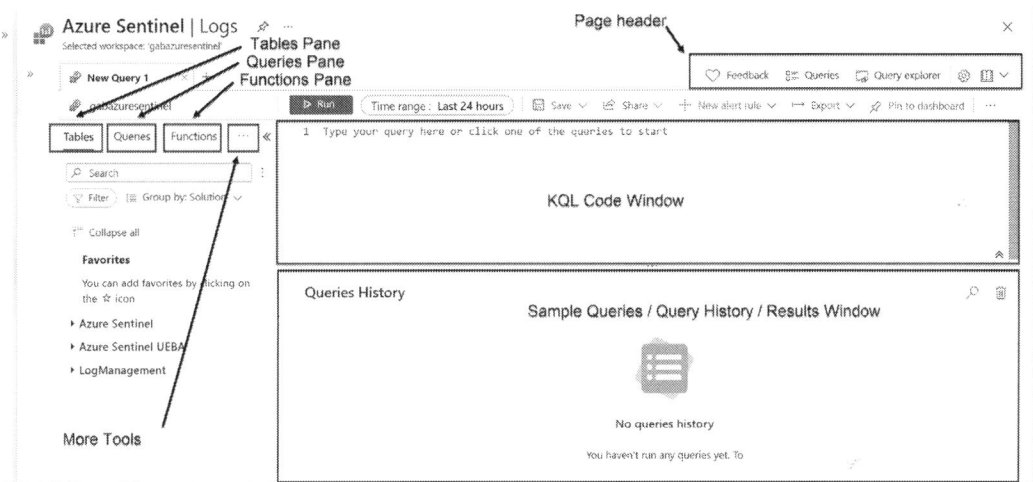

Figure 6.2 – Microsoft Sentinel Logs page sections

Let's describe each of these sections in more detail.

The page header

The page header is located at the top of the page and contains useful links, such as feedback, sample queries, query explorer, settings, and help, as shown in the following screenshot:

Figure 6.3 – Logs page header

You will not need to use these links to create new queries, although they can assist with some predefined code, as you will read about. We will look at each individual button, starting from the left side.

146   Microsoft Sentinel Logs and Writing Queries

Feedback

This feature allows you to send feedback to Microsoft regarding the Logs page. If this is clicked, you can select what you were doing, whether you liked it or not, provide a description, and select whether it is OK for Microsoft to contact you.

This is a great way to provide feedback as to how well you feel a feature is working, or to request new features.

Queries

Microsoft Sentinel has a few sample queries that have been provided to help you get started looking at tables. Follow these steps to use them:

1. Click on the **Queries** button. This will open a new window and show some sample queries as follows:

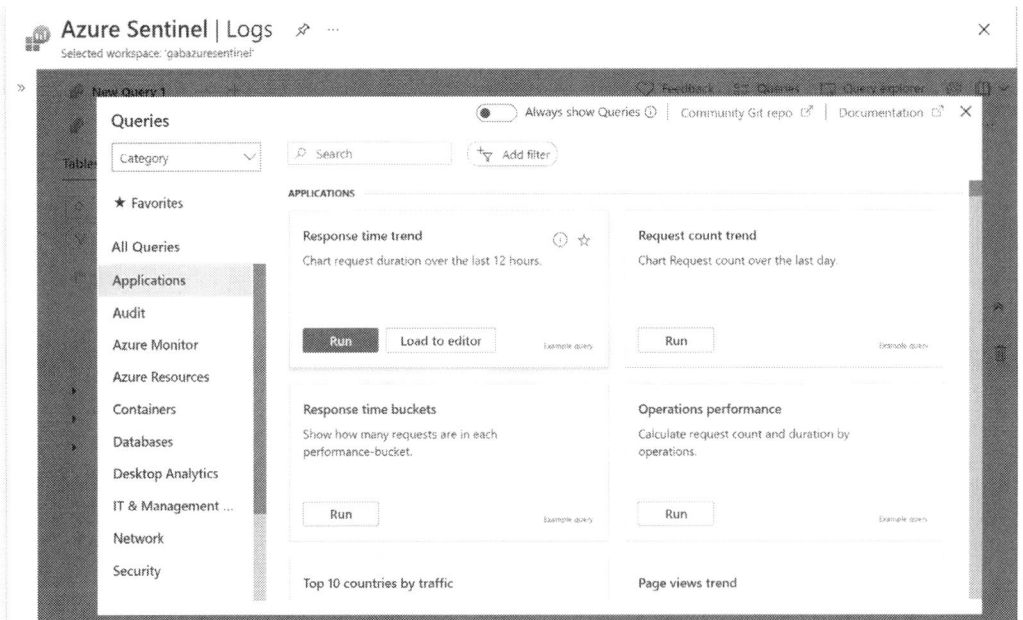

Figure 6.4 – Logs page sample queries

> **Note**
> You may have seen this page when you first went into the **Logs** page. If you notice at the top of the screen, there is a slider called **Always show Queries**. If this is enabled, this page will show up each time you go into the **Logs** page. By disabling this, the page will not show up automatically.

Also, the **Applications** tab will be shown by default. The queries are all related to showing information on the various applications that are logging data in your Log Analytics workspace.

If you hover over one of the queries, it will look like the **Response time trend** query shown in *Figure 6.4*. You can run the query, load the query's KQL code in the editor without running it, get more information on the query (that is the icon that looks like a letter **i** inside a circle), or mark it as a favorite, which is the icon that looks like a star, in which case this query will show up when you click on the **Favorites** link in the menu.

You can either scroll through the entire listing of queries or you can select one of the entries in the navigation menu, that is, **Applications**, **Audit**, **Azure Monitor**, and so on, to jump to that section.

2. Click the **Run** button on any of the entries to load the query and run it. In the following screenshot, the **Last heartbeat of each computer** query under the **Azure Monitor** section was run. Your results will vary depending on how many computers are reporting. If you do not see any results, it may be that you do not have the proper data connector set up – in this case, you need to have at least one computer associated with this Log Analytics workspace. For a refresher, see *Chapter 3, Managing and Collecting Data*, on setting up data connectors, and *Chapter 2, Azure Monitor – Introduction to Log Analytics*, on attaching computers to the Log Analytics workspaces.

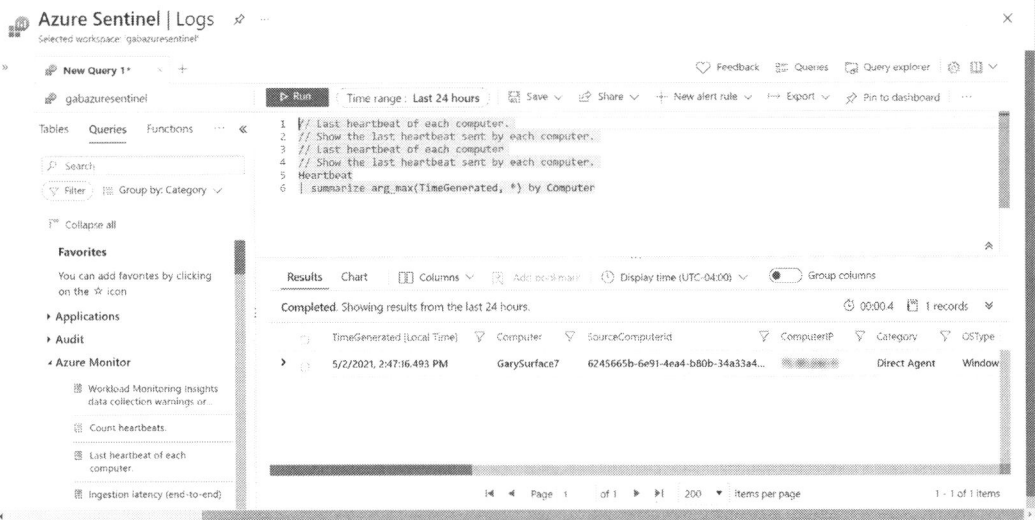

Figure 6.5 – Sample query results

Look at the other query sections to see what other queries are available to use.

> **Note**
> You can also access these same queries by going to the **Queries** tab that was called out in *Figure 6.2*.

Let's move on to the next button on the page header, which is the **Query explorer**.

Query explorer

The **Query explorer** button is like the **Queries** button, except that you can add your own queries to this list, which will be discussed later. If you have marked any queries as favorites or saved any queries yourself, these will show in this window:

1. Click on the **Query explorer** button. This will open the **Query explorer** blade as follows:

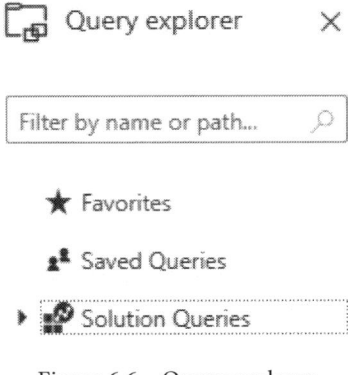

Figure 6.6 – Query explorer

2. Expand the **Solution Queries** tree; you will see that there are other groupings under it. Let's try this out. Expand the **Log Management** entry to see a list of queries that are related to log management, as shown in the following screenshot:

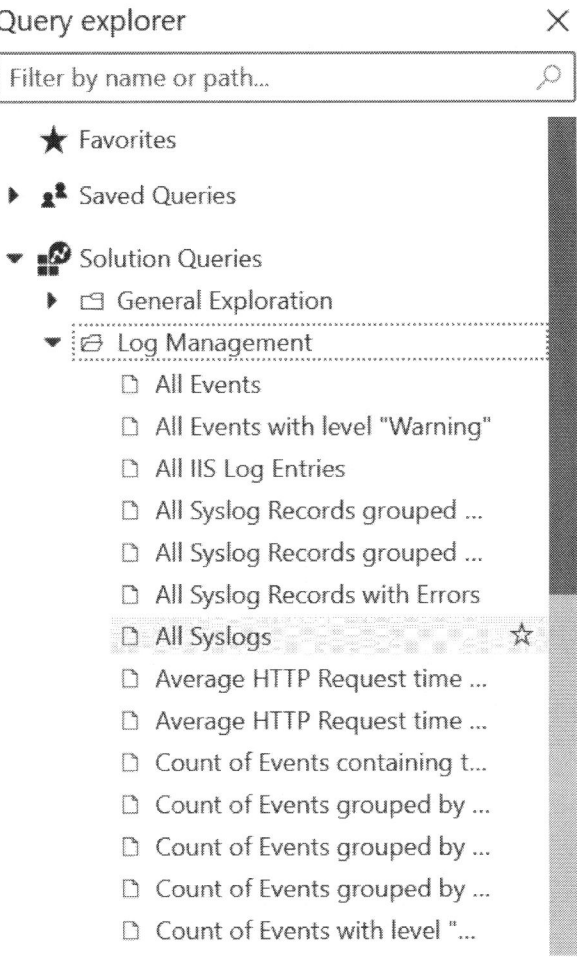

Figure 6.7 – Query explorer sample queries

3. As you can see in the preceding screenshot, the **All Syslogs** query has been selected. If the star on the right side of the name is selected, then that query will be saved as a favorite. The entry will be listed under the **Favorites** section, and the star will turn black, as shown in the following screenshot:

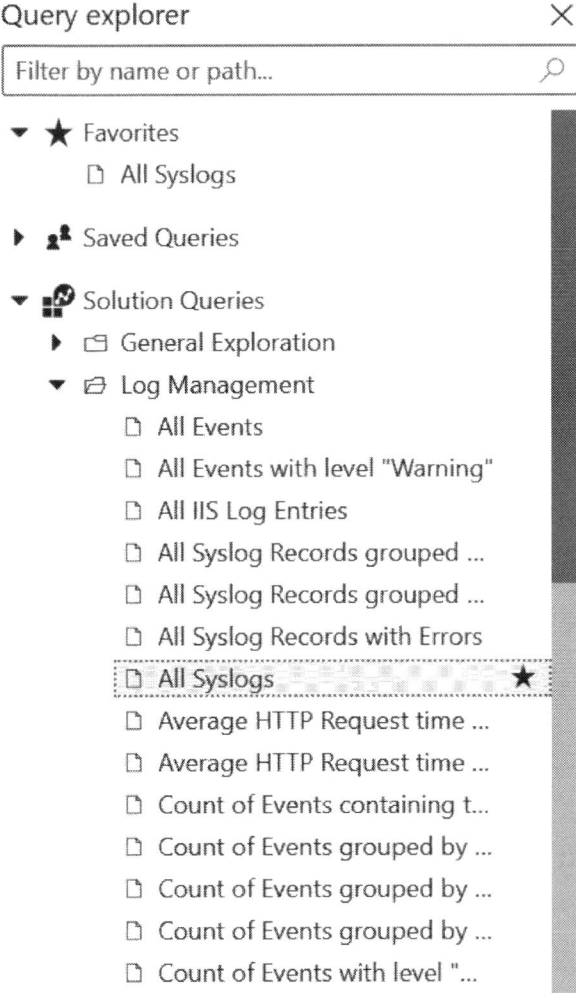

Figure 6.8 – Query explorer favorite query

4. Clicking on any entry will also load that query into the KQL window. In the following screenshot, the **All Syslogs** query was clicked on but not yet run. Notice that the title of the KQL code window has been changed to match the name of the selected query:

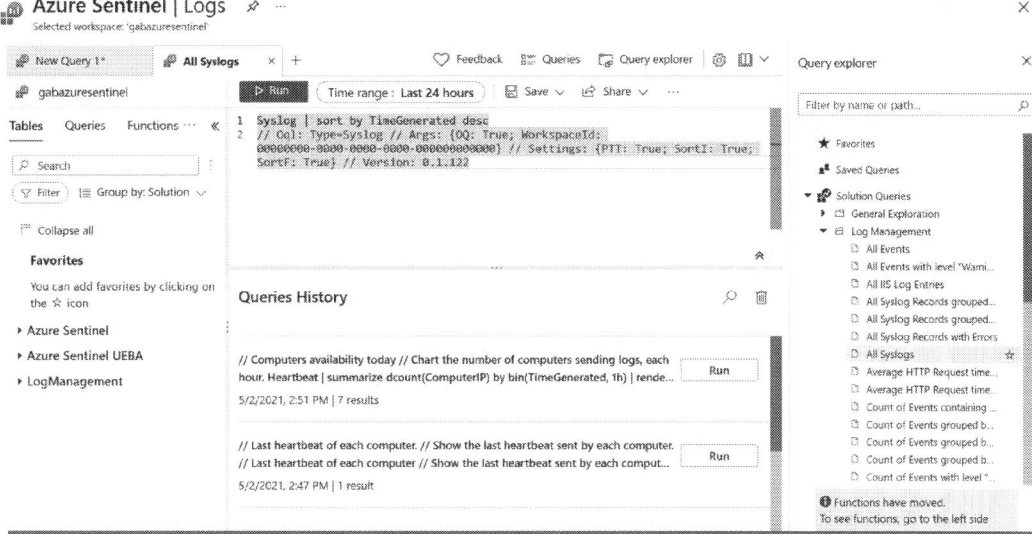

Figure 6.9 – Selected query from Query explorer

> **Important Note**
> It should be noted that when you click on the query, a new query tab will open. However, if you were to click the same query again, it would not open a new tab for that query again. It would switch back to the original tab that held the query.

Settings (the gear icon)

The Microsoft Sentinel **Logs** page has a few settings that can be modified.

Click on the **Settings** button. This will open the **Settings** blade as follows:

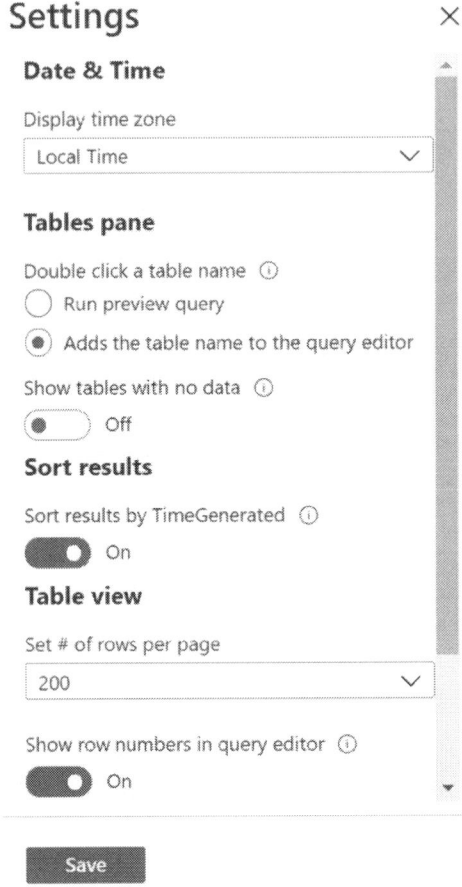

Figure 6.10 – Logs page Settings pane

Here you can choose from the following options:

- **Date & Time**: Select which time zone to use when displaying the date and time. This will change how any of the date and time fields, such as **TimeGenerated**, are displayed. By default, the fields will be displayed using **Universal Time Coordinated** (**UTC**), which is also known as **Greenwich Mean Time** (**GMT**) or **Zulu** (**Z**). Use the drop-down menu to change this to the time zone you desire. You can also use the **Local Time** entry to have the date and time displayed in whatever local time zone your computer is using.

> **Tip**
> Changing the date and time field here will change how the date and time are displayed whenever you show a time field in the results. You can also change the time zone used to display the time on a result-by-result basis in the header of the **Results** section. See The *results window* section for more information.

- **Tables** pane: Choose what happens when you double-click on a table in the **Tables** pane. If you select **Run preview query**, the KQL Query pane will have the table name followed by:

```
| where TimeGenerated > ago(24h)
| limit 10
```

  If you select **Adds the table name to the query editor**, then only the table name will be placed in the KQL Query pane and not any of the code.

  You can also determine if you want empty tables to show up or not. If you enable the slider called **Show tables with no data**, then any table that is part of your workspace, even if it has no data, will show up.

  This can be useful if you need to see what tables you have available to query, but could be frustrating if you are expecting to see data in all the tables.

- **Sort results**: Choose whether you want to automatically sort the results using the **TimeGenerated** field or not. If this is set to **On** (the default), then whenever the results are shown, they will be sorted using the **TimeGenerated** field. If this is set to **Off**, the results are shown in whatever order they were stored. Note that any sorting performed in the query will override this selection.

- **Table view**: How many rows to show on each page. The drop-down menu allows you to select **50**, which is the default, along with **100**, **150**, and **200**. Selecting higher values will allow more rows to be shown on a single page.

- **History Queries** (not shown in the screenshot): There is nothing to modify here; it is just to tell you how long the query history is stored for and how to clear the query history.

Let's look at the book icon next.

Help (the book icon)

This icon has no name assigned to it, but it is the one on the far-right side of the header that looks like a book.

Click on it to find other options that can help you learn more about the **Logs** page and writing queries in general:

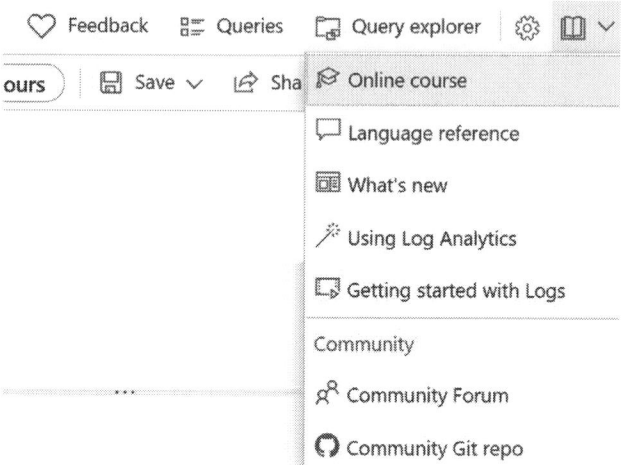

Figure 6.11 – Logs page help

Here you have the following options:

- **Online course** will open a new tab and will take you to **Pluralsight**'s page, where you can view the free *Kusto Query Language (KQL) from Scratch* course.
- **Language reference** will open the **KQL reference** page in a new tab.
- **What's new** will open the Azure Log Analytics updates page in a new tab.
- **Using Log Analytics** will open the Log Analytics tutorial page.
- **Getting started with Logs** will open a video on how to use Azure Monitor Log Analytics.
- **Community Forum** will open the Microsoft Sentinel tech community page where you can ask questions about Azure Monitor.
- **Community Git repo** will open the Microsoft Sentinel GitHub repository page.

> **Tip**
> Notice that all these entries are also duplicated on the right-hand side of the page under the **Learn more** heading.

That's it for the page header section of the **Logs** page. Next, we will look at the **Tables** pane, on the left side of the page.

The Tables pane

The **Tables** pane will list all the tables that are part of your Log Analytics workspace, grouped together using predefined groups.

Click on **Tables** and, looking at *Figure 6.12*, you will see that some of the logs are listed under a group called **Microsoft Sentinel**. There can also be groups called **Office365**, **SecurityInsights**, **WindowsFirewall**, and others.

> **Tip**
> Do not be concerned if you have greater or fewer groups than those shown here. The group will only be shown if there are any logs in it and the logs will only show if they are either part of Microsoft Sentinel or a connector is being used to populate them. For instance, the **Office365** group will only show if the underlying **OfficeActivity** log is present, and that will only show if the **Office365** connector has been enabled and has received data.

Expanding a group will show all the tables under that group. In the following screenshot, the **Microsoft Sentinel** group was expanded, showing all the logs under it:

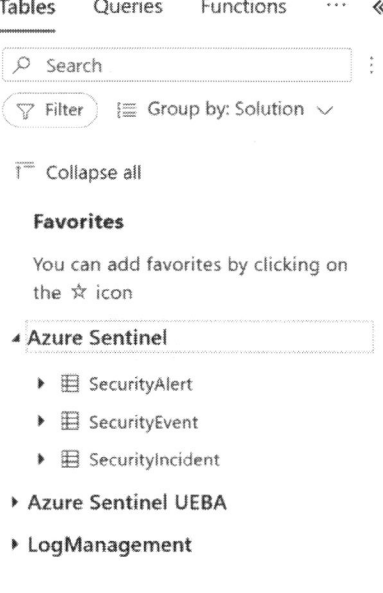

Figure 6.12 – The Tables pane

If you hover over any of the tables, a new window will pop up showing some information about the table, as shown in *Figure 6.13*.

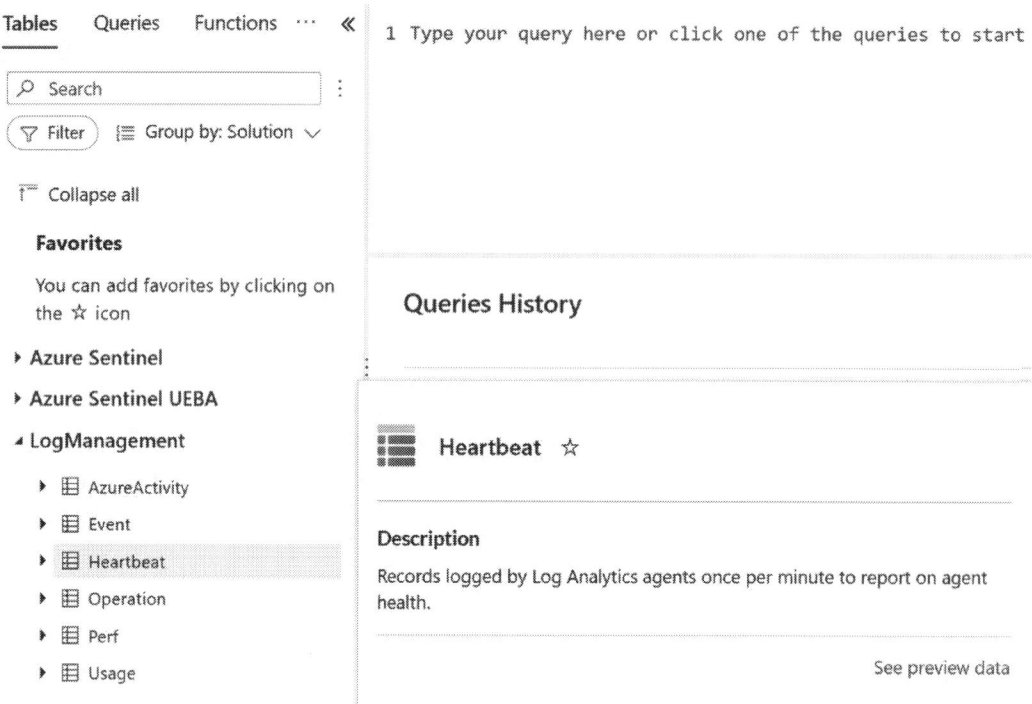

Figure 6.13 – Hover over table entry

Clicking on the star icon will save this entry as a favorite. It will show up at the top of the list under the **Favorites** section. This will be an identical entry so that you can expand it to see its columns and hover over it to see the eye icon, described next.

Clicking on the **See preview data** link will expand the pop-up window and will show the first 10 rows of the table, as shown in *Figure 6.14*. Notice that there are two new links added as well.

The **Use in editor** button, shown at the top of the window, will place the name of the table into the **KQL Query** pane. The name of the table, under the **Useful links** header, will take you to a page that has detailed information regarding the table, including the fields and descriptions.

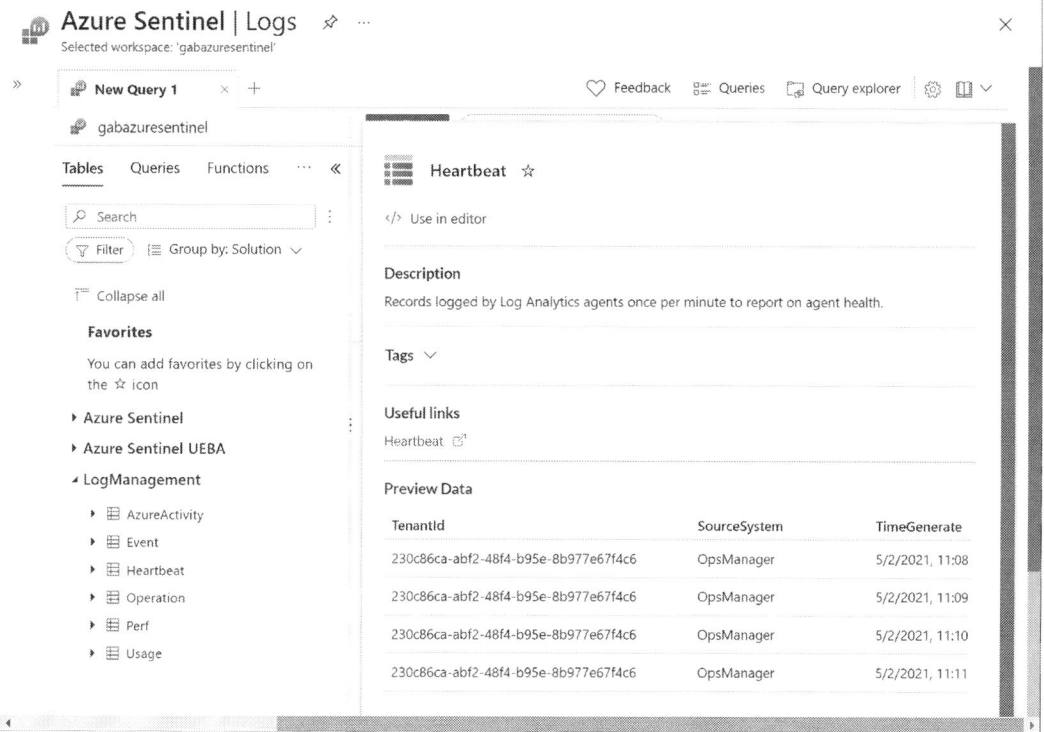

Figure 6.14 – Sample records from the log

> **Note**
> Some of the tables' pages are more complete than others with regard to the information provided.

There is also a section called **Tags** that, when expanded, will show you the tags that are used when grouping the tables. The current entries are **Solution** and **Category**. If you see multiple tags of the same type, that means the table will show up under multiple solutions or categories.

You can also expand a single table to see all the columns that make up the table, as well as the data type of the column. In the following screenshot, the **Event** log was expanded. You can see the various columns that make up the log and to the left of the name is an icon that shows the data type: an italic **t** for text, and a pound sign, #, for number. There is also a clock for date/time, **B** for Boolean, and {} for the dynamic type:

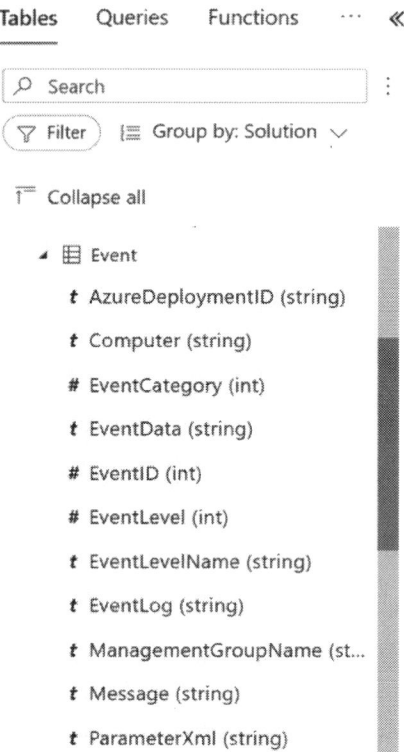

Figure 6.15 – Event log columns

Next, let's move on to the **Queries** pane.

The Queries pane

Selecting the **Queries** pane will show the same information as if you clicked on the **Queries** entry in the page header. The only difference is that you only see the title in a tree-view format. If you click on the title, the query will be placed into the **KQL Query** window as shown in the following screenshot:

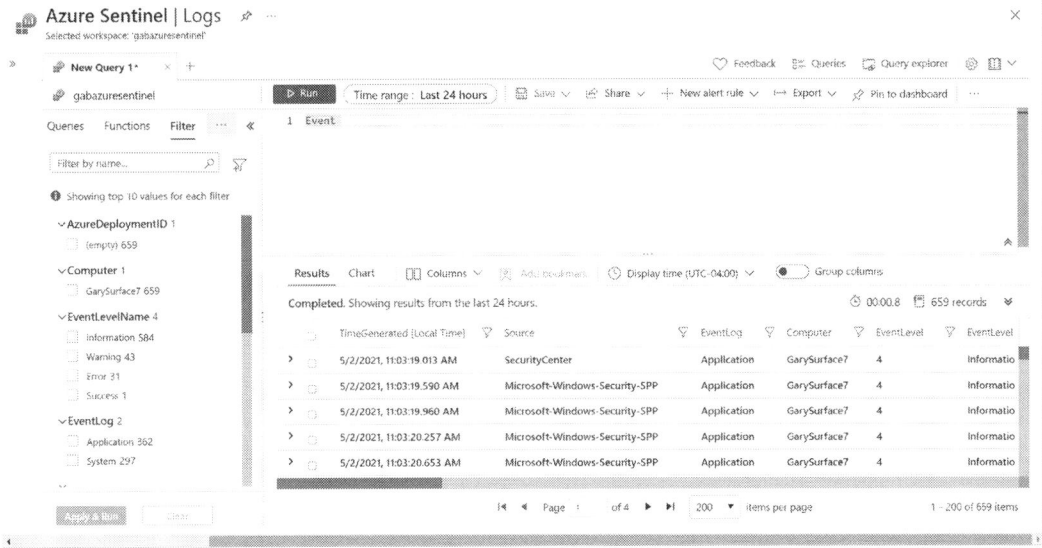

Figure 6.16 – Query pane

This shows the same query as was selected in *Figure 6.5* earlier. It is worth noting that to see the description, you must hover over the query name, much like mousing over a table name that was discussed in the previous section.

We saw how to look at the queries that have been saved. Now, let's look at any of the functions that are available.

The Functions pane

Functions are code that you have saved so that you can reuse them easily. Selecting the **Functions** pane will show you all the functions that have been created, grouped by their tags. Much like tables, you can change the grouping selection. However, with functions, there is an additional one called **Legacy category** that you can enter when creating your own functions, which is discussed later.

In the following screenshot, the `_GetWatchlist` function was double-clicked, to add the query to the KQL Query pane, and then hovered over, to show the description pop-up window.

If you notice in the pop-up window, in addition to the name and description of the function, any of the parameters that the function needs will be displayed. You can also see that the **KQL Query** window's help option, shows the needed variable. It also shows another function that has a similar name to make sure you did click on the correct one.

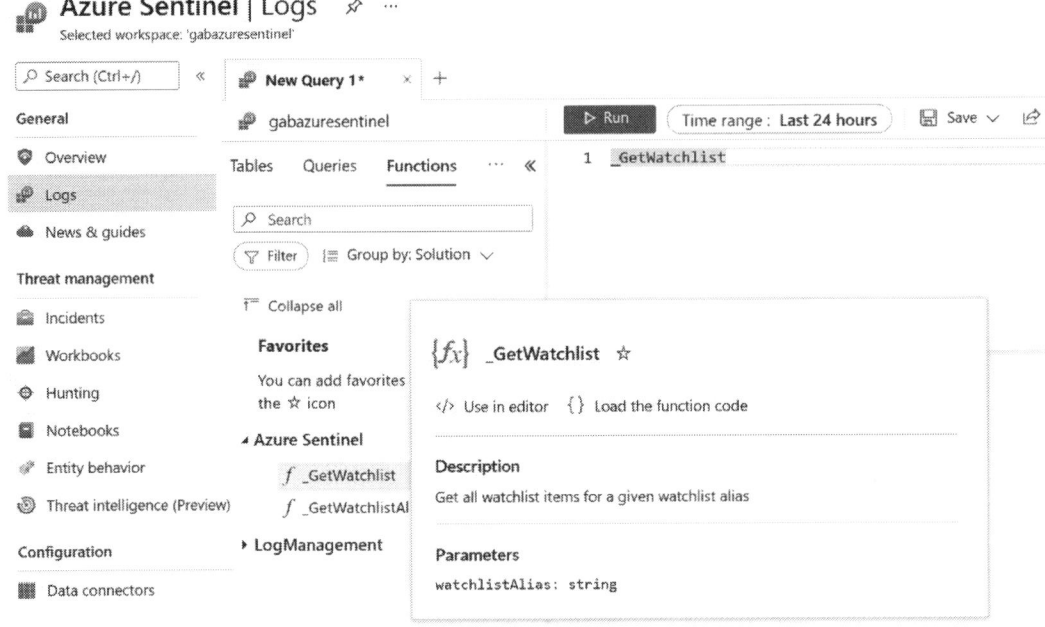

Figure 6.17 – Functions page

The last pane we need to look at is the **Filter** pane, and we discuss that next.

The Filter pane

You may have noticed that the Filter pane does not show up in *Figure 6.2*. This is because there are more tabs than can be shown in the space allocated to the panes. If you do not see the **Filter** pane, select the context menu (the three dots on the right side of the pane) and the panes that are not shown will be listed there. You can select the **Filter** pane from that list.

The **Filter** pane is useful after you run a query; before that, it will be empty. This pane will analyze the results of the query being run and generate useful filters for that query.

Clicking on any of the checkboxes in the **Filter** pane and then clicking **Apply & Run** at the bottom of the screen will modify the query to use those filters. Only the top 10 values for each filter will be shown, so it may be possible that you will not see the value that you want to use to filter. In that case, you will need to apply the filter on the individual column. Let's try this out.

In the following screenshot, a query to show entries from the **Event** table was run and the **Filter** pane was selected to show useful filters. A list of the columns that are part of the **Results** set will be shown and up to 10 entries that represent the values for the column will be displayed:

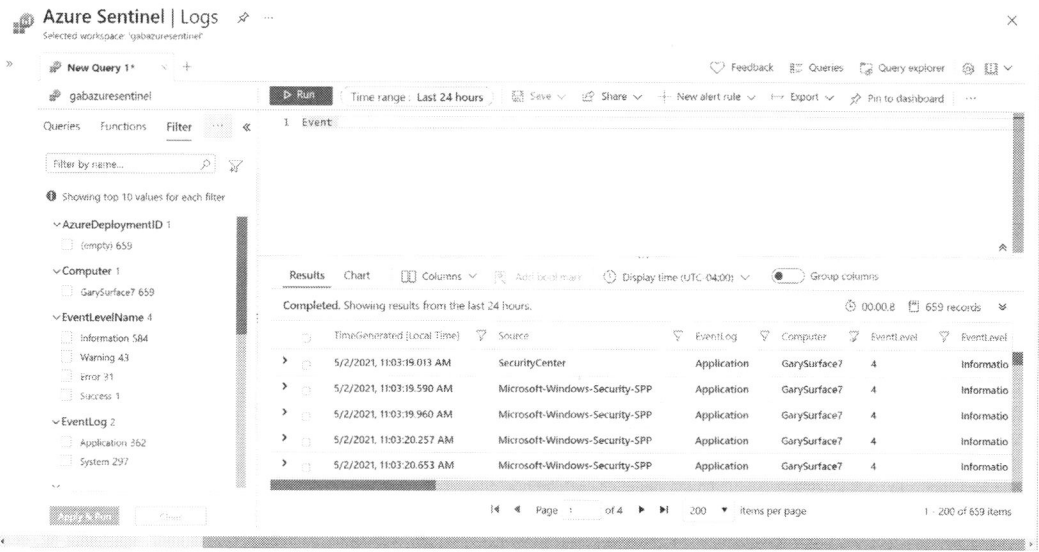

Figure 6.18 – Results filtering pane

If there are additional columns that you want to filter on that are not listed, click on the funnel icon to add them. This will open a new pop-up window that will show all the columns that are being returned by the query, as shown in the following screenshot. All the columns that are currently in use will be selected. Select any of the others that you wish to add and then click **Update**. The new columns will be shown as available filters now:

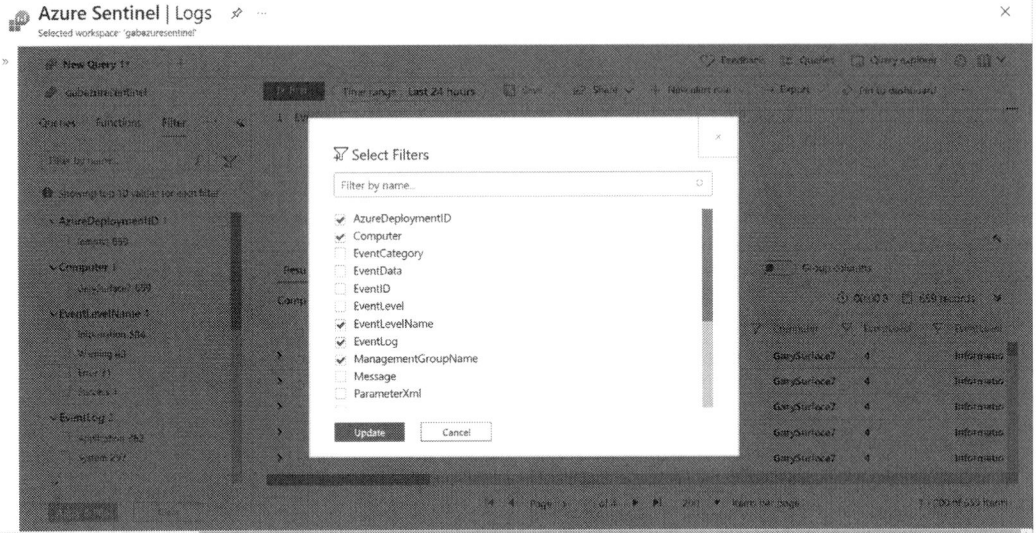

Figure 6.19 – Filter pop-up window

> **Tip**
> Be cautious when selecting new columns to show in the **Filter** pane. There is usually a good reason they were not chosen initially, including having too many entries, or just one entry.

To use a filter, select the checkbox next to the name. You can select any number of entries under any number of columns to perform a filter. Each entry you select will be treated as an `and` in the query, so that if you select an entry called `Alpha` and one called `Beta`, the row must have both `Alpha` and `Beta` in it for it to be shown in the result set.

When you have selected all the needed filters, click on the **Apply & Run** button to apply the new filters. You can also click the **Clear** button to remove all the selected filters.

In the following screenshot, the **EventLog** of **Application** and the **Source** of **Microsoft-Windows-Security-SPP** were selected and the **Apply & Run** button was clicked. It shows the new query and the updated results. Note that the **Filter** values have changed due to the new results:

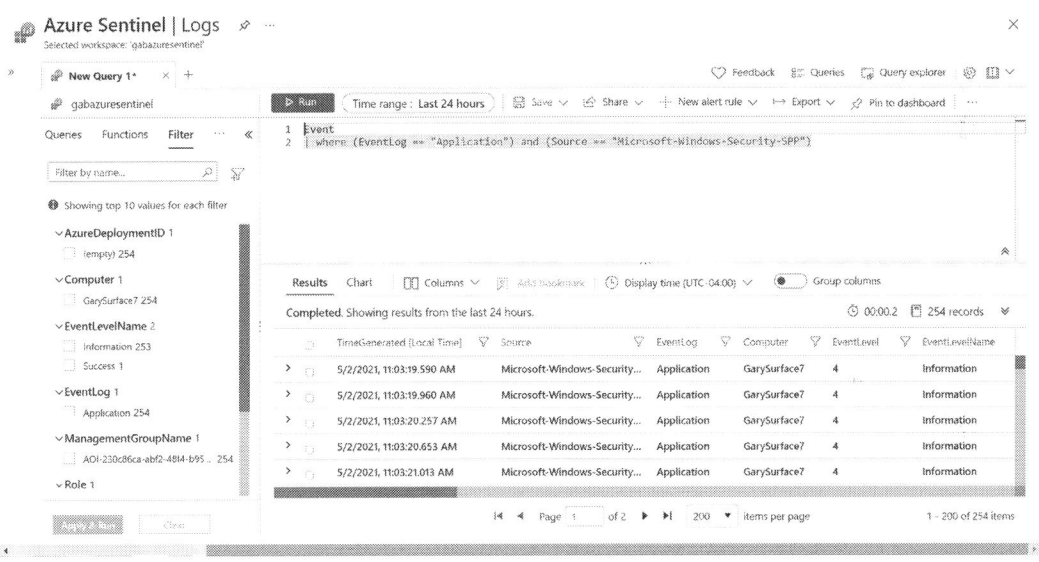

Figure 6.20 – Updated result-filtering pane

Next, let's explore the KQL code window.

The KQL code window

To the right of the **Schema** and **Filter** panes is the **KQL code** window. We have already worked a bit with this window previously when we were looking at predefined queries.

The KQL code window is where you enter the KQL code you want to run. While you can create your code using any text editor, including programs such as **Notepad**, **Notepad++**, and **VS Code**, there are some advantages to using the code window, including the following:

- The code window knows about your logs, so it can help you write your code by using a feature called *IntelliSense*. If you start typing Alert into an empty code window, you will see suggestions of logs that contain that phrase, as shown in the following screenshot. This makes it much easier to start writing your queries:

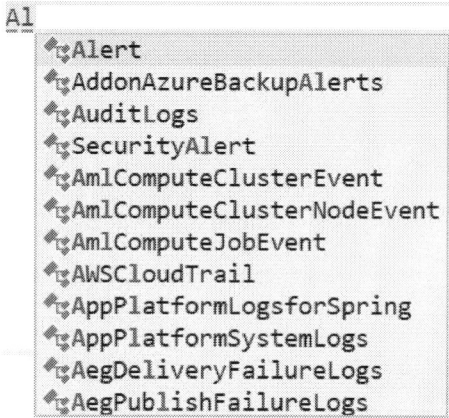

Figure 6.21 – Log IntelliSense

- The code window knows KQL, so it can help write your queries that way as well. If you type in Alert in an empty code window and press *Enter*, two things will happen. First, a new line is created with the | KQL delimiter already added. Second, a list of suggested KQL commands will be displayed, as shown in the following screenshot. You can start typing and the list will shorten to include only those entries that contain the text you have typed. If the command you want is highlighted, press the *Tab* key to have it automatically filled in.

This makes it much faster and easier to create your KQL query:

Navigating through the Logs page   165

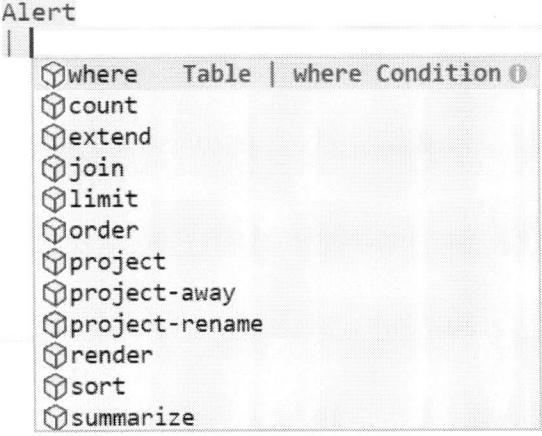

Figure 6.22 – Query IntelliSense

Just like the page header, the KQL code window also has its own header. Let's explore it.

The KQL code window header

The KQL code window has its own header comprised of buttons that allow you to perform actions against your queries, including running, saving, copying, and exporting them, as shown in the following screenshot:

Figure 6.23 – The KQL code window header

Each of the buttons will be discussed, working from the left to the right.

Run

Click on the **Run** button to execute whatever KQL code is in the window. Make sure that the query is selected before clicking this button to make sure your query is run.

It is worth noting that you can select just part of your query, and then if you click the **Run** button only the selected lines will run. In the same way, you can have multiple queries in the same window with at least one blank line separating them, and only the one that is selected will be run. This can save time if you find yourself needing to run different queries many times.

Time range

This will determine how far back your query will look, unless there is a statement in your KQL code that specifically states how far back to look. This works the same as all the other **Time range** buttons and will not be discussed here in more detail.

Save

This will allow you to save your query for future use. Clicking on this button will open the **Save** pane as follows:

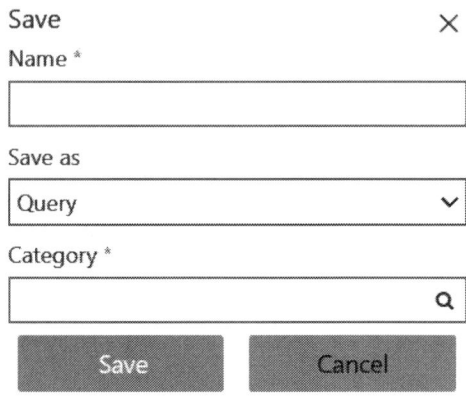

Figure 6.24 – The Save pane

Fill in the necessary fields as follows:

- **Name**: Provide a useful name for this query so that it can easily be determined what this query does.

- **Save as**: Select either **Query** or **Function**. If **Function** is selected, you will be asked to provide a **Function Name**, which is a short identifier so the function can easily be referenced in a query; a Legacy category that can be used for grouping; as well as a checkbox, asking whether this should be saved as a computer group. Refer to *Chapter 2, Azure Monitor – Introduction to Log Analytics*, for a refresher on computer groups. You can also enter whatever parameters the function will require.

- **Category**: Enter the name of the category that will be used to group queries together. You can use the lookup icon to find ones that have already been used.

Click the **Save** button to save your query or function.

Share link

This will allow you to copy either the link, the query, or the results to the clipboard. The options under this are as follows:

- **Copy link to query**: This will copy the URL for this specific query to the clipboard. This can be useful if you want to share a query with others.

- **Copy query text**: This will copy the query text to the clipboard. This is useful if you need to save your KQL query somewhere else.

- **Copy result**: This will copy the URL for the results (which is basically the same as the URL for the query) to the clipboard.

- **Share to community**: This will open an email that gets sent to the Microsoft Sentinel community email address and will include your query for submission to the Azure Monitor GitHub repository.

Let's look at the **New alert rule** button.

New alert rule

This has an entry under it called **Create Microsoft Sentinel alert** and once clicked, it will take you to the new **Analytics rule** page, where you can create a new scheduled rule that has the query already filled in. Refer to *Chapter 7, Creating Analytic Rules*, for more information.

Export

This will provide you with three options:

- **Export to CSV – All Columns**: This will export all the columns, visible and hidden, into a CSV file. When this is clicked, a file called `query_data.csv` will be created and downloaded with the actual step determined by your browser settings.

- **Export to CSV – Displayed Columns**: This will work as in the first bullet point, except that only those columns that are shown in the results window will be saved. Refer to the *The results window* section to see how to hide/show columns.

- **Export to Power BI (M Query)**: This will create and download a file called `PowerBIQuery.txt` and will provide you with instructions on how to load this query into the **Microsoft PowerBI** application.

Let's look at the **Pin to dashboard** option.

Pin to dashboard

This will allow you to pin this query to an Azure portal dashboard so that you can easily see the results of the query. The creation and usage of dashboards is out of the scope of this chapter. However, you can go to `https://docs.microsoft.com/en-us/azure/azure-portal/azure-portal-dashboards` for more information.

Format query

This will reformat the KQL code to make it more readable. It has internal rules that it uses to determine what is more readable, so you may or may not agree with how it reformats the code.

Running a query

Once you are satisfied with your query, click on the **Run** button to see the results. As stated previously, make sure that all the code in your query that you want to run is selected before clicking on the **Run** button. If you want to run all the lines in the query, you only need to make sure that the cursor is in the query and the UI will select the entire query for you.

The results will be shown in the **Results** window, which is described next.

The Results window

Immediately below the **Query** window is the **Results** window. As the name implies, this is where you will view the results of your queries. You can also perform tasks such as hiding or showing columns, filtering the results, and changing how the results look:

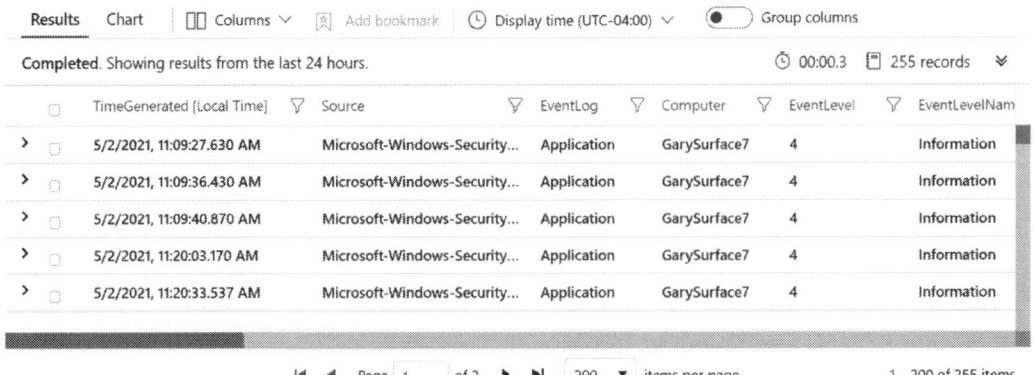

Figure 6.25 – Query results

> **Note**
> If you have not run any queries yet, this will display the **History** tab, which will show queries that you have run previously, if you have any, as well as the tabs for the various categories of sample queries.

The Results window header

At the very top of this window is a header that provides information regarding the results. On the left side is a message telling you information regarding the query. In *Figure 6.20*, the message states that the query is **Completed** and that it is showing a partial listing from the last 24 hours. The reason it is showing only partial results, in this case, is that there is a hard limit of 10,000 results that can be shown and there are more rows than the query can return. This message will change depending on the query results, and it provides valuable information regarding your query's results.

> **Important Note**
> The maximum number of records that are returned when running a query in the **Logs** page is 30,000.

To the right of that is a stopwatch icon and the time it took your query to run, just over 0.3 seconds in the preceding screenshot. This is a valuable tool to help determine whether your query is running inefficiently. While your query is running, this value will be updated periodically so you can see it is still running.

On the far right is the total number of records returned. This can be any number from 0 to 30,000 and lets you know whether you need to refine your query further.

If you click on the double down arrow icon to the right of the total numbers returned, you will be shown additional information regarding how long it took the query to run in milliseconds, as well as other information. For more information regarding these values and how you can use them to help optimize your query, see the *Optimizing log queries in Azure Monitor* link in the *Further reading* section.

The Results tab

On the left side of the page are two tabs to help you define and filter your queries. On the far left is a tab that shows the default **Results** view, which shows the results in a column/row format. Next to that is the **Chart** tab, which will try to show the results in a chart if possible.

Depending on which of those tabs is selected, there will be different information shown to the right. The following screenshot shows what it will look like when the **Results** tab has been selected:

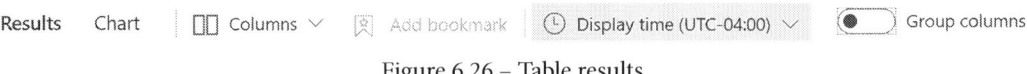

Figure 6.26 – Table results

The **Columns** drop-down menu will allow you to select which columns you want to show or hide.

To the right of the **Columns** drop-down menu is the **Add bookmark** link. This allows you to create bookmarks from selected result items. Refer to *Chapter 11*, *Threat Hunting in Microsoft Sentinel*, for more information on bookmarks.

No matter whether you have selected the **Table** or the **Chart** tab, the next two items will always be shown:

- **Display time**: This shows you what time zone is being used to show the time in the **Results** window. Use the drop-down menu to change the time zone. Refer to the **Settings** section to see how to change this for all the results windows.

- There is also a slider called **Group columns** that presents the option to group your results based on a column.

If this is enabled, then you will see a gray area under the **Results** tab where you can drag columns to categorize them by that column. The following screenshot shows the results when they are grouped by **Source**. Compare this to the results shown in *Figure 6.25*:

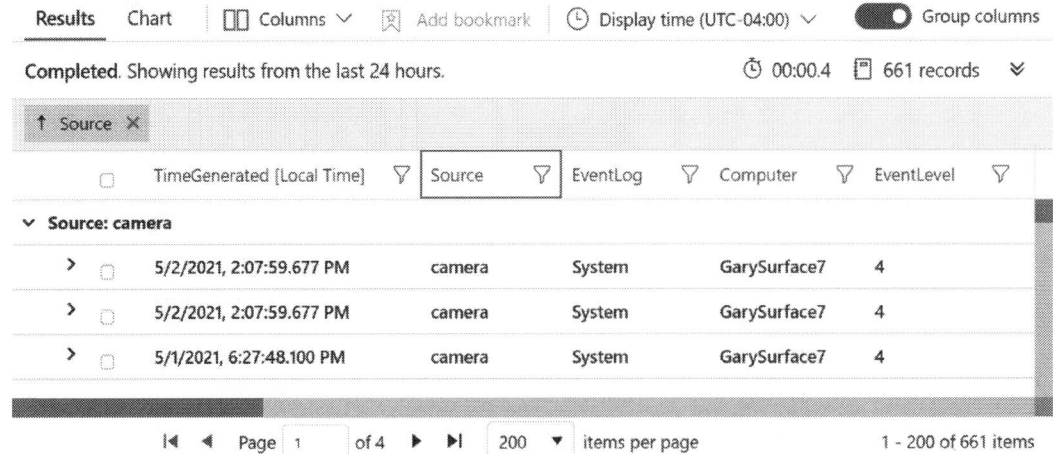

Figure 6.27 – Grouped query results

Underneath the grouping area, if it is enabled, is the listing of the result columns that have been selected to be shown. Click on the name of the column to sort the results using that column. The first time you click on the column, it will sort in ascending order. Clicking it again will sort in descending order.

Each column name will have a funnel icon to the right of the name. Click on the funnel icon to perform a filter on the column as shown in the following screenshot:

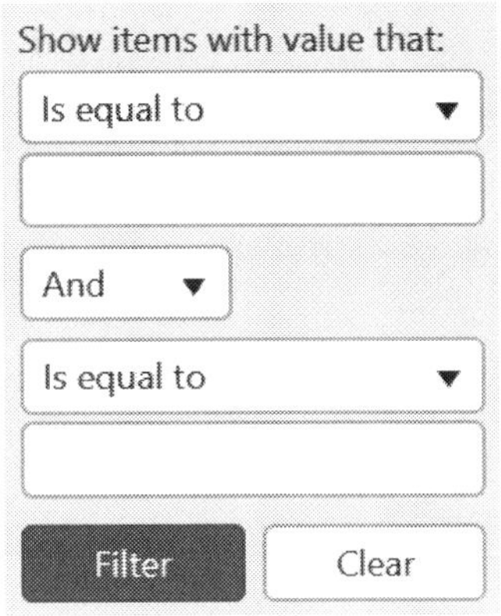

Figure 6.28 – Column filter

This is different than filtering using the **Filter** pane. If you were to select a value with which to filter a column using the **Filter** pane, the query itself would change, and the query would need to be rerun to see the changes. If you just enter a value to filter a column in the results window, the query itself will not change; only the rows displayed will change to match the filter immediately. Note that this will not be a list of possible values that you can filter on.

You can also change the comparison operator from **Is equal to** to other options, including **Not equal to**, **Contains**, **Has value**, **Has no value**, and others. This can give you a much more precise filtering experience than using the **Filter** pane, although it takes a bit more work to set up the filter since you have to know the filtering values.

To the left of each row is a greater-than button (>). Click on that to expand the result row to see all the data in it displayed as rows rather than columns. If any of the columns contain compound data, such as **JSON**, it will have another greater-than button which, when clicked, will expand that row to show the data inside of it (as shown in the following screenshot). This is very useful to see all the data that a row contains, whether or not the column is set to be visible in the **Table** view:

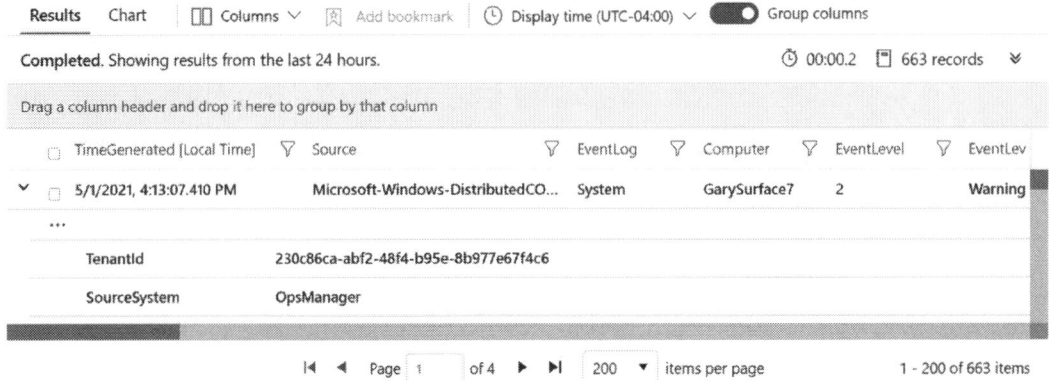

Figure 6.29 – Results row expanded

While being able to view your results in a table view is very useful, there are times when it is much easier to look at the results in some sort of graphical view, such as a line or pie chart. Let's see how to do this next.

The results footer

When you are looking at your results using the **Table** tab, at the bottom of the screen is the results footer, as shown here:

Figure 6.30 – Results footer

This footer will allow you to page forward and back through your results, showing you which page number you are on, as well as changing how many items to show on the page for this specific result window. Each part is described in the following list:

- The first button from the left is the *go to the first page* button, which will take you to the first page of results. This is only active if you have more than one page of results and you are not on the first page of results.

- Next is the *go to previous page* button, which will take you to the previous page of results. This is only active if you have more than one page of results and you are not on the first page of results.

- The page X of Y listing shows you the current page you are on (denoted by X), as well as the total number of pages (denoted by Y). In the preceding screenshot, we are on page **2** out of a total of **200** pages. You can enter the page number you wish to go to, and press *Enter* to go directly to that page.

- Next, we have the *go to next page* button, which will take you to the next page of results. This is only active if you have more than one page of results and you are not on the last page of results.

- Then, the *go to the last page* button will take you to the last page of results. This is only active if you have more than one page of results and you are not on the last page of results.

- The drop-down menu for **items per page** will allow you to change how many rows of results are shown on this specific page of results. You can select from **50**, **100**, **150**, or **200** items per page.

Next, let's move on to the **Chart** tab.

The Chart tab

To view the results graphically, select the **Chart** tab. Depending on the type of chart that is selected, the fields in the **Chart formatting** pane will be different. There will always be a drop-down menu where you can change the type of chart being shown, which will be called the name of the currently selected graphical choice, but the fields will differ after that.

As you can see in the following screenshot, a **Pie** chart has been selected, and the fields are specific to a pie chart. In this case, it is showing the fields that are being used to generate the chart's data.

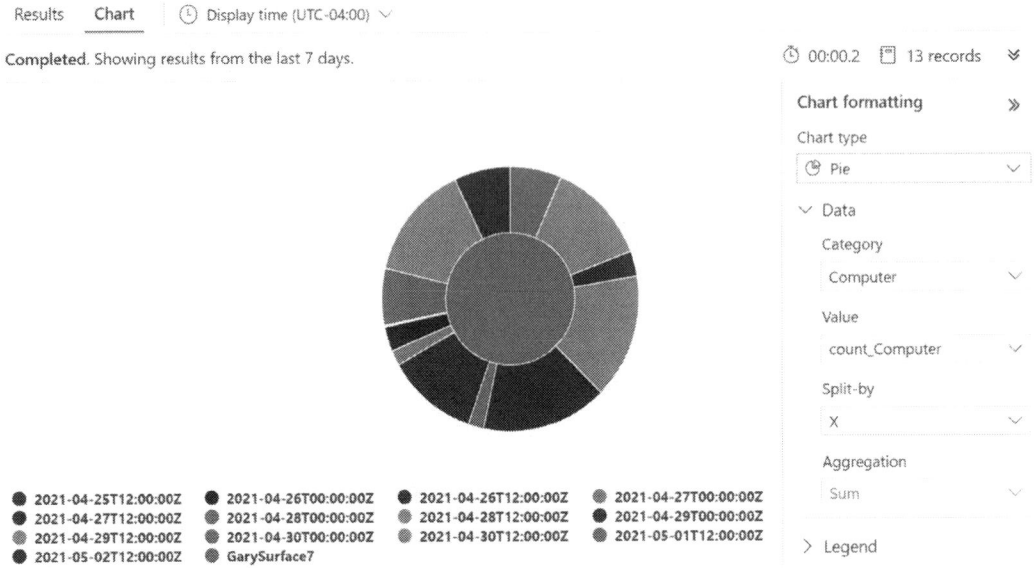

Figure 6.31 – Pie chart

This chart was generated by running the following code:

```
Heartbeat
| summarize count() by tostring(startofday(TimeGenerated))
| render piechart
```

This will generate a pie chart showing the percentage of how many times a computer added its heartbeat in a day during the selected time. It will look like the preceding screenshot. Again, the values shown may be different than what is shown in the screenshot, depending on what activity your tenant has had during the selected time.

> **Note**
> This is an interactive chart, so if you were to hover your mouse over one of the rows in the legend, that slice of the pie would be shown, and the others would become dimmer to make it easier to see that one slice. Likewise, when you hover your mouse over a slice of the pie chart, it will highlight the selected row in the legend.

Click on the chart type drop-down menu. You will be presented with the graphical representations of the available charts, as shown in the following screenshot. Keep in mind that not all charts will make sense for the data you have selected. Also, remember that the button will represent the currently selected graphical choice, which is a pie chart in this case:

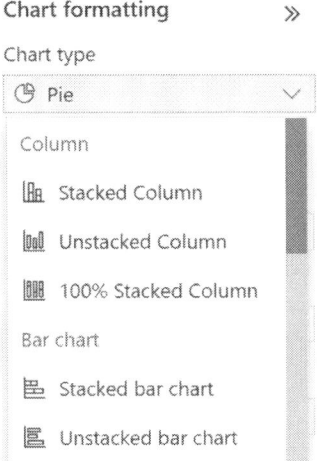

Figure 6.32 – Graphic view choices

You can use the chart type drop-down menu to change what type of chart is being shown or use the other drop-down menu(s) to change what column is being used to display the data, although for this query, no other columns are available.

> **Important Note**
> While you are limited to just those chart types available in Microsoft Sentinel when running your queries, you can use **Jupyter Notebooks** or third-party charting tools such as **Grafana** to access the same data and use third-party charting tools to get different chart types. For more information, refer to *Chapter 11, Threat Hunting in Microsoft Sentinel*.

Now you have learned how to use a pre-built query (or use your own) to generate results. You can manipulate these results to perform actions, including limiting what columns are shown or expanded after a single-result row to see all the columns that it contains. You have also learned how to change the view of the results from a straight text view into a graphical representation such as a pie chart.

Learn more

This section contains all the same links as the book icon in the page header. Refer to the *Help* (the book icon) section for a refresher.

The information is duplicated here as an easy way to refer to the links when entering the **Logs** page for the first time. As soon as a query is run, the results window will expand to overwrite this area, so you will need to use the book icon to get to these links.

You have learned quite a bit about the Microsoft Sentinel **Logs** page and how to select and run built-in queries to get the results. You have also learned how to manipulate those results further and how to change how they are displayed.

Now it is time to start learning how to write your own queries. You already have the basic knowledge of KQL from *Chapter 5, Using the Kusto Query Language*, so now let's go over the steps to consider when writing your own query.

Writing a query

Now that you have seen how to use the **Logs** page in Microsoft Sentinel, it's time to use your new skills to write your own queries. No matter what the query is, there are a few basic steps you will take to create your query:

1. Have an idea of what information you are looking for. Do you need to know which computers are currently active? What actions a user performed in SharePoint? What data has been ingested? This will give you an idea of what log(s) you will need to look at. Look at *Chapter 11, Threat Hunting in Microsoft Sentinel*, for information on one way to keep track of this data.

2. Once you have an idea of which table you want to look at, the next step is to look at a small number of rows in that table to get a better understanding of the data that is stored in it.

   One of the easiest ways to do this is to find the table in the **Tables** pane, hover over it, and click on the **See preview data** link in the pop-up window. This will show up to 10 rows from the selected log. Look at some of the rows. Is this some, or possibly, all the information that will be needed?

3. If it is, now you can create the query using the table and applying any filtering that may be needed.

4. Finally, determine what would be the best way for these results to be displayed. If you are using these in an analytics query, then they must be returned as a table view. However, if this is for threat hunting or for use in a workbook, then possibly a graphical view would be better.

Now that you have seen how to write your own queries, here are some that are not part of Microsoft Sentinel that you may find useful. As you are reading these, keep in the back of your head what steps would have been needed to develop these queries. What table would be needed? What information would be needed from the table? How would you filter it? How would you display it?

The billable data ingested

You have already seen the query to get a pie chart based on the amount of data being ingested. While this is useful, it only shows the percentage against the total; it does not show the size of the data being ingested.

If you want to see how much billable data has been ingested in the last 31 days, use the following query:

```
Usage
| where TimeGenerated > startofday(ago(31d))
| where IsBillable == true
| summarize TotalVolumeGB = sum(Quantity) / 1024 by bin(TimeGenerated, 1d), Solution
| render barchart
```

This will look at the `Usage` log, which holds all the information regarding log ingestion for the last 31 days and check the `IsBillable` column to make sure the ingested data is billable. If you want to see all the data, billable or not, remove the following line:

```
| where IsBillable == true
```

It then summarizes the data by gigabytes (the `Quantity` field stores information in megabytes, hence the division by `1024`), by the day that the data was ingested, and by the solution, which is where the data came from. Finally, it will generate this data in a stacked column bar chart for easier viewing.

If you want to see the amount of data from a single solution, you can add the following line after the other lines that begin with `where`, substituting `Security` for whichever solution you wish to view:

```
| where Solution == "Security"
```

This query is very useful to make sure that you are ingesting the amount of data you have planned to ingest.

Map view of logins

Another query that is useful when used in conjunction with the map visualization in the workbooks (see *Chapter 8, Creating and Using Workbooks,* for more information) is one that looks at all the Azure sign-ins and gets the latitude and longitude so the location can be mapped. This query will look at all the sign-ins and shows a summary of the location where the user logged in on a map:

```
SigninLogs
| extend latitude = toint(LocationDetails.geoCoordinates.latitude), longitude = toint(LocationDetails.geoCoordinates.longitude)
| extend country = strcat(tostring(LocationDetails.countryOrRegion)," - ",tostring(LocationDetails.state))
| summarize count() by latitude, longitude, country
```

This query will look at all the entries in the `SigninLogs` log, which holds all the login information. Since there is no time limit applied in the code, it will use the default time limit based on the **Time range** drop-down menu.

Rather than having to pass in the long string to obtain the latitude and longitude, it creates new variables for the latitude and longitude. A `toint()` function is used to convert `LocationDetails.geoCoordinates.latitude` from a dynamic data type into an integer data type so they can be used in the `summarize` command at the end:

```
| extend latitude = tostring(LocationDetails.geoCoordinates.latitude)
```

The same conversion will take place for the `longitude` variable.

There is a new feature of KQL exposed here: using a period to access information stored within a dynamic type. In the case of the `latitude` value, it is part of the `geoCoordinates` value, which is in turn part of the `LocationDetails` value, hence the need to traverse down the variable chain using the period to get to the value that is needed.

You could use a `where` command to make sure that both the `latitude` and the `longitude` variables have values. However, you may miss some logins, as there are cases where the `latitude` and `longitude` values are not passed into the log. It is up to you whether you consider that important or not.

Another new variable is created that takes the country and adds the state to the end. This was done to provide some names for the locations on the map:

```
| extend country = strcat(tostring(LocationDetails.countryOrRegion)," - ",tostring(LocationDetails.state))
```

Finally, it does a summary based on the variables, so the total number of logins per `latitude`, `longitude`, and `country` will be returned:

```
| summarize count() by latitude, longitude, country
```

This is just an incredibly small sampling of some useful queries. There are many, many more in the **Query explorer** that was discussed earlier. Go ahead and play around with some to get a better idea of how to interact with the log tables to get the information you need.

Other useful tables

As you can see, the `Usage` table is quite useful to determine how your data is growing and `SigninLogs` is useful to determine when and where your users signed in. You can imagine using the first query shown to see how your data is growing daily, and we will do just that in *Chapter 8, Creating and Using Workbooks*.

There are other tables that are just as useful. The following table lists just a few of them:

Name	Description
AzureActivity	View the activity within Azure along with the category of the action performed.
AzureDiagnostics	Look at the actions in Azure and whether they succeeded or not.
Event	Windows Events.
Heartbeat	The heartbeat of the computers that are attached to this Log Analytics workspace.
Perf	Performance counters of the computers that are attached to this Log Analytics workspace.
SigninLogs	Azure Active Directory Sign-in logs.
W3CIISLog	IIS Web server logs from any computer running IIS if that data is being collected.
SecurityAlert	The Alerts generated by Azure Sentinel including any other Azure security systems if the Analytic queries for those systems are being used.
OfficeActivity	Office 365 logs. Requires that the Office 365 connector be enabled.

Table 6.1 – Useful tables

This is just a small sampling of the tables that you will encounter when working on your queries. As you monitor more and more systems with Microsoft Sentinel, this list will grow.

Summary

In this chapter, we explored the **Logs** page of Microsoft Sentinel. We saw how to use the various sections of the page, such as the page header, the **Tables** pane, the **Filter** pane, and the code and results pages to run built-in queries and determine the way results are displayed. Besides this, we also learned how to write our own queries using KQL.

With the help of the **Logs** page and by writing useful queries, you are now ready to carry out your own table analysis for investigation. You can use it to your advantage for trend analysis, visualizations, and troubleshooting.

In the next chapter, you will learn how to take the queries you build in the **Logs** page and use them in analytics queries.

Questions

1. What are two ways you can see the out-of-the-box queries?
2. If I am viewing the results from a query that shows me a list of all the computers on a network, how can I filter the results to show only specific computers without changing the query?
3. What is the easiest way to see a preview of the entries of a table?
4. What is the easiest way to show up to 200 results on a page when viewing all results pages?
5. How can I show up to 200 results on a page when viewing a single results page?

Further reading

- Overview of log queries in Azure Monitor:

    https://docs.microsoft.com/en-us/azure/azure-monitor/logs/log-query-overview

- Getting started with log queries in Azure Monitor:

    https://docs.microsoft.com/en-us/azure/azure-monitor/logs/get-started-queries

- Logs in Azure Monitor:

    https://docs.microsoft.com/en-us/azure/azure-monitor/logs/data-platform-logs

- Optimizing log queries in Azure Monitor:

    https://docs.microsoft.com/en-us/azure/azure-monitor/logs/query-optimization

Section 3: Security Threat Hunting

In this section, you will learn how to use the tools available to create analytics, hunt for threats, and respond to security incidents.

This section contains the following chapters:

- *Chapter 7, Creating Analytic Rules*
- *Chapter 8, Creating and Using Workbooks*
- *Chapter 9, Incident Management*
- *Chapter 10, Configuring and Using Entity Behavior*
- *Chapter 11, Threat Hunting in Microsoft Sentinel*

7
Creating Analytic Rules

Now that you have connected your data to **Microsoft Sentinel** and know how to write your own **Kusto Query Language** (**KQL**) queries, you need to know how to use those queries to detect suspicious events. This is where **Microsoft Sentinel Analytics** comes into play.

Analytics is the heart of Microsoft Sentinel. This is where you will set up analytic rules that can run automatically to detect potential issues that you may have. These rules can run queries, which you build on your own, or they can come from the ever-growing list of templates that **Microsoft** provides. This is exactly what we will learn to do in this chapter.

This chapter will take you through the following topics:

- An introduction to analytic rules
- Creating an analytic rule
- Managing analytic rules

An introduction to Microsoft Sentinel Analytics

Microsoft Sentinel Analytics is where you set up rules to find potential issues with your environment. You can create various types of rules, each with their own configuration steps and unique options for the types of abnormalities you are trying to detect.

Types of analytic rules

There are currently five types of rules: **scheduled**, **Microsoft Security**, **machine learning**, **Fusion**, and **anomaly**. Each type of rule fills a specific niche. Let's explore each of these in turn.

Scheduled

As the name suggests, these rules run on a set schedule to detect suspicious events. For instance, you can have a rule run every few minutes, every hour, every day, or at another interval. The queries for these rules will use KQL to define what they are trying to find. These rules will make up a large proportion of your analytic rules and, if you have used other **Security Information and Event Management** (**SIEM**) systems, these are probably the ones you are most familiar with.

Microsoft Security

Microsoft Security rules are used to create Microsoft Sentinel incidents from alerts generated from other Microsoft Security solutions.

> **Note**
> Microsoft has recently renamed some of its Azure security offerings. While most documentation has been updated to use the new names, the Microsoft Sentinel rule templates have not. In the following list, the actual name of the rule temple is spelled out with the new name of the product in parentheses. It is recommended that when you create an alert rule from the template, you rename it to use the new name to avoid confusion.

At the time of writing, the following security solutions can have their alerts passed through the following:

- **Microsoft Defender for Cloud Apps**
- **Microsoft Defender for Cloud**
- **Microsoft Defender for Identities**)
- **Microsoft Defender for Endpoint**
- **Microsoft Defender for Office 365**
- **Microsoft Defender for IoT**

These rules are very useful to set up to provide a single location to go to see all the alerts from Azure Security and Microsoft 365 applications.

Machine learning behavioral analytics

Currently, these rules can only be created from templates that Microsoft provides. They use proprietary Microsoft machine learning algorithms to help determine suspicious events. By harnessing the power of artificial intelligence and machine learning, these queries can help to detect abnormalities in how your users behave. For example, if a user normally only logs in to a server Monday to Friday and then starts logging in on the weekend, this could be an action worth investigating.

Fusion

Fusion is another Microsoft machine learning technology that will combine information from various alerts to generate alerts about things that may otherwise be exceedingly difficult to detect. This can be immensely powerful as some lower-severity alerts may not mean much looking at each one separately, but when combined, they can indicate a much larger issue.

Even with the machine learning advances that Microsoft Sentinel has made regarding removing false positive results, **Security Operation Centre (SOC)** analysts may still not have time to look at all the lower-severity alerts. With the Azure Fusion rules, these may be combined with other rules to indicate a larger issue than what the lower-severity alert is specifying.

> **Note**
>
> For more information on the Fusion technology in Microsoft Sentinel, look at this page: `https://docs.microsoft.com/en-us/azure/sentinel/fusion`.

Anomaly

Anomaly detection is yet another way that Microsoft Sentinel uses machine learning to benefit you. Each of the provided templates has its own machine learning module that can process many events in your environment to detect anomalous behavior.

While you cannot change the rule configuration in these templates, you are able to copy the existing rule and then change the parameters. As each rule can have different parameters, we will not be walking you through the steps required to do so.

188   Creating Analytic Rules

Another difference that this type of rule has is the ability to set its **mode**. The mode can either be **Flighting** or **Production**. Production mode means the rule is running in production, while Flighting mode means you are testing your changes to see whether the changes work the way you desire. While you could have many different copies of a specific rule, only one of them at a time can be set to run in Production mode. If you set one of your copies to Production mode, then the one that was running in Production mode previously will be set to Flighting mode.

Those are the various types of analytic rules available. As you can see, they cover a wide variety of use cases, from fully automated machine learning to scheduled rules that you create yourself. In the next section, we will look at the **Analytics** home page.

Navigating through the Analytics home page

The **Analytics** home page is where you can view, create, and manage various alerts. Let's navigate through this page.

To access the **Analytics** home page, select **Analytics** from the left-hand navigation bar. The following screen will open:

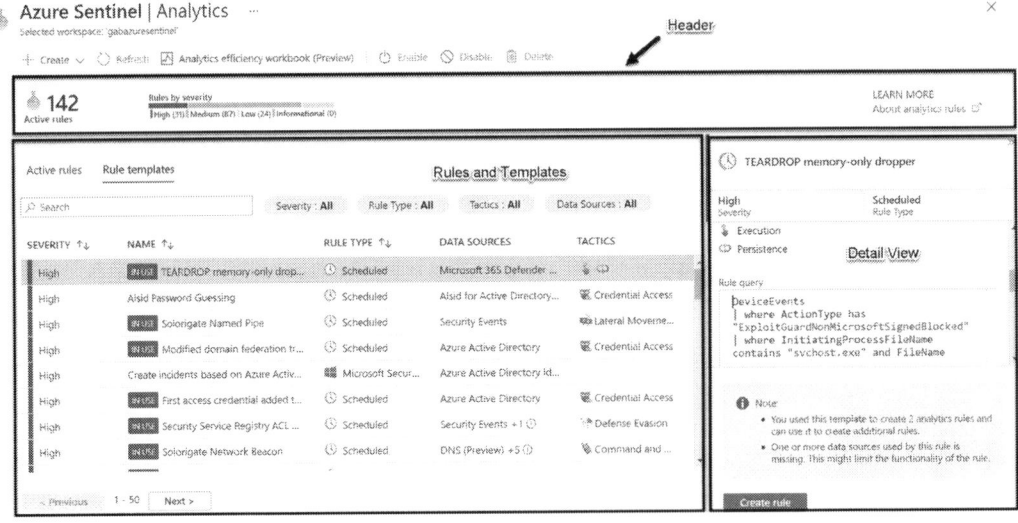

Figure 7.1 – Analytics home page

An introduction to Microsoft Sentinel Analytics   189

You will notice that the home page is arranged into three main parts:

- The header bar
- The listing of rules and templates
- The detailed information section

Each of these parts will be described in further detail in the following sections.

The header bar

The following screenshot shows the header bar. Take a closer look at it. On the left is the number of **Active rules**; this is the number of rules that are currently in use. To the right of that is a listing of those rules broken down by the severity of the alert they will create. On the far right is a link that will open a new tab where you can learn more about analytic rules.

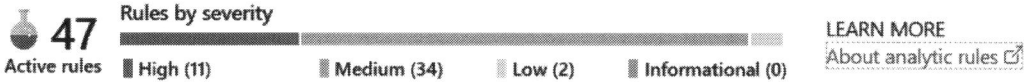

Figure 7.2 – Analytics header bar

Under the heading bar is a selector to select either **Active rules** or **Rule templates**. Each of these tabs has different information. Let's look at them now.

Rule and template listings

Click on **Rule templates**. This will show all the rule templates that Microsoft has pre-loaded from Microsoft Sentinel's GitHub repository for you to use. Note that these are templates only – you must create a rule from them to use them. There will be more on this later.

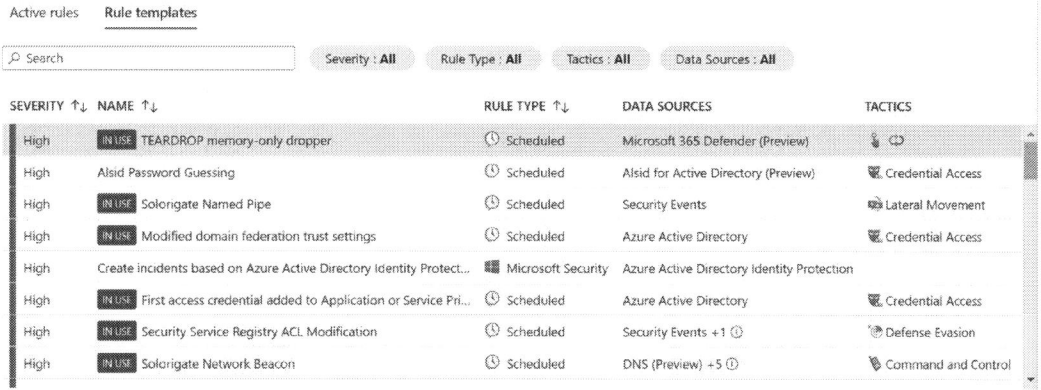

Figure 7.3 – Active rules/rule templates

190   Creating Analytic Rules

If you observe in the preceding screenshot, the first rule template in the list states it is **IN USE**. This means that a rule has been created from this template already. Some of the rule templates, mainly any machine learning behavioral analytics or Fusion rules, will only allow you to create a single rule from the template, so if you see this message on those rule types, you know you cannot create another rule from the template. The other rule types have no such restrictions, so the message is more of a notification that there is at least one rule created from that template. Refer to the *Creating a rule from a rule template* section for more information.

You may also see a **NEW** indicator on some of the rule templates. This means that the rule template has been recently added and you should probably look to see whether it is a rule that you can use.

For each rule, the name, rule type, required data sources, and tactics (see the **MITRE ATT&CK®** callout later) will be displayed. You can sort the name and rule type fields but not the required data sources or tactics fields since they can have multiple values.

Now, click on **Active rules** and you will see those rules that you have either created yourself or have used a rule template to create. The following screenshot shows an example of what this looks like. We will go into more detail about this view later in this chapter.

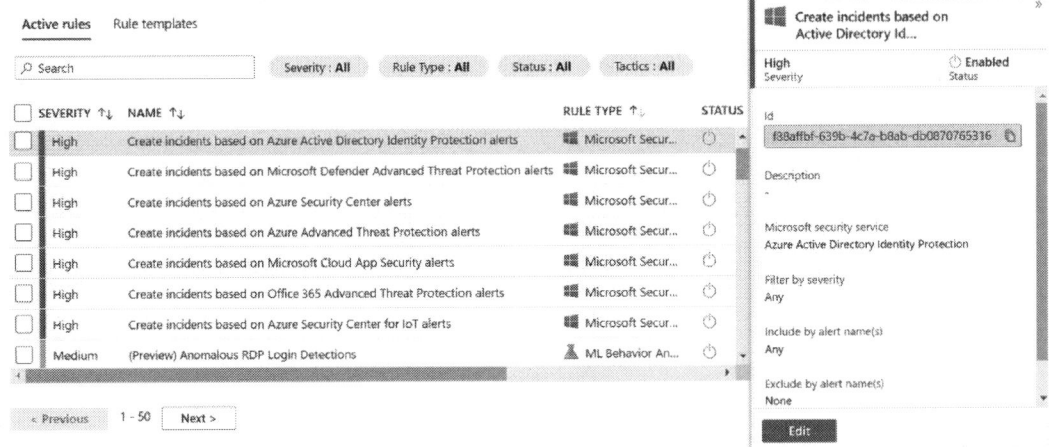

Figure 7.4 – Active rules

Immediately under those tabs are a search box and filters, as shown in the following screenshot. The tab you are viewing will determine where the search and filters will look. If you are viewing the **Rule templates** tab, then the filter and search will only look for rule templates that match. Likewise, if you are viewing the **Active rules** tab, the search and filter will only look for active rules that match.

Use the search box to search for the Rule templates or Active rules for which you know at least part of the title. Filters allow you to filter your view based on **Severity**, **Rule Type**, **Tactics**, and/or **Data Sources**. If you are looking at the **Active rules** tab on the **Data Sources** filter, it has been replaced by **Status**. Click on the filter to see a drop-down list of all the available options.

Figure 7.5 – Active rules search box and filters

Under the filters is a listing of either **Rule templates** or **Active rules**, depending on which tab you are in. Let's explore these next.

Now, draw your focus to the left of the **NAME** field in both the tabs (**Active rules** and **Rule templates**). There is a color-coded column. This shows the severity of the alert that will be created. Red is for high, orange for medium, yellow for low, and gray for informational. This field is used as the default for sorting the rows.

Details pane

Click on any row (in the following screenshot, we clicked on the **Alsid Password Guessing** template from the rule templates). This will show the details pane to the right of the listing, as shown in the following screenshot. In that pane, you can see as much of the full name that fits, preceded by an icon to match the rule type.

192   Creating Analytic Rules

Under the name are the severity and the rule type.

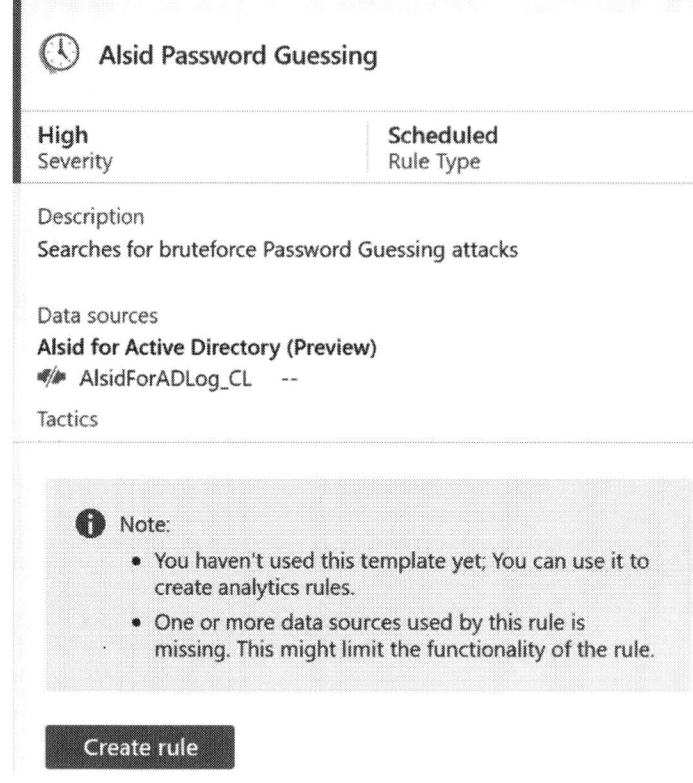

Figure 7.6 – Rule detail pane

There are currently five icons, and they represent the rule types discussed in the *Types of analytic rules* section from earlier. The icons are as follows:

Icon	Description
	Scheduled
	Microsoft Security
	ML Behavior Analytics
	Fusion
	Anomaly

Figure 7.7 – Icons for each rule type

The description is provided below that line and gives you more information regarding what the rule will be doing and any other useful information.

Below that is a listing of any data sources. If the icon to the left of the data source name is gray, that indicates that the data source is not available. If the icon is green, then the data source is present. This information will not be shown when looking at **Active rules**.

Now, scroll down the page. You will see that under the required data sources is a listing of tactics that this rule uses, as shown in the following screenshot. This will show what types of tactics this rule is associated with.

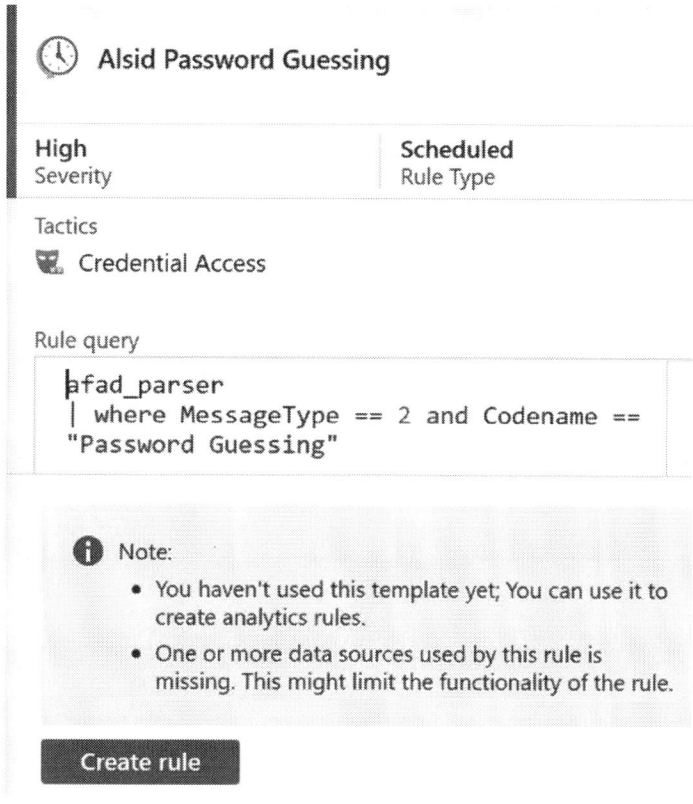

Figure 7.8 – Rule detail pane continued

Keep in mind that if you do not have the required data source now, you may have it in the future as new data connectors are added. It may also be that an existing data connector has yet to ingest the required data.

> **MITRE ATT&CK® tactics**
>
> The MITRE organization describes the ATT&CK® tactics as follows: *"MITRE ATT&CK® is a globally accessible knowledge base of adversary tactics and techniques based on real-world observations. The ATT&CK knowledge base is used as a foundation for the development of specific threat models and methodologies in the private sector, in government, and in the cybersecurity product and service community."* While a full discussion of tactics is beyond this book, it needs to be understood that these are standard ways of designating how adversaries are trying to access your system and can be used to denote what your rules are attempting to detect. For more information, visit `https://attack.mitre.org/`.

The rest of the fields depend on the type of rule being looked at.

If the rule is a scheduled rule, then the rule query will be shown under the tactics listing, as shown in the following screenshot. This is the KQL query that will be run to determine whether an alert needs to be generated. Only scheduled rules will have this field as other rule types hide their queries.

An introduction to Microsoft Sentinel Analytics   195

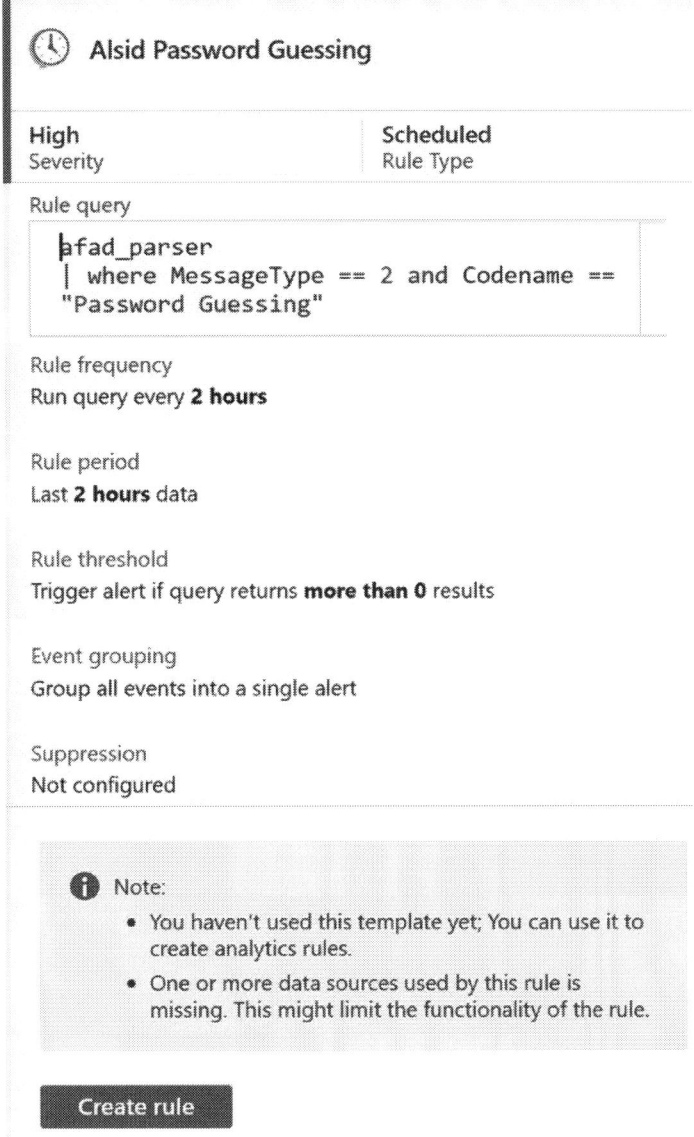

Figure 7.9 – Rule detail pane continued

Below the rule query are a few additional details:

- **Rule frequency**: This determines how often the query will be run.
- **Rule period**: This is how far in the past the query will look for its data. In this case, it will look through the data that was ingested on the last day.

- **Rule threshold**: This determines how many occurrences of the query finding a result are required for an alert to be generated.

- **Event grouping**: This determines whether all the events go into a single alert or whether each event goes into its own alert.

- **Suppression**: This will state whether the analytic rule has been suppressed and, if so, for how long. This will take effect after triggering for the first time. This can be useful if you are testing a new rule. After it triggers the first time, you would want time to investigate the incident to make sure the analytic rule is working correctly before it triggers again, otherwise you could have several false positive incidents.

If the rule is a Microsoft Security rule, then instead of the fields discussed earlier, the **Filter by Microsoft security service** field will state which other Microsoft service is being used to generate the alerts, as shown in the following screenshot:

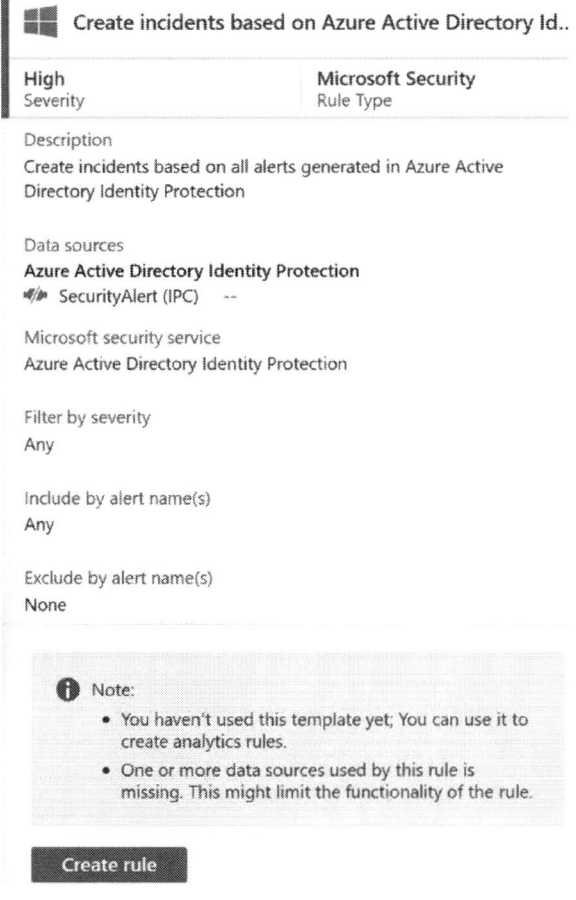

Figure 7.10 – Microsoft Security detail pane

The **Filter by severity** field will show which levels of severity are being used to filter the incoming alerts, and **Filter by alert name** will do the same for the names of the alerts. These fields will be discussed in the *Creating a Microsoft incident rule* section later.

You may also see a **Note** box at the bottom of the screen. This can tell you information about whether you have used this rule template before and if you can use it again. It will also tell you if you are missing any required data sources.

You have now learned about the Microsoft Sentinel Analytics home page, including how to view the various rules that have been created, both in the summary and detail views. You understand what a rule template is and now it is time to learn how to use those rule templates to create a new rule and how to create a new rule from scratch using the built-in wizards.

Creating an analytic rule

As mentioned before, there are two ways to create rules. You can either use a rule template to create a rule or you can create a new one from scratch using the built-in wizards. Let's first try and do this using a rule template.

Creating a rule from a rule template

To use a rule template to create a rule, all you need to do is to select the rule in the list of rule templates. If you can't create the rule, and if you have not already used this rule template to create a rule, then, at the bottom of the rule details pane on the right side of the screen will be a **Create rule** button. Click it to create the rule.

> Note
> As stated previously, if this button is grayed out, then there will be some highlighted text above it explaining why. Referring to *Figure 7.8*, you will notice that we are able to create a rule from the selected template since we meet all the criteria.

When you click on **Create rule**, you will be taken to the **Rule creation wizard** page. Depending on the type of rule you are creating, there will be different questions on the pages that need to be answered, and these pages will be discussed in the next section. Note that the name and description will be automatically filled in and cannot be changed.

For instance, the rule templates based on the Fusion and machine learning rule types only allow you to select whether the rule is enabled when creating a rule from the template. Both the schedule and Microsoft Security rule types allow you to modify all the fields, although a lot of default values have already been filled in for you. The following section covers what the fields are and how to fill them in.

Creating a new rule using the wizard

Microsoft Sentinel provides a wizard to help you create new analytic rules. This wizard comprises either two or four pages depending on the type of rule being created. As shown in the following diagram, there are two different types of rules that can be created using the wizard: scheduled query and Microsoft incident creation. The creation of each is presented here:

Figure 7.11 – Creating a new analytics rule

We will create a new rule using the **Scheduled query rule** link first.

Creating a scheduled query rule

Remember, a scheduled rule is one that will run on a set schedule and uses KQL code to perform the query. It also has the added benefit of being able to associate an **Microsoft Sentinel Playbook** to perform actions when this rule generates an alert.

This allows you to create a rule where you enter your own KQL query. Let's see how to do it:

1. Click on the **+ Create** link at the top of the page. This will present you with a drop-down list where you can select **Scheduled query rule**.

2. Once you select the option from the drop-down list, you will be presented with the **General** screen, as follows:

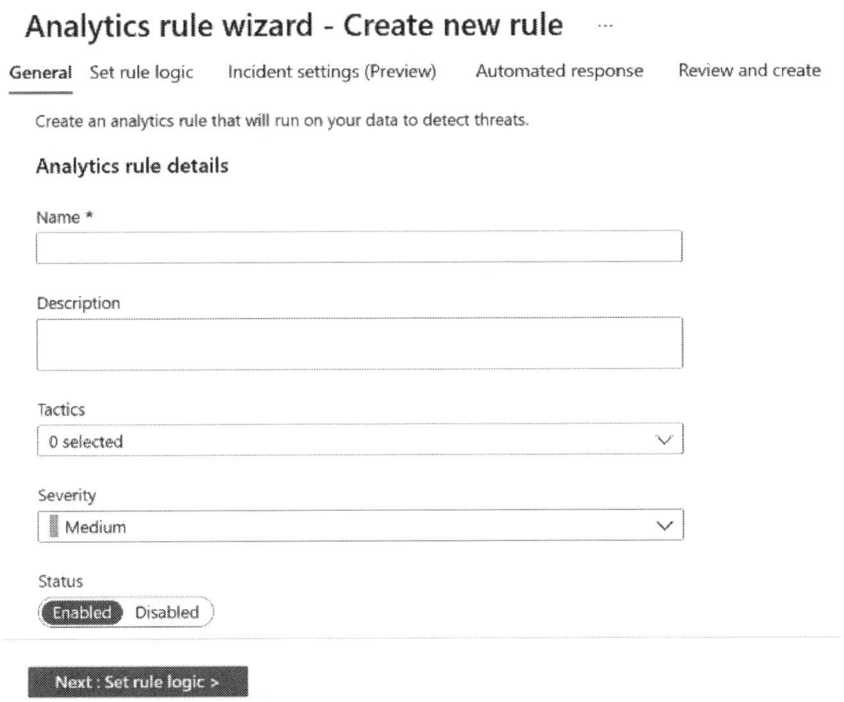

Analytics rule wizard - Create new rule

General | Set rule logic | Incident settings (Preview) | Automated response | Review and create

Create an analytics rule that will run on your data to detect threats.

Analytics rule details

Name *

Description

Tactics
0 selected

Severity
Medium

Status
Enabled | Disabled

Next : Set rule logic >

Figure 7.12 – Create new rule, General page

Fill in the details for each field. The following table provides further details to help you out:

Field name	Description
Name	This is the name of the rule. Make this as descriptive as possible. The user should be able to easily tell what type of activity the rule is trying to find. For example, `Security Event log cleared` clearly tells you it is checking to see whether the security event log has been cleared.
Description	This is the description of the rule. Add enough information so that whoever is reading the description knows what the rule does.
Tactics	These are the MITRE tactics that this rule uses. Go to `https://attack.mitre.org/tactics/` for more information.

Field name	Description
Severity	What is the severity of the alert that gets created by this rule? There are no hard and fast rules for what severity to choose, but make sure the severity matches what you are looking for. Having someone fail to log in to their account 5 times in 10 minutes is probably not a high severity issue since it could be the user just changed their password and is trying to remember it. However, having someone fail to log in 5 times in 10 minutes and then log in to a server they have not logged in to before could indicate a brute-force password attack and would merit high severity. Here are some recommendations that Microsoft has when determining the severity: **Low**: Could potentially cause noise or is a detection that would need additional detections to raise the overall severity. **Medium**: These are generally quiet but may require some additional investigation to verify the impact of the attack. **High**: These are rare, high-confidence detections that are generally guaranteed to indicate compromise or a high-level impact of an attack.
Status	This is either **Enabled** or **Disabled**. You can disable a rule if you expect to perform actions that would result in many false positives being generated. Just remember to enable the rule when you are done testing.

Table 7.1

3. When you have all the fields filled in, click on **Next: Set rule logic >** to continue. The **Set rule logic** page is where you add your KQL code and entities and set the schedule and alert threshold. The screen is shown here, followed by a description of the fields:

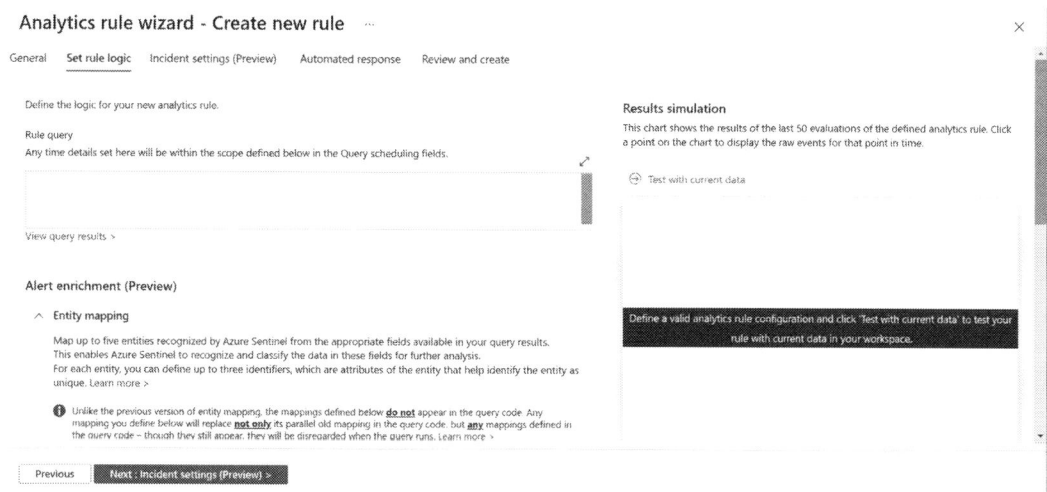

Figure 7.13 – Create new rule, Set rule logic page

Once again, fill in the details for each field. The following table provides further details to help you out:

Field Name	Description
Rule query	This is where you enter your KQL query string. Once it has been entered and you leave this field, the **Results simulation** on the right will show the number of results in a graph. Click on the section **Test with current data** link to see these results.

Table 7.2

4. Let's take a minute to talk about entities. Entities are very important when creating scheduled rules. They are used when performing graphical investigations of incidents (see *Chapter 9, Incident Management,* for more information). To perform a graphical investigation, there must be at least one entity type with a value filled in for the incident to be investigated.

As shown in the following screenshot, you must first select an entity type. There are many different types that you can select from including **Account**, **Host**, and **IP**. See the *Microsoft Sentinel entity types* reference in the *Further reading* section for more information.

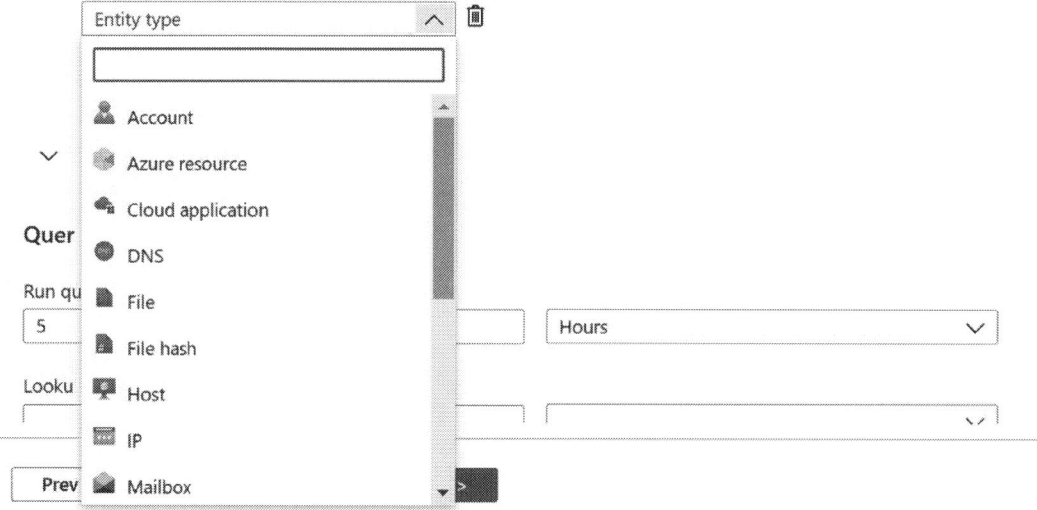

Figure 7.14 – Create new rule, Entity mapping

Once you have selected the entity type, you must select the identifier as shown in the following screenshot. Different entities can allow for multiple types to be selected, so you must specify which one this is. For instance, you could have an entity for both the account's **FullName** as well as one for the account's **Azure Active Directory identifier**.

Once you have the identifier selected, select the appropriate column from the **Value** dropdown.

> **Note**
> While you must add the identifier when creating an entity, the identifier is not currently shown in the incident's **Entities** tab, nor in the graphical investigations.

Remember that you want to add as many entities as you can to make it easier to do your investigations later. Being able to use the entities in the graphical investigation and in entity behavior will make your investigations much easier and faster.

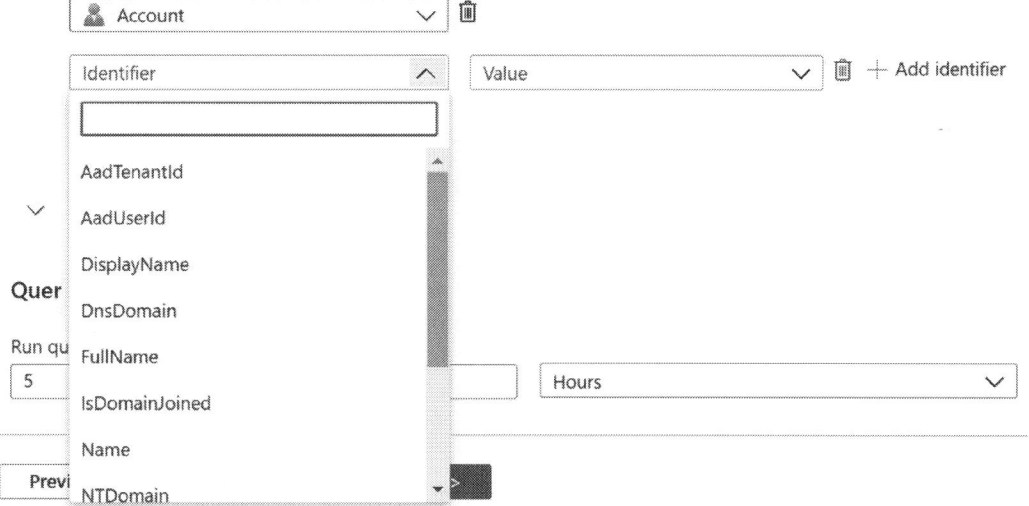

Figure 7.15 – Create new rule, Entity identifier

The following screenshot shows one entity filled in. It also shows a section called **Custom details** where you can add your own custom entities. However, as of the time of writing this chapter, this custom entity does not show up anywhere.

To add a custom entity, just add a name for the field **Key** and select a value from the **Value** dropdown.

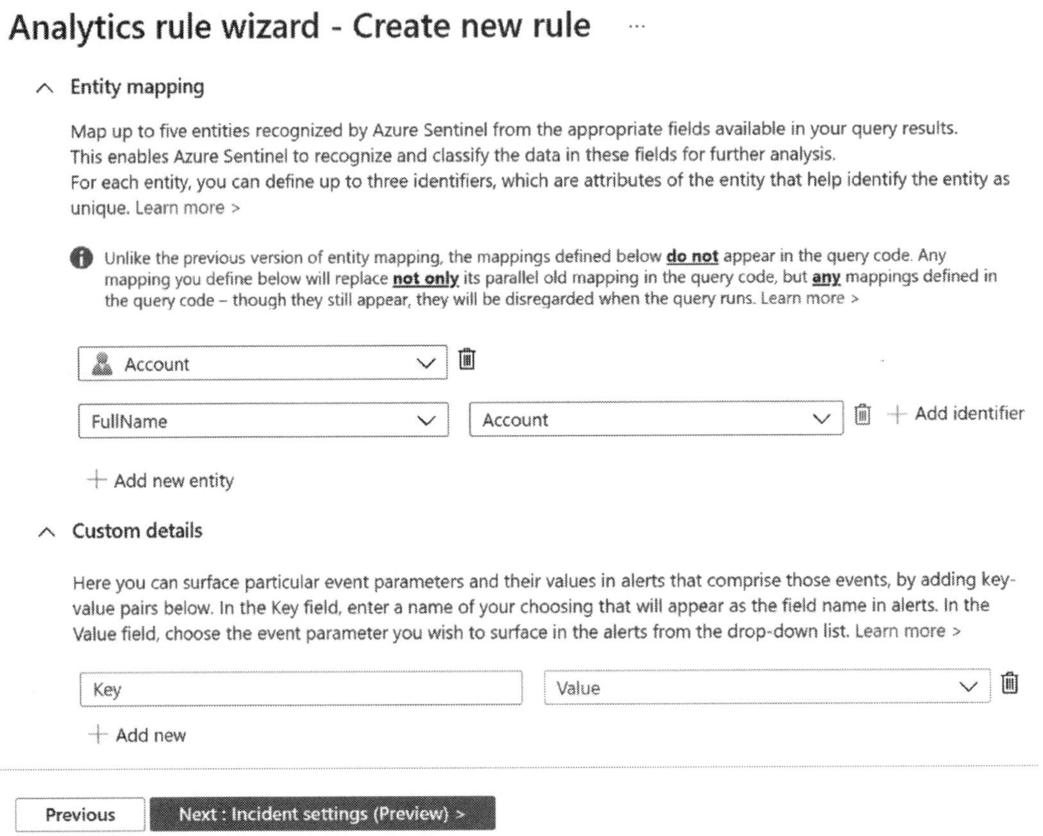

Figure 7.16 – Create new rule, Entity mapping and Custom details page

Now, scroll down the page and you will find some more fields related to **Query scheduling** and **Alert threshold**, as shown here:

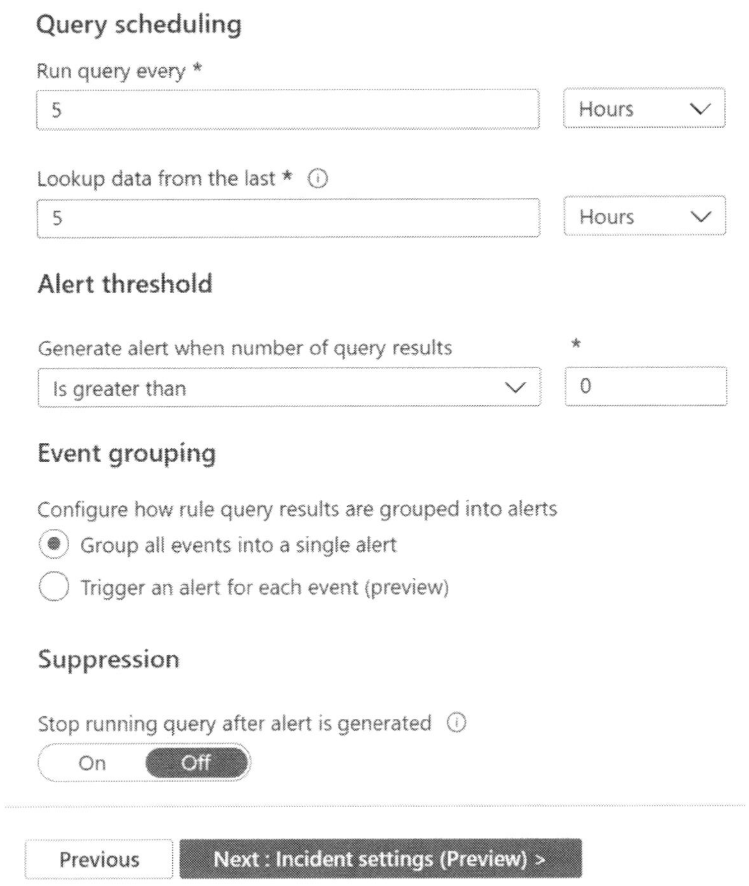

Query scheduling

Run query every *

| 5 | Hours ∨ |

Lookup data from the last * ⓘ

| 5 | Hours ∨ |

Alert threshold

Generate alert when number of query results   *

| Is greater than ∨ | 0 |

Event grouping

Configure how rule query results are grouped into alerts

- (•) Group all events into a single alert
- ( ) Trigger an alert for each event (preview)

Suppression

Stop running query after alert is generated ⓘ

(On **Off**)

[Previous] [**Next : Incident settings (Preview) >**]

Figure 7.17 – Create new rule, Set rule logic page continued

The following table provides further details for each entry:

Field Name	Description
Run query every	Select the numeric value and the time span (minutes, hours, or days) to determine how often the query runs. While there are no additional charges for running a query often, consider how often the suspicious activity would occur and how quickly you need to know about it. It is tempting to run every query as quickly as possible, but that can lead to alert overload. Do you need to be notified as quickly as possible of the low-severity event of someone entering the wrong password 5 times in 10 minutes? This is the rule frequency when viewing the rule on the **Overview** page.

Field Name	Description
Lookup data from the last	Select the numeric value and the time span (minutes, hours, or days) to determine how far back in time to look for data. Usually, this will be the same as the rule frequency. This is the rule period when viewing the rule on the **Overview** page.
Stop running query after alert is generated	This determines whether the rule will be paused after an alert has been generated. This can either be on or off. If on, elect the numeric value and the time span (minutes or hours) to determine how long the rule will be paused before reactivating. This can be very useful when testing a new query. You want to be able to validate that it is working correctly and that the alert generated, and possibly the incident, is accurate before continuing. So, by setting this, you can get one new incident that you can investigate to make sure the query is accurate.
Alert threshold	This determines how many times the rule finds a positive result before an alert gets generated. This can be set to **Is greater than**, **Is less than**, **Is equal to**, or **Is not equal to** a numeric value. This can be used to limit the number of incidents that get generated to avoid overload. For instance, you may set the number of times a failed login occurs before generating an incident much higher than you would set something like a new account being granted admin rights. This is the alert threshold when viewing the rule on the **Overview** page.
Event grouping	By default, every event found when this rule's query runs will be placed into the same alert. There may be times when you will want each event to have its own alert (for instance, to keep the various entities separated). If that is the case, select the **Trigger an alert for each event (preview)** radio button. It should be noted that only the first 20 events will get their own alert and then the 21st alert will include all the events.
Suppression	Enable this if you want to stop running the analytic rule after it has created an alert. This is especially useful for testing purposes to make sure that all the data is correct before having this run and potentially create false positives.

Table 7.3

5. When you have all the fields filled in, click on **Next: Incident settings (Preview) >** to continue. If you need to change some values on the previous screen at any moment, click on the **Previous** button.

    The **Incident settings (Preview)** page allows you to determine whether you want this alert to create an incident and whether you want this alert to group incidents together. It is shown here:

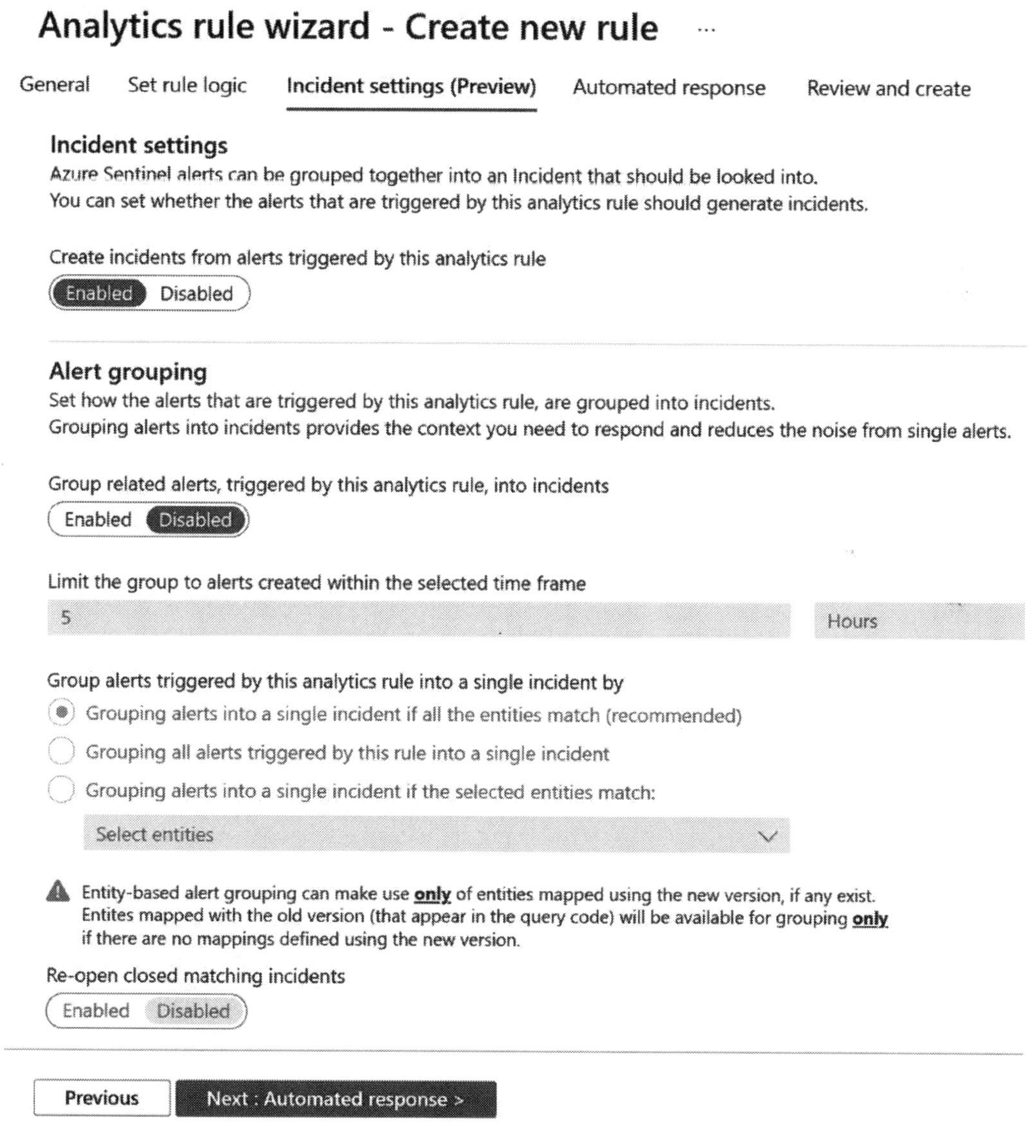

Analytics rule wizard - Create new rule

General   Set rule logic   **Incident settings (Preview)**   Automated response   Review and create

Incident settings
Azure Sentinel alerts can be grouped together into an Incident that should be looked into.
You can set whether the alerts that are triggered by this analytics rule should generate incidents.

Create incidents from alerts triggered by this analytics rule

(**Enabled**   Disabled)

Alert grouping
Set how the alerts that are triggered by this analytics rule, are grouped into incidents.
Grouping alerts into incidents provides the context you need to respond and reduces the noise from single alerts.

Group related alerts, triggered by this analytics rule, into incidents

(Enabled   **Disabled**)

Limit the group to alerts created within the selected time frame

| 5 | Hours |

Group alerts triggered by this analytics rule into a single incident by

- (•) Grouping alerts into a single incident if all the entities match (recommended)
- ( ) Grouping all alerts triggered by this rule into a single incident
- ( ) Grouping alerts into a single incident if the selected entities match:

    Select entities   ⌄

⚠ Entity-based alert grouping can make use **only** of entities mapped using the new version, if any exist. Entites mapped with the old version (that appear in the query code) will be available for grouping **only** if there are no mappings defined using the new version.

Re-open closed matching incidents

(Enabled   **Disabled**)

[Previous]   [**Next : Automated response >**]

Figure 7.18 – Create new rule, Incident settings page

The following table provides further details for each entry:

Field Name	Description
Create incidents from alerts triggered by this analytics rule	By default, each alert that gets triggered will create an incident. If this is not the desired functionality, select **Disabled**. One reason you may want to disable this is if you want to perform more computations on the alert in a playbook before creating the incident.
Group related alerts, triggered by this analytics rule, into incidents	Enable this if you want all the alerts that this alert will create to be grouped into one incident. This can make it easier to perform the investigation if there are multiple occurrences of the alert that are identical.
Limit the group to alerts created within the selected time frame	Select how far back to look for matching alerts. Enter the number and then select either minutes, hours, or days from the drop-down list. This has three options that you can select to determine how the alerts are matched: **Grouping alerts into a single incident if all the entities match (recommended)**: Selecting this will match the alerts if, and only if, all the entities in the alerts match. **Grouping all alerts triggered by this rule into a single incident**: This will match all the alerts created by this rule into the same incident, regardless of whether the entities match. **Grouping alerts into a single incident if the selected entities match**: If this is selected, then the drop-down list under it will list all the entities that have been associated with this rule. Select the one or more that you want to match.

Field Name	Description
Re-open closed matching incidents	Enable this if you want previously closed incidents to re-open when a new alert is matched. You may want to do this if you feel that having additional alerts that match previously closed ones would warrant further investigation into those that were previously closed.

Table 7.4

6. When you have all the fields filled in, click on **Next: Automated response** > to continue. If you need to change some values on the previous screen at any moment, click on the **Previous** button.

   The **Automated response** page allows you to select which playbooks and/or automation runs automatically when an alert is generated, as shown here:

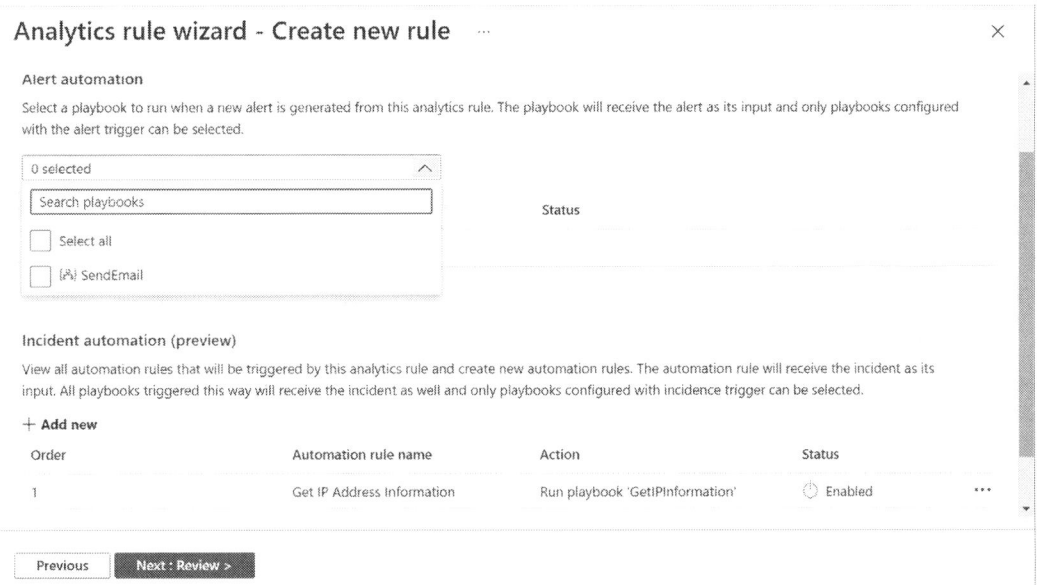

Figure 7.19 – Create new rule, automated response

In the preceding screenshot, there are multiple playbooks available to be selected. If there are no Playbooks listed, then you have not created any that have **When a response to an Microsoft Sentinel alert is triggered (Preview)** set as the **Trigger** kind. For more information on creating Microsoft Sentinel Playbooks, see *Chapter 12, Creating Playbooks and Automation*.

To choose the Playbook that you want to run when this analytic rule generates an alert, click on the name of the Playbook. The screen will then change to show the selected Playbook, as shown here:

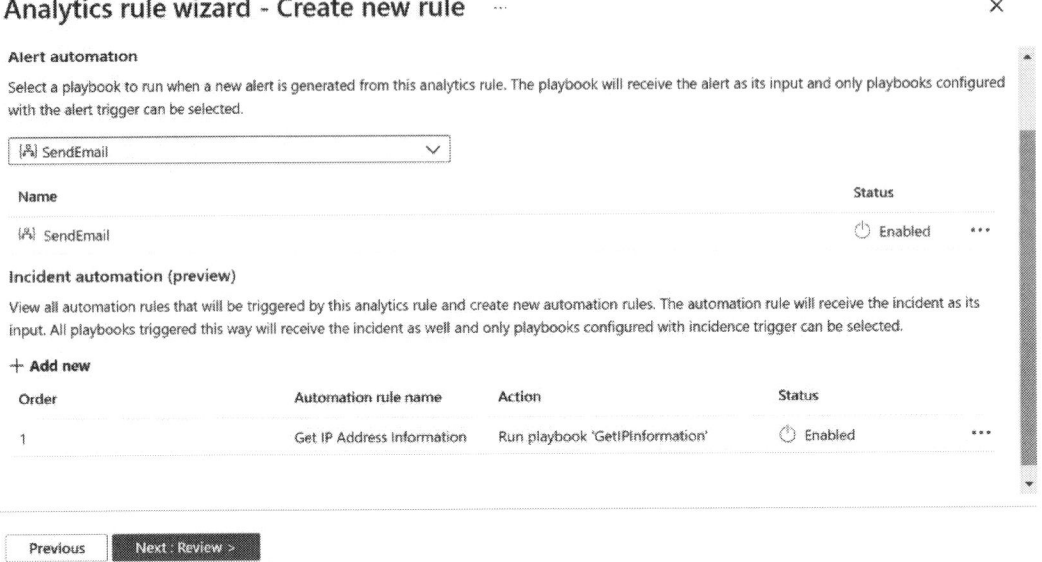

Figure 7.20 – Create new rule, automated response with the selected Playbook

You can also see any incident automation rules that have been associated with this alert rule. You can click the **Add new link** button to add a new automation rule. Refer to *Chapter 12, Creating Playbooks and Automation*, for more information on creating automation rules.

There are different reasons for using one rule type over another. An **Alert automation** Playbook can be run manually, so you would be able to run this on any alert that you wish when viewing the alert.

An **Incident automation** rule can be easily assigned to all alert rules automatically and can perform some actions automatically. Again, refer to *Chapter 12, Creating Playbooks and Automation*, for more information.

7. When you have all the fields filled in, click on **Next: Review** > to continue. If you need to change some values on the previous screen, click on the **Previous** button.

   The **Review and create** screen will show you a review of all your choices and validate your entries to make sure they are valid. If there are issues, you will see a screen like the one shown here:

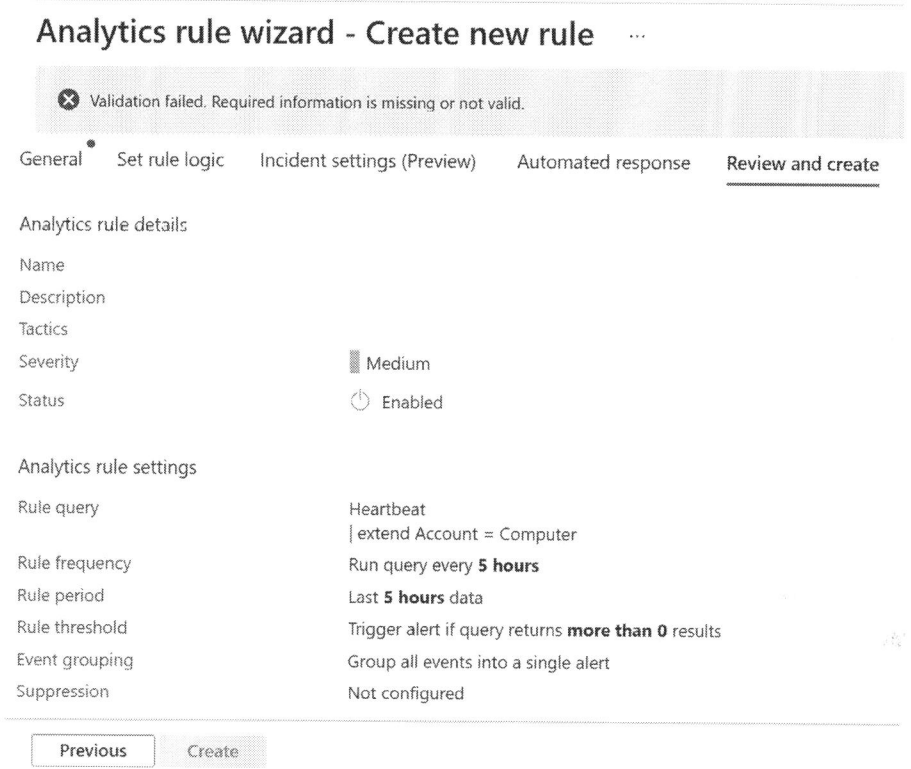

Figure 7.21 – Create new rule, Review and create page with an error

You can see an error message telling you that there is a validation failure and a red dot next to the page name that has an error. In this case, it is the **Set rule logic** page, as indicated by the red dot to the right of the tab's name. If there are no errors, you will see a page like the one shown here:

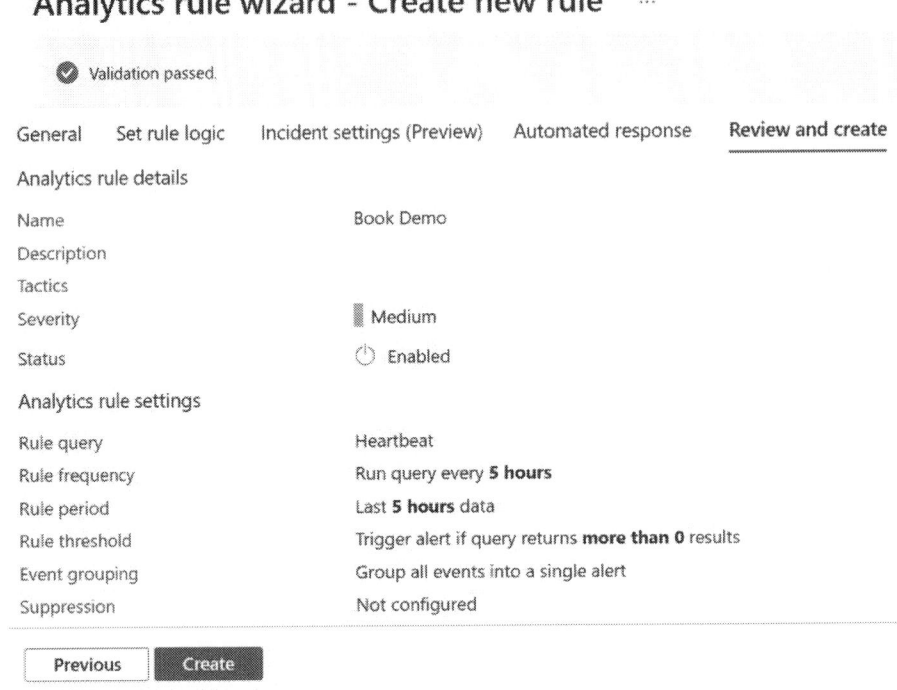

Figure 7.22 – Create new rule, Review and create page with no errors

8. Finally, after all the details have passed validation, you can then click on the **Create** button to create your rule.

Now you know how to create a scheduled rule. These are going to be most of the rules that you create and use. As you can see, they are quite flexible, not only in terms of the KQL query that gets run, but in terms of when it runs, whether it creates a new incident or adds new information to an existing one, and what happens automatically when this rule generates an alert. Next, we will look at creating a Microsoft incident rule.

Creating a Microsoft incident rule

When creating one of these rules, you are telling Microsoft Sentinel to take the alerts passed in by another Azure security system such as Microsoft Cloud App Security, apply any filters, and create the alert in Microsoft Sentinel. To create this type of rule, follow along with these steps:

1. Click on the **+ Create** link at the top of the **Analytics** page. This will present you with a drop-down list where you can select **Microsoft incident creation rule**.
2. Once you select the option from the drop-down list, you will be presented with the **General** screen, as follows:

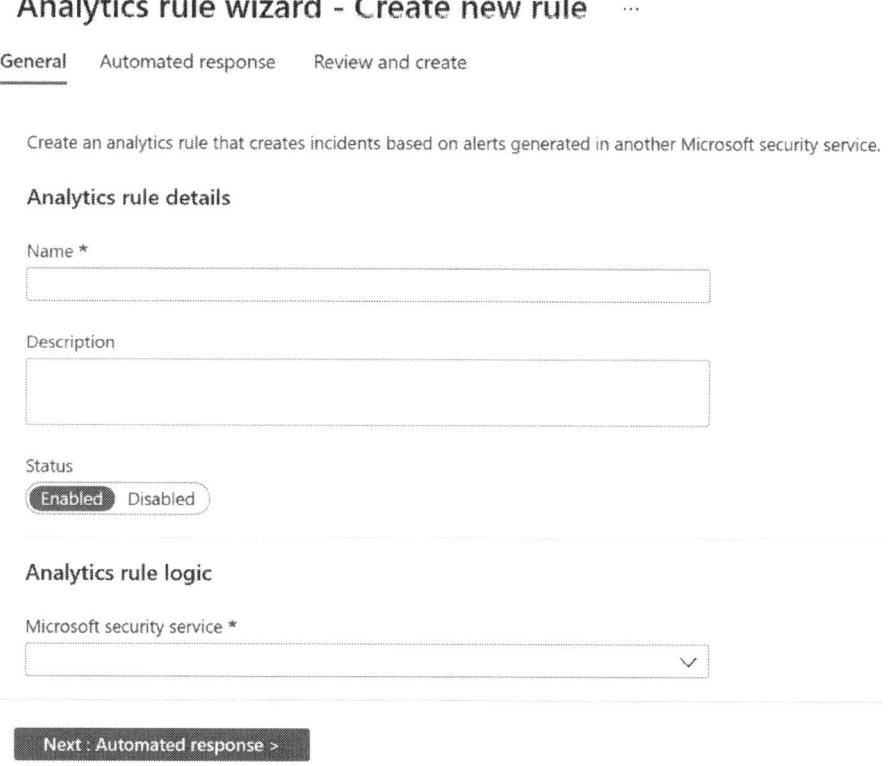

Figure 7.23 – Creating a Microsoft incident rule

Creating Analytic Rules

The following table provides further details for each entry:

Name	Description
Name	This is the name of the rule. Make this as descriptive as possible.
Description	This is the description of the rule. Add enough information so that whoever is reading the description knows what the rule does.
Status	This is either enabled or disabled. You can disable a rule if you expect to perform actions that would result in many false positives being generated. Just remember to enable the rule when you are done.

Table 7.5

Scroll down and you will see more fields to fill in, as shown here:

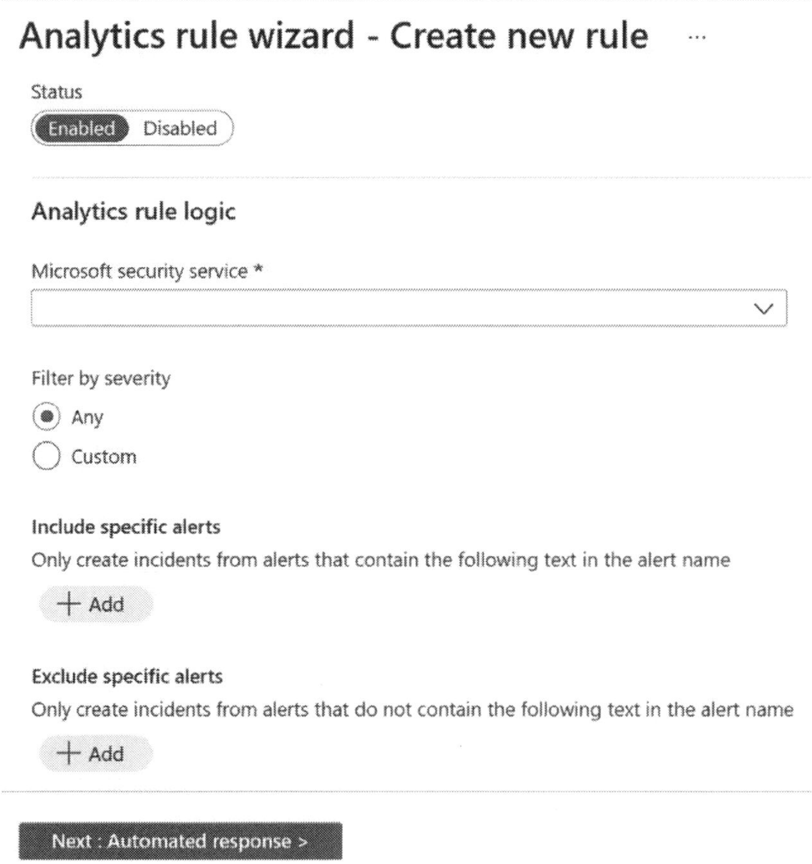

Analytics rule wizard - Create new rule

Status

Enabled Disabled

Analytics rule logic

Microsoft security service *

Filter by severity
- Any
- Custom

Include specific alerts
Only create incidents from alerts that contain the following text in the alert name

+ Add

Exclude specific alerts
Only create incidents from alerts that do not contain the following text in the alert name

+ Add

Next : Automated response >

Figure 7.24 – Creating a Microsoft incident rule continued

The following table provides further details for each entry:

Name	Description
Microsoft security service	Use the drop-down list to select the Azure resource from which you want to ingest the alerts. This includes Microsoft Cloud App Security, Azure Security Center, Azure Advanced Threat Protection, and more.
Filter by severity	This can either be **Any** or, if you select **Custom**, you can select one or more from **High**, **Medium**, **Low**, or **Informational**. This will filter those alerts to only allow the selected severity to pass through.
Include specific alerts	If this is selected, only those alerts that you have selected will trigger this rule. Enter the specific alert rule name in a textbox that opens in a pop-up window. There can be multiple specific rules selected.
Exclude specific alerts	If this is selected, all the alerts will trigger this rule *except* for those you have selected. Enter the specific alert rule name in a textbox that opens in a pop-up window. There can be multiple specific rules selected.

Table 7.6

3. When you have all the fields filled in, click on the **Next: Automated response >** button to continue. The **Automated response** screen will open, as shown in the following screenshot, where you can view and add new incident automation rules.

216 Creating Analytic Rules

4. You can click the **Add new** link to add a new automation rule. Note that you will not see the Playbook section that you saw when creating a scheduled rule since they cannot run on a Microsoft incident rule type. Refer to *Chapter 12, Creating Playbooks and Automation*, for more information on creating automation rules.

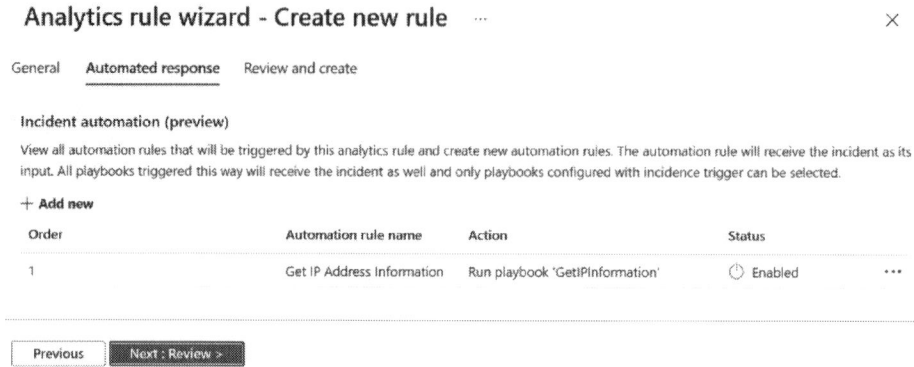

Figure 7.25 – Creating a Microsoft incident rule, Automated response page

5. When you have all the fields filled in, click on **Next: Review** > to continue. The **Review and create** screen will open, which shows you a review of all your choices and allows you to check your entries to make sure they are valid. If there are issues, you will see a screen like the one shown here:

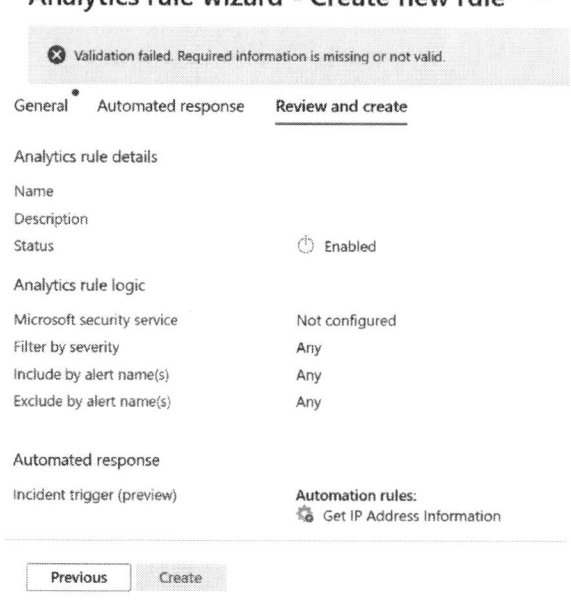

Figure 7.26 – Creating a Microsoft incident rule, Review and create page with an error

You can see an error message telling you there is a validation failure and a red dot next to the page name that has an error. In this case, it is the **General** page, as indicated by the red dot next to the tab's name. If there are no errors, you will see a page like the one shown here:

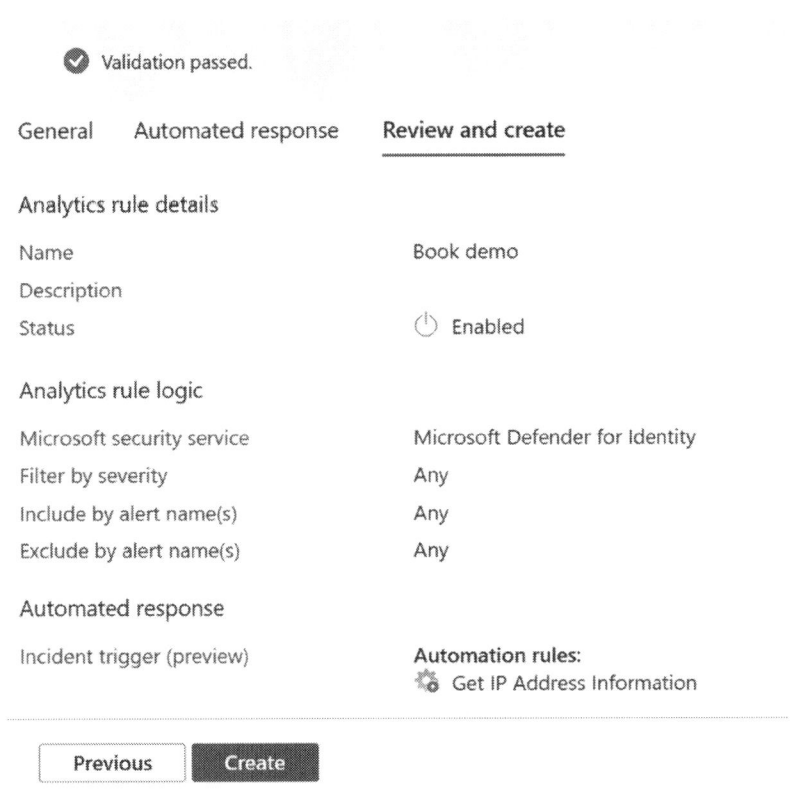

Figure 7.27 – Creating a Microsoft incident rule, Review and create page with no errors

6. Finally, click on the **Create** button to create your rule.

We have looked at the three different ways to create a new analytic rule: using a template, creating a new scheduled rule from scratch, and creating a new Microsoft incident rule from scratch. All three ways have their uses, and you will most likely use all three while setting up Azure in your environment. Next, we will look at how to manage existing analytic rules.

Managing analytic rules

Once your rules are created, you will need to manage them on an ongoing basis to ensure they remain useful. You may need to tweak a rule to give better results, change the Playbooks assigned to a scheduled rule, disable a rule, or even delete ones that are no longer needed.

You can only manage those rules listed in the **Active rules** tab. So, follow along to complete these two simple steps:

1. First, click on the **Active rules** link.
2. In the listing of rules, to the right of the **LAST MODIFIED** column, is the context menu, and the three periods in a row, for each rule. Click on it and you will see a drop-down list, as shown in the following screenshot:

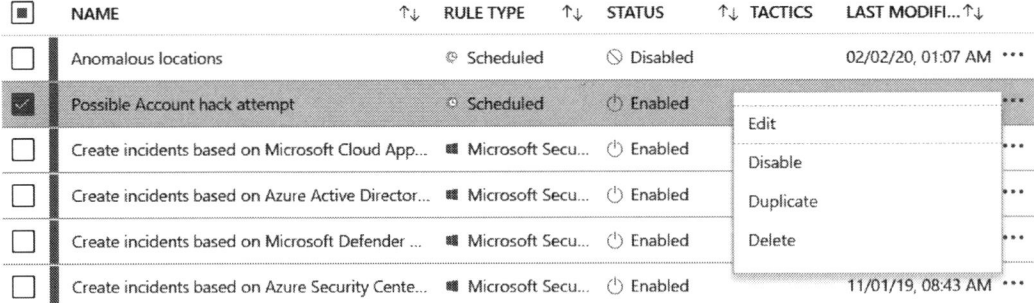

Figure 7.28 – Analytic rule context-sensitive menu

Let's see how to use these options:

- **Edit**: This entry will allow you to edit the rule so that you can modify any of the fields as needed. You can also edit the rule by clicking on the **Edit** button on the details blade. Editing a rule will take you through the same pages as creating the rule with all the saved parameters filled in. Make the necessary changes and save them.

- **Disable**: This entry will allow you to disable the rule. If the rule is disabled, then this entry will be labeled **Enable** and it will allow you to enable the rule. You can disable a rule if you think it is no longer needed before deleting it or if you are going to perform operations that you know will trigger the rule unnecessarily. Just remember to re-enable it when you are done!

- **Duplicate**: This button will create an exact copy of the selected rule that you can then edit. The name will be that of the existing rule appended with `- Copy X`, where X is the next number in the series starting with `1`. So, if there is a rule called **Test Rule** and the **Duplicate** entry is selected, the new rule will be named `Test Rule - Copy 1`, and if **Duplicate** is selected again, the new rule will be called `Test Rule - Copy 2`, and so on.
- **Delete**: This entry will allow you to delete the rule. A pop-up box will ask for confirmation before the rule is deleted. For example, if you have a rule set up to check for abnormalities in equipment that is no longer running, you can delete the rule as it is no longer needed. A best practice is to disable the rule for some time to make sure that the rule isn't needed anymore before deleting.

By effectively managing your rules, you can make sure your rules stay valid. You can modify the queries as needed and update any actions that get taken when a new alert is created from a scheduled rule. You can help to avoid alert overload by reclassifying an alert's severity if it is deemed to be too high (or too low). You can also delete any rules that are no longer needed.

Summary

This chapter introduced you to Microsoft Sentinel Analytics queries and the Analytics page. You not only learned about the different rule types but also how to create your own rules using the analytic rules templates that Microsoft has provided to make it easier. In addition, you learned how to create both a scheduled and a Microsoft incident creation rule. Finally, you learned how to manage your existing analytic rules.

You are now ready to start creating the rules needed to monitor your environment. Look at the extensive list of rule templates that Microsoft provides and see which of those will be useful. Then, create your own rules to fill in the blanks.

The next chapter will introduce Azure workbooks, which allow you to create very useful tables, charts, and graphs to get a better understanding of your data.

Questions

1. What are the five different rule types?
2. If I want a rule to run on a set interval, which rule type should I use?
3. Can you have alerts from other Azure security systems create incidents in Microsoft Sentinel?
4. What would you need to do to have a Playbook run automatically when a scheduled alert fires?
5. What are the two ways of deleting a rule you no longer need?

Further reading

You can refer to the following links for more details:

- *Creating custom analytic rules to detect suspicious threats*:

    https://docs.microsoft.com/en-us/azure/sentinel/tutorial-detect-threats-custom

- *Microsoft Sentinel correlation rules: Active List out; make_list() in, the AAD/AWS correlation example*:

    https://techcommunity.microsoft.com/t5/ azure-sentinel/azure-sentinel-correlation-rules-active-lists-out-make-list-in/ba-p/1029225

- *Microsoft's Microsoft Sentinel Query Style Guide*:

    https://github.com/Azure/Azure-Sentinel/wiki/Query-Style-Guide#severity

- *Microsoft Sentinel entity types reference*:

    https://docs.microsoft.com/en-us/azure/sentinel/entities-reference

8
Creating and Using Workbooks

Microsoft Sentinel workbooks are a way to create and show customizable and interactive reports that can display graphs, charts, and tables. Information can be presented from Log Analytics workspaces using the same **Kusto Query Language** (**KQL**) queries that you already know how to use. These workbooks are based on the workbook technology that has already been used with other Azure resources, including Azure Monitor and Log Analytics workspaces.

Microsoft Sentinel provides several templates that are ready for use. You can use these templates to create your own workbook that can then be modified as needed. Most of the data connectors that are used to ingest data come with their own workbooks, to allow you better insight into the data that is being ingested using tables and visualizations, including bar and pie charts. You can also make your own workbooks from scratch, if required.

In this chapter, you will learn the following topics:

- An overview of the Workbooks page
- Walking through an existing workbook
- Creating workbooks
- Editing a workbook

- Managing workbooks
- Workbook step types

An overview of the Workbooks page

To go to the **Workbooks** page, select **Workbooks** from the **Microsoft Sentinel** navigation blade. A new screen will appear that will look like the one shown in the following screenshot:

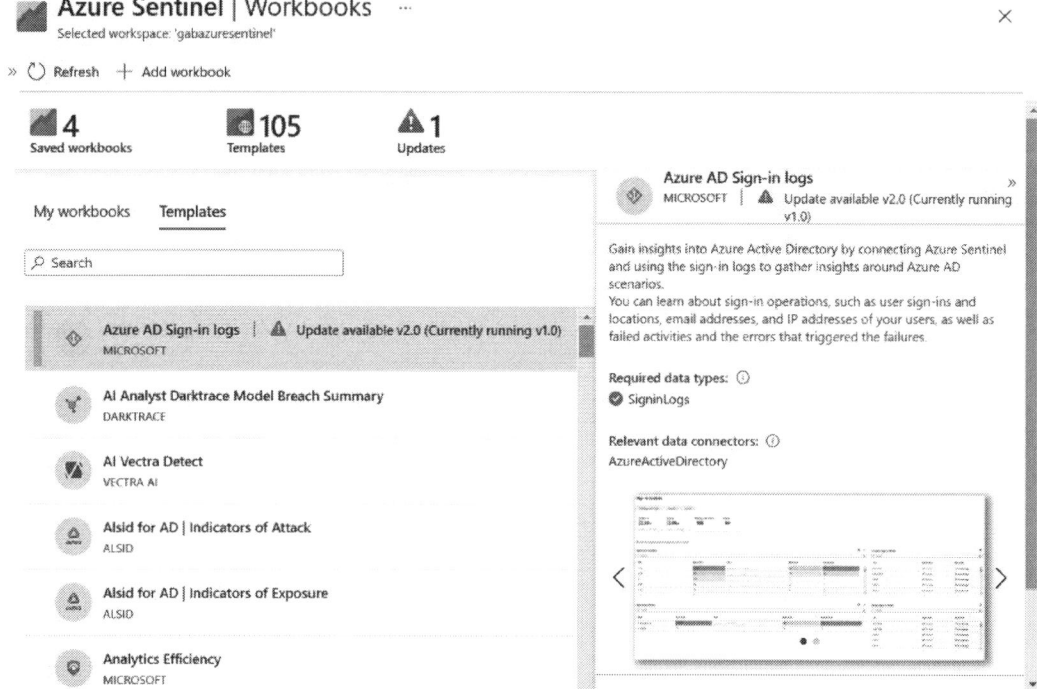

Figure 8.1 – Microsoft Sentinel Workbooks page

The header at the top of the page in the preceding screenshot shows the **Refresh** and **Add workbook** buttons. Adding a new workbook will be discussed in the *Adding a new workbook from scratch* section.

Let's discuss the different components of the **Workbooks** page in detail in the following sections.

The workbook header

Under the **Refresh** and **Add workbook** buttons is the total number of workbooks that have been saved. The number **9** in the following screenshot includes all the workbooks that have been saved on our instance:

Figure 8.2 – Workbook header

To the right of that is the total number of templates available to use. This number may change as new workbook templates are added.

On the far-right side is the total number of templates that can be updated. As you can see in *Figure 8.1*, there is an update available for the **Azure AD Sign-in logs** workbook. If you select the workbook, there will be a button at the bottom of the details pane that reads **Update**. Click it to update the workbook.

> **Note**
> Note that this will update the template and the saved version of this template if there is one. This will overwrite any changes made to the saved version. To avoid this, it is considered a best practice to change the name of the workbook that you saved from a template so it will not get overwritten.

Let's look at the **Templates** view.

The Templates view

Below the workbook header are two tabs, **My workbooks** and **Templates**, as shown in the following screenshot. The **My workbooks** tab will show all the workbooks to which the user has access. The **Templates** tab shows all the templates that are available for use:

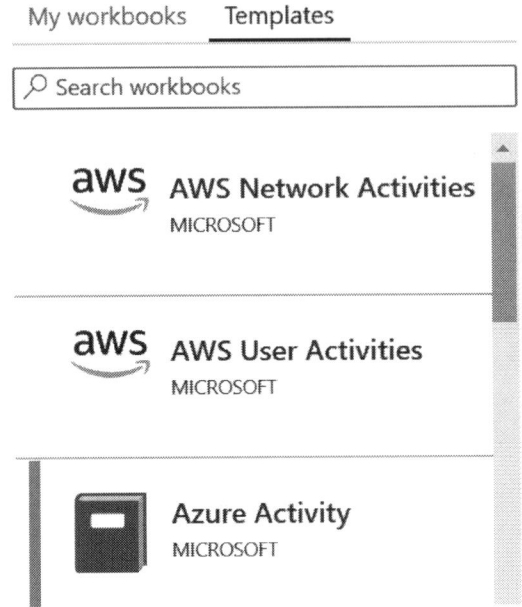

Figure 8.3 – Templates view

No matter which tab you select, each template or report will be shown on a single row. On the far left of each template you may see a vertical green bar, indicating that this template has been saved previously and can be viewed under **My workbooks**, or a yellow bar to indicate that template has an update waiting. If you are looking at the **My workbooks** tab, then every report will have a green bar since every report is available to view, or maybe an orange bar if there is an update available to the template. To the right of the colored bar is an icon representing the company that created the template, followed by the template name, and the name of the company under this.

Looking at the first template listed in the preceding screenshot, you can see the icon for **Amazon Web Services** (**AWS**). This is followed by the template name, **AWS Network Activities**, with the company that created it, **MICROSOFT**, under the template name.

Workbook detail view

Selecting a workbook will show its information in the details window on the far-right side of the **Workbooks** page, as shown in the following screenshot:

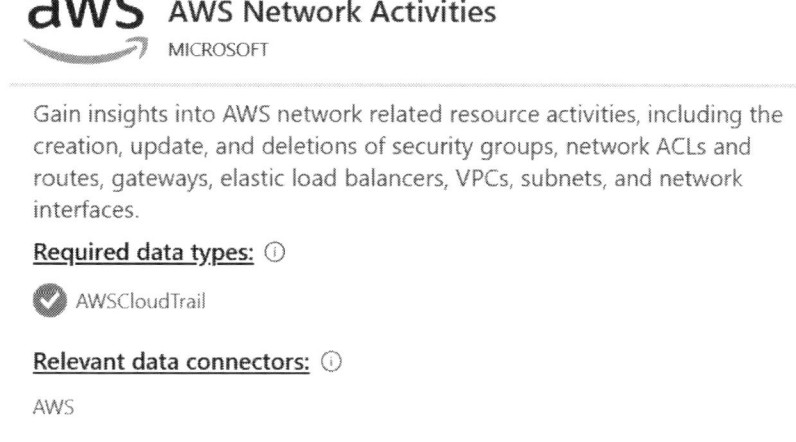

Figure 8.4 – Workbook detail view

This window will again show the icon, name, and company name at the top of the screen. Under that is a detailed description of the workbook.

Missing required data types

Below the workbook detail view is the list of required data types. This will list one or more data types that are needed for this workbook to function correctly. If your environment has the required data source, a green checkbox icon will show, but if it does not, then a red cross icon will show in its place, as shown in the following screenshot:

Figure 8.5 – Missing required data types

Unlike the analytics query templates discussed in *Chapter 7*, *Creating Analytic Rules*, you can create a workbook from a template, even if you do not have the required data types. The only thing that will happen is that no information will be shown in the workbook, and there may be an error.

Below the **Required data types** field are the relevant data connectors that show which data connector(s) are used to ingest the needed data.

Scrolling down in the details pane will show one or more reports that represent how the report will look. This can be very useful to see what the workbook would look like, especially if you do not have the requisite data source populated yet, and an example of this can be seen in the following screenshot:

Figure 8.6 – Workbook detail view (continued)

Clicking on the left and right arrows will switch the displayed report if there is more than one available.

Saved template buttons

At the bottom of the screen are a series of buttons that change depending on whether you have saved the template or not. *Figure 8.6* in the preceding section shows the buttons for a template that has not been used to create a workbook, and the following screenshot shows the buttons for a template that has been saved:

Figure 8.7 – Saved template buttons

Let's discuss each of these buttons in detail:

- If you have saved the template as a workbook, the first button that will be shown is **View saved workbook**. This will allow you to look at the workbook you have created from the template, including any changes that you have made to it. This activity will be discussed in the *Creating workbooks* section later in this chapter. If you have not saved the template as a workbook, then the **Save** button will be displayed, as shown in *Figure 8.6*. Clicking this will allow you to create a new workbook from a template. Refer to the *Creating a workbook using a template* section for more information.

- The next button is **View template**. This will show whether you have saved the template as a workbook already, as you can see in both *Figures 8.6* and *8.7*. This will allow you to view the template. This is a fully interactive view of the template, although the only action you can perform is to refresh the template. You will not be able to save or modify the template from this view.

- The next button will depend on whether you have saved the template as a workbook. If you have saved the template, the **Delete** button will be displayed, as shown in *Figure 8.7*. Clicking this will cause a validation popup to appear. If you confirm the deletion, the saved workbook, including any changes you have made, will be deleted.

The **My workbooks** tab will show the same information as the **Templates** tab, except that it will only show those workbooks that have been saved from a template or created from scratch. Also, at the bottom of the detailed description window, the buttons have changed.

If you have created a workbook from scratch, without creating it from an existing template, then the buttons will be shown as in the following screenshot. Since there is no template to view, the **View template** button will not be shown:

Figure 8.8 – Buttons for creating a workbook from scratch

You now have a good understanding of the workbook's overview page. You know how to look at a workbook template, determine whether you have the needed data sources, and create a new workbook using a template. Next, we will look at an existing workbook to give you an idea of what you can do with workbooks.

Walking through an existing workbook

We are going to look at an existing template that has most of the features available to workbooks. This may give you an idea of what you can do with your workbooks, or at least show you how to set up a workbook to do what you want.

The **Azure Active Directory (Azure AD) Sign-in logs** template has a wide variety of charts and graphs in it. In addition, it shows how to allow users to change parameters, and it shows how you can make columns in a table and display information in a more graphical way.

If you do not have the `SigninLogs` data type available, which the **Azure AD Sign-in logs** workbook uses to get its information, it is recommended that the Azure AD connector be enabled for your Microsoft Sentinel instance. Refer to *Chapter 3, Managing and Collecting Data*, for guidance on how to do this. If you cannot get this connector activated, for whatever reason, you can follow along in the book. However, you will have a better experience if you can look at the workbook yourself.

Select the **Azure AD Sign-in logs** template and click the **View template** button. If you have created a workbook from this template, you can click the **View saved workbook** button. It will make no difference in this case. You will see a screen like the following. It is expected that the values will be different for you, and some of the columns may not display the same graphics seen in the following screenshot:

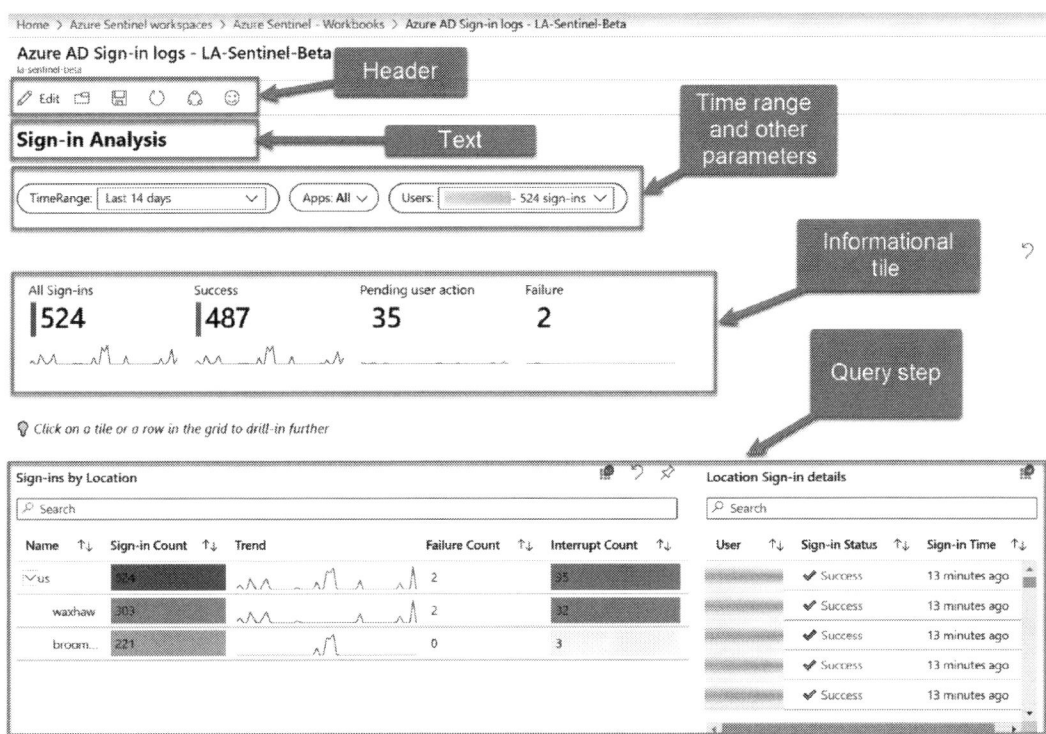

Figure 8.9 – Azure AD Sign-in logs workbook

A workbook is made up of small sections called **steps**. Each step has a unique name that can be pretty much anything, and this name can be referenced in other steps. Each step can run on its own, although some may require parameters either from a parameter step, as with the one discussed later, or from other steps.

The header at the top of the page does not concern us at this point. It will be explained in the *Editing a workbook* section later in this chapter. Notice that the page has a title called **Sign-in Analysis**. This is an example of straight text being shown.

Beneath that are some parameters that allow you to change what the workbook is looking at—in this case, **TimeRange**, **Apps**, and **Users** can be changed. In this way, the user can either select to look at the entire report, or narrow it down to a specific date, app, or user, or anything in between.

Under that is the first example of a query section. This uses a KQL query to obtain the data, and then displays it in different ways. In this case, the information is displayed as tiles; one tile per column is returned.

Below that is another example of a query section. In this case, the information is displayed as a table, but the individual columns have been modified to show graphical information, while other columns show as straight text. If you look at the second column from the left, it shows a heatmap along with the textual value. The third column, called **Trend**, shows a sparkle line instead of text values.

Another interesting thing to note about these query sections is that they are shown side by side. Normally, when a new query is added to a workbook page, it is set to take up the entire width of the page. This can be modified so that the individual queries take up as much or as little width as desired. If another query can fit beside the first one, it will do so.

Remember that workbooks are interactive, meaning that they can be defined in such a way that if you click on one value, others can change. In this workbook, if you select a row from the **Sign-ins by Location** query shown in the preceding screenshot, **Location Sign-in details** will be filtered to show only those users who belong to the selected location.

The rest of the workbook's sections are pretty much the same as the ones already discussed. This should give you an idea of what you can do with your workbooks to display relevant information.

Go ahead and look at some of the other workbook templates available to see what else you can do. Remember: you can just click on the template and look at the provided report to get an idea of what the workbook will look like. You will see that you can show bar charts, pie charts, area charts, and more.

Now that you know how to look at an existing workbook to see how they work, let's look at how to create your own workbooks.

Creating workbooks

Now that you have an idea of what you can do with workbooks, it is time to see how to create your own. There are two ways of doing this:

- Using a workbook template
- Creating one from scratch

Either way, we will get a working workbook; however, you may find it easier to create workbooks from templates to begin with, to get a better understanding of how workbooks function and what you can do with them. There is no reason why you cannot create your own workbook using the queries from a workbook created from a template as your starting point.

To be able to create a new workbook, you will need to have the proper rights. Refer to `https://docs.microsoft.com/en-us/azure/sentinel/roles#roles-and-allowed-actions` to see the rights that are required to create and edit workbooks.

Creating a workbook using a template

The following steps show how to create a workbook using a template. This makes it easier to create a new workbook, as it gives you a basis to start from:

1. While looking at a template's details page, click on the **Save** button.
2. A pop-up window, as shown in the following screenshot, will ask you which location to use to save the new workbook. Select the appropriate location. This should be the same location as where your Log Analytics workspace resides, to avoid egress charges:

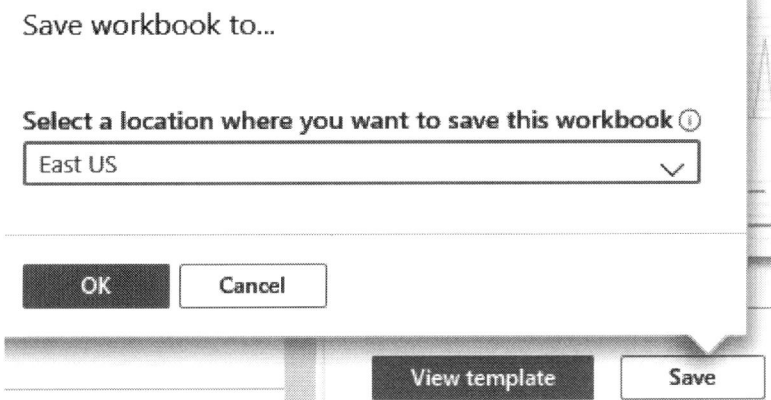

Figure 8.10 – Choosing your workbook location

3. Click **OK**. This will cause a new workbook to be created under **My workbooks**, with the same name as the template.

You now know how to create a workbook using a template as the baseline. This is a very easy method to get a workbook created that you can then modify as needed. Next, we will discuss creating a workbook from scratch, without using a template as the baseline.

Creating a new workbook from scratch

Creating a workbook from scratch is a bit more complicated. It involves creating the workbook, and then you need to edit it, since the workbook created is already saved with a default query assigned to it. To create a workbook from scratch, perform the following steps:

1. Click the **Add workbook** button in the header. This will create a workbook like the one shown in the following screenshot. Note that your actual values will most likely be different:

Figure 8.11 – A new workbook created from scratch

2. Notice that it comes already populated with text and with a query step already included, to get you started.

3. Click the **Save** icon in the header to save this workbook. Clicking it will open the **Save** dialog box, as follows:

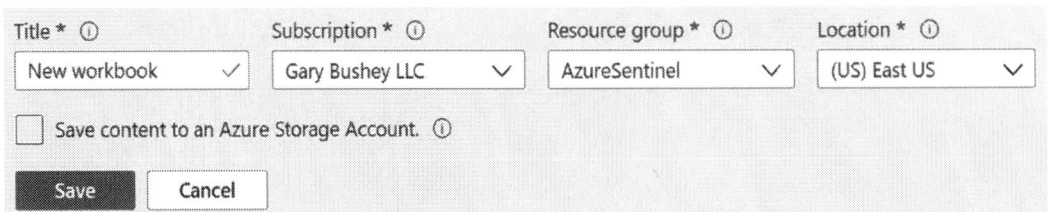

Figure 8.12 – Save workbook screen

The relevant field options are discussed in the following table:

Name	Description
Title	The name of the workbook. This should be descriptive enough so that users can easily tell what kind of information will be shown.
Subscription	Select the subscription where this workbook will reside. It should be the same subscription as your Log Analytics workspace.
Resource group	Select the resource group where this workbook will reside. It does not matter if it resides in the same resource group as your Log Analytics workspace. For instance, you could have one resource group for all resources related to your Microsoft Sentinel instance, or one resource group just for your workbooks, or a combination of both. Follow your corporate standards on where to place items if these apply.
Location	Select the location where your workbook will reside. You will want this to be the same location as your Log Analytics workspace to avoid egress charges.

Table 8.1

Below that is a checkbox labeled **Save content to an Azure Storage Account**. If you need to protect the information stored in the workbook, you can secure it by saving the workbook's content to an Azure Storage account. See the *Further reading* section at the end of this chapter for a link to get more information on how to do this.

4. Click **Save** to save the workbook.

> **Note**
> It is not actually necessary for you to save the new workbook before you edit it. It is generally recommended that you do so to make sure you have a saved copy of it that you can revert to should your edits not work correctly.

That is all there is to it. Now, you will need to edit the workbook so that you can edit or remove the existing steps or add your own new steps. Refer to the next section, where we will cover more details on what can be done to modify your workbook.

Editing a workbook

There will be times when you need to edit a workbook. As you saw in the previous section, you need to edit a workbook created from scratch to add what you need to it. You can also edit workbooks created from templates to modify them to suit your needs.

If you are not already viewing your workbook, you will need to view it first. If you are already viewing your workbook, you can skip this next step and move directly to the editing portion.

To edit a workbook, perform the following steps:

1. Go to either the **My workbooks** or the **Templates** tab.
2. Select the workbook in question.
3. Then, select the **View saved workbook** button in the workbook's detail pane.

> **Note**
> You cannot edit a workbook template directly. It must be saved first, and then the saved workbook can be edited. If you have created a workbook from scratch, you must go to the **My workbooks** tab since these workbooks have not been created from a template and only show up there.

At the top of the page is a header containing buttons, shown as follows. The one we care about in this section is the first one on the left, called **Edit**:

Figure 8.13 – Saved workbook header bar

When you click the **Edit** button, the workbook view will change to edit mode, which will look like the following screenshot:

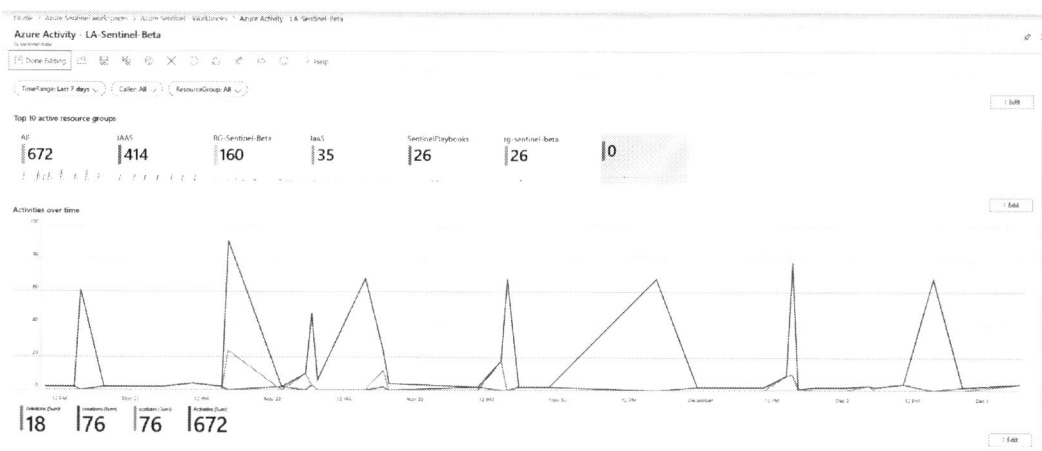

Figure 8.14 – Workbook in edit mode

Each step in the workbook will have its own **Edit** button so that you can make changes to that individual step. More information on the various types of steps can be found in the *Workbook step types* section. Note that all the steps will be displayed, even those that have been set to be hidden when viewing the workbook.

The buttons in the edit mode header look as follows:

Figure 8.15 – Edit mode header buttons

The following table briefly describes each button:

Icon	Name	Description
Done Editing	Done Editing	This button will change from edit mode to view mode. All the individual edit buttons will disappear.
	Open	Open another dashboard. See the *Managing workbooks* section for more information.
	Save	Save all the changes made to this workbook.
	Save as	Save this workbook with another name.
	Settings	Allows you to change some of the advanced settings for this workbook, including resources, styles, tags, and trusted hosts. The discussion of these topics is outside the scope of this chapter.
X	Revert changes	Discard any changes made and revert to the last saved version.
	Refresh	Refresh the page. This will recalculate any queries on the page.
	Share	Allows you to share this workbook directly with others. This will open a pane with the URL, which you can copy and send to others. Note that a workbook must belong to the Shared Workbooks group before you can share it. If the workbook is not shared, you will be prompted to move it to Shared Workbooks before you can share it.
	Show pin options	This will open the pin options, where you can pin the entire workbook to a dashboard or pin each section that can be pinned to a dashboard.
</>	Advanced editor	Switches the screen to show the JSON or *Azure Resource Manager* (*ARM*) code that gets generated automatically. See the *Advanced editing* section for more information.
	Feedback	This allows you to provide feedback to Microsoft about workbooks. This works here as it does throughout the rest of the Azure portal.
? Help	Help	Opens the Microsoft workbook documentation page in another tab.

Table 8.2

If you look at the bottom of the workbook you are editing, you will see a list of links matching the following screenshot. This is how you will add new steps, and each step will be described individually in the *Workbook step types* section:

Add text | Add query | Add metric | Add parameters | Add links/tabs

Figure 8.16 – Edit mode add links

Once you have finished making all your changes, click on the **Done Editing** button in the header bar to revert to the view mode. All the individual edit buttons will disappear, as will any steps, parameters, or columns that have been set to be hidden.

Look at your workbook to make sure the edits you just made are working as desired. Once you are satisfied with your changes, click on the **Save** button to save your changes.

Advanced editing

While the workbook's editing **graphical user interface** (**GUI**) allows you to completely create and edit an Microsoft Sentinel workbook, there may be times when you need to tweak a setting directly in the code. You may also wish to get the ARM template, which will allow you to easily reproduce this workbook elsewhere or store it as part of your DevOps process.

In either case, clicking on the **Advanced Editor** button will allow you to do that. When you click on the button, you will be taken to the **Gallery Template** view of the advanced editor, as shown in the following screenshot. This view will allow you to directly modify the JSON code. When you are done making the changes, click the **Apply** button to apply your changes, or the **Cancel** button to return to the GUI without saving your changes:

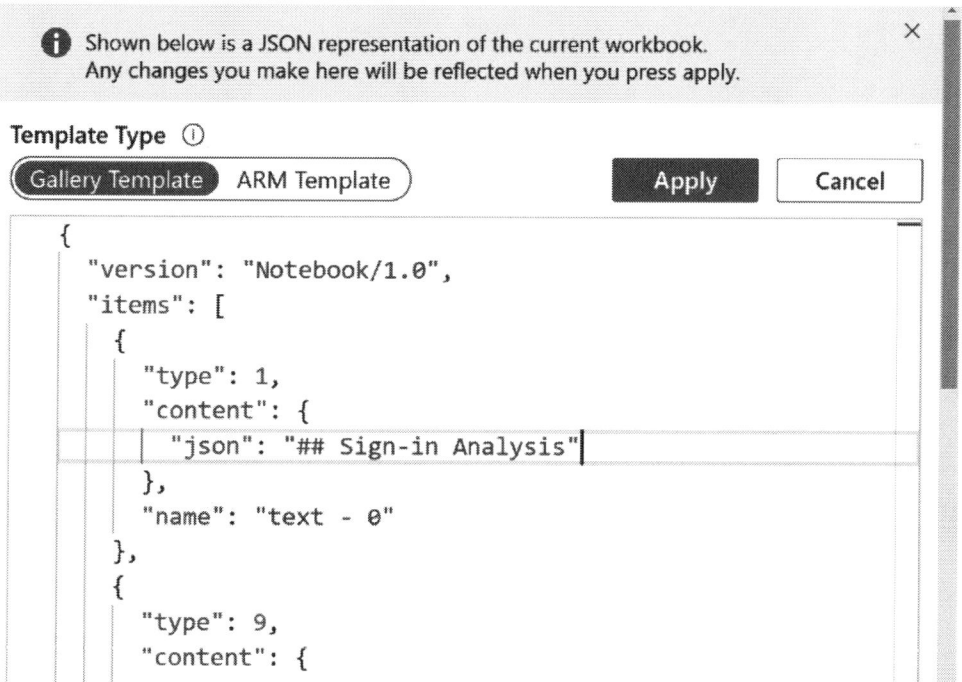

Figure 8.17 – Advanced Editor – Gallery Template view

> **Note**
> Do not modify the JSON code directly unless you are familiar with JSON and what needs to be changed. Any changes made here will apply to the GUI view as well, and if a mistake is made, you could render the workbook unusable.

If you want to see the ARM template that gets generated, click on the **ARM Template** button. This will switch the view to show you the ARM template that can be used to reproduce this. Copy the code and paste it into another file to recreate your workbook as needed. The **ARM Template** view can be seen in the following screenshot:

```
Shown below is an ARM template compatible representation of the current workbook.

Template Type
 Gallery Template   ARM Template                                          Cancel

  "contentVersion": "1.0.0.0",
  "parameters": {
    "workbookDisplayName": {
      "type": "string",
      "defaultValue": "Azure AD Sign-in logs - LA-Sentinel-Beta",
      "metadata": {
        "description": "The friendly name for the workbook that is used in the Gallery or Saved List.
      }
    },
    "workbookType": {
      "type": "string",
      "defaultValue": "sentinel",
      "metadata": {
```

Figure 8.18 – Advanced Editor – ARM Template view

> **Tip**
> The discussion of ARM templates and how to use them is beyond the scope of this book. Go to `https://docs.microsoft.com/en-us/azure/azure-monitor/visualize/workbooks-automate` to learn more about them.

When you are done, click the **Cancel** button to return to the GUI view.

You have now seen how to edit a workbook using both the GUI and the advanced view, where you can edit the underlying code directly. You have also learned how to copy the JSON code that can be used in an ARM template to recreate this workbook as needed. Next, we will look at managing your existing workbooks.

Managing workbooks

You have seen how to add a new workbook, and now, you will learn how to manage the ones you have. This will include deleting, moving, and sharing workbooks. As a reminder, go to `https://docs.microsoft.com/en-us/azure/sentinel/roles` to make sure you have the proper rights needed to manage workbooks.

As stated earlier, clicking on the **Open** button when looking at a saved workbook will allow you to manage workbooks. Clicking on it will open the **Saved Workbooks** blade, which will look like the following screenshot:

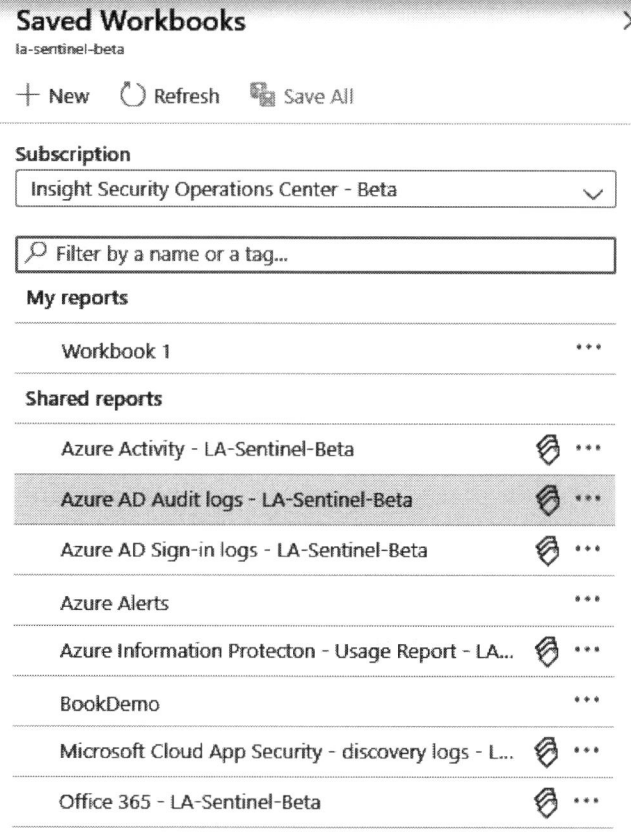

Figure 8.19 – Managing workbooks

At the top of the screen is the **New** button, which will allow you to create a new workbook; the **Refresh** button, which will refresh this view; and the **Save All** button, which will save all the changes made. Under that is the **Subscription** dropdown, which will allow you to change the subscription you are looking at, followed by a search box where you can search for specific workbooks.

Below that is a listing of all the workbooks. Clicking on any of the workbooks will change the workbook that you are viewing.

Each workbook will be shown in a separate row. It will display the name, and then an icon that will show whether the workbook has been created from a template, and then a context-sensitive menu. Clicking on the context-sensitive menu icon will show the menu as shown in *Figure 8.20*.

This menu will allow you to delete this workbook, rename it, move it to **Shared reports** (or if this workbook is already shared, it will allow you to move it to **My reports**), share it with others (or if it is not a **shared report**, you will be asked to make it a **shared report** before you can share it), and pin it to a dashboard, which provides a shortcut to get directly to this workbook. All of this can be seen in the following screenshot:

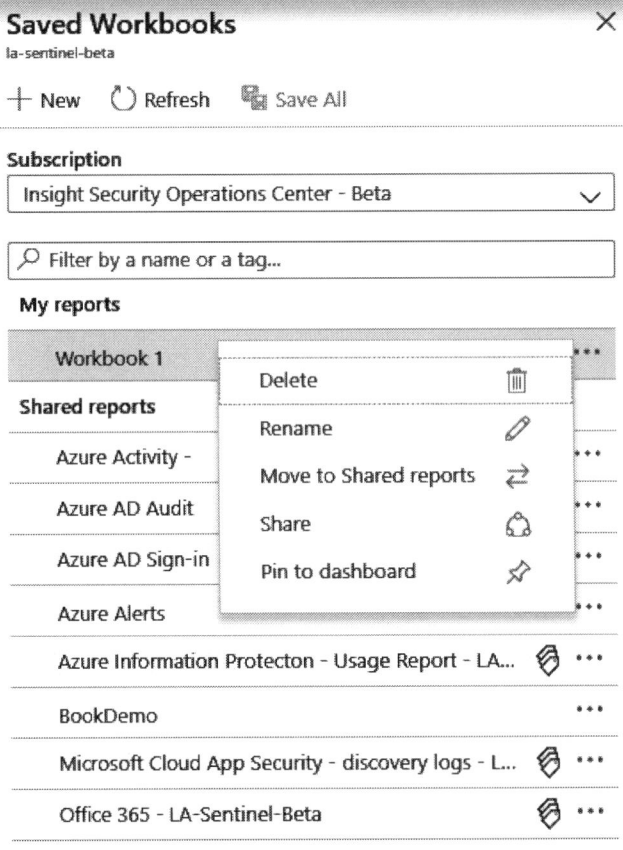

Figure 8.20 – Managing the workbook context menu

We have finished looking at how to manage your existing workbooks. You have learned about the **Saved Workbooks** pane, as well as the context-sensitive menu that will allow you to perform various management tasks on a workbook. Now, it is time to look at the various parts that make up a workbook, and how to use them.

Workbook step types

Each workbook is comprised of one or more steps. As stated earlier, a workbook is made up of small sections called steps. Each step has a unique name, which can be pretty much anything, and this name can be referenced in other steps. Each step can run on its own, although some may require parameters, either from a parameter step or from other steps.

There are six different types of steps: **text**, **query**, **metric**, **parameters**, **links/tabs**, and **groups**. Each type of step will be discussed in more detail in the following sections.

To add a new step when editing a workbook, at the bottom of the screen is the **+Add** button, which, when clicked, will present a listing of the step types, as shown in the following screenshot. Click on the appropriate option for the type of step you wish to add:

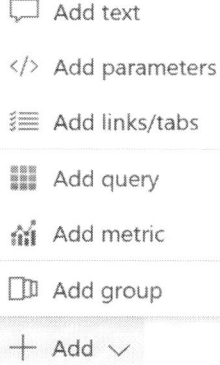

Figure 8.21 – Edit mode Add option

No matter which links you click, the step will have a list of options at the bottom of the step that looks like the following screenshot:

Figure 8.22 – Edit mode add options after adding a step

Clicking the **Done Editing** button will change the selected step to view mode so that you can see how your changes look.

Click the **Add** button to add a new step.

The **Move** button, when clicked, will show the **Move Up** and **Move Down** options. If there is a step below the one that you are editing, **Move Down** will be enabled, otherwise it will be grayed out. If this step is at the top of the page, the **Move Up** link will be grayed out. There is also a **Move into group** entry that will allow you to move this step into a group or create a new one if there are no groups.

The **Clone** button will create a duplicate of the step you are editing. This can be useful if you need to have two steps that are very similar, with only a few changes between them. Rather than having to create the two steps individually, you can create one, click the **Clone** button, and then make the necessary changes on the second one.

The **Remove** button will remove this step. Note that there is no verification that you need to perform for this step. Clicking on it will automatically remove this step. It pays to save often just in case you accidentally delete a step you didn't intend to, so that you can revert to a prior saved version.

Now that you know how to add a step, let's discuss each type in detail.

Text

As you may have guessed from the name, clicking the **Add text** link will add a step that displays text using the Markdown language. Clicking the link will add a new step with an empty textbox where you can enter your text, as shown in the following screenshot:

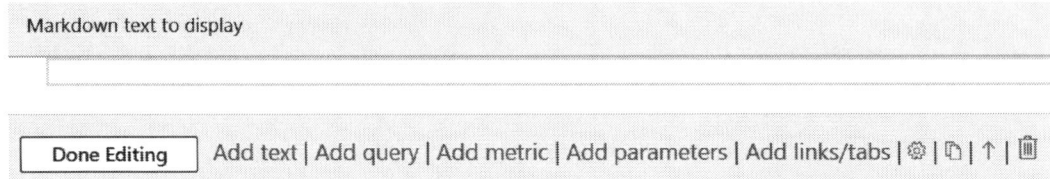

Figure 8.23 – New text step

Enter the text you want, along with any of the Markdown formatting commands, and then click the **Done Editing** button to see your changes with the formatting applied.

The Markdown language is a text-based language that is used in many different systems, most notably GitHub. It was developed to allow people to write plaintext documents that contain the same formatting you would see in HTML documents. To see the various formatting commands, go to `https://www.markdownguide.org/`.

Query

The query step is the mainstay of the workbook. By using KQL queries, you can display data from the logs in various formats, including grids (or tables), area charts, various types of bar charts, line charts, pie charts, scatter charts, time charts, and tiles.

Currently, most of the visualization types are supported, with two of them—graph and map—in preview. Microsoft may make changes from time to time, so please refer to the official workbook docs for up-to-date information. The graph format allows you to show information in a graph view, much like what you see when investigating an incident. Refer to the *Investigating an incident* section in *Chapter 9, Incident Management*, to see what this looks like. The map format will show information in a non-interactive map. This means that you cannot adjust the scale to zoom in or out.

After you click on the **Add query** link, you will see that a new step has been added, which looks as follows. Note that a lot of white space has been removed from the screenshot so it can all be shown:

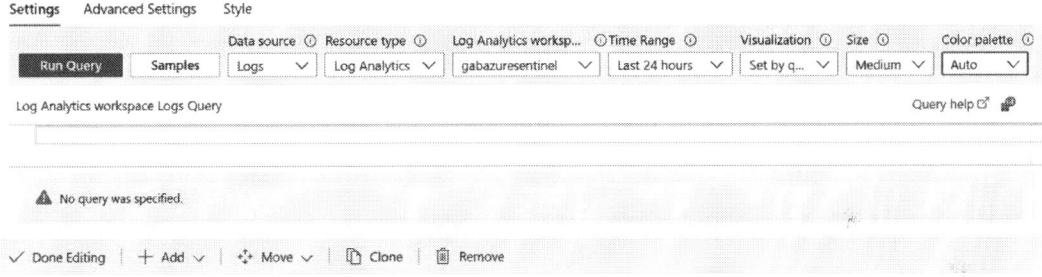

Figure 8.24 – New query step

Let's have a look at the different fields of the header bar:

- The **Run Query** button will run the query that has been added to the query window. In the preceding screenshot, there is no query, so clicking on the button will return an error.

- The **Samples** button will open a new pane and show some sample code. The code for the default query step that is added to a new workbook created from scratch is one of the samples available.

- The **Data source** dropdown will show a list of all the data sources that are available to query. Because of the other Azure technologies that use workbooks, there are more choices than just **Logs** being available. However, for this chapter, that is the only data source we are concerned with.

- The **Resource type** dropdown will list what kind of resources can be used in the queries. Much like the **Data source** dropdown, this is used in other Azure resources, although we are only concerned with using the **Log Analytics** entry.
- The **Log Analytics workspace** dropdown shows a listing of all the available workspaces that are available to use. Most of the time, you should be using the one that your Microsoft Sentinel instance is using.
- The **Time Range** dropdown will show the various time ranges you can select, as shown next. If a value is selected here, it will tell your query to only look as far back as the value that has been set, with a few exceptions.

Most of the entries should already be familiar to you. However, the top one, **Set in query**, and the bottom one, **TimeRange**, need some explanation. You may not see the **TimeRange** value listed, and the reason is explained here.

The **Set in query** value will read the time span directly from the query itself. If you have a query such as `Heartbeat | where TimeGenerated < ago(1d)`, then because the time is set in the code, any value in the dropdown will be ignored. A best practice in cases such as this is to set the dropdown to the **Set in query** value so that anyone needing to edit this step can easily tell that the time span is set in the code.

The **TimeRange** value is added because there is a parameter called **TimeRange** that is set to be a time-range picker. This is explained more in the *Parameters* section. If you do not see this value, then you do not have a time-range picker set up as a parameter.

Remember that **TimeRange** is just the name given to the parameter. It could be called something else in your case. If there is anything listed under the **Time Range Pa…** header (which is a shortened version of **Time Range Parameter**), then that too can be used as the time range value.

> **Tip**
> It is a best practice to use a time range picker parameter in your workbooks as much as possible so that the workbooks can be as flexible as possible.

The **Time Range** dropdown is shown as follows:

Figure 8.25 – Time Range dropdown

- The **Visualization** dropdown determines how the output will be displayed. The values have already been discussed, but another entry that is available is **Set in query**. If this value is selected, then it means that the code itself has determined how to visualize the data using the `render` command.

- The **Size** dropdown is used to determine how much vertical space the step will take up, with the values shown in the following screenshot. Select the value that makes the most sense to you, and notice that the actual amount of space may vary, depending on the type of visualization selected:

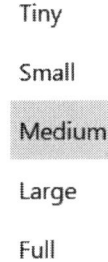

Figure 8.26 – Available sizes

There is one more button that can be shown on the header, which is based on the type of visualization selected, and is used to change the settings of the visualization. The grid, pie chart, tiles, graph, and map each have their own buttons shown to change the settings for that specific visualization.

The book would be far larger if we were to discuss every individual setting for each of these visualizations, so you will need to play around to see what the different settings do. See the link in the *Further reading* section for more information.

One that we will discuss, since it is very useful and is used to create some of the visual representations discussed in the overview of the **Azure AD Sign-in logs** workbook, is the grid's column renderer.

To see this in action, perform the following steps:

1. Enter `Heartbeat` into the **Log Analytics workspace Logs Query** area.
2. Change **Time Range** to **Last 24 hours**.
3. The query should run automatically, but if it does not, click on the **Run Query** button to start the query.
4. When the query has finished, select **Grid** from the **Visualization** dropdown.
5. You will see a new button called **Column Settings** show up in the header. Click it to open the **Settings** pane.
6. Select any column, and then the **Column renderer** dropdown will activate.
7. Click on it to see the listing of choices, including **Automatic**, **Text**, **Right Aligned**, **Date/Time**, and many others.

Most of the available entries will not make sense for an Microsoft Sentinel workbook, but others are useful. Some of the more useful ones are **Heatmap** and **Spark line**, which were used in the **Azure AD Sign-in logs** workbook, as well as **Text**, **Date/Time**, **Thresholds**, **Timeline**, **Icon**, and **Link** (which works like the links/tabs step type described in the *Links/tabs* section).

> **Note**
> Depending on which one you select, other choices for settings can show up or disappear.

One other useful entry is **Hidden**. Selecting this will cause the column to not display in the grid. There may be times when you will need to have the column around, but do not want to show it. Set the column's renderer to **Hidden** for this to happen. It's outside the scope of the book to go into more detail on how to use these different renderers but look at the **Azure AD Sign-in logs** workbook to get an idea of how to use **Heatmap** and **Spark line**.

Beneath the header bar is the **Log Analytics workspace Logs Query** area. This is where you enter your KQL query to be run. On the right side of this screen are three icons, as shown here:

Figure 8.27 – Query step results buttons

The preceding list of buttons is explained as follows:

- The **Query help** icon will open a new tab and will take you to a page discussing how to write KQL queries.

- The icon next to it will open the **Logs** page, in the same tab, and load the query you have in the **Log Analytics workspace Logs Query** area. This can be useful if you are having issues with your query and need to figure out what the problem is.

- The last icon will only show up once you have run a query. It will allow you to export your results into Excel for further processing.

The area directly under the **Log Analytics workspace Logs Query** area is where your results will show up. They will be displayed according to the value selected in the **Visualization** dropdown. Run the Heartbeat query we used earlier, and then change the values in the **Visualization** dropdown to see how this area changes.

Metric

The metrics step allows you to view metrics on different Azure resources. This step type is not used that much in Microsoft Sentinel, so we will not discuss it in this chapter. To get more information on how to use the metrics step, refer to `https://docs.microsoft.com/en-us/azure/azure-monitor/app/usage-workbooks#adding- metrics-sections`.

Parameters

As much as the query step is the mainstay of Microsoft Sentinel workbooks, they would not be as useful without parameters. A workbook that cannot change any of its inputs may just as well be an image rather than an interactive workbook that you can manipulate to query the results in different ways.

There are two types of parameters: those that get set in a parameter step, which we will discuss here, and those that are populated when an item in a query step is selected, which will be discussed in the *Advanced Settings* section later in this chapter.

When you click the **Add Parameter** link, you will see the following screen. Note that a lot of white space has been removed from the screenshot so it can all be shown:

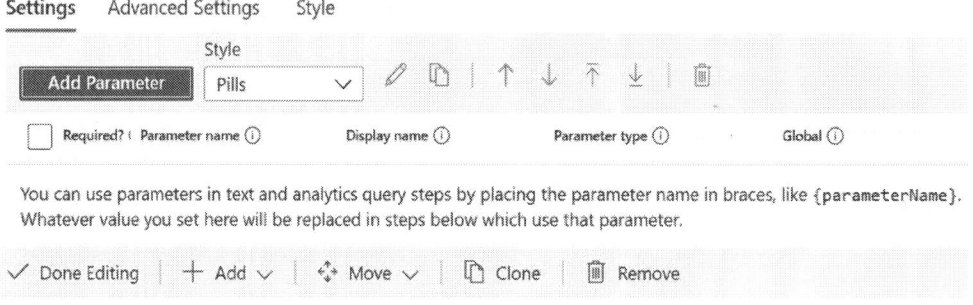

Figure 8.28 – New parameter step

Once you have entered the parameters, they will be displayed in a table, one per row, as shown in the following screenshot. You can select a single checkbox to edit all the settings of an individual parameter. You can also change the **Required?**, **Parameter name**, and **Display name** fields directly from this screen. It will show the **Parameter type** and **Explanation** fields, although you cannot edit those fields from this screen. Refer to the *Adding a new parameter* section for an explanation of these fields:

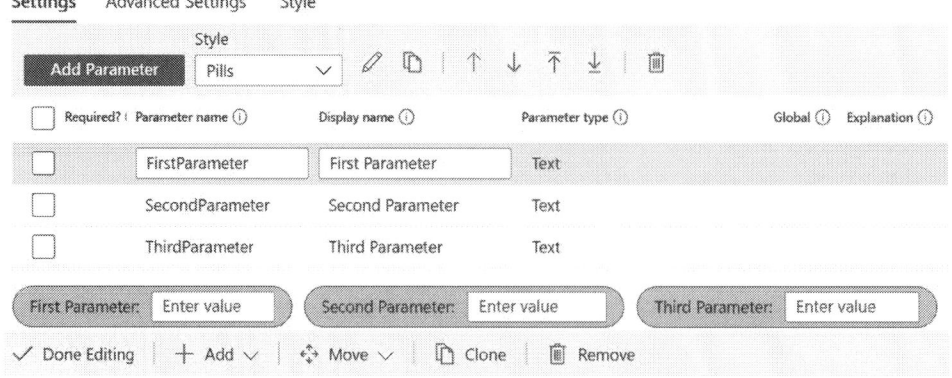

Figure 8.29 – Parameter step with sample parameters

Click on the **Add Parameter** button to add a new parameter. When you do, a new pane will open. This is where you will set up your new parameter. Refer to the *Adding a new parameter* section for more information.

The **Style** dropdown allows you to change how the parameters are displayed. By default, they are displayed as pills, as shown in the following screenshot.

When you click the **Add parameter** link, you will see the following. The parameters are displayed in a single line as much as possible. If they cannot fit on one line, then multiple lines will be used:

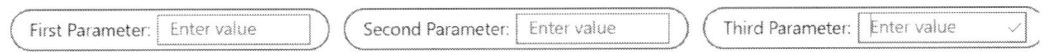

Figure 8.30 – Parameter inputs using the pill style

The other option is **Standard**, which will display the parameters as follows, with no border around them:

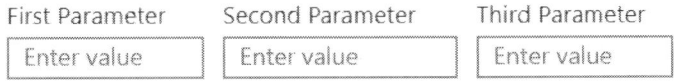

Figure 8.31 – Parameter inputs using Standard style

Notice that you do not need to click the **Done Editing** button to see the changes. The parameters will show right above the button. This will be true even if you change **Parameter name** or the **Display** name as well. The header buttons are shown as follows:

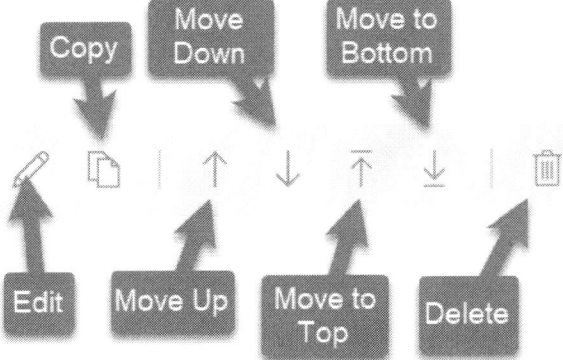

Figure 8.32 – Parameter header buttons

The header buttons are further discussed as follows, from left to right:

- The **Edit** button will allow all the entries to be edited in a single selected row.
- The **Copy** button will create a new copy of the parameter. This will open the same pane as when adding a new parameter, where the other fields are filled in from the original parameter, except for the parameter's name. Fill in those details and click the **Save** button to create the copy.
- The **Move Up** and **Move Down** buttons will allow a parameter to be moved up and down in the list, respectively.
- The **Move to Top** and **Move to Bottom** buttons will move the parameter to the top of the list or the bottom of the list, respectively.
- The **Delete** button will delete the parameter.

Now that you have seen how the parameter step works, let's see how to add new parameters. These parameters will allow your users to have a more interactive experience with your workbooks.

Adding a new parameter

To add a new parameter, click the **Add Parameter** button. This will open the **New Parameter** screen with a description of fields, as shown in the following screenshot:

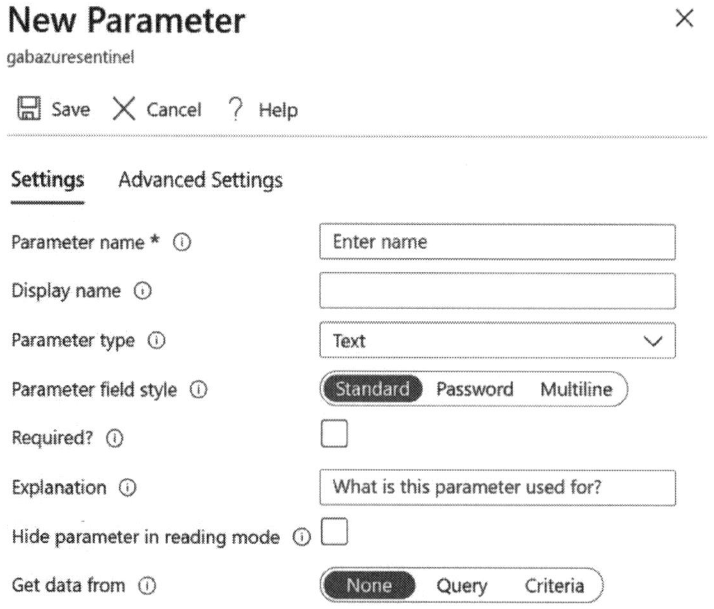

Figure 8.33 – New Parameter screen

The different fields of the **New Parameter** window are described in the following table:

Name	Description
Parameter name	This is the name of the parameter that you will use when you need to reference the parameter. No whitespace is allowed in the name, although underscores are allowed. Make the name descriptive enough to allow other users to know what it is used for.
Display name	This is the name of the parameter that will show on the screen when in reading mode. If this is left empty, the parameter name will be used as the display name.
Parameter type	This will determine how the parameters are populated and what type of input is displayed. These types will be discussed in more detail later.
Required?	Select the checkbox if this is a required parameter.
Get default value from query	If this is selected, then there will be a new section of the screen that will open so that a KQL query can be entered. This works like entering a query for a query step, except there are no **Visualization** or **Size** dropdowns. The query should return a single row and a single value.
Explanation	Provide a brief explanation of the purpose for this parameter. It will show up as a tooltip when the parameter is selected.
Hide parameter in reading mode	If this is selected, then this variable will not be visible when in reading mode but can still be used in other queries. This is a way of tricking the workbook itself into accepting parameters. Set up the parameter so it is not visible and set it to have a default value. Set your KQL query to return the value you would want as the parameter.
Previews	These fields are read-only and will give you an idea of how the parameter will look when in edit and reading modes. It will also show you how to use the variable in your other steps, and what the value will be when the parameter is used.

Table 8.3

Let's look at the different parameter types.

Parameter types

There are seven different parameter types:

- **Text**
- **Drop down**
- **Time-range picker**
- **Resource picker**
- **Subscription picker**
- **Resource-type picker**
- **Location picker**

Each works differently and can have additional fields show up in the **New Parameter** pane when selected. For instance, the **Text** type is very basic and will show a textbox for input, while the **Drop down** type will show the KQL window so that its values can be populated from a query; there will be a new field asking whether multiple selections can be made. These are discussed as follows:

- **Text**: This is the basic parameter type. It will allow you to enter text—for instance, an email address—that can then be used to filter other queries.
- **Drop down**: The **Drop down** type allows you to enter a KQL query, or a JSON string, to provide the choices for the dropdown. This type will also have five additional fields:

Name	Description
Allow multiple selections	If selected, the user can select more than one entry from the dropdown.
Limit multiple selections	If selected, this will set the upper limit to how many items a user can select from the dropdown. Another field will show where the upper limit number can be entered.
Delimiter	If multiple entries are allowed to be selected, this is the delimiter that will be used to distinguish one entry from another.
Quote with	If multiple entries are allowed to be selected, this is the character that will wrap each entry at the beginning and end of that entry.
Include in the drop down	If the **Any one** checkbox is selected, then this parameter will not be used to filter.

Table 8.4

- **Time Range**: This is probably the most widely used parameter type, and one that you will see on most—if not all—workbooks. It allows you to select how far back in time to look for your information. This type will also show several time ranges—stretching from 5 minutes to 90 days—that can be selected to show as available choices, as well as one that allows users to enter a custom range.
- **Resource Picker**: This type allows you to choose what types of Azure resources to show, and then the user will be able to choose one or more of them. For instance, it could be set up to allow users to choose from **virtual machines** (**VMs**). This type will also have the same five additional fields as the **Drop down** type.
- **Subscription Picker**: This type allows you to select one or more subscriptions from a list. This list can either be default subscriptions, all subscriptions, a KQL query, or a JSON string. This type will also have the same five additional fields as the **Drop down** type.
- **Resource Type**: This type allows you to choose a resource type from a list. This list can either be **known resource types**, a KQL query, or a JSON string. This differs from **Resource Picker** in that this one allows you to pick the type of the resource (that is, VMs, virtual networks, Logic Apps, and so on), while **Resource Picker** selects individual resources from a given type. This type will also have the same five additional fields as the **Drop down** type.
- **Location Picker**: This type allows you to pick Azure locations such as East US, East US 2, and West US, among many others. This type will also have the same five additional fields as the **Drop down** type.

> **Note**
>
> For those parameter types that have the **Include in the drop down** field, care must be taken in the KQL query that uses that parameter to account for the case where **All** is selected. The following code comes from the **Azure AD Sign-in logs** workbook and uses the **Apps** parameter. It can be filtered based on the selection, or can look for all apps:
>
> ```
> |where AppDisplayName in ({Apps}) or '*' in ({Apps})
> ```
>
> It is the second part, after or, that allows the code to use the **All** entry.

That is all the various parameter types that can be selected. Notice that when you change the parameter type, the **Previews** section will change to show how each type of parameter will look, and this is described next.

The Previews section

The second part of the **New Parameter** blade, at the bottom of the screen, shows a preview of how the variable will be displayed and how to use the variable in code. The following screenshot shows a parameter with no values filled in:

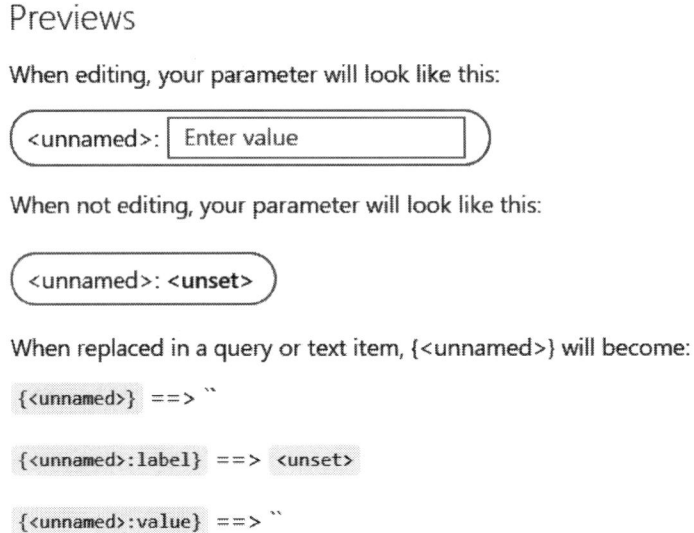

Figure 8.34 – New Parameter screen – Previews section

The last part is very important as it shows how to use the variable in code. This is the **parameter name**, not the **display name**, surrounded by brackets, { }.

Links/tabs

The links/tabs step allows you to either display links in different formats, or tabs. This allows you to open a new website to show more information, show details about a selected cell, or display different tabs.

When you click on the **Add links/tabs** button, a new step will be added, as follows:

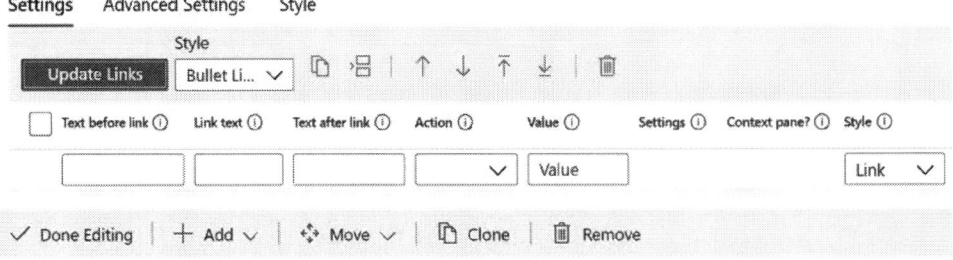

Figure 8.35 – New links/tabs step

This screen will allow you to add, edit, delete, or change the order of the links that you have added. Keep in mind that as far as workbooks are concerned, tabs are links that are displayed differently.

The **Update Links** button will update the links with any modifications that have been made during the edit process. The **Style** dropdown will change how the links will be displayed in the list. The following table shows how the various styles will affect how the links are shown:

Display Name	Sample
Bullet List	• First Link • Second Link • Third Link
List	First Link Second Link Third Link
Paragraph	First Link Second Link Third Link
Navigation	First Link | Second Link | Third Link
Tabs	First Link Second Link Third Link

Table 8.5

The rest of the header buttons are as follows:

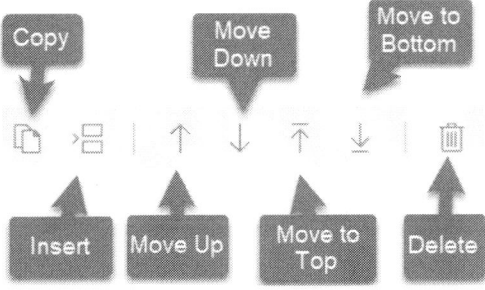

Figure 8.36 – Links/tabs step header buttons

The header buttons are discussed as follows, from left to right:

- The **Copy** button will create a duplicate of the selected link.
- The **Insert** button will insert a blank row above the selected row to allow for a new link to be created.
- The **Move Up** and **Move Down** buttons will allow a link to be moved up and down in the list, respectively.
- The **Move to Top** and **Move to Bottom** buttons will move the link to the top or to the bottom of the list, respectively.
- The **Delete** button will delete the link.

Let's look at how to add a new link.

Adding a new link

To add a new link, start entering information in the blank row shown in the list. The different fields are described as follows:

- **Text before link**: Information entered into the **Text before link** textbox will be shown before the actual link. This field will not show if the selected **style** is **Tabs**.
- **Link text**: The **link text** is the actual text of the URL that will be shown.
- **Text after link**: Information entered into the **Text after link** textbox will be shown after the actual link. This field will not show if the selected **style** is **Tabs**.
- **Action**: This is the action that will be performed when the link is selected. There are many different entries to choose from, but for this chapter, we will only look at **Url**, **Set a parameter value**, and **Scroll to a step**. Depending on which value you select, there may be a button or textbox showing up on the **Settings** field to provide more information, but a brief description of these fields is given in the following table:

Name	Description
Url	This will allow you to create a URL that you are used to seeing in internet browsers such as Edge and Chrome. You will need to set the URL in the **Value** field.
Set a parameter value	This allows you to set a parameter's value and is useful when working with tabs. You will need to set the parameter's name in the **Value** field and the value for the parameter in the **Settings** field.
Scroll to a step	This will allow you scroll directly to a step without the need to scroll manually. This is useful if you want the user to go to a specific step in a workbook without having to hunt for it. You will need to select the step from a dropdown that shows up in the **Value** field.

Table 8.6

- **Value**: As discussed previously, this field changes dynamically depending on which **action** was selected.
- **Settings**: As discussed previously, this field changes dynamically depending on which **action** was selected.
- **Context Blade**: This field is only available when certain values in the **Action** field are selected. If enabled, any action that would cause some new blades to show—that is, **Cell Details** and **Generic Details**—will show in a pop-up window rather than a new blade appearing up the left-hand side of the screen.
- **Style**: The style that is in the header of the step deals with how the links are shown in a list. This style determines how an individual link is presented. Only certain values selected in the **Action** field will allow all the entries in the **Style** field to be selected. For instance, if **Url** is selected in the **Action** field, then the only available style will be **Link**. However, if the **Set a parameter** value is selected, then both **Button (primary)** and **Button (secondary)** will be shown. The following screenshot shows how the selected value changes how the link is displayed:

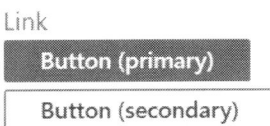

Figure 8.37 – Link formats

Let's now discuss groups.

Groups

Groups allow multiple controls to be treated as one unit. This will make it much easier when needing to perform the same task (for instance, setting up the conditionally visible setting) for multiple steps.

When you click on the **Add group** button, a new window will be added as shown in the following screenshot:

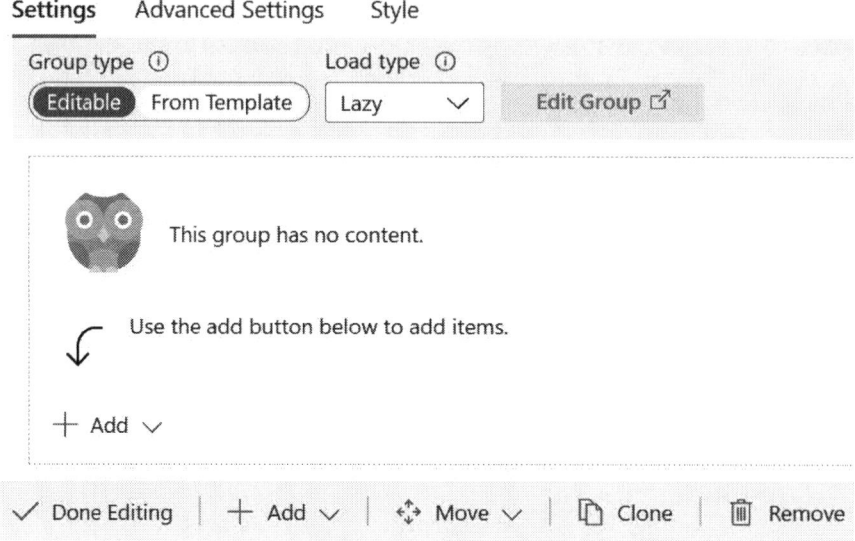

Figure 8.38 – New group

There are two different group types: **Editable** and **From Template**. The **Editable** group type is the default and allows you to make all the changes to your group in this workbook.

If you select **From Template**, then you will be asked for the template ID, which is the resource ID for the workbook. You can obtain this by going to the workbook's resource group, selecting the workbook in question, and then selecting the resource ID that is displayed in the **Overview** page.

You can use this setting if you have multiple workbooks that may use the same grouping of steps to avoid having to create the steps each time. Keep in mind that if you want to make a change to the template, you will have to go to the template to make the actual change and it will affect all the workbooks that are using this template.

The **Load** type will determine when to load the group. Refer to the following table for the values:

Name	Description
Lazy	The group will only load when it becomes visible onscreen. This can lead to faster initial loads but there will be a delay the first time this group is displayed.
Explicit	There will be a **Load More** button and the group will not load until that button is clicked. This gives you much more control over when the group will load but requires a manual step to load the group.
Always	The group will load when the workbook opens. This is the opposite of the **Lazy** option in that it may slow down the initial loading of the workbook but there will not be a delay when the group is displayed.

Table 8.7

There is also a link called **Edit Group** that allows you to open just this group in another window where you can make the edits. This can be useful if you have a lot of steps to make it easier to see just those steps that belong to this group. Once you have finished your edits, you can close the window to return to the main edit screen. Note that this button will only become active if you have at least one step inside the group.

It is worth noting that if you remove a group, you will also remove all the steps that are inside the group.

Now, let's look at how to add a new tab in the following section.

Adding a new tab

When adding a new tab, the **Style** field in the header needs to be set to **Tabs**. The only fields that will be shown are **Tab Name**, **Action**, **Value**, **Settings**, and **Context Pane**. You cannot set any text to show before or after the tab.

> **Note**
> There is no reason why you cannot use any of the other styles to do the same thing as the **Tabs** entry. The **Tabs** style is set up to minimize the amount of work needed to create a tab interface, including hiding unneeded fields, and changing how the links are displayed to look like a traditional tabbed interface.

The value for the **Action** field for the tab will be the **Set a parameter** value, as you will be using this value to either show or hide steps to make the tabs work. Enter the name of the parameter in the **Value** field and the value in the **Settings** field. It is recommended that you use the same parameter for all the tab entries, just changing the value to designate different tabs to show. This will be used along with the **Make this item conditionally visible** option in the advanced settings discussed in the following section.

Advanced Settings

All steps have an **Advanced Settings** tab in the step's header that shows when the step is being edited. This will allow you to set items, including the step's name and visibility; whether it exports parameters; what information to show when in view mode; as well as the step's width and other style settings. Not all step types will show the same fields, although all fields will be discussed here.

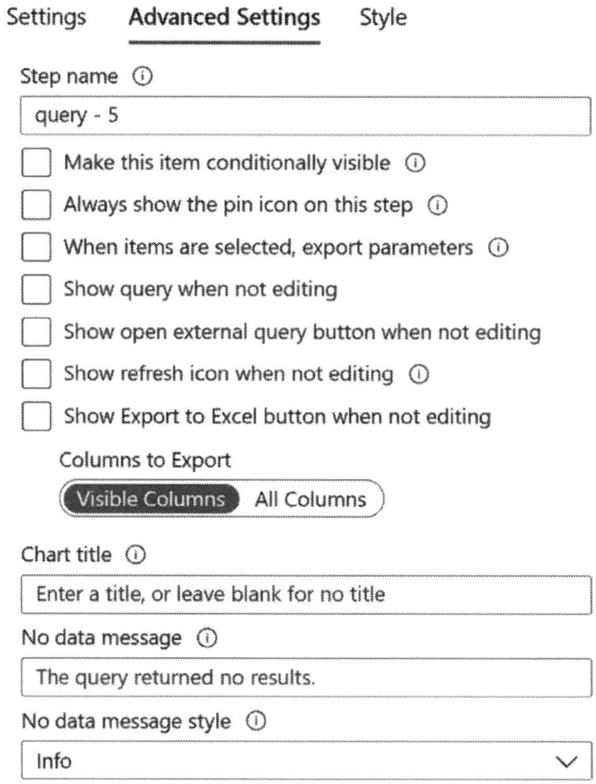

Figure 8.39 – Advanced Settings

The different fields on the **Advanced Settings** tab are explained as follows:

- **Step name**: This is where the name of the step is set. It can be any text and should be descriptive enough so that users can easily tell what the step does. This is especially useful when used in dropdowns in links.

- **Make this item conditionally visible**: This will determine whether the step is always visible or is displayed only when certain conditions are met. If this is selected, a new button will show under it, called **Add Condition**. Clicking on that will open a new window where you can set the condition, as shown in the following screenshot:

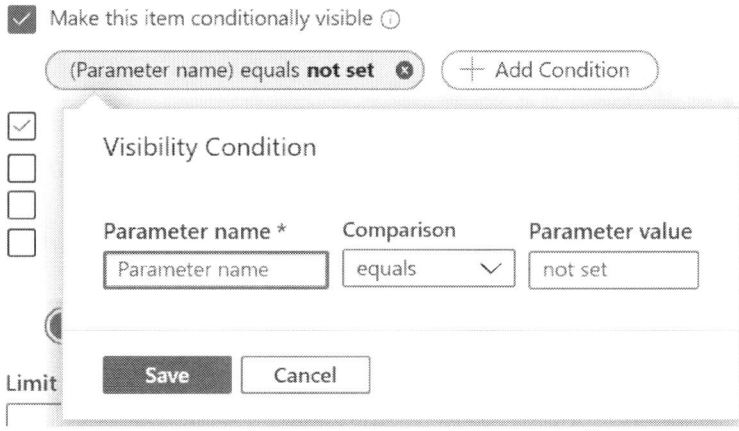

Figure 8.40 – Advanced Settings – adding a conditionally visible condition

This is where you set the condition. You need to enter the **parameter name**, the **comparison** (equals to or not equals to), and then the **parameter value**.

This is the field you will use when working with tabs. Each tab will have the **parameter name** set to a different value, so when that tab is selected, the parameter will have a specific value, and that value will determine which step(s) to show.

You can have multiple conditions, and *all* of them must be met for the step to show.

- **Always show the pin icon on this step**: This will determine whether the pin icon will always show or whether it will follow the workbook's setting for when to display the pin. Clicking on the pin icon will allow a user to pin this step to a dashboard so that a shortcut is created to this step.

- **When items are selected, export parameters**: If this is selected, when an item in this step is selected, a parameter will be set to the corresponding value. This allows functionality such as filtering a listing of users based on status. If this is selected, a new button will show under it, called **Add Parameter**. Clicking on that button will open a new window where you can set the parameter, as shown in the following screenshot:

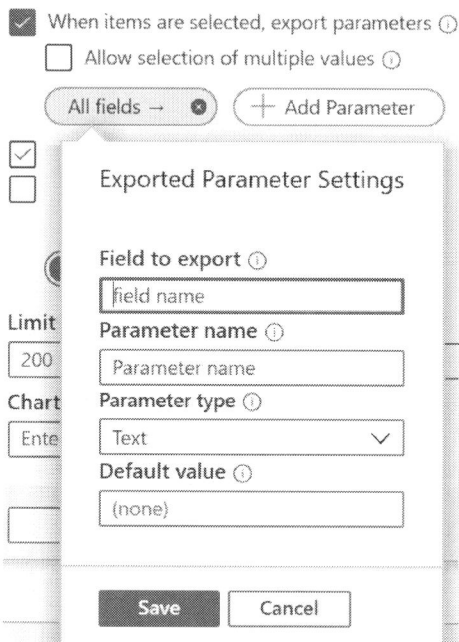

Figure 8.41 – Advanced Settings – adding a new parameter to export

Field to export is for the name of the field from the query that will be used to populate the parameter's value. **Parameter name** is for the name of the parameter, and **Parameter type** is for the type of the parameter. For this book, we will always use text that includes integer, date/time, and Boolean values.

You can have multiple parameters exported at the same time. Remember to use the parameter in a query, surrounding the parameter name with brackets, { }.

- **Show query when not editing**: If this is selected, the KQL query will always be displayed. This is not usually a good idea as it may confuse the casual user.

- **Show open external query button when not editing**: If this is selected, then the open external query button in the header will always be displayed.

- **Show Export to Excel button when not editing**: If this is selected, the **Export to Excel** button will always be displayed. This allows the results to be exported into Excel for further analysis.

- **Columns to Export**: This allows you to export either only the columns that are shown in reader mode or all the columns, whether they are visible in reader mode or not.

- **Chart title**: This is the text that will appear at the top of a chart as its title.

- **No data message**: This is the text that will display if the query should return no results.

- **Show filter field above grid or tiles**: If this is selected, a search bar will appear above the results when the visualization type is set to a grid or tiles. Enter text into this field to filter based on that text.

- **Limit grid rows to**: This decides how many rows will be displayed in a grid. You want this set to a high enough value that the user can get useful information, but not so high that it takes too long for the grid to display.

- **Show open in Metrics Explorer button when not editing**: This setting is only available when looking at a metrics step and will determine whether the **Metrics Explorer** button will always be displayed.

- **Limit resources to**: This setting is only available when looking at a metrics step and will limit the number of resources that will be shown at one time. You want this set to a high enough value that the user can get useful information, but not so high that it takes too long for the grid to be displayed.

That is everything you can do using the **Settings** tab. As you can see, each step in a workbook can be customized considerably. Next, we will look at the style changes you can make.

Style

The **Style** tab will allow you to change how the step will look when displayed. Unlike the **Advanced Settings** tab, all the fields are present in all the step types, as shown in the following screenshot. Note that the **Make this item a custom width** option is selected in this screenshot to show all the fields. By default, it is not selected:

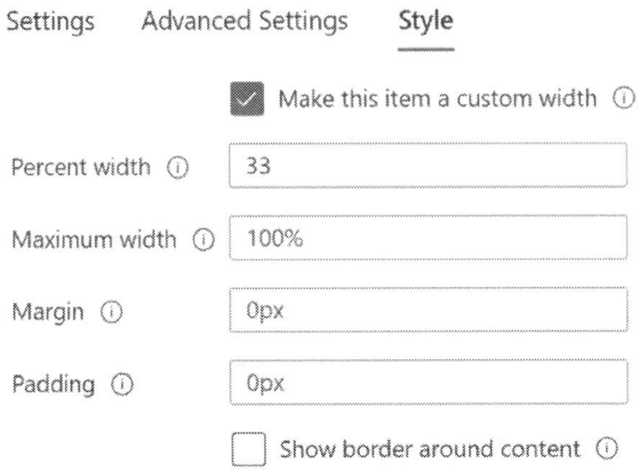

Figure 8.42 – Style

The different fields from the preceding screenshot are explained as follows:

- **Make this item a custom width**: If this item is selected, two new fields show up under it: **Percent width** and **Maximum width**. The **Percent width** field determines how much of the overall width this step takes. If it is less than 100 and the previous or next step's width is also less than 100, the two steps will show side by side, assuming the sum of the widths is less than or equal to 100. Look at the **Azure AD Sign-in logs** workbook for examples of steps being displayed side by side. **Maximum width** determines how wide a step can possibly be. It can either use a specific value, such as 150px, or a percentage.

- **Margin**: This specifies the margin that will show outside of the border of the step. Enter a value followed by a unit, such as px for pixels.

- **Padding**: This specifies the padding that will show inside the border of the step. Enter a value followed by a unit, such as px for pixels.

- **Show border around content**: This determines whether there will be a border shown around this step. Select it to show a border.

That ends our discussion of the advanced settings for steps. As you have seen, these settings allow you to perform many actions, including specifying when the step is to be visible, being able to export variables that other steps in the workbook can use, and determining how much of the width of the page the step will take up.

Summary

In this chapter, you learned about Microsoft Sentinel workbooks and how their interactive display is used to show information to users. Workbooks can be used to help determine whether there is something in your environment that needs investigation.

You learned how to create and edit a new workbook using the various step types provided. You learned how to define parameters using a new step, as well as coming from a query, and how to use those parameters to further filter your queries.

They can display a combination of texts, various graphs, metrics, and links including tabs. Using parameters, we can change what information is presented in our workbooks to help us determine whether there is an incident that needs to be investigated.

Finally, you learned how to change the advanced settings of a step to modify how it operates and looks. You learned how to get multiple steps to show up on the same row in a graph, and how one graph can communicate with another through parameters.

In the next chapter, you will learn about Microsoft Sentinel incidents, which are generated from alerts and other queries, along with how to manage and investigate them.

Questions

1. What are the two ways to create a new workbook?
2. If I wanted to show the user instructions on how to use a workbook, what would be the best step type to use?
3. If I want to allow a user of a workbook to be able to change how far back in time every query in the workbook looks, which two actions would I need to take? (Hint: The second action would need to be performed on every query step.)
4. Is it possible to have a workbook step only show up when certain conditions are met?
5. How can I have two steps in the same workbook show side by side?

Further reading

For more information, you can refer to the following links:

- Azure Monitor workbooks: `https://docs.microsoft.com/en-us/azure/azure-monitor/visualize/workbooks-overview`
- Azure Monitor workbook visualizations: `https://docs.microsoft.com/en-us/azure/azure-monitor/visualizations`
- Microsoft Sentinel's GitHub repository for sample workbooks: `https://github.com/Azure/Azure-Sentinel/tree/master/Workbooks`
- Azure Monitor's GitHub repository for sample workbooks: `https://github.com/Microsoft/Application-Insights-Workbooks`

9
Incident Management

In *Chapter 7*, *Creating Analytic Rules*, you learned that rules in analytics create incidents. These incidents can represent potential issues with your environment and need to be looked at to determine whether they are indeed an issue. Are they false positives, irrelevant to your environment, or actual issues? The way to determine this is through incident management.

There are no hard-and-fast rules for incident management, other than to look at the incidents and determine whether they are actual issues. There are various ways to do this, and this chapter will look at the options Microsoft Sentinel provides to perform these investigations, including a graphical representation of the incident, viewing the full details of the incident, and running other queries to obtain more information.

In this chapter, we will cover the following topics:

- Using the Microsoft Sentinel **Incidents** page
- Exploring the full details page
- Investigating an incident

Using the Microsoft Sentinel Incidents page

To look at the Microsoft Sentinel **Incidents** page, click on the **Incidents** link in the left-hand navigation panel. This will take you to the **Incidents** page, as shown in the following screenshot. The actual numbers and incidents listed may be different, of course:

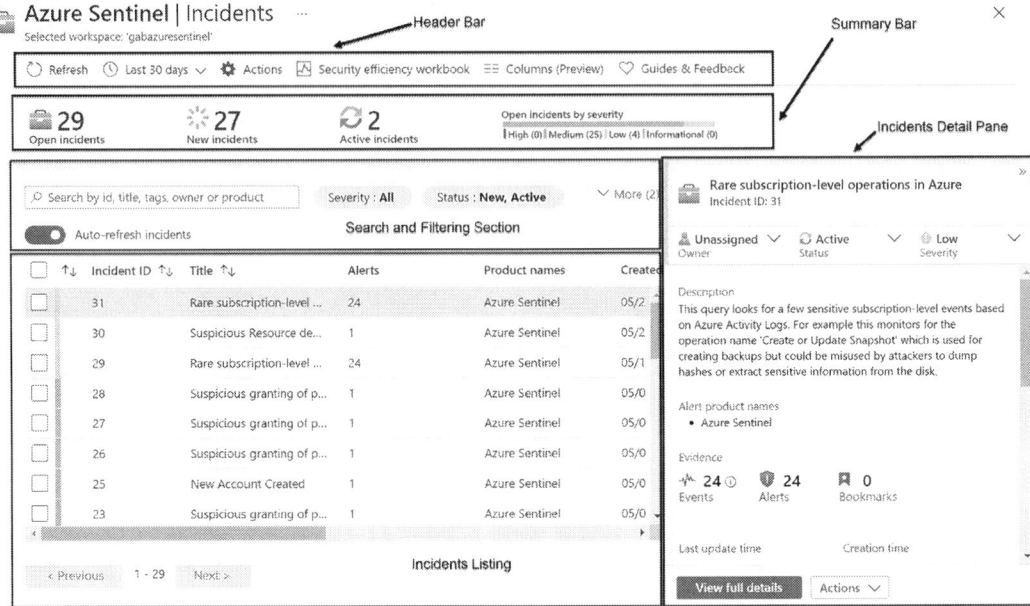

Figure 9.1 – The Microsoft Sentinel Incidents page

The page has been broken up into the header bar, the summary bar, the search and filtering section, the incidents listing, and the incident details pane. Each of these sections is described in more detail next.

The header bar

The header bar at the top of the page, shown in the following screenshot, has the usual **Refresh** button and timespan drop-down option. There is also another button called **Actions**:

Figure 9.2 – The Incidents page's header bar

The **Actions** button will allow you to perform actions against multiple incidents at once, including changing the severity, assigning an owner, changing the status, and adding tags. See the *Using the Actions button* section for more information.

To the right is the **Security efficiency workbook** button. Clicking this will take you to the Security Operations Efficiency workbook, which will give you a general overview of the incidents, including a timeline of when they were created, the closing classification (if any) of the incidents, breakdowns by severity, owner, status, and much more.

The **Columns** (preview) link will allow you to select which columns to show in your view. This will allow you to customize the view of the Incidents page, and the changes will persist. See the *Incident listing* section in this chapter for a listing of all the columns.

On the far right is the **Guides & Feedback** button. Clicking this will open a pane that has some guides on incidents and will allow you to share feedback with Microsoft regarding the **Incidents** page.

The summary bar

Under the header bar is the summary bar, shown in the following screenshot. This shows the total number of open incidents, the number of new incidents, and the number of incidents that are in progress:

Figure 9.3 – The Incidents page's summary bar

On the right side of the summary bar is a listing of the open incidents, broken down by severity. By looking at the two different summaries of the incidents, you can get an idea of how your incidents are broken down.

The search and filtering section

Below the summary bar is the search and filtering section. This is where you can filter what results you see in the listing of all the incidents:

Figure 9.4 – The Incidents page's filtering section

Let's look at all the parameters under the search and filtering section:

- **Search by id, title, tags, owner or product**: This filter allows you to enter a search term to find specific incidents. This can either be text found in the title of the incident(s) or the incident ID number.

    > **Important Note**
    > If you search by ID number, the value entered must be an exact match to an incident's ID number.

    You can also filter by the various fields that make up the incident display, discussed next. As you can see, you can filter by **Severity**, **Status**, **Product** name (which product generated the incident), and/or **Owner** (which is the person that is assigned to the incident).

- **Severity**: This filter allows you to select one or more of **Select All**, **Informational**, **Low**, **Medium**, **High**, and/or **Critical**. By default, **Select All** is selected, which appears as just **All** in the summary bar, as shown in the preceding screenshot.

- **Status**: This filter allows you to select one or more of **Select All**, **New**, **In Progress**, or **Closed**. By default, only the **New** and **In Progress** values are selected.

- **Product Name**: This filter allows you to select one or more of **Select All, Defender for Cloud Apps, Microsoft Defender, Defender for Identities, Microsoft Information Protection, Defender for Endpoint, Defender for IoT, Defender for Office 365, Microsoft 365 Defender, and/or Microsoft Sentinel**. By default, **Select All** is selected, which appears as just **All** in the summary bar, as shown in the preceding screenshot.

    > **Additional products**
    > As Microsoft adds more security-related products to Azure and the ability to create alert rules based on those products are added to Microsoft Sentinel, it is expected that this list will expand to include them.

- **Owner**: This filter allows you to select one or more people to filter. Since anyone could be an owner of an incident, the actual list is too long, and the values will not be listed here. Note that there are some special entries, including **All Users** and **Assigned to me**. **All Users** will show the incidents assigned to anyone, including those that are unassigned. **Assigned to me** will just show those incidents that are assigned to the user currently logged in.

> **Select All / All Users**
>
> The **Select All / All Users** entry in the filters section is a shortcut that allows you to select all the entries in the listing rather than having to select each one individually. By deselecting it, all the individual entries will be deselected as well, and each one can then be selected individually.

The search and filtering section is very useful for finding a specific incident. You can make use of these features to help you quickly locate incidents when there is a long list, especially if you just need to view those incidents to which you are assigned. Next, we will discuss what you do when you've found the incident you want.

Incident listing

Below the search and filtering section is a list of each incident, one per row, shown in the following screenshot. Here, you can see a summary of the incident, including the incident ID, title, the number of alerts that make up the incident, the product names that created the incident, the date and time of creation, the owner, and the status:

	Incident ID	Title	Alerts	Product names	Created time	Last update time
	31	Rare subscription-level operations in Azure	24	Azure Sentinel	05/22/21, 11:08 AM	05/23/21, 10:08 AM
	30	Suspicious Resource deployment	1	Azure Sentinel	05/21/21, 08:03 AM	05/21/21, 08:05 AM
	29	Rare subscription-level operations in Azure	24	Azure Sentinel	05/16/21, 02:08 PM	05/17/21, 01:08 PM
	28	Suspicious granting of permissions to an ac...	1	Azure Sentinel	05/09/21, 12:13 PM	05/09/21, 12:13 PM
	27	Suspicious granting of permissions to an ac...	1	Azure Sentinel	05/09/21, 11:13 AM	05/09/21, 11:13 AM

Figure 9.5 – Incident listing

On the far left is a checkbox. This checkbox is used to state that you want to perform an action on this incident. Refer to the *Using the Actions button* section for more information. You can also check the **Select All** checkbox at the top of this section to select all the incidents at once.

After that is a colored strip. The colored strip indicates the incident's severity: red for high, orange for medium, yellow for low, and gray for informational.

The remaining fields are described in the following table:

Name	Description
Incident ID	This is the ID number of the incident that is publicly shown.
Title	The title of the incident. This will match the name of the alert rule that generated it.
Alerts	The number of alerts that created this incident.
Product names	The name of the product that generated this incident.
Created time	The time this incident was created.
Last update time	The time this incident was last updated.
Owner	The name of the person that owns the incident.
Status	The status of the incident.
Tags	Any tags associated with the incident.
Tactics	Any of the MITRE ATT&CK tactics that are associated with this incident.
Reason for closing	If this incident has been closed, the reason for closing will show here.
Analytic rule name	The name of the analytic rule that created this incident
Incident team	The name of the Microsoft Teams team that has been created to investigate this incident.

Table 9.1

You can sort by the **Incident ID**, **Title**, **Created time**, **Last update time**, **Owner**, and **Status** fields. Clicking on any of these fields will sort the listings in ascending order. Clicking again will change the sort to descending order.

Each incident has its own row in the listing with its own properties, as we have just seen. You can use most of these properties to sort the rows to help you find the incident you want. Next, we will look at the incident details pane, which will provide even more information about the selected incident.

Incident details pane

When you select any incident from the list, the incident details pane will open, which shows more information about the selected incident. Of course, the information will be different depending on which incident you select:

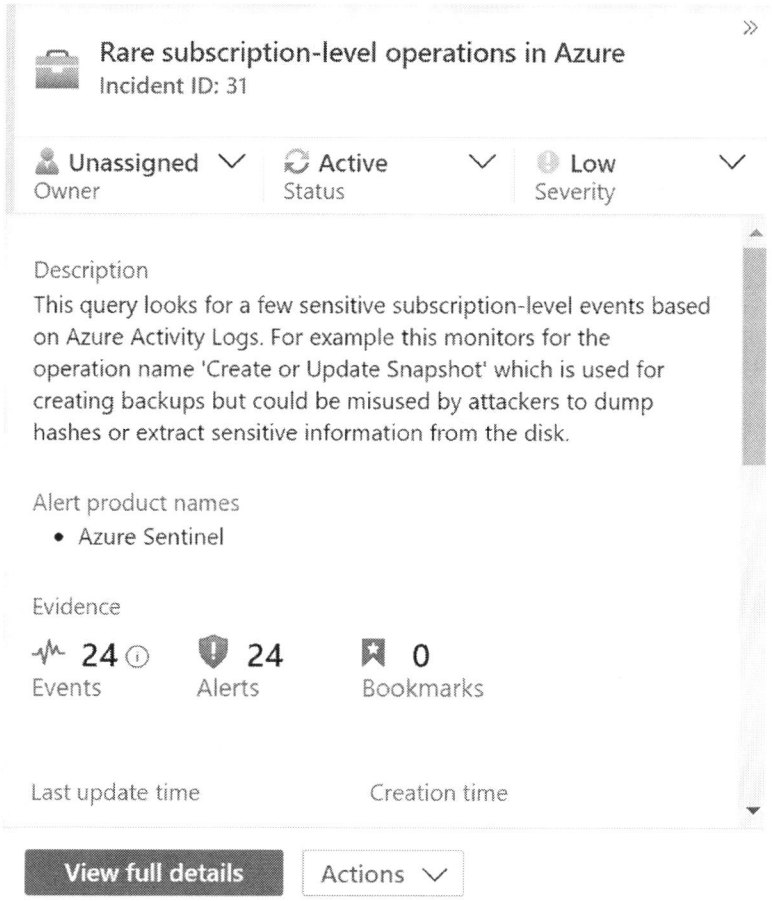

Figure 9.6 – Incident details page

At the top of the page is the title, and the incident number appears directly beneath it. To the left of the title is a colored strip, indicating the severity of the incident: red for high, orange for medium, yellow for low, and gray for informational.

Under that, on the left, is the owner of the incident. This is the person assigned to handle the investigation of the incident. Click the drop-down option to be presented with a list of possible owners, including an entry called **Assign to me**, which will assign the incident to the currently logged-in user, and **Unassign Incident**, which will remove the current owner of the incident. Click **Apply** once the owner has been selected to assign the incident to that user. Note that there can only be one owner for an incident, but it does not stop others from working on the incident:

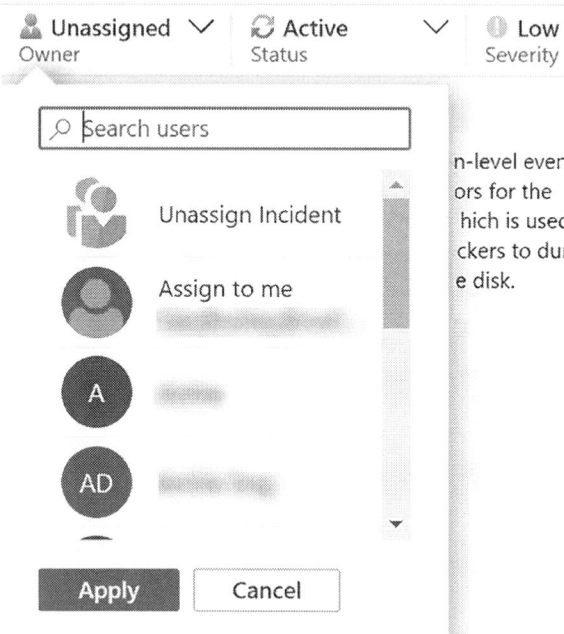

Figure 9.7 – Owner options

To the right of **Owner** is **Status**. This indicates whether the incident is new, being worked on, or closed. Again, you can change the value by using the drop-down list to select the new status, and then click the **Apply** button to change the value. Note that if you select the **Closed** status, a new pop-up window will appear, asking you to select the reason, either **True Positive** or **False Positive**, and add a comment. You will then have to click **Apply** again for the new status to take effect:

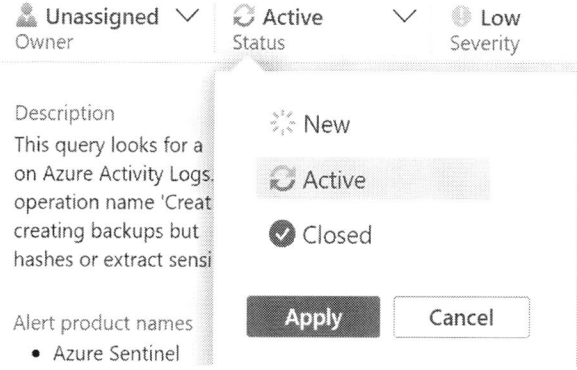

Figure 9.8 – Status options

> **Important Note**
> For a discussion on the importance of using the correct closing classification, go to *How and Why to Use the Closed Classification Properly for Microsoft Sentinel Incidents – Azure Cloud & AI Domain Blog* (`azurecloudai.blog`).

On the far-right is the **Severity** value of the incident. This indicates how big of an issue this incident is and is defaulted from the analytic rule used to create this incident. You can change this value by using the drop-down list to select the new **Severity** value and then clicking on the **Apply** button to change the value, as shown in the following screenshot:

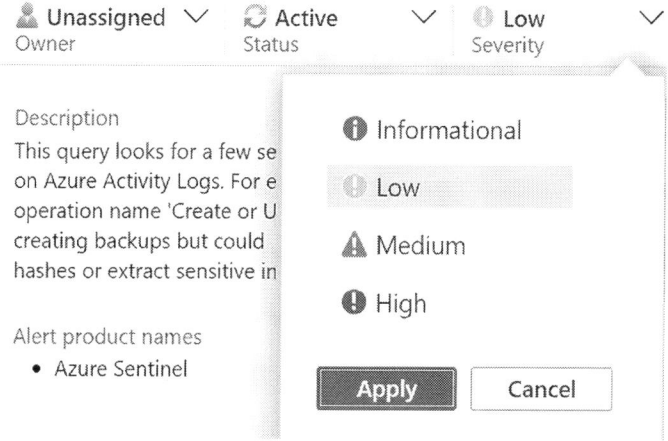

Figure 9.9 – Severity options

Under those dropdowns are descriptions of the incidents. This provides more details about an incident and can include items such as what the incident is looking for, how it was determined, and even external links to get more information.

Directly below that is the name of the product that created this incident under the **Alert product names** header. This information is useful in that it can help you determine if there will be more information that is stored in Microsoft Sentinel. If this incident is coming from another Azure security product, chances are there will not be as much additional information in Microsoft Sentinel, if any.

Under that is the **Evidence** section. This is where you will find the number of events, alerts, and bookmarks that are in this incident. As shown in *Figure 9.6* previously, the incident being looked at has 24 events, 24 alerts, and no bookmarks. Click on any of these entries to get more information.

Scrolling down the details pane, we find **Last update time**, **Creation time**, **Entities**, **Tactics**, the **Incident workbook** link, the **Analytics rule** link, and **Tags**, as shown in the following screenshot:

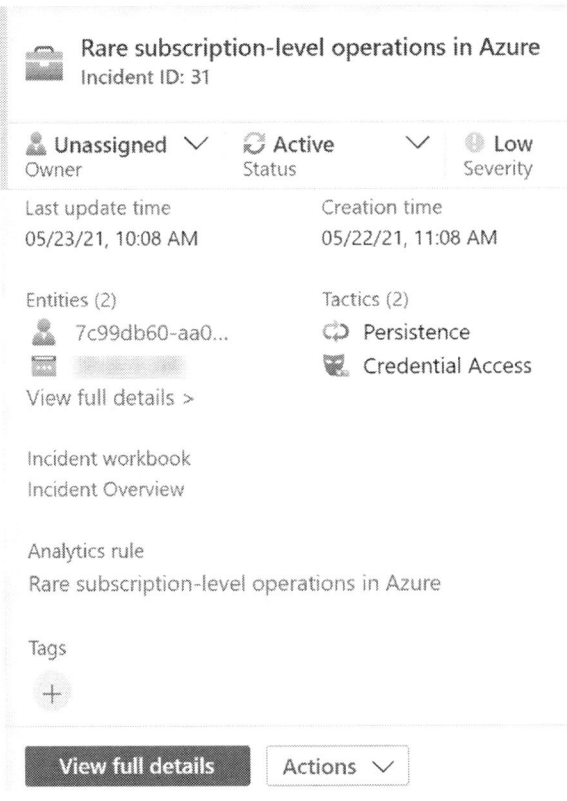

Figure 9.10 – Incident details page continued

As you would expect, the **Creation time** and **Last update time** fields show when the incident was created and when it was last updated.

The **Entities** section shows some of the entities that are associated with this incident. Remember that they need to be mapped when creating an analytics rule and at least one must be filled in so that the **Investigate** link, described in the following figure, will be enabled. Click on the **View full details** link to see all the information about the incidents. Refer to the following *Entities tab* section for more information.

The **Tactics** section shows the MITRE ATT&CK tactics that are associated with this incident. Both an icon and text are used to describe the various tactics.

The **Incident workbook** link will take you to the Incident Overview workbook, where you can obtain additional information about the incident, including the reasons why similar incidents were closed, a log of all the activity that has occurred with this incident, and all the comments.

The **Analytics rule** link will take you to the analytics rule that created this incident. This will allow you to see the query and other parameters that were used in the analytics rule.

The **Tags** section will show you all the tags that are associated with this incident, if any. Click on the + button to add a new tag.

Scrolling down again, we find **Incident link** and **Last comment**, as shown in the following screenshot:

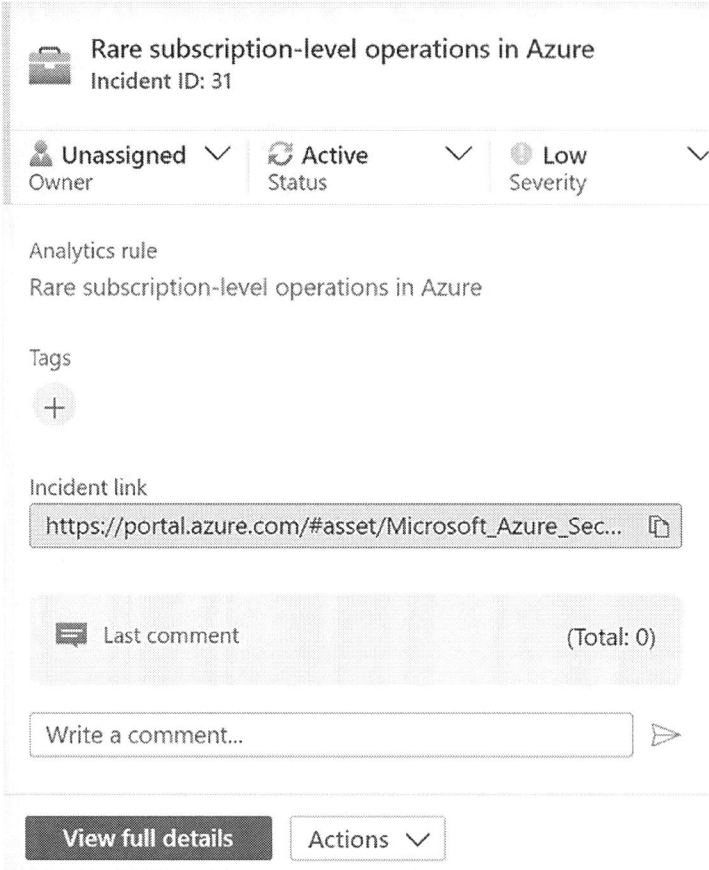

Figure 9.11 – Incident details page continued

The **Incident link** field provides a URL that you can provide to others that will take them directly to the incident's full details page, described in the *Exploring the full details page* section. This makes it easier to get to an incident, as the person will not need to traverse the Azure portal's menus and then search for it.

At the bottom of the page is the last comment that has been added to the incident. To the right of the **Last comment** field is the total number of comments associated with this incident. Clicking on this number will take you to the **Comments** tab in the full details page, described in more detail in the *The Comments tab* section. To add a new comment, enter the text in the **Write a comment** textbox and click on the **submit** button on the right. It will look like an arrow pointing to the right.

The **View full details** button will open the full details page, which will be discussed in the *Exploring the full details page* section.

The **Actions** button (not to be confused with the **Actions** button in the header) will show the following actions:

Name	Description
Investigate	This will open the graphical incident investigation page. Refer to the following *Investigating an incident* section for more information.
Create automation rule	This will allow you to create an automation rule specifically for this incident type. Refer to *Chapter 11, Creating Playbooks and Automation*, for more details.
Create team	This will allow you to create a Microsoft Teams team to facilitate the investigation of this incident. The use of this feature is outside the scope of this book.

Table 9.2

Now that you have seen how to look at and update a single incident, let's look at how you can update multiple incidents at once. This is done by using the **Actions** button in the page's header.

Using the Actions button

You have just learned how to change a single incident. What if you need to change more than one at a time? The **Actions** button from the header bar will allow you to do that.

The **Actions** button will allow you to make changes to multiple incidents at once. Looking back at the header in *Figure 9.2*, you will see the **Actions** button. This button will allow you to perform the same action on multiple selected incidents.

First, in the listing of all the incidents, select the checkbox to the left of the incidents on which you want to perform the action. You can also select the **Select All** checkbox to select all the incidents shown in the list.

After selecting the incidents that you want to handle, click on the **Actions** button and the **Actions** pane will open on the right, as the following screenshot shows:

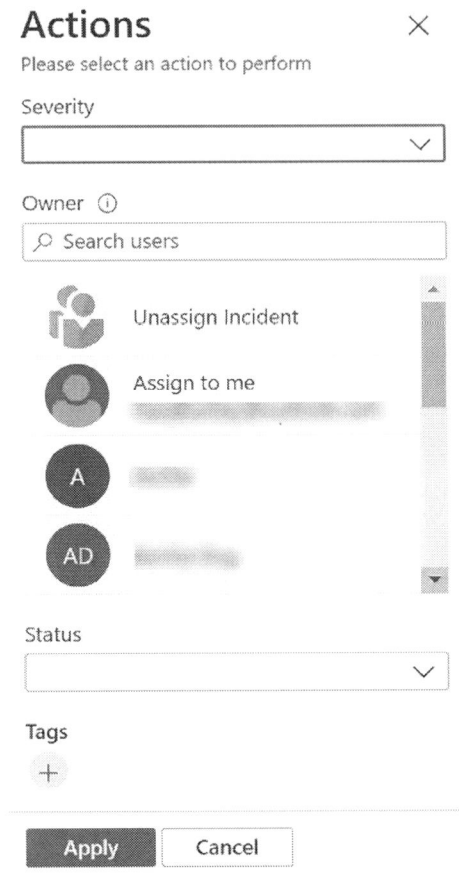

Figure 9.12 – Incident actions

Make any changes to **Severity**, **Owner**, **Status**, or **Tags** that you wish, and then click **Apply**. Refer to the *Incident details pane* section for a refresher on any of the fields.

Now you know how to change some of the settings, not only for a single incident but also for multiple incidents. This will help you keep your incidents up to date. Next, we will look at the full details page, which will show us even more information regarding an incident.

Exploring the full details page

The full details page shows you a lot more information about the incident than you would see in just the incident listings and the incident details pane. Some additional information includes details on the alert(s) that make up the incident, any bookmarks associated with this incident, details on any entities that are part of this entity, and any comments added to this incident.

Clicking on the **View full details** button in the incident details pane will take you to the incident's full details page, as shown in the following screenshot:

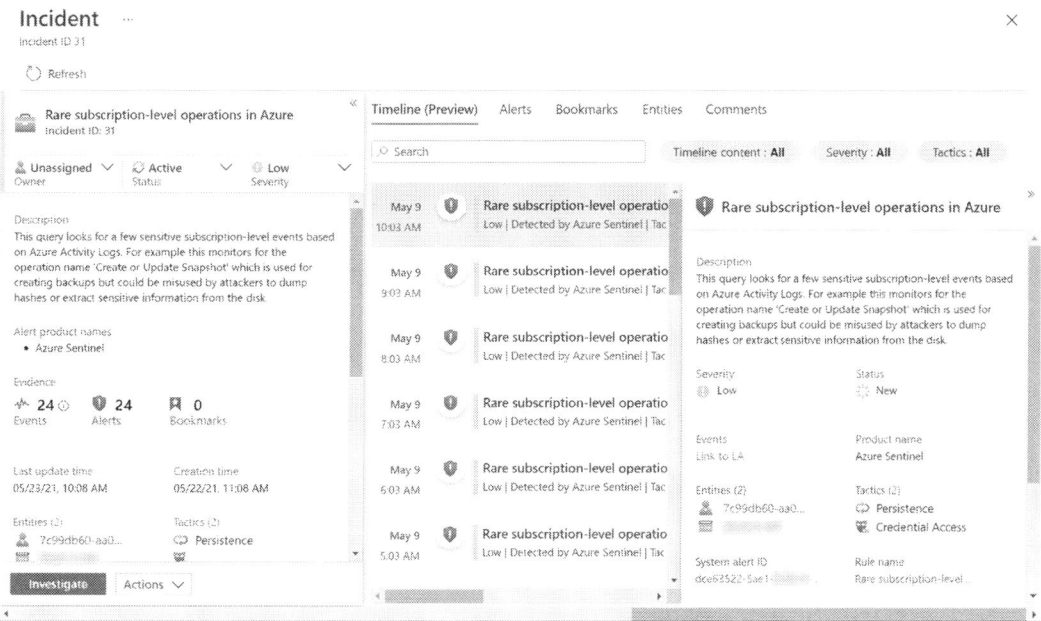

Figure 9.13 – Incident full details page

The left side of the page will show the same information as we saw in the *Incident details pane* section. As a matter of fact, the left side of the page is the same as the incident details pane. The right side of the page is broken up into tabs that show information about the alert itself, any bookmarks for this incident, the entities for this incident, and a list of all the comments. Each tab is described in further detail in the following sections.

The Timeline tab

This is a new tab; as you can see, it was still in preview when this chapter was written, which presents a different way of viewing the alerts associated with an incident:

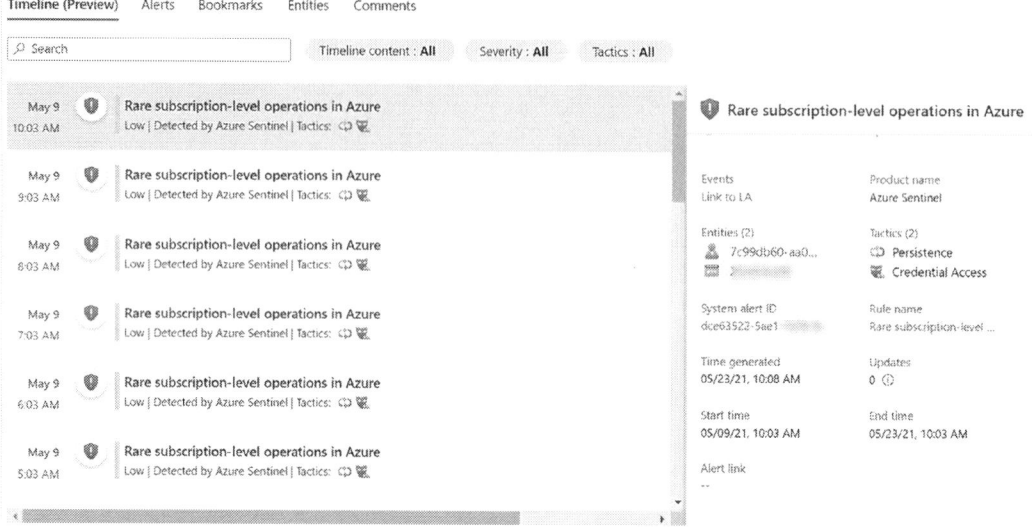

Figure 9.14 – The Timeline tab

This tab will show you all the alerts that make up this incident in a timeline view. The newer alerts will show up at the top and the older ones will show up at the bottom. Clicking on an alert will show you more information, as shown in *Figure 9.13* and *Figure 9.14*.

Many of the fields are the same as were just described in the previous section on the incident details pane, so we will only discuss the different fields here.

The **Link to LA** link under the **Events** section will take you into the **Logs** page, and a query that is associated with this alert will be run to show you the information on the event(s).

The link under the **System alert ID** section will take you into the **Logs** page, and a query that shows this alert will be run to show you the information about this alert.

The **Updates** section will show the number of updates that have occurred to this alert.

On the far-right side of the page, not shown in the preceding figure, is the **View playbooks** link that will function just like the **View playbooks** link described in the next section.

The Alerts tab

This tab will show the one or more alerts that make up this incident. The following screenshot shows what it looks like, with a description of the fields following:

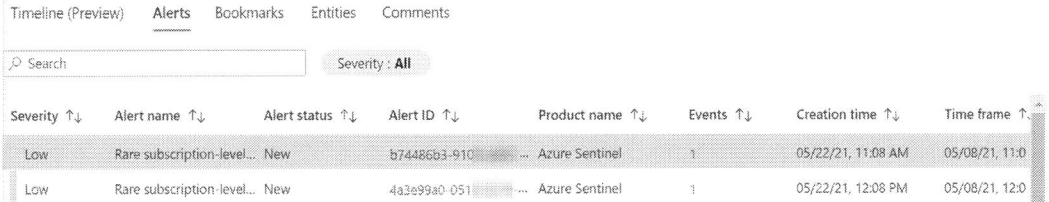

Figure 9.15 – Incident Alerts tab

First is a colored strip. The colored strip indicates the alert's severity: red for high, orange for medium, yellow for low, and gray for informational.

The rest of the fields are described in the following table:

Name	Description
Alert name	The name of the alert that generated this incident.
Alert status	The status of the alert.
Alert ID	The internal ID of the alert. Clicking on it will take you to the Logs page, where a query will automatically be generated and run to show you more information regarding this alert.
Product name	The name of the product that was used in the alert rules to generate this incident.
Events	The number of events that the analytics rule found when generating this alert. Clicking on the number will take you to the Logs page, where a query will automatically be generated and run to show you more information on the events.
Creation time	The creation time of the alert that generated this incident.
Time frame	This will show the beginning and end dates that the alert looked at when generating this incident.

Table 9.3

At the far-right of this screen is the **View playbooks** link. Clicking on it will open a new pane, showing all the playbooks:

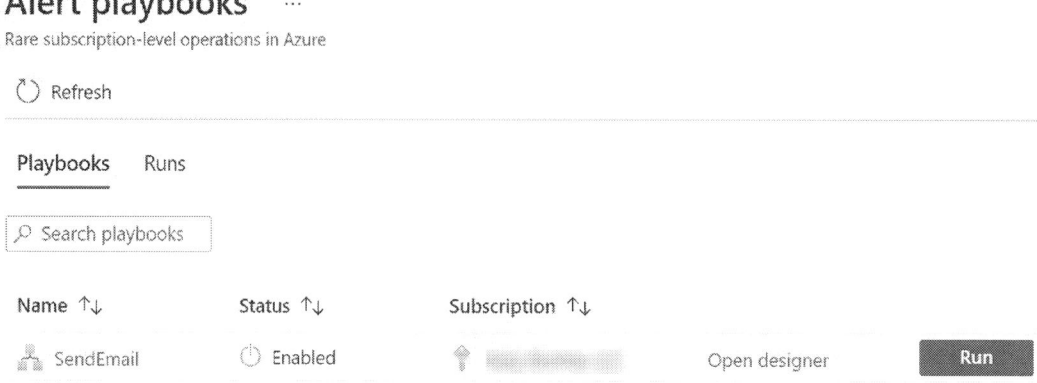

Figure 9.16 – Incident alert playbooks

You can click the **Run** button in each playbook's row to run the playbook against the alert's information, even if this is not the playbook associated with the analytics rule. Refer to *Chapter 12, Creating Playbooks and Automation*, for more information on playbooks.

> **Important Note**
>
> As will be described in more detail in *Chapter 12, Creating Playbooks and Automation*, there are currently two types of playbooks – those that use the Microsoft Sentinel **alert trigger** and those that use the Microsoft Sentinel **incident trigger**. At the time of writing, only those playbooks that use the Microsoft Sentinel alert trigger will show here. In the future, it is expected that both types will show and be available for use here.

As you have just seen, the **Alert playbooks** tab provides a lot of useful information regarding the alerts and events that make up an incident. It is a good place to go when you need to see all the data associated with the incident.

The Bookmarks tab

Clicking on the **Bookmarks** tab will show you all the bookmarks associated with this incident, as shown in the following screenshot. For more information on creating bookmarks, refer to *Chapter 11, Threat Hunting in Microsoft Sentinel*:

Exploring the full details page   285

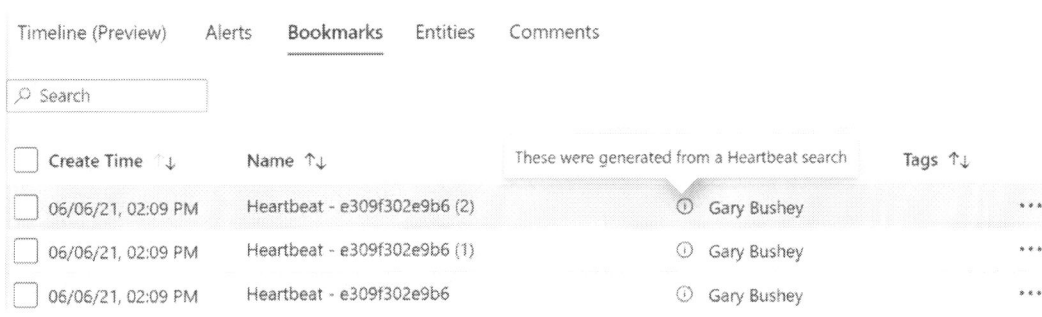

Figure 9.17 – Incident Bookmarks tab

You can use the **Search** textbox to search for a specific bookmark. For each bookmark, the **Create Time**, **Name**, **Created By**, and **Tags** fields will be displayed. At the far-right side of each listing is a context-sensitive menu where the only option is **Remove from incident**.

Note that just to the right of the **Created By** entry for each row is the information icon. Mousing over that icon will show the note that was associated with the bookmark when it was created. If there is no note, this icon will not be shown.

Clicking on the context-sensitive menu will automatically select the bookmark and clicking on the **Remove from incident** entry will prompt you to confirm that you meant to remove the bookmark. Selecting **Yes** will remove the bookmark from this incident. Note that if you have selected multiple bookmarks, the entry will change to say **Remove X bookmarks from incident**, where **X** is the number of selected incidents.

The Entities tab

This tab will show all the entities associated with this incident, as shown in the following screenshot. There will be one row for each of the entities associated with the incident:

Figure 9.18 – Incident Entities tab

286   Incident Management

You can use the **Search** textbox to search for specific entities. The **Entities** filter allows you to select one or more of **All**, **Account**, **Host**, **IP**, and/or **URL**. By default, **All** is selected.

Each entity will be listed on a separate row. The name of the entity (which is also its value) and the type will be shown. If the entity is shown as a URL, you can click on it to go to the **User Entity Behavior Analytics** (**UEBA**) page to obtain more information about this entity. Refer to *Chapter 10*, *Configuring and Using Entity Behavior*, for more information.

Entities are very useful pieces of information to look at when starting your investigation. They provide the basic information that the analytics rule has exposed to allow you to see what the incident pertains to.

The Comments tab

This tab will show all the comments associated with the incident. Note that the link will also show the total number of comments – in this case, **1**. You can also use this page to add new comments if desired:

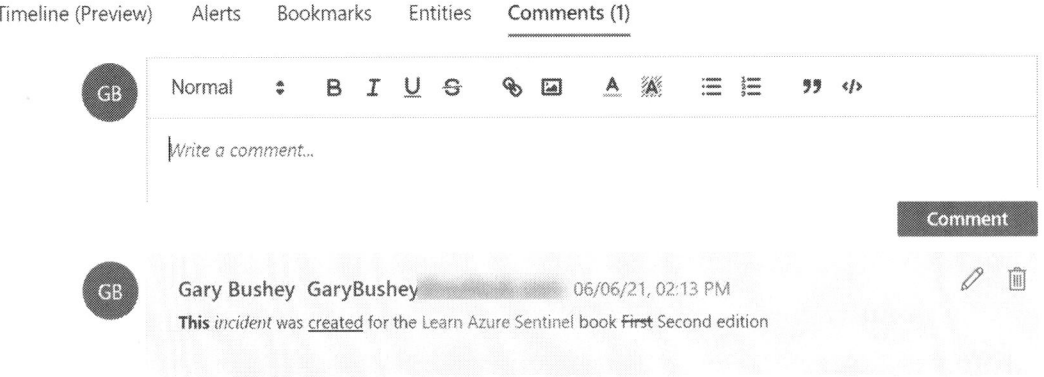

Figure 9.19 – Incident Comments tab

As you can see in the preceding figure, you have some limited formatting capabilities available to you when you create a comment. The comment that has been added has made use of the bold, underline, and strikethrough text modification, and also added a link.

Adding comments while performing your investigation will help you remember what you were doing. They will also help others that may need to come in later and either look at the same incident or investigate one that is similar. Next, we will look at how to go about investigating an incident.

Investigating an incident

Remember how in *Chapter 7, Creating Analytic Rules*, you learned that the rules in analytics create incidents? Incidents are not worth anything if they just sit there without being investigated; after all, that is the reason they were created. An investigation is used to determine whether the incident is an issue. For example, an incident describing failed logins could be as simple as someone forgetting their password, or it could be someone trying to crack a password. You will not know which until an investigation is performed.

Now that you know how to look at an incident and retrieve all the information relating to it, it is time to see how to investigate an incident. The main way this is done in Microsoft Sentinel is via the graphical investigation page. This is a graphical interface that not only shows you the incident in question but can also be used to find related information.

When you are looking at an incident's details, at the bottom of the screen is the **Investigate** button. You click this to start the graphical investigation. If this button is grayed out, that means there are no entities associated with this incident. There needs to be at least one entity for the graphical investigation to work.

Depending on the entities associated with your incident, the actual information presented will likely look different, but the functionality will be the same. Clicking on the button will take you to a page that looks something like the following:

Figure 9.20 – Incident investigation screen

288　Incident Management

The header bar gives you general information regarding the incident, including the title, severity, status, owner, and last update time.

On the right side of the screen are two columns of buttons. The column on the left contains the screen control buttons. The top button will fit your diagram to the screen. This is useful if you zoom in or out too far. Under that is the zoom-in button, and at the bottom is the zoom-out button. You can also use your mouse's middle button to perform zooming if you have one. On the far right of the page are the buttons related to the incident itself, and each is described in more detail in the following sections.

This is an interactive UI, so you can move the various objects shown on the screen around as needed, as well as the entire image. This can make it easier to see the part you are interested in when you zoom in.

While being able to see the incident graphically is nice, the real benefit comes when you look at the related alerts to get a bigger picture of the incident.

Showing related alerts

If you hover your mouse over an entity, this will show a pop-up window with more options. This will vary a bit depending on the type of entity you have selected, but they will all show the **Related alerts** actions, as shown in the following screenshot:

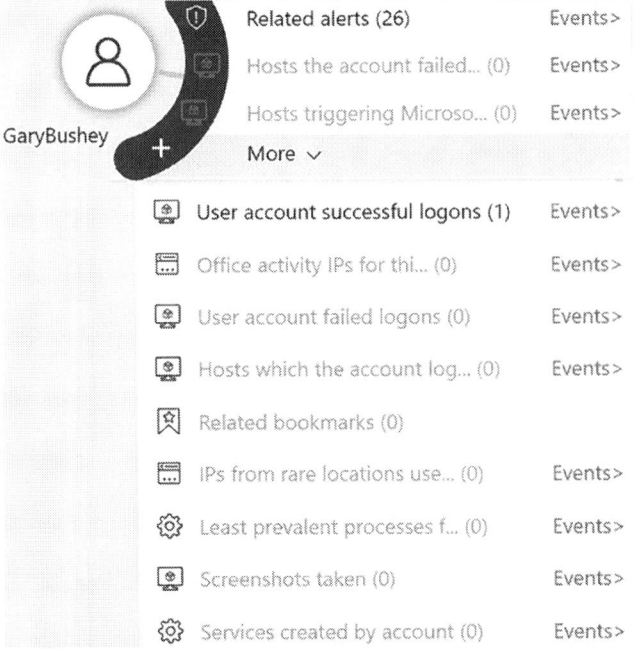

Figure 9.21 – Related alerts

Selecting this will bring up all the alerts related to that entity. In the following screenshot, the related alerts for the user entity are shown:

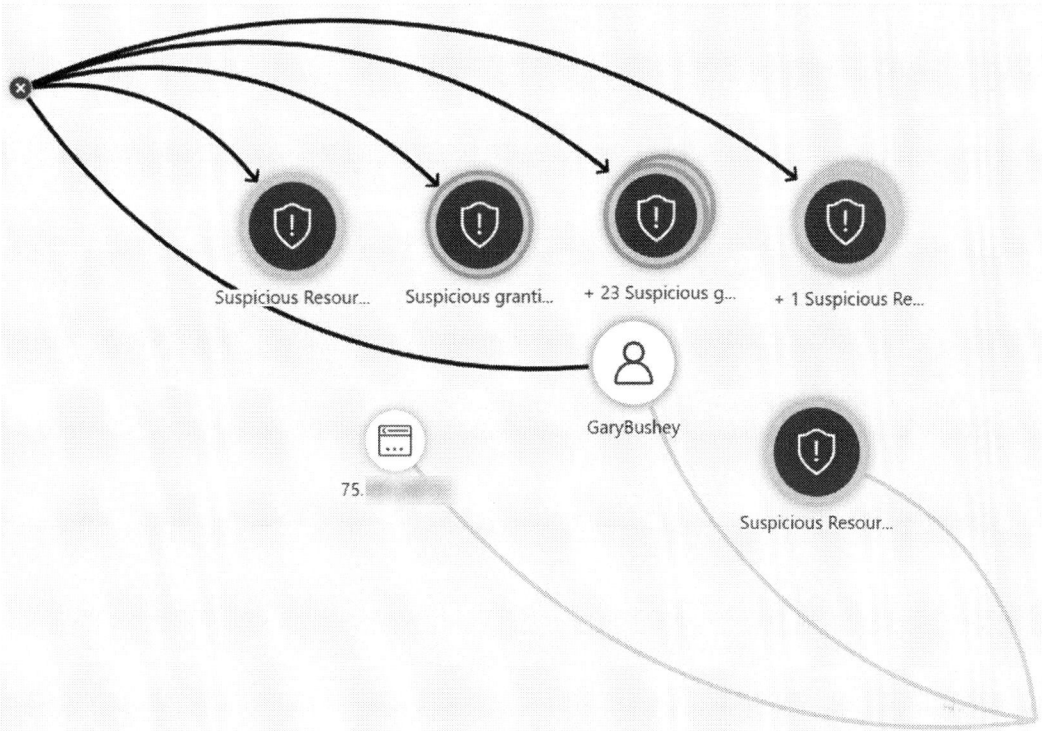

Figure 9.22 – Alerts related to the selected user entity

This will help you determine what else has occurred that is related to this entity. By seeing what other alerts are related to this user, in this example, you can see what else they have done. We can see that the user entity is also an entity in other alerts, so we could look at those to get more information.

290   Incident Management

Although it is called **related entities**, since you are looking at an alert rather than an entity, you can perform the action that we just discussed. In the following screenshot, **Suspicious granting of rights** was expanded. This shows that the alert uses the same entities as the incident we are investigating:

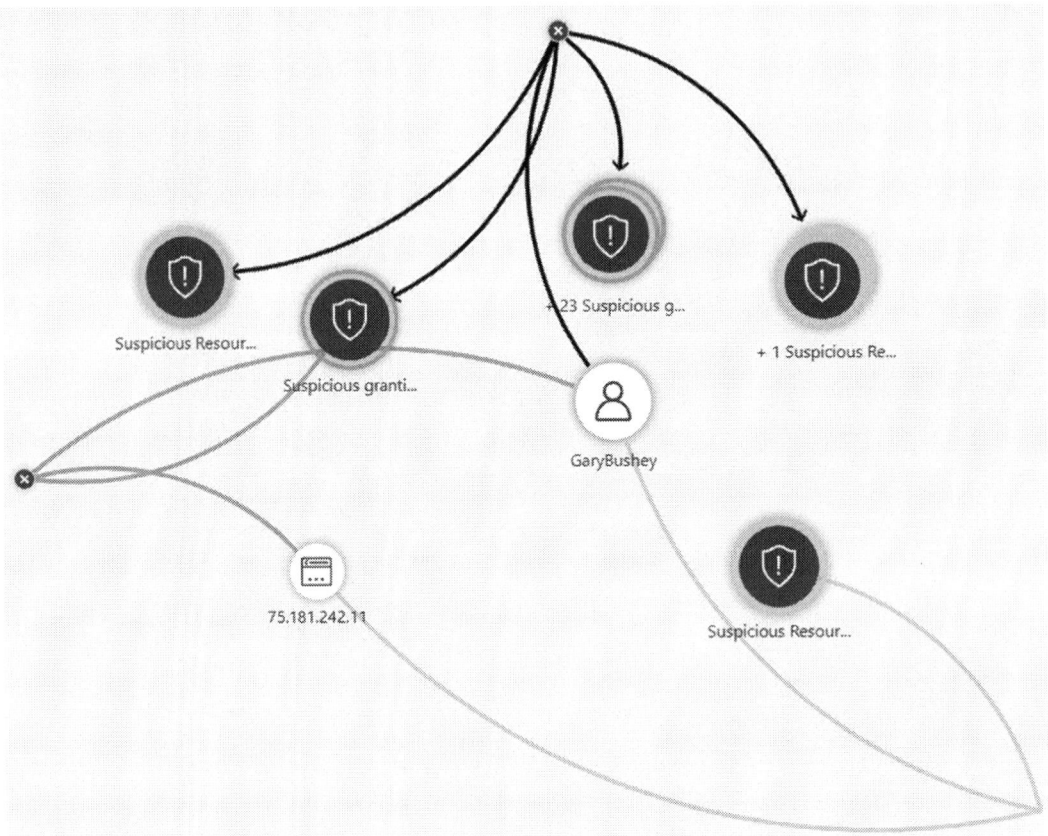

Figure 9.23 – Investigating user activities

The other actions available when you move the mouse over an entity, called **exploration queries**, will work similarly to how the **Related alerts** action works. Looking back at *Figure 9.21*, you can see that there are entries called **User account successful logons**, and more. In this case, this entry has one entry, designated by the **(1)** value after its name, and all the entries have **(0)** after the name, indicating that the query did not find any results. If any of these entries had one or more results, it would be worth selecting it to see what the results are as part of your investigation.

Now that we know how to look at an incident, its related incidents, and its exploration queries, let's discuss the incident buttons located on the far-right side of the screen in detail.

The Timeline button

The **Timeline** button shows the timeline of all the incidents being shown on screen. If this incident was just opened, then there will probably only be one incident shown, but if you show a lot of related alerts, then the timeline will show a history of when the alerts occurred, as shown in the following screenshot:

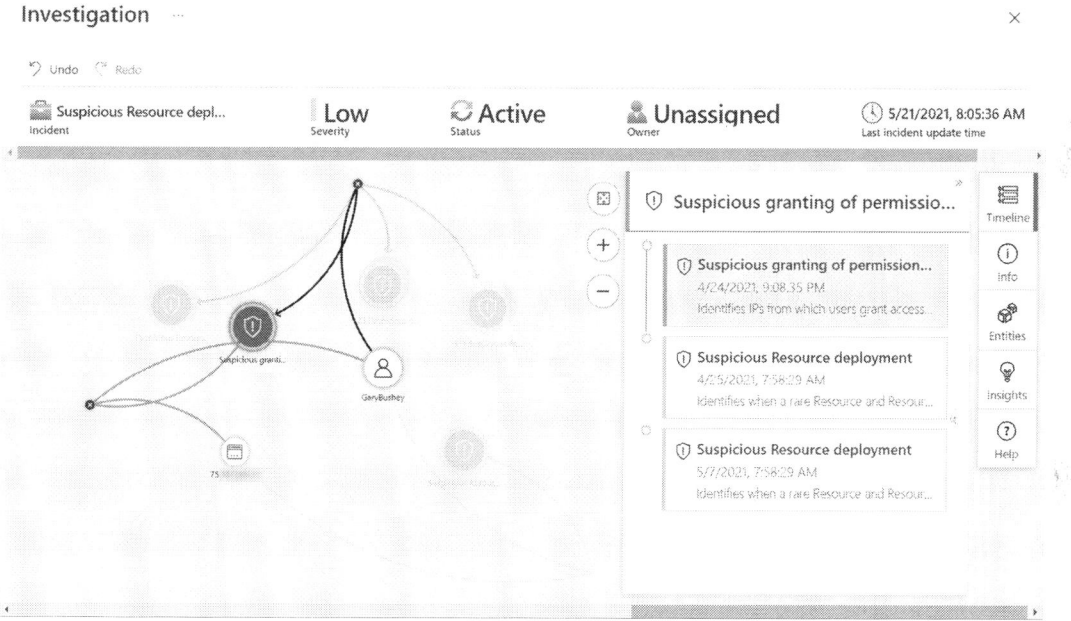

Figure 9.24 – Investigation timeline

In the preceding screenshot, notice that the **Suspicious granting of permissions** incident is selected in the **Timeline** list. When you select a single incident, only those entities related to that incident will be highlighted in the view; the rest will be grayed out, as shown. This makes it easy to progress through the timeline and see what entities are related to which incidents.

The Info button

The **Info** button will show information on whichever entity you have selected. For the IP, host, and account, this will show either **Address**, **Hostname**, or **AccountName**, depending on which type you have selected, as shown in the following screenshot:

Figure 9.25 – Entity information

Notice at the bottom of the blade is the **View full details** button. This will show up for the IP address, host, and account entries. This will take you to the **Entity Behavior** screen, where you can get more information about the selected entity. Refer to *Chapter 10, Configuring and Using Entity Behavior*, for more information.

The Entities button

The **Entities** button will show a list of all the entities, alerts, and bookmarks related to all the information being shown on the screen. If you are just starting to investigate this incident, then this will most likely just be the information for your incident. However, if you are looking at a lot of related alerts, this will show all the information for those alerts as well:

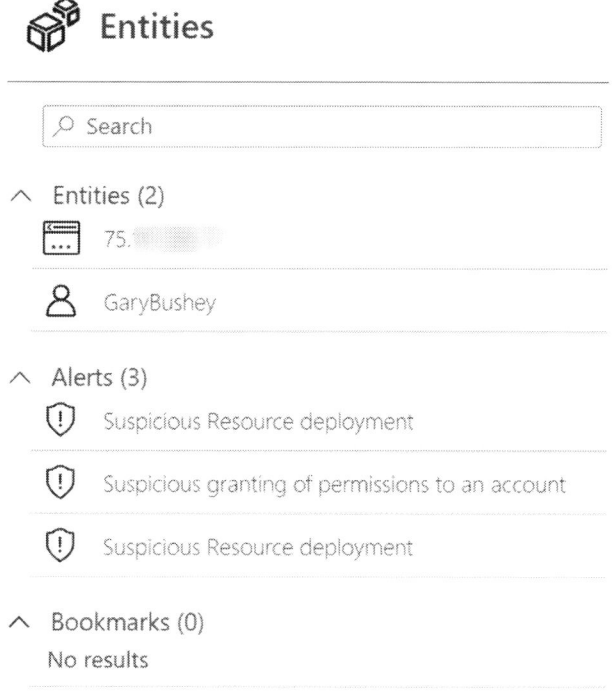

Figure 9.26 – List of related entities

If you hover your mouse over any of the items listed, the UI will highlight the entities related to the item, much as it did for **Timeline**.

The Insights button

The **Insights** button will show some additional information about the selected entity if there is anything. This information will vary depending on the selected entity type and will be covered more in *Chapter 10, Configuring and Using Entity Behavior*.

The Help button

The **Help** button shows general help for this screen. The main screen of this page shows the entities and how they are related to each other. This is a fully interactive screen, which means you can move around the objects to get a better view, as well as zoom in and out.

That was an introduction to how to start performing an investigation into an incident in Microsoft Sentinel. There is much more to performing investigations, and the links in the *Further reading* section should help.

Summary

In this chapter, you learned about the Microsoft Sentinel **Incidents** page and its various components. You learned how to view an incident and change its values, including who owns that incident, its severity, and how to close an incident.

You also learned how to view more details about the incident along with the alert(s) that generated it, any bookmarks associated with it, the entities that the incident contains, and all the comments added to it.

Finally, you learned about Microsoft Sentinel's graphical incident investigation feature. This allows you to not only view the incident in question but also the related alerts, the timeline of those alerts, and more information about the entities.

In the next chapter, you will learn about hunting for issues that alerts and incidents may not have found.

Questions

1. If I only want to see a listing of incidents that are in progress, what should I do?
2. Looking at an incident in the details pane, in which two ways can I tell what the incident's severity is?
3. I am looking at an incident in the incident's full details page and the **Investigate** button is grayed out. What does that indicate?
4. If I want to get full details of the first alert that generated an incident, what should I do?
5. I need to look at the analytics rule that created an incident I am looking at. What is the easiest way to do that?

Further reading

You can refer to the following links for more information on the topics covered in this chapter:

- *Use tags to organize your Azure resources*: https://docs.microsoft.com/en-us/azure/azure-resource-manager/management/tag-resources?tabs=json
- *Keep track of data during hunting with Microsoft Sentinel*: https://docs.microsoft.com/en-us/azure/sentinel/bookmarks

- Five steps of incident response: https://digitalguardian.com/blog/five-steps-incident-response
- SANS Incident Response Policy template: https://www.sans.org/security-resources/policies/general/doc/security-response-plan-policy
- SANS Sample Incident Handling forms: https://www.sans.org/score/incident-forms
- NIST Incident Response Guide: https://nvlpubs.nist.gov/nistpubs/SpecialPublications/NIST.SP.800-61r2.pdf

10
Configuring and Using Entity Behavior

In the previous chapters, you learned about incident investigation and how to obtain more information regarding the incident. By using KQL queries and performing a graphical investigation, you can get more information about the incident. You learned how to find alerts and incidents related to the one you are investigating and learned how the entities are related.

In this chapter, you will learn about another way to obtain more information about your incident by using Entity behavior.

We will cover the following topics in this chapter:

- Introduction to Azure Entity behavior
- Enabling Entity behavior
- Overview of the Entity behavior page
- Overview of the Entity behavior details page
- Creating Entity behavior queries

Introduction to Microsoft Sentinel Entity behavior

Entity behavior, also known as **User and Entity Behavior Analytics** (**UEBA**), allows you to gather more information about the entities that have been exposed in your incident. You will not only see the other alerts that this entity is associated with, but you will also see the other activities that this entity has performed.

For more information on the various types of entities that are available, see the *Further reading* section.

Other information will be exposed, depending on the entity type being viewed. For instance, if you are looking at a user account, you will see information that's been gathered from Azure Active Directory.

However, to use Microsoft Sentinel Entity behavior, you must enable it. It is not enabled by default. The next section will tell you how to do just that.

Enabling Entity behavior

By default, Entity behavior is not enabled. You must go in and enable it. To do so, you will need to have either **Global Admin** or **Security Admin** rights.

Select **Settings** from the **Microsoft Sentinel** navigation menu. Then, on the new screen, select **Settings** in the header. This will take you to the **Settings** page. The **Entity behavior analytics** section should be open, as shown in the following screenshot, but if not, select it:

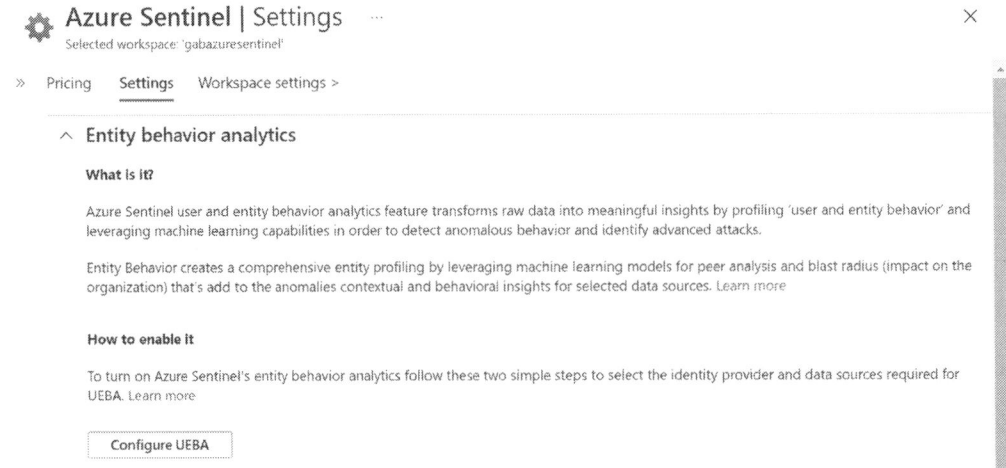

Figure 10.1 – Azure entity behavior analytics settings

Click on the **Configure UEBA** button to activate and configure Entity behavior. When you do so, you will be taken to the **Entity behavior configuration** page, as shown in the following screenshot. First, you must enable Entity behavior:

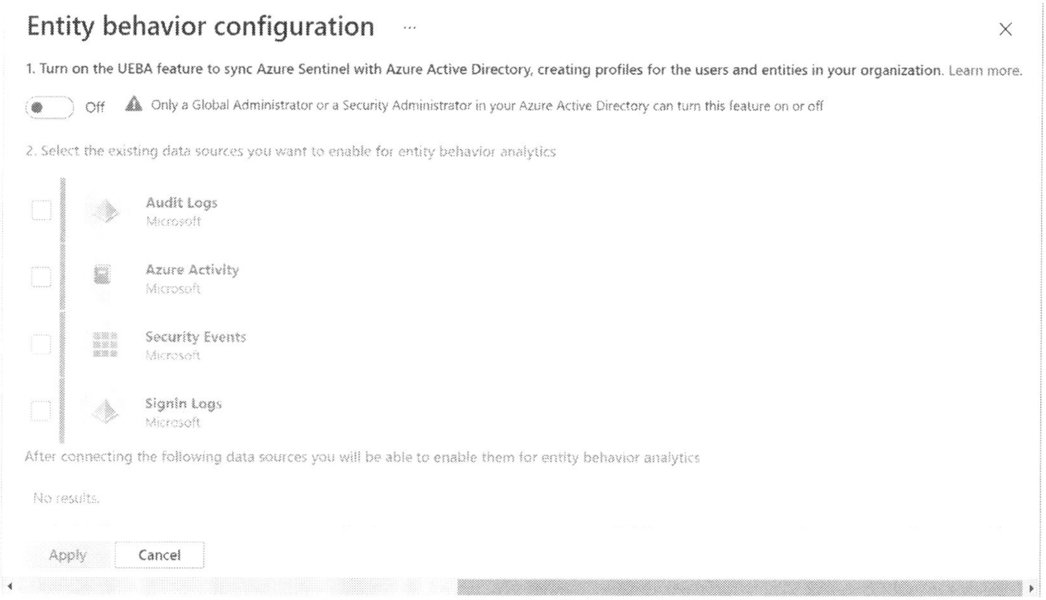

Figure 10.2 – Entity behavior configuration

To enable Entity behavior, move the slider under *Step 1* to the **On** position. Once you have done that, the data sources under *Step 2* will be enabled.

Select any of the data sources that you want to use with Entity behavior. It is recommended that you select all of them so that you can get the best results.

If there are some data sources listed under the **After connecting the following data sources you will be able to enable them for entity behavior analytics** section, this means that the data connectors aren't enabled to ingest that type of data. Enable the data connector if possible and then come back to this screen to select those data sources.

> **Note**
> When you are enabling these data sources, they may provide you with the option to enable them in Entity behavior, right from the **Data connector** page.

Once you have selected all the data sources, click the **Apply** button to start using those data sources in Entity behavior.

300 Configuring and Using Entity Behavior

You now have your data flowing into Entity behavior. Next, we will look at how you can use this data in your investigations.

Overview of the Entity behavior page

There are a few ways to get to the **Entity behavior** page:

- When looking at the **Entities** tab of the incident's **View full details** page
- When looking at a specific entity's information on the incident graphical investigation screen and then clicking on the **View full details** button
- Selecting the **Entity behavior** link via the **Microsoft Sentinel** navigation menu

The main difference between these three ways is that the first two will take you directly to the entity's details page, while the third will take you to the main screen of **Entity behavior**, as shown in the following screenshot. Note that some of the white space on the screen has been removed:

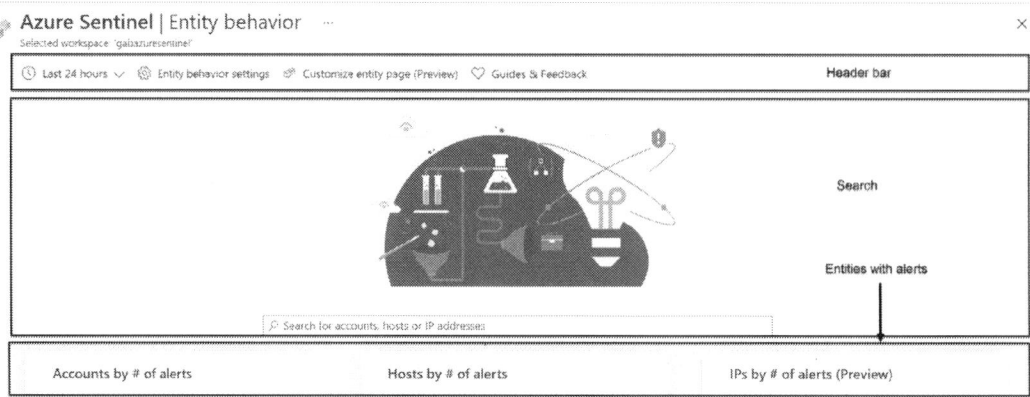

Figure 10.3 – Entity behavior main screen

> **Note**
> At the time of writing, only the **Account**, **Hosts**, and **IP Address** entity types can be viewed on the **Entity behavior** screen. Others may be added in the future.

Let's look at each of these sections in more details.

The header bar

The header bar is located at the top of the page and contains useful links, such as the timeframe to look for data, configuring Entity behavior, customizing the entity page, and providing feedback, as shown in the following screenshot:

Figure 10.4 – Entity behavior header bar

The timeframe dropdown for determining how far back to look for data should be familiar to you by now as it is used almost everywhere in Microsoft Sentinel. Use this drop-down to determine how far to look for the data, keeping in mind that the further you look back, the longer it will take for the data to show up.

The **Entity behavior settings** link will take you to a page where you can find what data sources to ingest, as described in the previous section.

The **Customize entity page (Preview)** link will take you to a page where you can add queries to run against the entities, as well as view out-of-the-box ones. See the *Creating Entity behavior queries* section of this chapter for more information.

The **Guides & Feedback** link will open a new pane that contains more information about Entity behavior and will allow you to send feedback to Microsoft.

The search section

The search section will allow you to search for entities. This is the one place where you can find information regarding those items that are not entities associated with an incident.

302 Configuring and Using Entity Behavior

If you start typing in the search text box, suggestions will start to show up below it, as shown in the following screenshot. You can select any of those suggestions to see the information about them. As you can see, it will suggest any of the entity types as you perform your search:

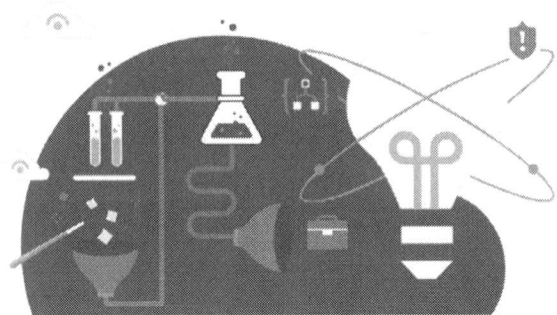

Figure 10.5 – Entity behavior search

Clicking on any of the entries listed will take you to the entity details page described in the *Overview of the Entity behavior details page* section of this chapter.

Entities with alerts

At the bottom of the screen are those entities that have the largest number of alerts. It shows how many alerts each entity has, as shown in the following screenshot. You can click on any of the entities to go to the details page for that entity:

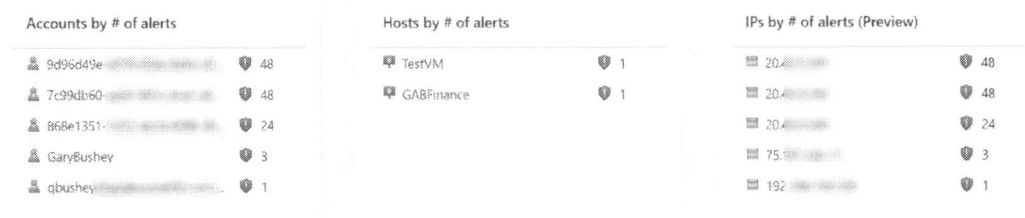

Figure 10.6 – Entities with alerts

Now that you have seen the different ways to find an entity to look at, let's look at how each one will look when viewing them.

Overview of the Entity behavior details page

No matter how you have selected the entity, the Entity behavior details page is where you will see all the information about that entity. Depending on what type of entity you have selected, the actual data will vary, but the page will follow the same format as the one shown in the following screenshot:

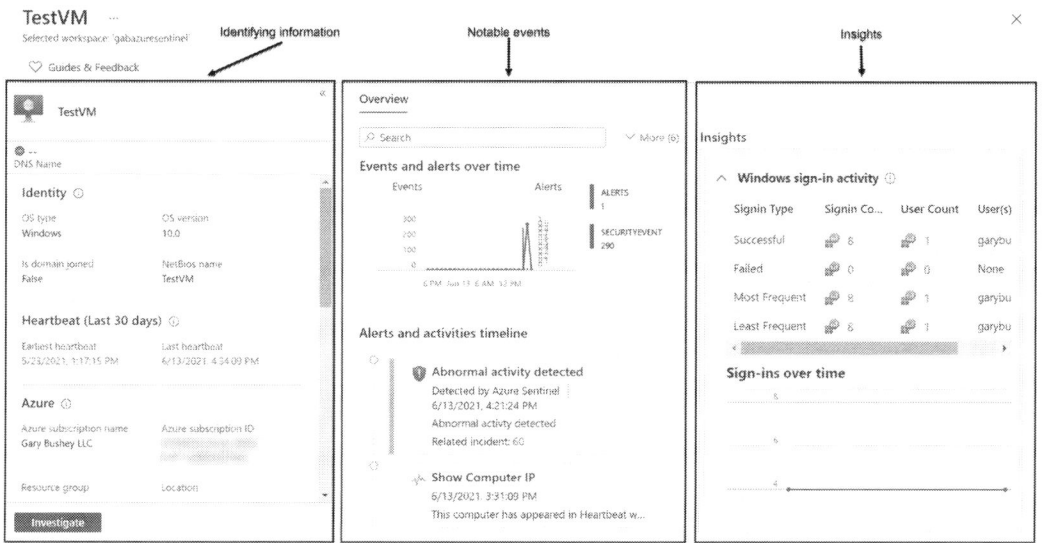

Figure 10.7 – Entity behavior details page

As you can see, there are three sections to this page, each of which will be described in more detail in the sections that follow.

Identifying information

This pane will show the data that can be used to identify the entity to make sure you have the correct entity and can gather more information about the entity.

Depending on the entity type, the data shown will vary, as will the source of the data. For instance, as shown in the preceding screenshot, the host type will show information regarding the OS, the last time its heartbeat was sent, as well as Azure-based information (if it is a VM hosted in Azure).

If the entity type is an account, there will be information from Azure Active Directory, including its email address and contact information. An IP address would show information including the geolocation data, log activity, and which hosts this IP address was connected to.

Regardless of what type of entity is being shown, they will all have an **Entity link**, which provides a link directly to this page with the entity already selected, as well as an **Investigate** button, which will take you into the graphical investigation portion, which is used for incidents. However, instead of having the incident shown with all its entities, the entity will be shown with all its alerts:

Figure 10.8 – Entity link and the Investigate button

As you can see, this section will provide a lot of information regarding the identity of the entity. Use this section to make sure that the entity you are viewing is the one that you want to investigate. You can also use it to determine which one you are looking at if you are coming in from any of the incident screens.

Notable events

This section is a major part of the entity's information. It will show not only the alerts that this incident is associated with but also other activities. As described in the next section, *Creating Entity behavior queries*, you can even add custom activity queries.

While the actual information shown will depend on the entity type being viewed, the format of the information will be the same. The following screenshot shows a detailed view of this section:

Figure 10.9 – Notable events

As you can see, this section is broken into three main subsections: the search and filter area, **Events and alerts over time**, and the **Alerts and activities timeline** subsection. Each subsection will be described in more detail in the following sections.

Search and filter subsection

This area allows you to search for a specific alert or action. In addition, you can filter the information that's shown using the various filters described in the following table:

Filter Name	Description
Time range	This allows you to specify what time range you want to use. When you click on it, you will be shown a pop-up window that will allow you to select what time range you want to use. This can be different from the time range that was selected on the main page.
Timeline content	This allows you to select which items to show on the timeline. The options are Security Alerts, Bookmarks, Activities, and Select All.
Alerts	Selecting this will allow you to filter which alerts to show. You can select the individual alert names to show or Select All to see all the alerts. Note that if this entity does not have any alerts, then this filter will be disabled.
Actions	Selecting this will allow you to filter which actions to show. You can select the individual action names to show or Select All to see all the alerts. Note that if this entity does not have any actions, then this filter will be disabled.
Alert Severity	Selecting this will allow you to filter which alert severities to show. You can select the individual severity names to show or Select All to see all the severities. Note that if this entity does not have any alerts, then this filter will be disabled.
Bucket size	Selecting this will allow you to change the bucket size that is used to group activities. This will determine how the various items are grouped.

Table 10.1

Let's now discuss about the other subsections.

Events and alerts over time subsection

This presents a timeline that shows how much activity this entity has had on certain tables over the selected time range. This works just like **Events and alerts over time**, which is shown on the **Microsoft Sentinel** overview page, but it just shows the information for the selected entity.

The actual table(s) displayed will depend on which entity is being viewed, as well as what data connectors are enabled.

Alerts and activities timeline subsection

This will show all the alerts, activities, and bookmarks that this entity belongs to unless they've been set to be hidden based on the filters described in the preceding sections. All the information will be presented in chronological order with the newest information at the top.

By looking at this information, you can get an idea of what has happened with this entity over time. In addition, if you click on either an **Alert** or a **Bookmark**, you will be taken to the **Logs** page and the query that was used to determine the item will be shown.

In addition, the alerts shown will provide a link to the incidents they are associated with. Clicking on that link will take you to the incident's full details page.

Insights

The **Insights** section shows those queries that have been defined by Microsoft security researchers to help you investigate the entities more efficiently and effectively. They provide valuable information on the hosts, users, and IP addresses and display this information through tables and charts.

These insights should help reduce the number of additional queries that would need to be run. This is another location where Microsoft Sentinel will utilize machine learning to help detect anomalous behavior.

That is the overview of the **Entity behavior details** page. This page can provide a lot of information in one location to make it easier to perform your investigations.

Next, we will look at how to create activity queries.

Creating Entity behavior queries

If you look back at *Figure 12.2*, you may notice that all the data sources you can select come from Microsoft sources. What if you are getting your data from other sources that are not listed or you want to query other Microsoft data? That is where the **Customize entity page** link from the main **Entity behavior** page comes into play.

> **Note**
> At the time of writing, this feature is in preview, so the features may have changed.

308   Configuring and Using Entity Behavior

Clicking on the **Customize entity page** button from the **Entity behavior** main page will take you to the **Entity Settings** page, as shown in the following screenshot:

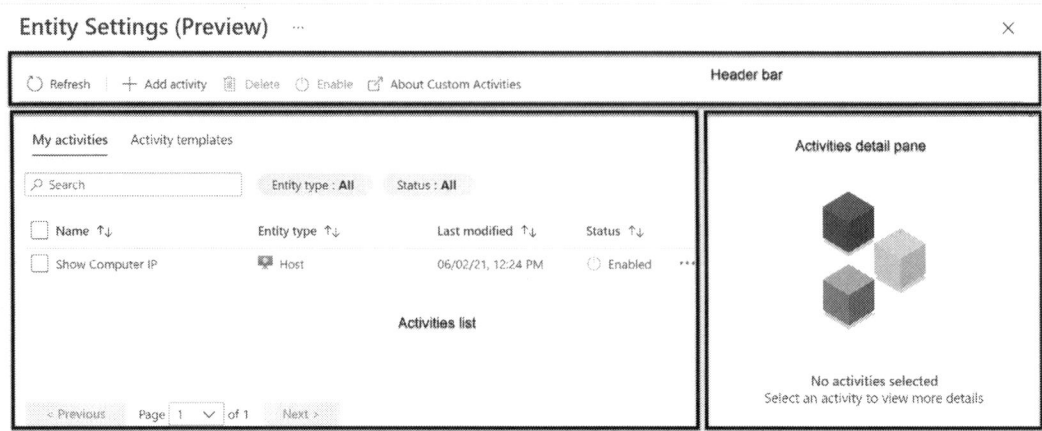

Figure 10.10 – Entity Settings page

The page is broken into three sections: the header bar, the activities list, and the activities detail pane. Each section will be described in the following sections.

Header bar

The header bar allows you to refresh the page, add a new activity, delete an activity, disable/enable an activity, and learn more about custom activities, as shown in the following screenshot:

Figure 10.11 – Entity Settings header bar

The **Refresh** button will allow you to refresh the page.

The **Add activity** button will start the new activity wizard. See the *Adding a new activity* section for more information.

The **Delete** button will delete the selected activity or activities. If none are selected, this button will be disabled.

The **Enable/Disable** button will enable a disabled activity or activities or disable enabled ones.

The **About Custom Activities** button will open a new tab in the browser and show a page that provides more information on how to add custom activities.

Activities list

This section is broken into two tabs. The **My activities** tab will show all those activities that you have created, while the **Activity templates** tab will show those activities that came with Microsoft Sentinel out of the box.

The main difference between the two tabs is the **My activities** tab, as shown in *Figure 12.10*, which will show the **Name**, **Entity type**, **Last modified**, and **Status** fields, as well as a context-sensitive menu that will allow you to edit, disable/enable, duplicate, or delete the activity.

The **Activity templates** tab, as shown in the following screenshot, will show the **Name**, **Entity type**, and **Data sources** fields; there is no context-sensitive menu here:

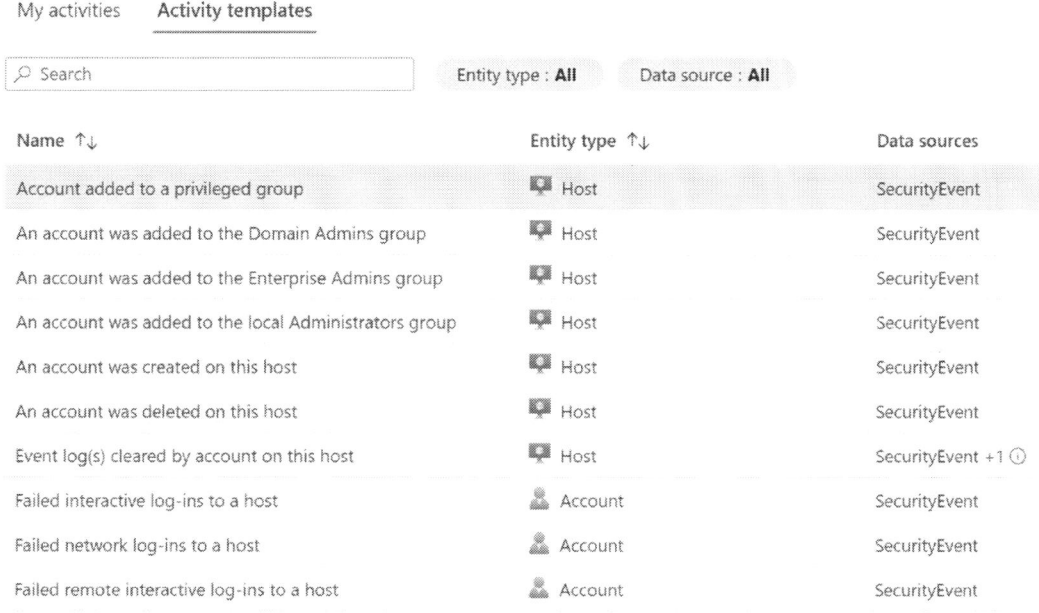

Figure 10.12 – Activity templates tab

Note that the filters will change, depending on the tab. The **My activities** tab will allow you to filter by **Entity type** and **Status**, while the **Activity templates** tab will allow you to filter by **Entity type** and **Data source**.

Clicking on any of the entries will populate the **Activity details** pane, as discussed next.

Activity details pane

This pane will show information about the activity and will allow you to edit a custom activity or create a custom activity from an out-of-the-box one. The following screenshot shows what the pane will look like when looking at a custom activity (left-hand side) as opposed to an out-of-the-box activity (right-hand side):

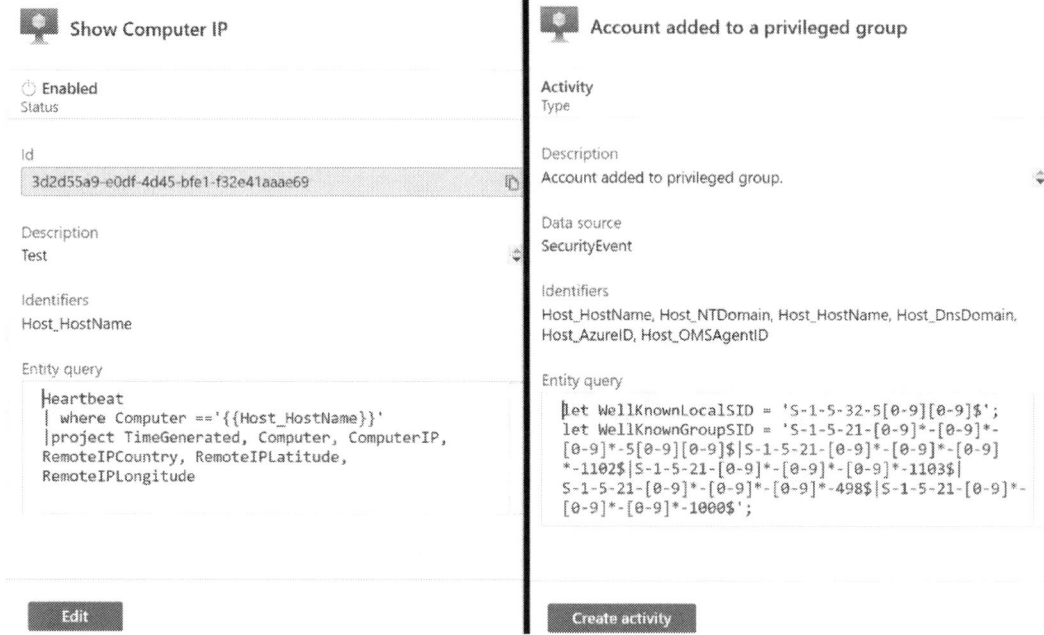

Figure 10.13 – Activity details pane

They both show a lot of the same information, including **Name**, **Description**, **Identifiers** (more on those later), and the query that is being used. However, the custom activity also shows the **Id** property, while the out-of-the-box activity shows the **Data source** property.

You can modify an existing activity by clicking on the **Edit** button. If you are looking at an out-of-the-box activity, you can create a custom activity by clicking on the **Create activity** button which, will start the **Activity wizard** window with a lot of the fields already filled in. See the *Adding a new activity* section for more details.

Here, you will see an overview of the **Entity Settings** page. It shows a lot of information regarding not just the out-of-the-box activities but also those that you have created.

Next, we will look at how to create a custom activity.

Adding a new activity

As we mentioned previously, there are two ways you can open the **Activity wizard** window. You can either click on the **Add activity** button from the header bar or you can click on the **Create activity** button when looking at an out-of-the-box activity. The only difference is that when you click on the **Create activity** button, the fields in the wizard will already be filled in.

Clicking either button will start the wizard. We will walk through creating a new activity from scratch since it will be easy to see how creating a new activity from an out-of-the-box activity will work.

General tab

The **General** tab of the wizard is where some of the basic information is filled in, as shown in the following screenshot:

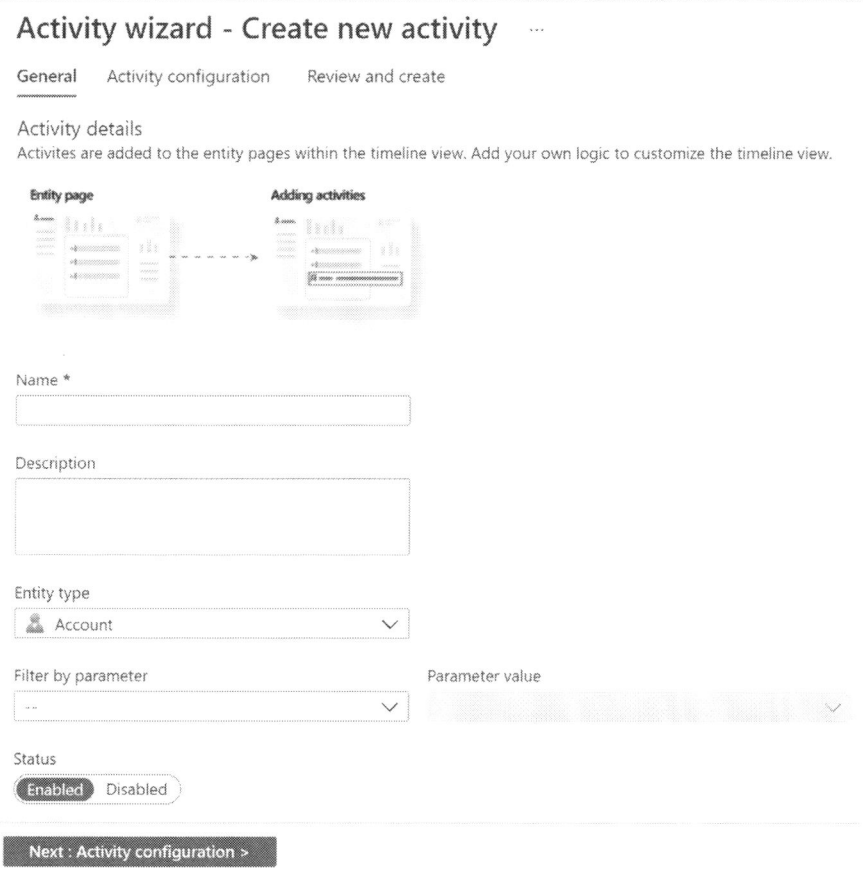

Figure 10.14 – Activity wizard – General tab

312　Configuring and Using Entity Behavior

This is the first tab of the wizard. It provides some basic information regarding the purpose of the wizard. You must also fill in the following fields:

- The **Name** field is where you enter the name of the custom activity. Make it descriptive enough that it gives someone a good idea of what this activity will do.
- The **Description** field can contain a more detailed description of this activity.
- The **Entity type** dropdown lists all the different entities that you can use when writing the custom activity. Currently, only **Account** and **Host** are available.
- The **Filter by parameter** dropdown allows you to filter the entity by an additional parameter. The list of parameters will vary, depending on which entity type was selected. If a parameter is selected, then the **Parameter value** dropdown will activate, and the available options will be listed.
- The **Status** field allows you to select whether the action is **Enabled** or **Disabled**.

Once you have entered all these values, click on the **Next: Activity configuration** button to go to the next page of the wizard.

Activity configuration

This page allows you to enter the query for your activity and other information, as shown in the following screenshot:

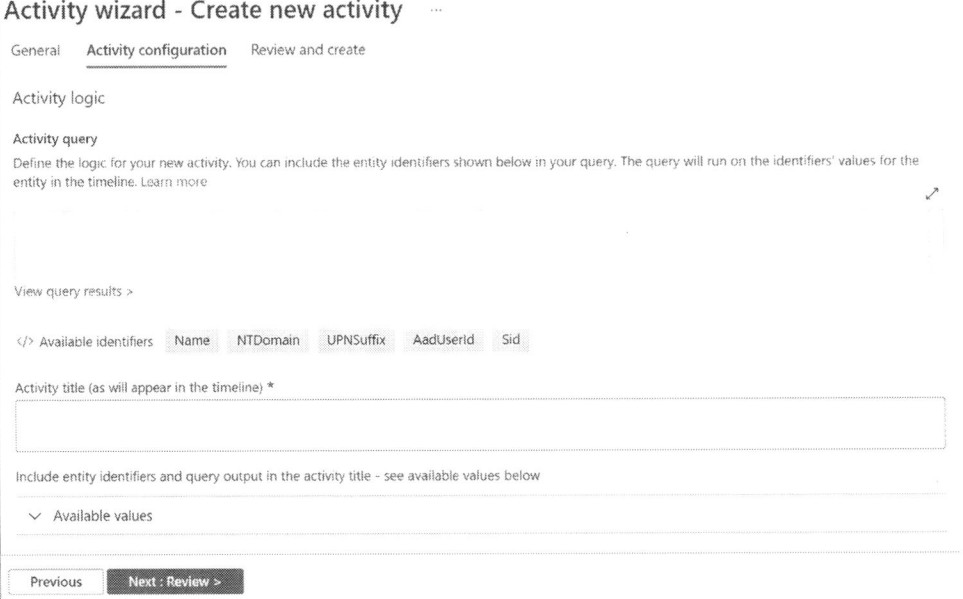

Figure 10.15 – Activity wizard – Activity configuration tab

Each field is described as follows.

Activity query is where you will enter the KQL query that this activity will be used for. This text box will provide information about the KQL you are entering, much like you were when working on the **Logs** page of Microsoft Sentinel. Notice at the top right-hand corner of the text box that there is an icon that looks like a double-headed arrow. Clicking on that will allow you to expand or contract this text box to make it easier to see all your code.

You will be using variables that get passed into the query to work against a specific entity. For instance, if I am writing an action to work against a Host entity type, I could write my query like so:

```
Heartbeat
| where Computer == '{{Host_HostName}}'
```

This investigates the `Heartbeat` table and filters by the current host entity. Notice that the variable is surrounded by { { and } }. This is used to designate the variable's name. You are not limited to just using one variable and, in many cases, you will have many different variables in your query.

Note that if you use this query, an error and a warning message will be displayed. The error message will tell you that you are only allowed to return a maximum of 10 columns from your query, so you should use the `project` command to filter your results.

> **Note**
> While the error message will say you are limited to 10 columns being returned, **TimeGenerated** must be one of them, so you technically only have nine columns that you can choose to return.

The warning will say that the identifier you have chosen is weak and that you should consider using additional identifiers to ensure the reliability of the results. You can use the query with just the identifier you have selected if you so choose but the results may not be accurate.

If you look below the **Activity query** text box, you will see a line of text that lists the available identifiers. This listing will be different, depending on which entity type you selected on the previous screen.

Since, in this example, the Host entity type was selected, the available values are **Name**, **NTDomain**, **UPNSuffix**, **AadUserId**, and **Sid**. Clicking any of these entries will add the appropriate code to the **Activity query** text box, making it much easier to create your queries.

Directly underneath the **Activity query** text box is the **View query results** link. Clicking on that will take you to the **Logs** page, with the query filled and automatically running. This can be useful to test your queries but remember that the variables will not be filled in, so no data will be returned when running the query as-is.

Activity title will allow you to enter the title that you want to appear in the timeline. One great feature of this is that you can use the variables that have been returned from your query in the title. Keep in mind that you are limited to 10 columns being returned (as per the error message we discussed previously), so determine which columns you will want to use in your title when writing your query.

Looking under **Activity title**, which can be expanded or collapsed, is a subsection called **Available values**. Clicking on it will show the fields that you can use, as shown in the following screenshot. These fields will be taken from the query you have entered, so the actual entries will be different. Other variables will be available as well, including the identifiers you can use in your query, some different time fields, and a count of the number of results. You can click on the **Copy to clipboard** icon (which looks like two sheets of paper) on the right of each value so that you can then paste them into the **Activity title** text box. The actual value of the variable will be filled in when the activity is displayed in the timeline:

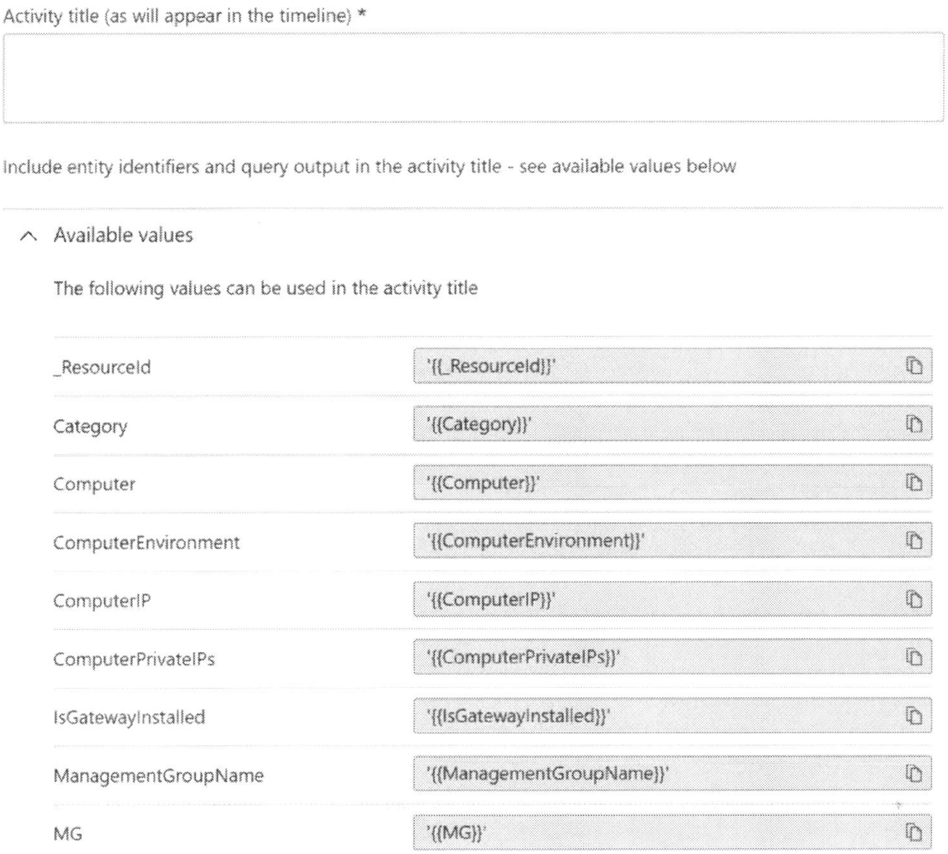

Activity title (as will appear in the timeline) *

Include entity identifiers and query output in the activity title - see available values below

∧ Available values

The following values can be used in the activity title

_ResourceId	'{{_ResourceId}}'
Category	'{{Category}}'
Computer	'{{Computer}}'
ComputerEnvironment	'{{ComputerEnvironment}}'
ComputerIP	'{{ComputerIP}}'
ComputerPrivateIPs	'{{ComputerPrivateIPs}}'
IsGatewayInstalled	'{{IsGatewayInstalled}}'
ManagementGroupName	'{{ManagementGroupName}}'
MG	'{{MG}}'

Figure 10.16 – Activity wizard | Available values

Once you have filled in all the fields in this tab, click on the **Next: Review** button to review your choices.

316   Configuring and Using Entity Behavior

On this tab, all the values you have entered will be reviewed to make sure there are no errors. If there are none, you will see a screen like the following. In this case, everything was entered correctly, so a message at the top of the screen will inform you of that fact and the **Create** button will be activated:

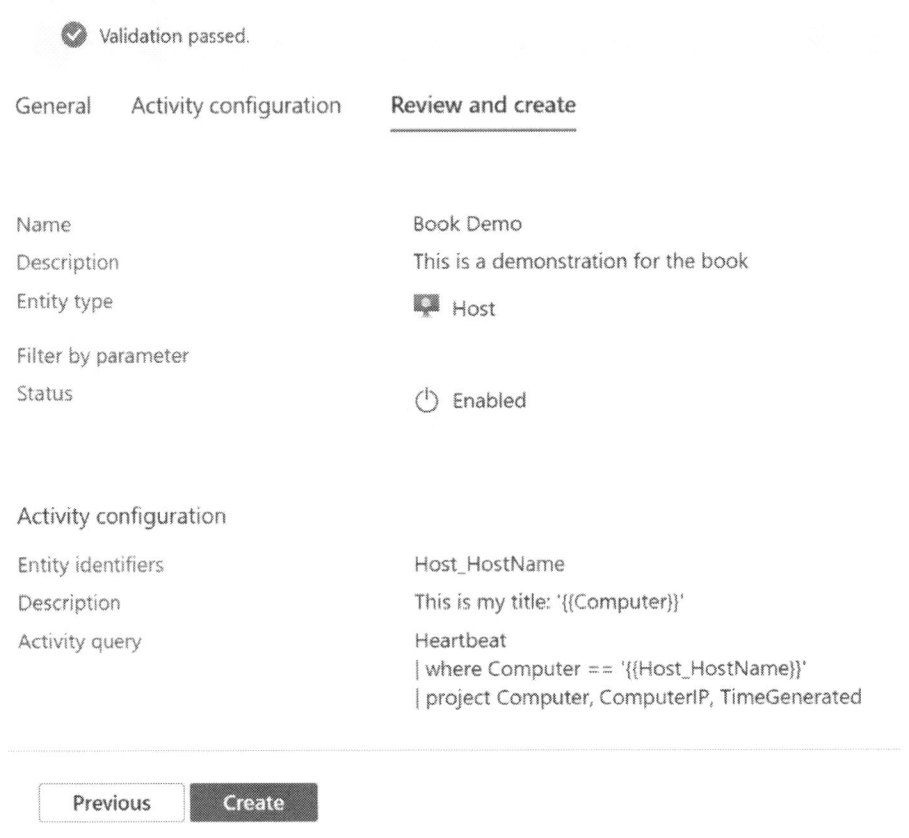

Figure 10.17 – Activity wizard – Review and create – good entries

If there are any errors, the message at the top of the screen will state that there is an error and the **Create** button will be disabled. You will need to go back and review your entries to see where any errors may have occurred. It will likely be in the query itself, as shown in the following screenshot. Notice that there is no `project` command to limit the number of columns being returned:

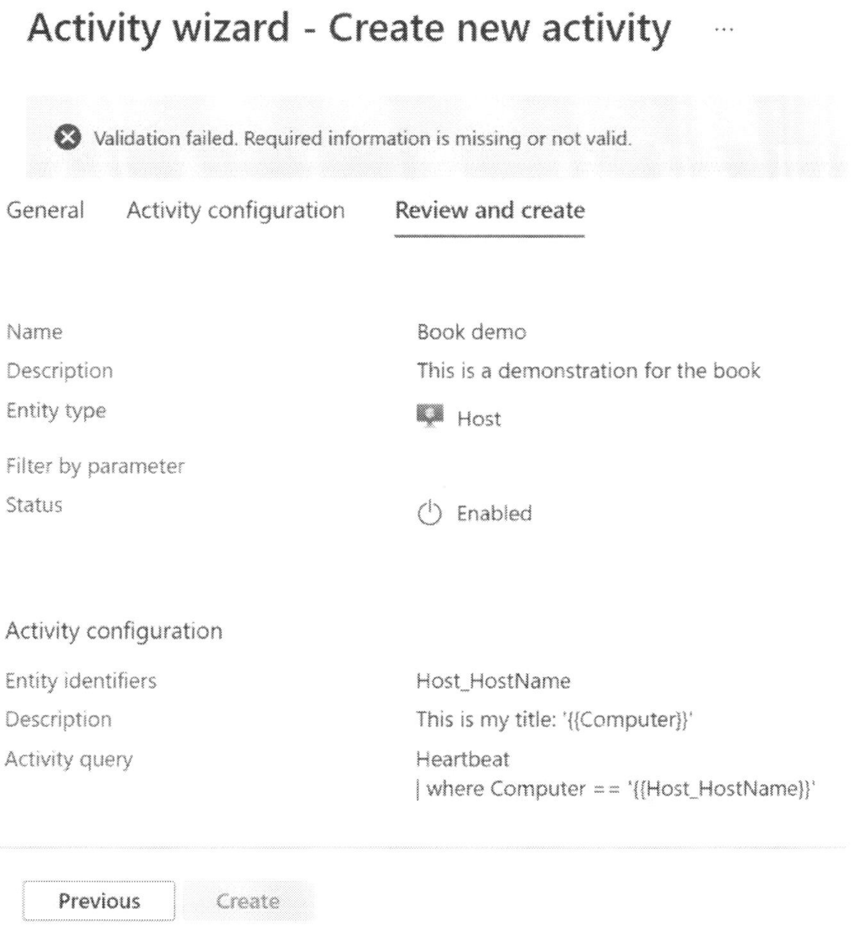

Figure 10.18 – Activity wizard – Review and create – bad entries

Once everything is ready to go, click on the **Create** button to create your new activity. Again, the only difference between creating a new activity from scratch and one from an existing out-of-the-box template is that when you're doing this from a template, the fields will already be filled in for you.

With that, you know all about Microsoft Sentinel's Entity behavior and how to use it. This will make your investigations much easier in the future.

Summary

In this chapter, you learned how to activate and configure Microsoft Sentinel's Entity behavior functionality. You learned how to view information when looking at an entity and the different ways to find the entities to view. You also learned how to write activities to use in your investigations.

With what you have learned, you can now perform investigations using entities quickly and easily. You can use the out-of-the-box activities, plus the ones you have written, to get detailed information about your entities.

In the next chapter, you will learn about the operational tasks you must perform to keep your Microsoft Sentinel instance running smoothly.

Questions

Answer the following questions to test your knowledge of this chapter:

1. What three types of entities can be viewed in Entity behavior?
2. What are the three types of information that can be presented in the entity's timeline?
3. If I am looking at an entity and only want to see its activities, how would I do that?
4. In which two ways can I create a custom activity?
5. What are the two entity types that can be used to create a custom activity?

Further reading

Please refer to the following links for more information on the topics that were covered in this chapter:

- *Enable User and Entity Behavior Analytics (UEBA) in Microsoft Sentinel*: `https://docs.microsoft.com/en-us/azure/sentinel/identify-threats-with-entity-behavior-analytics`
- *Microsoft Sentinel UEBA enrichments reference*: `https://docs.microsoft.com/en-us/azure/sentinel/ueba-enrichments`
- *Customize activities on entity page timelines*: `https://docs.microsoft.com/en-us/azure/sentinel/customize-entity-activities`
- *Microsoft Sentinel entity types reference*: `https://docs.microsoft.com/en-us/azure/sentinel/entities-reference`

11
Threat Hunting in Microsoft Sentinel

Threat hunting is part science, part art, and part intuition. Usually, you are looking for something that may have happened in your environment. It may be that you think something has happened due to external events, such as something odd showing up in the workbooks, a notice from a threat intelligence feed, or even something you just read about on the internet, and you want to investigate. No matter what the reason is for performing your hunt, the tools in Microsoft Sentinel, including queries and the **Jupyter Notebook**, remain the same.

Threat hunting is a series of activities that you will perform during your investigation. While there is no set guidance on how to perform threat hunting, this chapter will introduce you to the tools that are available in Microsoft Sentinel to help you perform your investigations.

A brief introduction on how to perform threat hunting activities will also be discussed, which will include aspects such as how to determine where to look for information. The cyclic process of threat hunting will be introduced as well.

In this chapter, we will cover the following topics:

- Introducing the Microsoft Sentinel Hunting page
- Working with Microsoft Sentinel hunting queries
- Working with livestream
- Working with bookmarks
- Using Microsoft Sentinel notebooks
- Performing a hunt

Introducing the Microsoft Sentinel Hunting page

To access the **Microsoft Sentinel | Hunting** page, select the **Hunting** link in the Microsoft Sentinel navigation menu. This will show the **Microsoft Sentinel | Hunting** page, which will look like the following screenshot:

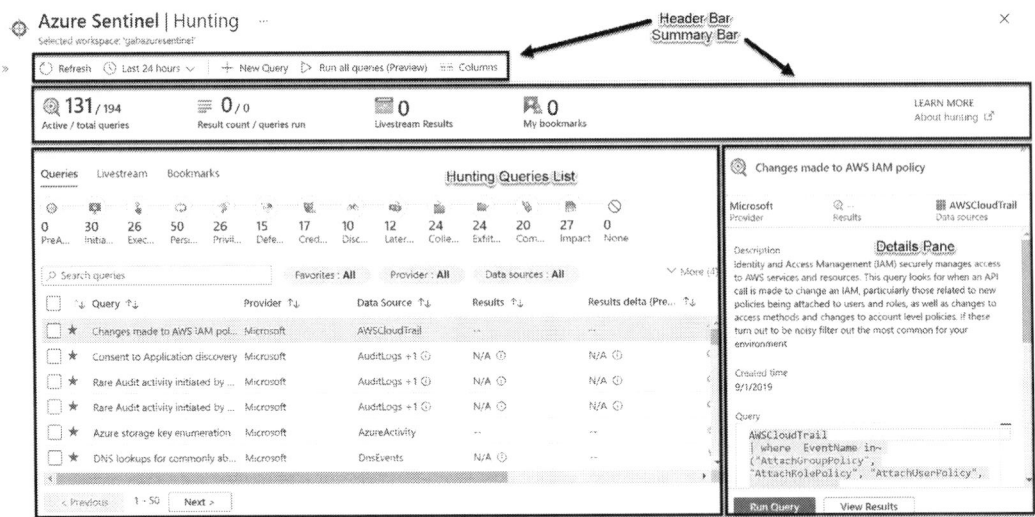

Figure 11.1 – Hunting page overview

Each of these sections will be described in more detail in the following sections.

The header bar

The header bar, at the top of the page, has the usual **Refresh** button and timespan dropdown. There is also a **New Query** button that will allow you to create a new query (refer to the *Adding a new query* section for more information). The header bar can be seen in the following screenshot:

◯ Refresh   ◯ Last 24 hours ∨ | ＋ New Query   ▷ Run all queries (Preview)   ☰ Columns

Figure 11.2 – Hunting page's header bar

Next, we have the **Run all queries (Preview)** button. This button will run all the hunting queries in the background and will then update the hunting query list section with the number of results found. This is easier than running each query one after another. You can also select which queries you want to run; in which case the button will be relabeled to read **Run selected queries (Preview)** and will only run those queries you have selected.

> **Important Note**
> If you have read the first edition of this book, you may have noticed that this button used to be **Run all queries**. The reason this is now called a preview feature is that between the time the first edition was released and when this edition was being written, this button was changed to only run those queries that are shown on the page, so you would have to go to the next page if you wanted to run the fifty-first query. Due to overwhelming customer demand, this has recently been changed back to run all queries. You can also select just the ones you want to run.

There is also the **Columns** button, which will allow you to select or unselect which columns you want to see. Keep in mind that, depending on the number of columns you select, you will need to scroll to the right to see some of them.

The available choices are as follows:

Name	Description
Favorites	The star icon determines whether this is a favorite, in which case it will be filled in, or not, and only the outline will show. Favorites will also appear first in the listing of queries.
Query	This is the title of the query and not the KQL query.
Provider	This is who provided the query. This will typically be either Microsoft or Custom Queries.
Created By	This is who wrote the query. It will either contain the name (or email) of the person who created the custom threat hunting query or be blank if it was provided by Microsoft.
Created Time	The date and time the query was created.
Entities	This will show which entities the query will provide.
Data Source	This will list the data source that this query requires. If there is more than one data source required, the first one will be listed along with a number telling you how many more data sources there are. You can mouse over the information icon, which looks like an i inside a circle, to see the other data sources.
Results	If the query has not yet been run, this will show two dashes to indicate that. If it has been run, it will either show the number of results returned or N/A if it was unable to run due to missing data sources.
Results delta (preview)	This will show the delta between the results from the current run of the queries and the results from the last run of the queries.
Tactics	This will show the MITRE ATT&CK® tactics that this query uses.
Techniques (preview)	This will show the MITRE techniques that this query uses. Note that these will only show up for Microsoft-provided queries, as there is no way to select these when creating your own queries.

Table 11.1

The header bar shows the links needed to start your query. It also can change what information the threat hunting screen shows by showing or hiding specific columns.

The summary bar

The summary bar shows the total number of queries that are active and the number that are available to run, the total number of queries that have results and the total number of queries run, the total number of livestream results (refer to the *Working with livestream* section for more information), the total number of bookmarks that you have (refer to the *Working with bookmarks* section for more information), and, on the far right, a link to learn more about threat hunting, as shown in the following screenshot:

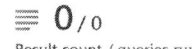

LEARN MORE
About hunting

Figure 11.3 – Hunting page's summary bar

You may have noticed in the previous screenshot that while there are 194 queries in total, only 131 are listed as active. This is due to the Microsoft Sentinel environment where this screenshot was captured not having all the needed tables for the queries to run.

The hunting queries list

Below the header is a listing of all the hunting queries. At the top of the listing is the MITRE ATT&CK® breakdown. Clicking on any of the icons in the MITRE ATT&CK® breakdown will show you only those queries that have that specific attack type associated with them. So, if you click on the **Initial Access** icon (the first icon that looks like a monitor), it will only show those hunting queries that have **Initial Access** as one of their entries in the **Tactics** field.

The summary bar gives you a good overview of how your hunting queries are broken down. This can make it easier to find those queries that you need in your investigations.

> **Important Note**
> You can visit `https://attack.mitre.org/tactics/enterprise/` to learn more about MITRE ATT&CK®.

Below that is the search and filtering section. This works like other pages' search and filtering sections, so it will not be described in detail here. Refer to the *Search and filtering* section in *Chapter 9*, *Incident Management*, for a refresher on how this works.

Each row will show a star icon that shows whether it is a favorite. If it is a favorite query, the star will be selected; otherwise, it is not. Another benefit of making a query a favorite is that each time you visit the **Hunting** page, the favorite queries will automatically run.

Each row will also list the name of the query, where it came from, the first data source that is required (note that in the following screenshot, the *more information* icon was shown with the mouse placed on it to display what the tooltip would look like if there are multiple data sources required), the number of results found for the query, the results delta, any of the MITRE ATT&CK® tactics selected for this query, and then the MITRE techniques, as follows:

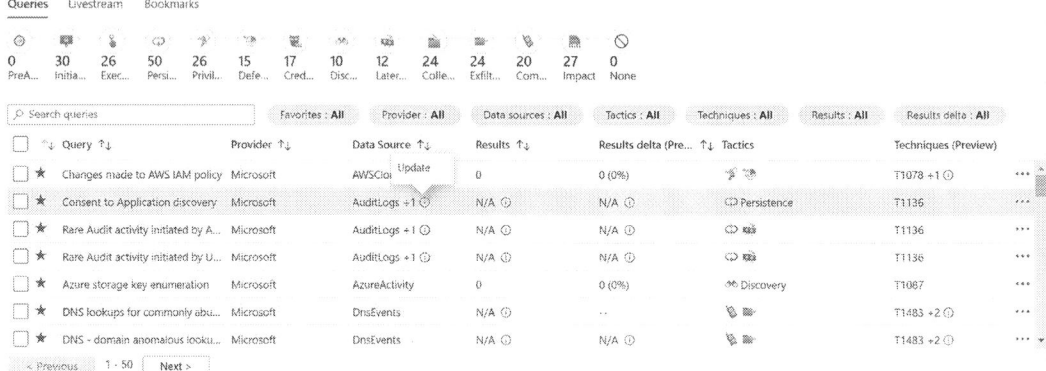

Figure 11.4 – Hunting queries list

You can look at the table in the *The header bar* section above to see what other columns may be shown and their purpose.

At the very end, on the right-hand side, is the context-sensitive menu, where you can run the query, add/remove the query to your **FAVORITES** list, edit the query (if you created it), clone the query (so that you can edit it), delete the query (again, if you created it), add the query to Livestream, and create an analytics rule from the query. Refer to the *Working with Microsoft Sentinel Hunting queries* section for more information.

This covers all the fields of the **Microsoft Sentinel | Hunting** page. As you saw, you can learn a lot about each hunting query from here. However, there is more information pertaining to queries, and you will read about that in the next section.

Hunting query details pane

When you select any query from the list, the hunting query details pane will open the query and will show more information about it. Naturally, the information shown will depend on which query was selected. An example can be seen in the following screenshot:

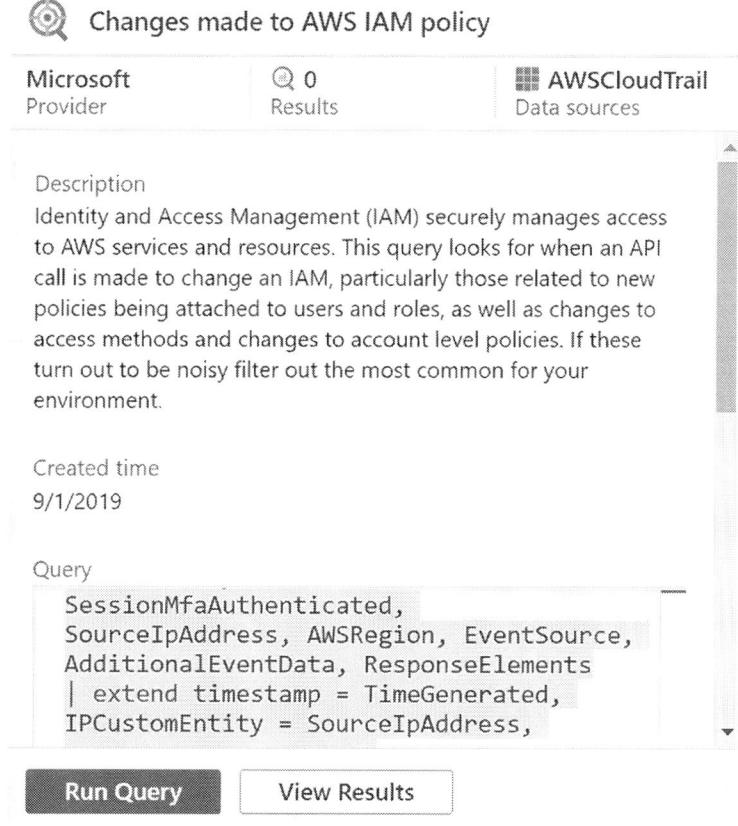

Figure 11.5 – Hunting query details pane

At the very top of the page is the title of the query. Immediately under that is the name of who wrote the query. In this case, it is **Microsoft**, but if it is a query that you created, it will say **Custom Queries**. Next to that is the number of results for this query. On the right of that is the first data source that this query is using. If there is more than one data source for this query, you will need to hover your mouse over the *more information* icon to see them, as shown in *Figure 11.4*. Under that is the description of the query. This will provide you with information about how the query works and what it is looking for.

Under the **Description** field is the **Created time** field, which will tell you when this query was created. For any of the queries that came with Microsoft Sentinel, this will be when this Microsoft Sentinel instance was created.

The **Query** field will show the **Kusto Query Language** (**KQL**) query that this query will run. Under this is a link called **View query results** (not shown), which will take you to the **Logs** page and run this query. Refer to *Chapter 6, Microsoft Sentinel Logs and Writing Queries*, for more information on the **Logs** page:

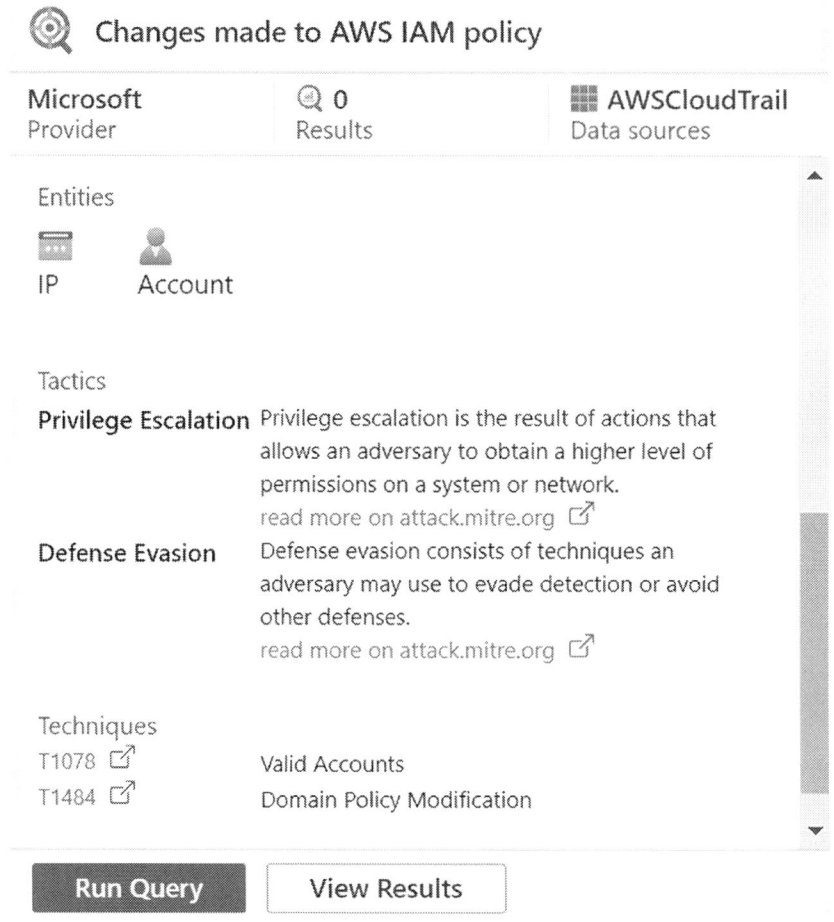

Figure 11.6 – Hunting query details pane (continued)

By scrolling, you will find more fields, as shown in the preceding screenshot. There is a listing of **Entities** that will be filled in when this query is run.

> **Important Note**
> If there are no entities, this section will not appear at all.

Under that is the **Tactics** section, which will provide more details about each tactic that is associated with this query, as well as a link to get more information on the tactics. If there are none, this section will not appear at all.

Finally, there is a section for **Techniques** that are associated with this query. Clicking on one of the techniques will open a new page with a description of the technique in question.

At the bottom of the details page are the **Run Query** and **View Results** buttons. The **Run Query** button will run the query in the background and will show the number of results in the **Hunting Queries listing** section. The **View Results** button will work just like the **View query results** link described earlier.

Now that you have seen the various parts of the **Hunting** page, let's look at the hunting queries that you can run to start your investigation.

Working with Microsoft Sentinel hunting queries

While there are a lot of pre-existing queries, with more being added all the time, there may be times when you need to add your own or modify an existing query to better suit your needs.

Adding a new query

To add a new query, click on the **New Query** button at the top of the **Hunting** page. This will open the **Create custom query** page, as shown in the following screenshot. This is very similar to creating a new scheduled query, as discussed in *Chapter 7, Creating Analytic Rules*, so you can read the *Creating a new rule using the wizard* section as a refresher:

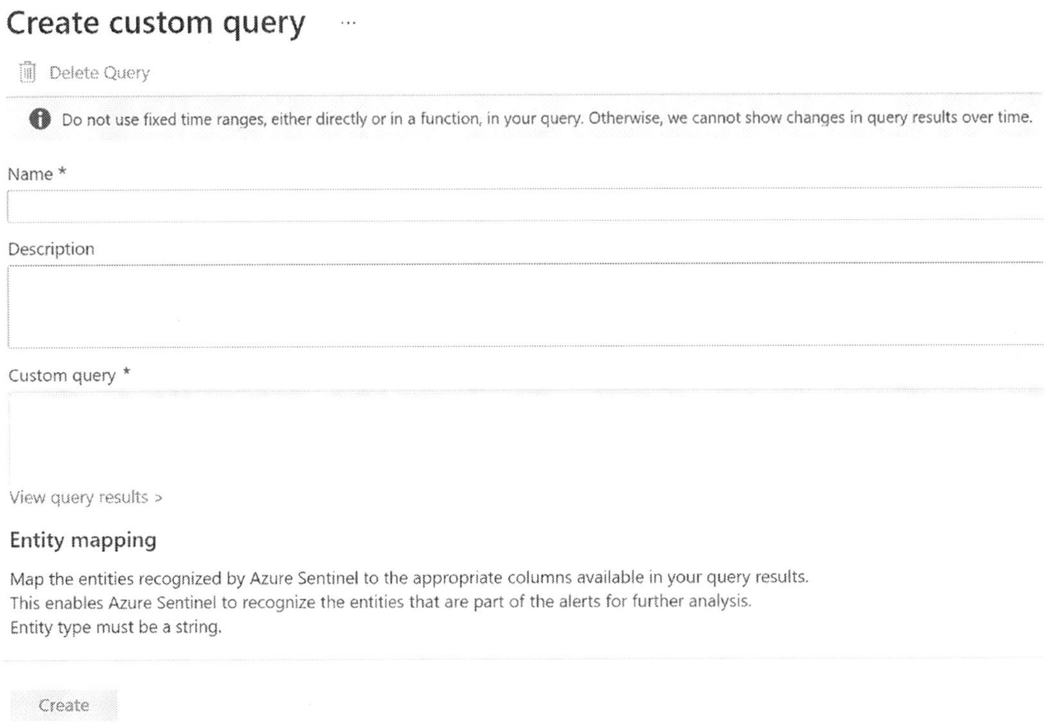

Figure 11.7 – Adding a new query

Fill in the **Name**, **Description**, and **Custom query** fields. If your query has any entities, use the **Entity mapping** section to add the entity mapping to the query. Remember to add them one at a time. Finally, select one or more tactics (not shown in the screenshot) that this query is using.

> **Important Note**
> At the time of writing this chapter, there is no place to enter or select MITRE techniques. These are only available with out-of-the-box hunting queries.

Once all the information has been filled in, click on the **Create** button to create the new query.

Now that you have added a new query, what happens if you need to make a change to it? The next section talks about editing a query and will answer that very question.

Editing a query

If a query is not working quite as you expect, or you want to update information about the query, you can edit it to make the needed changes.

To edit a query, click on the context-sensitive menu (denoted by the three periods at the far right of the line) to the right of the query's name in the **Query** list and select **Edit Query**, as shown in the following screenshot:

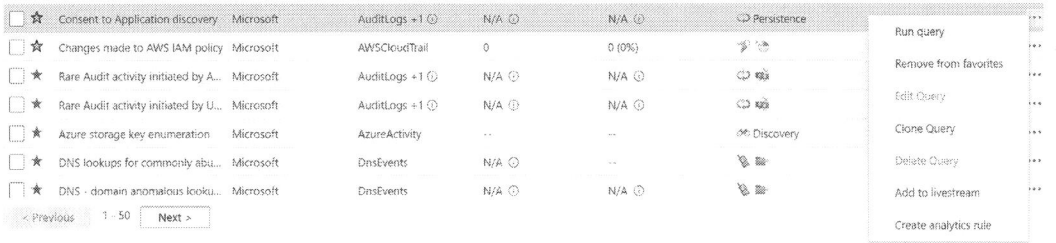

Figure 11.8 – Context-sensitive menu

This will bring up the same page that was shown in *Figure 11.7*, when adding a query was discussed earlier. Make the necessary changes and click on **Save** to save your changes.

You can always click on the **X** in the upper right-hand corner of the window to close the window without saving any changes. If you have made any changes, you will be prompted for verification that you want to close the window without saving your changes.

Now you know how you can change a query as needed. What if you want to make a new one and change the new one? You can clone the query, as described in the next section.

Cloning a query

You may have noticed that you cannot edit a pre-existing query. If you need to modify a pre-existing query, you will need to clone it first to make a custom query, and then change the new custom query.

To clone a query, click on the context-sensitive menu, as shown in the previous section, and click **Clone Query**. This will open the same window that is shown when adding a new query, and all the fields will be filled in with the same information that the original query has, except for the **Name** field.

The **Name** field will be filled in with the name of the original query but will have `Copy of` prepended to the name. This is done so that there are not two queries with the same name, which can lead to confusion, although there is nothing to prevent you from having multiple queries with the same name.

When you have made all the necessary changes, click the **Create** button to create the new query.

At this point, you can add a new query, edit a query, and create clones of the queries. You may find that some of the queries are no longer needed, and so you may want to get rid of them. The next section will tell you how to delete queries that are no longer needed.

Deleting a query

If you need to delete a query, click on the context-sensitive menu, and select **Delete**. This will bring up a pop-up window, asking you to verify that you want to delete the query. Click on **Yes** to delete it.

Now you know how to work with individual hunting queries. Running these queries can be the first step of your investigation. But what if you want to constantly run these queries? This will be discussed in the next section.

Adding to Livestream

This will allow you to add a query to a Livestream. See the next section for more information.

Creating an analytics rule

This will allow you to create an analytics rule from the query. See *Chapter 7*, *Creating Analytic Rules*, for more information.

The next section will discuss working with livestream, a new feature that allows you to watch the results of a query in real time.

Working with livestream

Livestream is a new feature for Microsoft Sentinel that will allow you to watch one or more hunting queries in real time, to see new results as they occur. This can be useful when performing an investigation and watching whether a query has any new results without having to constantly rerun the query.

Looking back at *Figure 11.8*, the last entry in the context menu is called **Add to livestream**. Selecting this will add the query to the Livestream window, as follows:

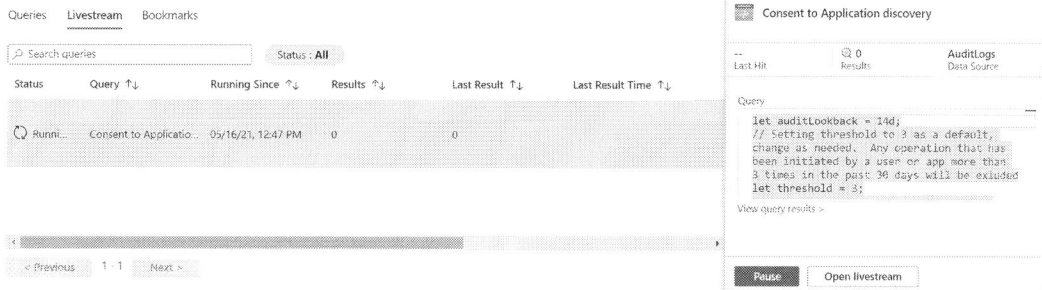

Figure 11.9 – Adding a query to Livestream

For each livestream that has been added, you can see its status, the query name, how long it has been running, how many results have been found, what the last result was, the time that the last result occurred, and a sparkline showing how many results were found along the timeline (not shown).

Clicking on each livestream will show the details pane where you get information about the query, including the full KQL code and the ability to view the query results as if you were running it from the **Queries** tab. At the bottom of this pane is the **Pause** button, which will pause a running livestream or, if it is paused, play the livestream, and the **Open livestream** button.

Clicking the **Open livestream** button will open the **Livestream** window. Here, you can start or stop the query, promote it to an alert rule, modify the query, and see the results, as shown in the following screenshot:

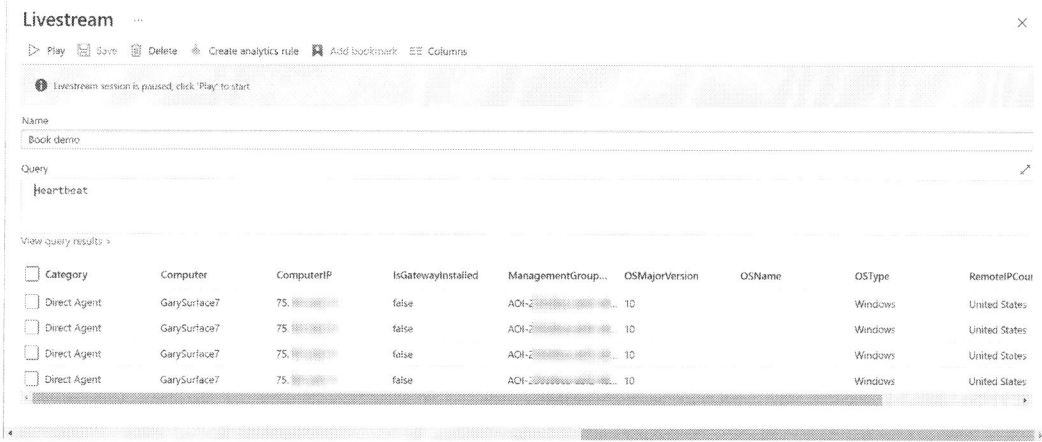

Figure 11.10 – Livestream page

At the top of the screen is the header bar where you perform actions against the livestream. You can play or pause the livestream, save the livestream, delete it, create analytics from the livestream, save any selected results as bookmarks, and show or hide the columns that the query returns.

At the bottom of the screen are all the results that have been added since the query started running. The columns that are displayed will depend on the query that is being run.

Adding a query to the **Livestream** and enabling it causes that query to be run every minute. If the query runs and the display increments, it means that a potential threat is active. Additionally, you can move away from the **Livestream** tab, and it will continue running. You will be notified through the Azure console notification system as new artifacts are incrementing during the **Livestream** session. You can also select the individual rows of the results and add them as bookmarks, which will be described in the next section.

Adding queries to **Livestream** can be a very useful tool to watch what is happening in your environment in almost real time. By watching one or more queries, you will get to see the results show up when they happen.

In the next section, we will discuss bookmarks, which allow you to save the results from queries and associate them with an incident, to assist you further with your investigations.

Working with bookmarks

While carrying out investigations, there may be times when you need to keep track of the results from previously run queries. It could be that you need to work on another project and will come back to this investigation later, or another user will be taking over the investigation. You may also need to keep certain results as evidence of an incident. In any case, using a bookmark will allow you to save this information for later.

Creating a bookmark

To create a new bookmark, you must run a query from the **Logs** page – refer to *Chapter 6, Microsoft Sentinel Logs and Writing Queries*, or, as we just saw, from the results of a livestream. While on the **Hunting** page, clicking the **Viewing Results** button in the query's details pane will open the **Logs** page, showing your results, as follows:

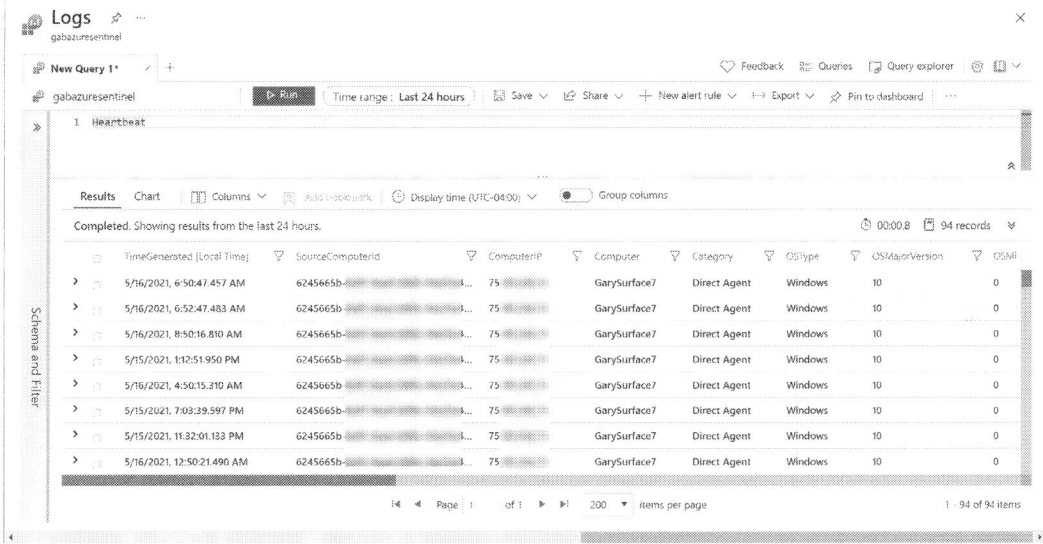

Figure 11.11 – Viewing query results

You may have noticed that there are checkboxes to the left of each result. To create a new bookmark, select one or more checkboxes. When at least one checkbox has been selected, the **Add bookmark** link will be enabled in the result's header bar.

When you click on **Add bookmark**, a new blade will open, as shown in the following screenshot (the actual title of the blade will be different if you select one checkbox instead of multiple checkboxes):

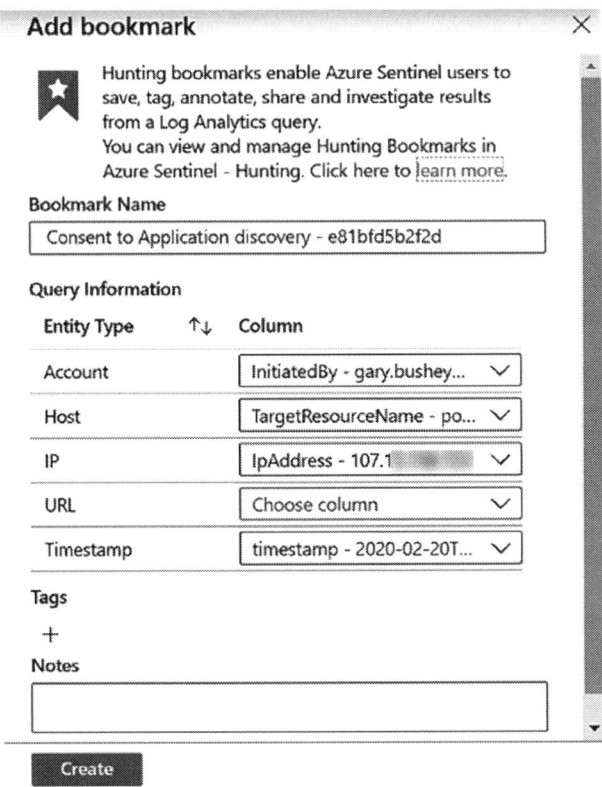

Figure 11.12 – Adding a bookmark blade

The **Bookmark Name** will be filled in with the name of the query, followed by a random 12-digit hexadecimal number so that if you create multiple bookmarks from the same query, they will each have a unique name. Below that is a list of all the available entities. If the query has any entities associated with it, they will be filled in. Of course, you can fill in any of the entities manually.

Add any **Tags** and **Notes** that are needed. When adding **Notes**, make sure they provide enough information so that when you or someone else comes back to this bookmark, it will be easy to understand what is going on. Enter any **Tags** that will be useful to filter to find the various bookmarks when needed.

Click **Create** to create the bookmark when all the fields have been filled in.

> **Important Note**
> If you select multiple checkboxes when creating a bookmark, the first bookmark created will follow the naming convention stated earlier. For the rest, a new bookmark will be created for each selected result, and the **Name** will have (x) appended to it, where x is the copy number of the bookmark. For example, if there are four checkboxes selected and the bookmark name was set to Test Bookmark - 123456789012, then the first bookmark will have that name; the second will be named Test Bookmark - 123456789012 (1), the third will be named Test Bookmark - 123456789012 (2), and the fourth will be named Test Bookmark- 123456789012 (3). This way, you can easily tell which bookmarks were created together.

It is very easy to add bookmarks when you are performing your queries. In the next section, we will discuss how to use them.

Viewing bookmarks

If you go back to the **Hunting** main page, you will see that there is a **Bookmarks** tab above the listing of all the queries. Clicking it will change the page to show the **Bookmarks** tab, as illustrated in the following screenshot:

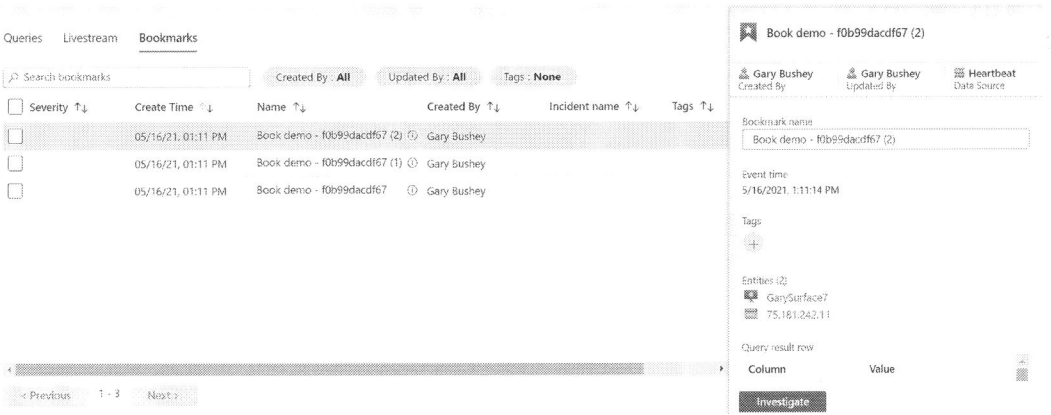

Figure 11.13 – Bookmarks tab

When a bookmark is selected, the details pane is opened on the right, showing more information about the bookmark, as illustrated in the following screenshot:

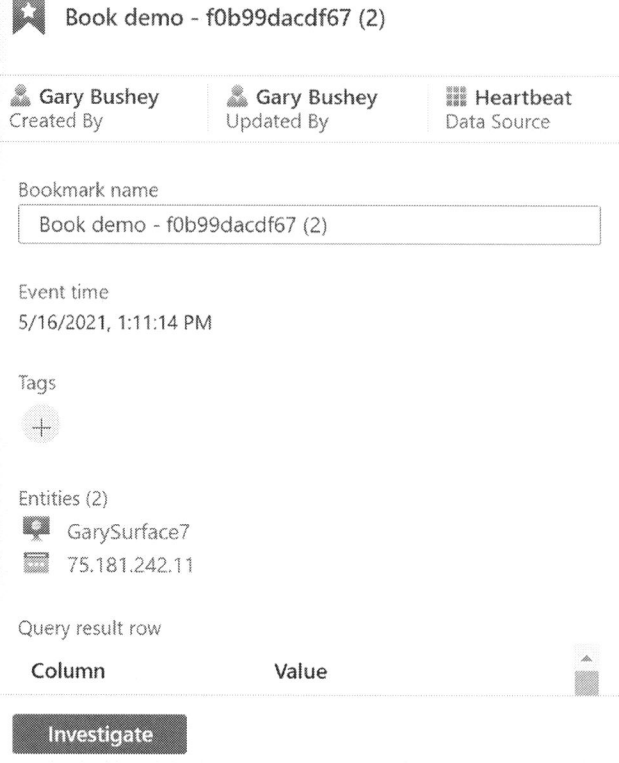

Figure 11.14 – Bookmark details pane

At the top of the page is the bookmark's name, and under that is who created it, who last updated it, and the data source used by the query that created the bookmark, or the first data source if there were multiple data sources.

Below that is another field that contains the bookmark name. This field is editable, so if you want to change the bookmark's name, you can make the changes here. Once you leave the field, the new change will be automatically applied, or press the *Enter* key to save the data without leaving the field.

Under that is the time the result was created, any tags associated with the bookmark, and the entities that are associated with this bookmark. You can click on a host, IP, or account entities to get more information about them. Refer to *Chapter 10, Configuring and Using Entity Behavior*, for more information.

Scrolling down, you will see additional fields, as shown in the following figure:

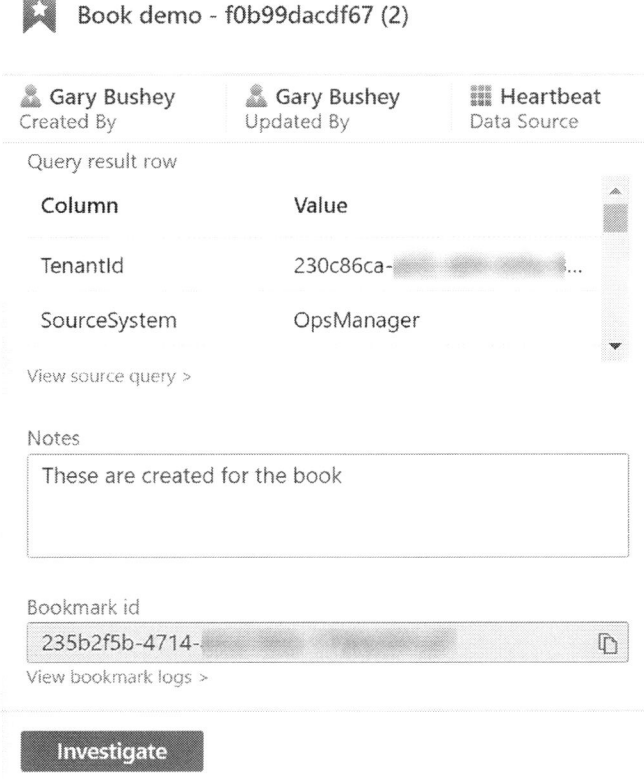

Figure 11.15 – Bookmark details pane (continued)

Under that is the **Query result row**, which contains the values for all the columns displayed for the query result. You will need to scroll down to see all the fields. Directly under that is a link called **View source query**, which will allow you to view the source query itself. The text for this link is in a very small font, so it is easy to miss.

There is also the **Notes** section, where you can add any notes that you need to. This is an editable field, and any changes you make in this field will automatically be updated when you leave the field, or press *Enter* to save the changes without leaving the field.

After that is the bookmark's internal ID, with a link to view the bookmark log for this query so that you can view the history of the bookmark. This will include items such as the creation of the bookmark, any changes to the bookmark's name, and when notes were added. Since there is nothing on the screen that tells you when notes were added or updated, this is a useful feature for determining when actions were performed against the bookmark.

> **Important Note**
> You may see a message stating **Investigation cannot be used to investigate this bookmark because some of the data related to this bookmark is no longer stored**. This can occur if the results that were stored in a bookmark have been deleted due to your data retention policy. Refer to *Chapter 2, Azure Monitor – Introduction to Log Analytics*, for information on setting your data retention policy.

At the bottom of the screen is the **Investigate** button, which will only be enabled if there is at least one entity with a value. Clicking the button will open the investigation screen, which was described in detail in *Chapter 9, Incident Management*.

There is one change to the **Investigate** screen; since you are working with bookmarks rather than incidents, the main icon will look as follows:

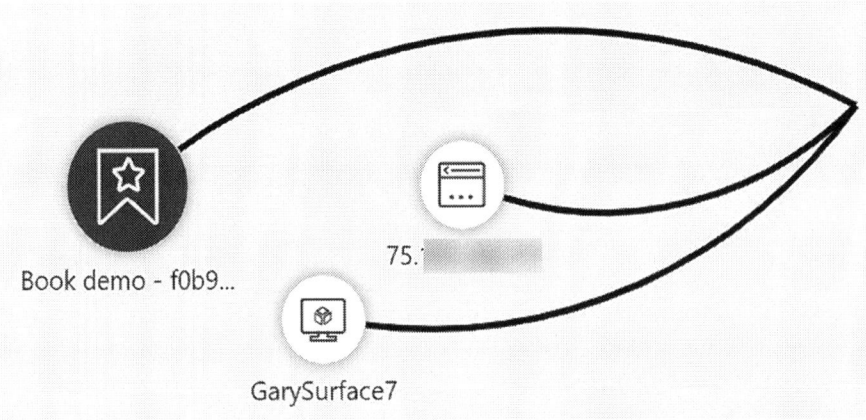

Figure 11.16 – Bookmark investigation

You now know how to view the bookmarks that you have created. You can get more details about them and see how to view the information using the **Investigate** button. Next, we will learn how to associate the bookmark with an incident.

Associating a bookmark with an incident

Bookmarks, by themselves, are not that useful. To be useful, they need to be associated with an incident, either a new incident or an existing one. This section will discuss the various ways to associate the bookmark with an incident.

No matter how you want to associate the bookmark with an incident, the first step is using the context menu. The context menu for each bookmark appears as follows:

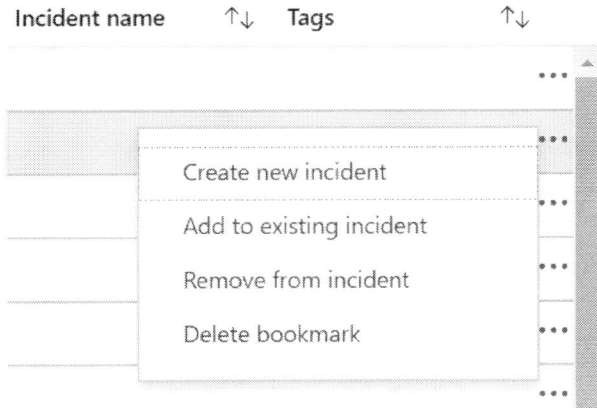

Figure 11.17 – Bookmark context menu

Make sure you have the correct bookmark selected when choosing the context menu to ensure you do not affect the wrong one.

> **Important Note**
> The context menu is only for working with individual bookmarks. If you want to work with multiple bookmarks, select the ones that you want to work on and click on **Incident actions** at the top of the page. All the actions will be the same, except for the ability to delete a bookmark; you will need to do that one at a time.

Let's now look at the different fields under the context menu in detail:

- If you select **Create new incident**, the new incident blade will open, as follows. This will allow you to create a new incident based on the selected bookmark:

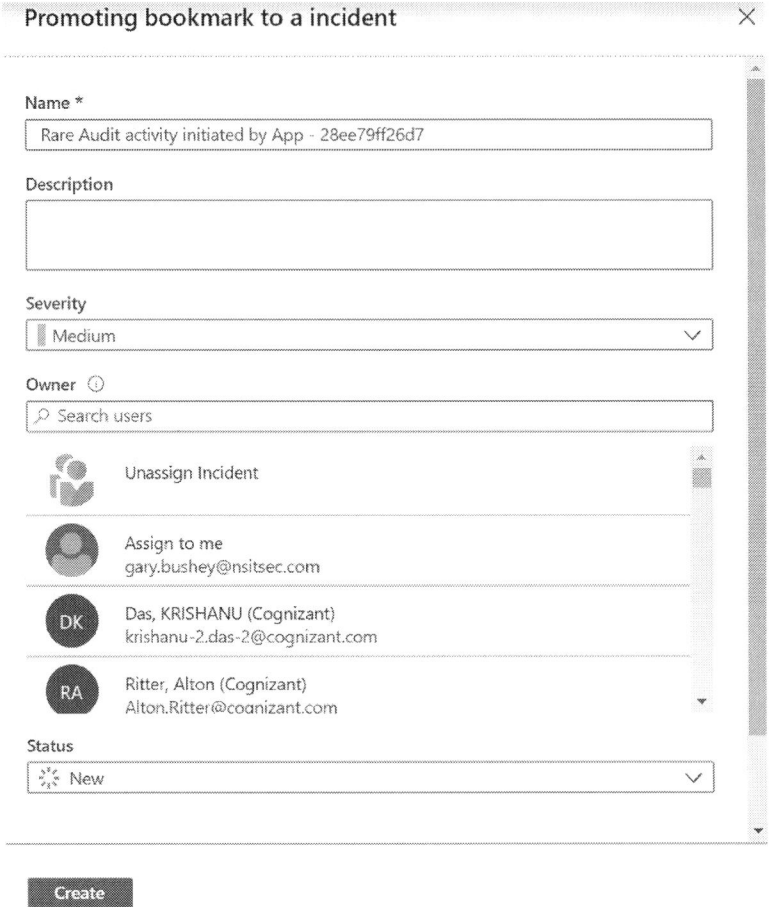

Figure 11.18 – Creating an incident from bookmark

These fields are the same as any other incident, so they will not be covered here. Refer to *Chapter 9*, *Incident Management*, for more information on incidents. Click **Create** to create a new incident from this bookmark.

- Clicking on **Add to existing incident** will open a new blade, allowing you to choose one or more incidents with which to associate this bookmark, as shown in the following screenshot. Select the incident with which you wish to associate this bookmark, and then click **Add**:

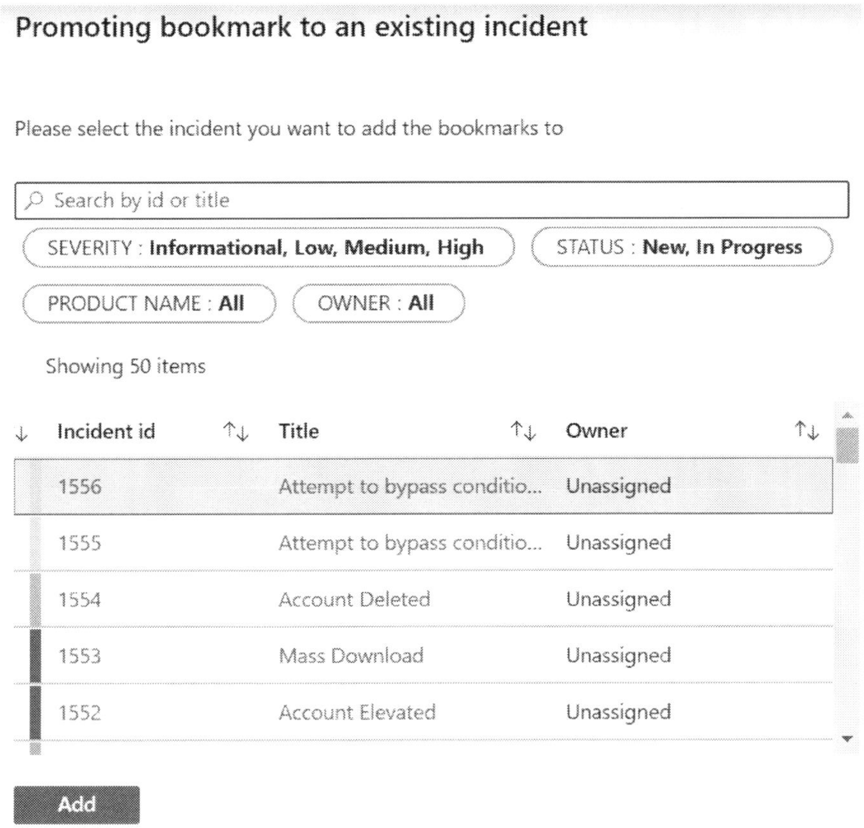

Figure 11.19 – Adding a bookmark to an existing incident

- Clicking on **Remove from incident** will cause a pop-up box to appear, asking you to verify that you do want to remove the bookmark from the incident. If you confirm the choice, the bookmark will be unassociated with the incident.

- Clicking on **Delete bookmark** will cause a pop-up box to appear, asking you to verify that you do want to delete the bookmark. If you confirm this choice, the bookmark will be deleted.

That is all there is to the **Microsoft Sentinel | Hunting** page. As you have read, it is quite useful, with many built-in queries and the ability to add your own queries and add a bookmark of results to help the investigation.

However, there may be times when this is not enough. Perhaps you need information that is only available outside of Microsoft Sentinel, or you want to use a visualization that is not part of Microsoft Sentinel. In cases like this, you can use the Jupyter Notebook, which is the topic of our next section.

Using Microsoft Sentinel notebooks

Sometimes, just using KQL queries against logs does not give enough information to assist with properly performing hunting activities. In cases such as this, you can use the Jupyter notebook, hosted in the **Microsoft Azure Machine Learning** (**AML**) service, to perform additional work. The Jupyter Notebook combines text with code to provide an overall view of your threat-hunting activities. The code can be written in Python, PowerShell, and other languages, so threat hunters can work with a language they are most likely already familiar with.

> **Important Note**
> The full scope of the Jupyter Notebook is beyond the scope of this book. For more information, go to `https://jupyter.org/`.

Click on **Notebooks** in the **Microsoft Sentinel** navigation area to go to the **Notebooks** page, which will look like the following screenshot:

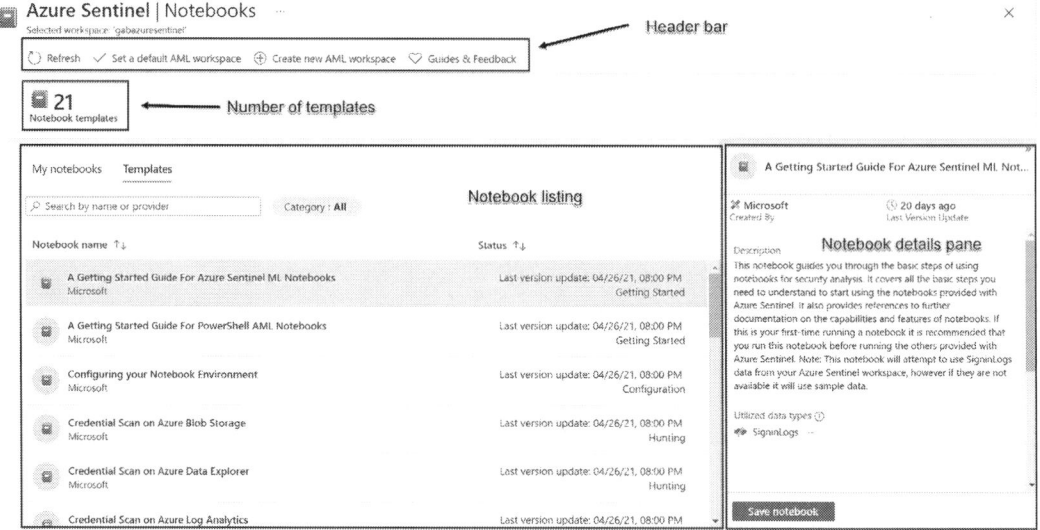

Figure 11.20 – Notebooks page overview

Each of the areas on this page is described in more detail in the following sections.

The header bar

The header bar allows you to work with the notebooks and is shown in the following screenshot:

Ⓒ Refresh   ✓ Set a default AML workspace   ⊕ Create new AML workspace   ♡ Guides & Feedback

Figure 11.21 – Notebooks' header bar

On the far left is the **Refresh** button that allows you to refresh the listing of notebooks.

Next to that is the **Set a default AML workspace** button. If you have multiple AML workspaces, you can use this button to select the default for you so that you do not need to always select the AML workspace you want to go into when you open a notebook.

To the right of that is the **Create new AML workspace** button. This will allow you to create a new AML workspace for the notebooks to use. See the *Creating a workspace* section below for more information.

On the far right is the **Guides & Feedback** button. If you click on this, a new pane will open on the right with some useful links and the ability to provide feedback to Microsoft.

The summary bar

The summary bar shows the number of notebooks templates, as illustrated in the following screenshot:

Figure 11.22 – Notebooks' summary bar

This summary bar is useful to see whether any new notebooks have been added to Microsoft Sentinel. You can view these new notebooks to see whether they may be something you can use.

The notebook list

Looking at the tab, you will see that all the available Jupyter Notebook templates are shown. These notebooks are provided by the Microsoft Sentinel GitHub repository, maintained by Microsoft, and updated regularly.

> **Important Note**
> While most of the Microsoft Sentinel information is stored in the Microsoft Sentinel GitHub repository, located at `https://github.com/Azure/Azure-Sentinel`, these notebooks are stored in the Microsoft Sentinel Notebook GitHub repository, located at `https://github.com/Azure/Azure-Sentinel-Notebooks`.

For each notebook, the name of the notebook will be shown with the authoring company underneath it. The last update time, with the type of notebook underneath it, will be shown on the right. There are currently four different options for type: **Getting started**, **Configuration**, **Hunting**, and **Investigation**. More may be added later.

The notebook details pane

Selecting a notebook will show the notebook details blade, as shown in the following screenshot. This will show the notebook's name at the top of the page. Under that is the name of who created it and the last time it was updated.

Beneath that is the description of the notebook, which will tell you what the notebook is trying to find. Under that is the **Required data types** field, which refers to the Microsoft Sentinel logs that it will be querying. Below that is a listing of the data sources (not shown) that are used to populate the data types and, finally, one or more images pertaining to the notebooks:

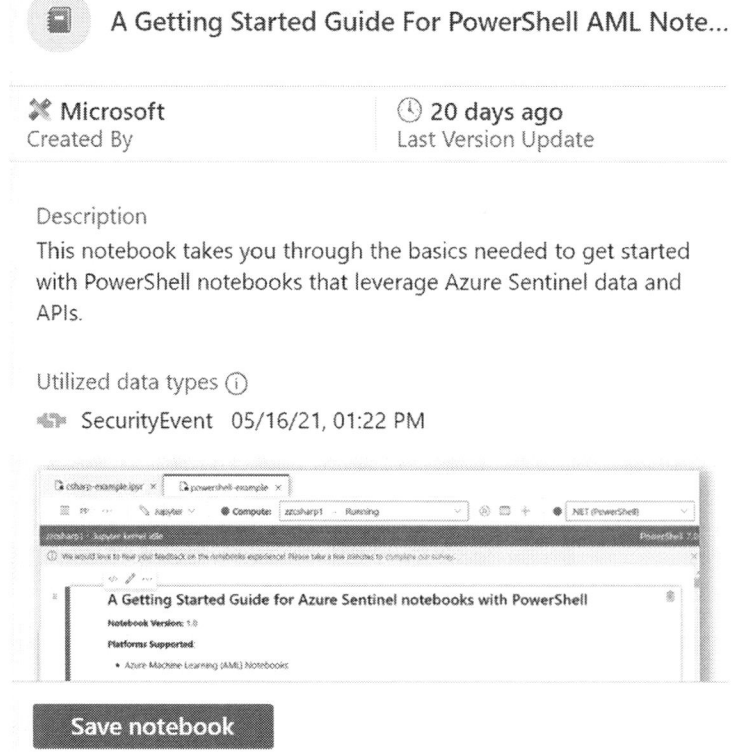

Figure 11.23 – Notebook details pane

At the bottom of this blade is the **Save notebook** button. This will save the selected notebook. You have the option to overwrite an existing notebook if you have saved this template already. If you do not choose to overwrite an existing notebook and one is present, then nothing will happen.

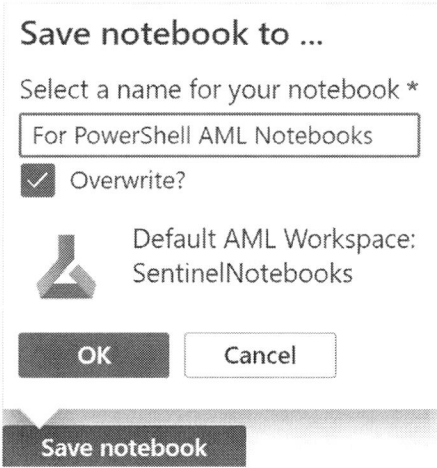

Figure 11.24 – Saving a notebook template

After you click on the **Save notebook** button, unless you cancel the action, it will change to **Launch notebook**. If you click the button now, the notebook will then be opened in the AML workspace. If you select a different notebook and return to this one, the button will revert to **Save notebook**.

> **Important Note**
> If you do not have an Azure Machine Learning workspace created, there will be a message stating that when you try to save the notebook, you will need to create the workspace first. See the following *Creating a workspace* section ahead for more information.

As stated previously, the best way to get to your notebooks is to use the **My notebooks** tab in the header. Clicking that will take you to a tab such as the following:

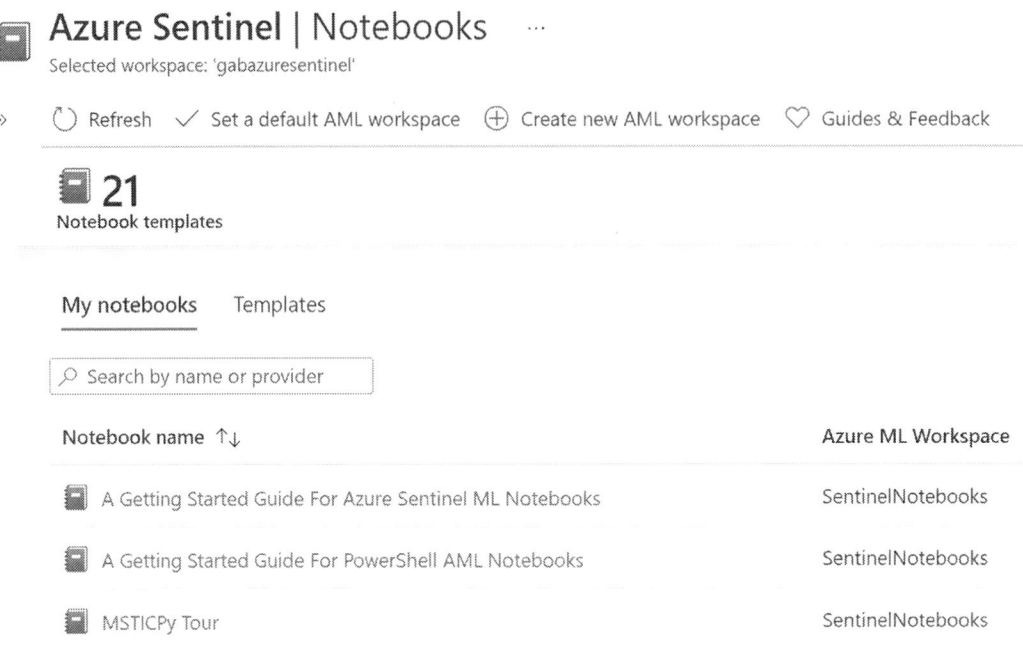

Figure 11.25 – My notebooks page

Click on one of the notebooks to start using it. This will open the Microsoft Azure Machine Learning page, as shown in the following figure:

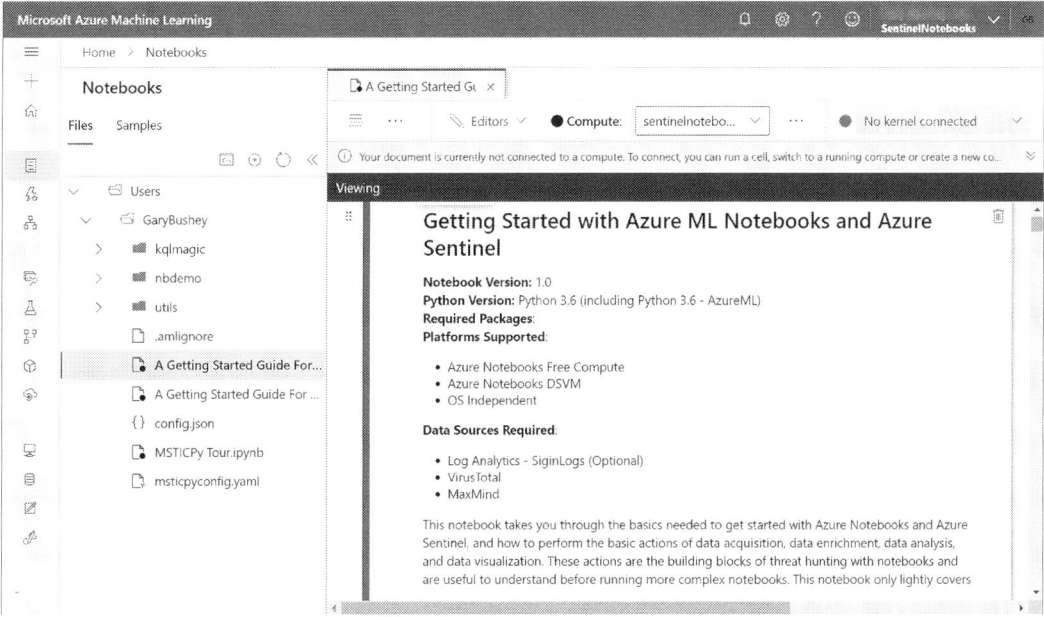

Figure 11.26 – Microsoft Azure Machine Learning page

From here, you can select your notebook and start working with it. The actual usage of the notebooks is outside the scope of this book.

Azure notebooks will allow you to perform queries outside Microsoft Sentinel. They can incorporate text and code and can include data internal and external to Microsoft Sentinel. They can also make use of graphics packages that are not available to Microsoft Sentinel to create graphs that you would not be able to create in Microsoft Sentinel.

Next, we will look at the mechanics of how to perform a threat hunt. This is going to focus on the tasks you will perform and not on how to do it inside Microsoft Sentinel.

Creating a workspace

As stated previously, you need to have a workspace created before you can save a notebook template. To start the process, click on the **Create new AML workspace** button in the header bar.

All the steps required to create a workspace are beyond the scope of this book. Refer to the **Create and manage Azure Machine Learning workspaces** link in the *Further reading* section for more information on the creation process.

Once the workspace is created, you will need to create a compute resource to host your notebooks. To do so, go into your workspace and click on the **Compute** link in the navigation menu, as shown in the following figure:

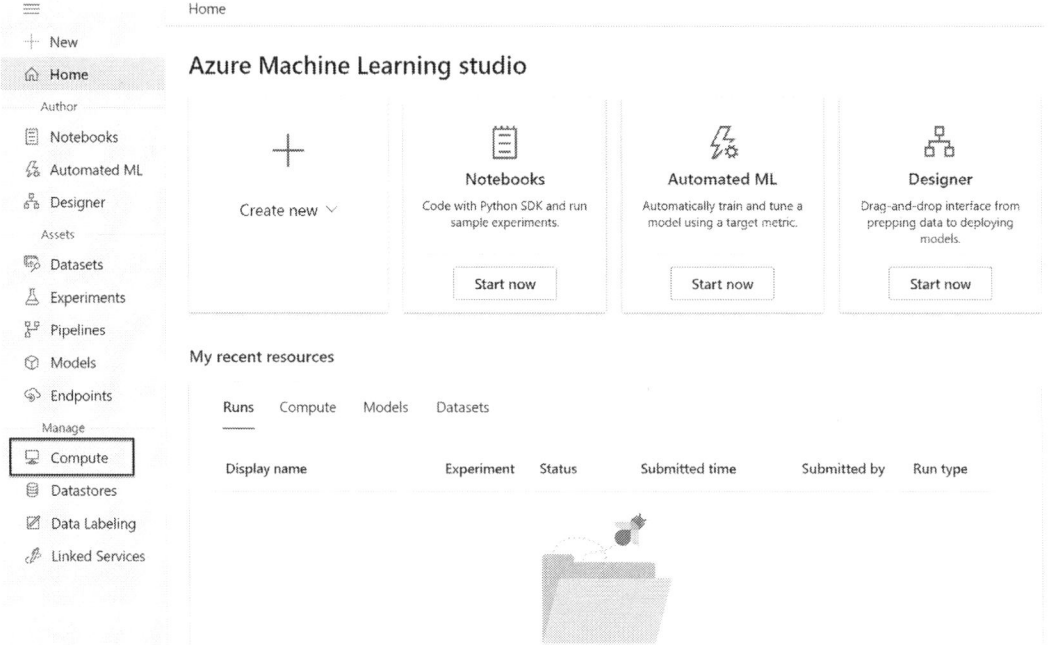

Figure 11.27 – Azure Machine Learning workspace home page

For Microsoft Sentinel notebooks, you will only need to create a single compute instance. On the new page that opens, click on the **+ New** button to create a new compute instance. There will be a new page that opens, asking you to select the type and size of the virtual machine, the name, and whether you want to be able to access the virtual machine via SSH.

Once you have the compute instance created and running, you can go back to the listing of notebook templates, save one or more, and then proceed to use the AML workspace to run it.

Performing a hunt

While there are no real set rules on how to run a hunt, there are some steps that you can take to focus your work: develop a premise, determine the data, plan the hunt, execute the investigation, respond, monitor, and improve.

As shown in the following diagram, this is a never-ending process. As new logs are added or new threats are recognized, this will be done repeatedly. Even something as simple as checking for a malicious IP address will most likely be done many times and based on previous findings, can be improved upon. You can find the logs that are most likely to contain the IP address and check those first, rather than blindly searching across all logs:

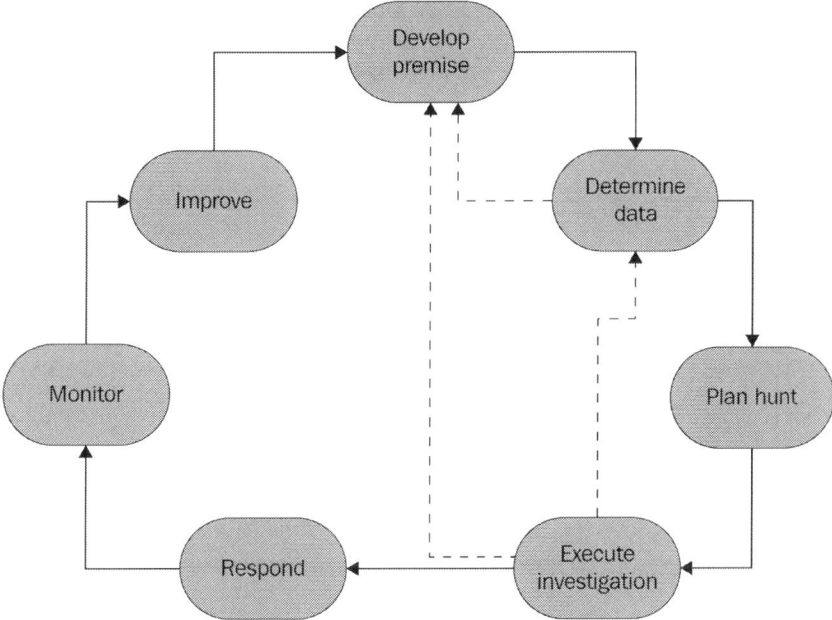

Figure 11.28 – Threat-hunting life cycle

As you can see from the preceding diagram, there are various steps to performing an investigation. Each step is described in further detail next.

Developing a premise

In this step, you need to determine what it is you are trying to find or prove. What is it you are trying to find out? Is it to determine whether a malicious IP address has been found in your environment? Did a new user account perform actions it should not have? Is someone from a foreign entity trying to gain access to your system?

When you develop a premise, you are specifying what it is you are trying to find. It may be that you are told what it is you are looking for, or it may be that you are looking for something that you think may have happened. Utilize tools such as threat intelligence sources as premises to being your threat hunt.

Keep in mind that threat hunting is a gap measure to ensure coverage of newly reported threats until analytics rules are available.

Determining data

In this step, you will determine which data you need to start your investigation. Which data will you need to look at to work your hypotheses? Is it all in Log Analytics, or will it be found elsewhere? What do you already know about your environment and what do you need to learn?

It may be that during your investigation, you determine that there is additional information that you may need, so do not feel that you are locked into just the data you have acquired in this step.

You may also find that you do not have all the data needed to work on your premise. It may be that there is data you need that is not being logged, in which case you will need to see whether you can start gathering that information. In any event, if you cannot obtain the needed data, you may need to go back and revise your premise.

Once you start finding specific types of activities in the various logs you have, it will make sense to keep track of these to make it easier to find the data in the future. The following screenshot shows the beginning of one method to track information: using Microsoft Excel to keep track of the log name, the type of data being queried, and whether the data is found in the log. If the data is found, the name of the column holding the data is entered:

Data Type	Domain	Host Name	IP Address	Account
AuditLogs	TargetResources*	TargetResources*	TargetResources*	InitiatedBy
AzureActivity	HTTPRequest		CallerIPAddress	Caller
AzureDiagnostics				
AzureMetrics				
Event	EventData	Computer	EventData	UserName
SigninLogs	ResourceDisplayName		IPAddress	UserPrincipalName
Not available				
Sometimes available				
Always Available				
* Compound Column				

Figure 11.29 – Data field tracker

Notice that the `TargetResources` column is entered for multiple data types for the `AuditLogs` log type. This is due to this column comprising other fields, so the actual information will need to be extracted from them. This is designated by having an asterisk, *, at the end of the column name.

Another point to note is that your data diagram may be different from the one shown here, even for the same logs. This is due to the type of data coming in and what resources you have in your subscription. For instance, in the preceding Excel sheet data, the `AzureMetrics` row does not find any of the data types in question, but that may be due to not having any Azure resources saving their diagnostic information to this Log Analytics workspace.

Planning a hunt

How will the hunt be performed? Can it all be done in Microsoft Sentinel, or will you need a notebook?

In this step, you will look at the data you gathered from the previous step and determine how you need to access it. It may be that you can access all required data via Microsoft Sentinel queries; however, many times, you will need to look at additional information outside of Microsoft Sentinel, in which case you will need to use a notebook. You will also write the queries and additional code that may be needed or use queries that were already written, if they work.

Executing an investigation

In this step, you will execute the queries that you obtained in the previous step, whether you wrote them or found ones that were already written that will work. You may be performing queries in Microsoft Sentinel as well as, or instead of, in a notebook. Wherever you run the queries, once you start looking at the results, you may find that you need to revise your premise or determine that you need more data, so you may need to go back to a previous step (refer to *Figure 10.24*).

Responding

Now that you have the information you need, you can respond to the results of the investigation. You may just have to plug the security gap you found, or you may need to escalate to another team and present what you found. This may be just your team, or in the event of a major breach, it could be the **Chief Information Security Officer** (**CISO**), **Chief Information Officer** (**CIO**), or even the board.

If the response is simple, such as blocking a port in a firewall or blocking an IP address range, most likely it is just a matter of notifying the appropriate people, updating the ticket, and moving on.

However, there will most likely be cases where you need to do a full presentation on your findings. This could be just to your team, but it could also be to a different audience. How you do the presentation is up to your company and its corporate culture; just keep thinking while you are doing your work, *Would this information be useful in a presentation?*, and think about how you would present it. A table of information may be enough when presenting to your team, but others who are not as familiar with the data may need graphs and charts.

At the very least, your findings and how you got to your results should be presented within your team if it is new information, so that everyone is kept up to date with the latest findings and can take the most appropriate action.

Monitoring

Develop new analytic queries if possible; otherwise, continue to periodically run the investigation to validate findings. Refer to *Chapter 7, Creating Analytic Rules*, for a refresher on creating analytic queries.

In this step, you will determine how you can perform continuous monitoring to help safeguard against the situation you were investigating or improve the ability to investigate again next time. Can you add more information to the log? Is there a change in the operating procedures that can be performed to help avoid this situation in the future? Is there a change to your network that can be performed?

One of the best outcomes would be to create an analytic query so that this situation can be found automatically and perhaps handled via a playbook. Refer to *Chapter 12, Creating Playbooks and Automation*, for more information on creating playbooks.

Improving

Based on any learnings that came from the investigation, improve the investigation code and techniques, if possible.

In this step, you – and, most likely, others – will work to determine how to improve the queries used in this hunt, as well as how to avoid needing this hunt in the future. It may be that the queries you used could be rewritten to be more efficient, changes could be made to operating procedures to avoid the situation altogether, or other recommendations may be made based on the skills and experience of your team, partners, and domain-specific experts.

Those are the steps that can be taken to start your threat-hunting investigation. Again, none of these are set in stone, and the steps are only provided for guidance. You may find that your company has its own steps or that you want to add your own. The real takeaway from this is that you should have a repeatable process that is always improving, enabling you to share your results at least with your co-workers and with the threat-hunting community at large, if you can.

Summary

Now, you have learned about how to start doing threat hunting in Microsoft Sentinel. You learned about the **Hunting** page, the **Notebooks** page with its Jupyter notebooks, and got a brief introduction on how to perform a threat-hunting investigation.

We looked at the tools that Microsoft Sentinel provides to assist with threat hunting. This includes queries that only get run periodically, either due to factors such as needing to look for a specific piece of information or the fact that they would return too many results to be useful on a scheduled basis.

Another tool that can be used is the hosted instances of Jupyter notebooks. These notebooks allow you to combine text and code into one location to make hunting easier and repeatable. In addition, notebooks can query not only Microsoft Sentinel logs but also third-party information using programming languages, including PowerShell and Python.

In the next chapter, we will look at using Microsoft Sentinel playbooks to help automate reactions to incidents.

Questions

1. How do I run a single hunting query?
2. How do I run all the hunting queries at one time?
3. How can I view the results of a single hunting query?
4. How do I create a new bookmark?
5. What are two ways in which I can associate a bookmark with an incident?

Further reading

You can refer to the following links for more information on topics covered in this chapter:

- *Hunt for threats with Microsoft Sentinel* (https://docs.microsoft.com/en-us/azure/sentinel/hunting).
- *Security Investigation with Microsoft Sentinel and Jupyter Notebooks – Part 1* (https://techcommunity.microsoft.com/t5/azure-sentinel/security-investigation-with-azure-sentinel-and-jupyter-notebooks/ba-p/432921)
- *Security Investigation with Microsoft Sentinel and Jupyter Notebooks – Part 2* (https://techcommunity.microsoft.com/t5/azure-sentinel/security-investigation-with-azure-sentinel-and-jupyter-notebooks/ba-p/483466)
- *Security Investigation with Microsoft Sentinel and Jupyter Notebooks – Part 3* (https://techcommunity.microsoft.com/t5/azure-sentinel/security-investigation-with-azure-sentinel-and-jupyter-notebooks/ba-p/561413)

- *Create and manage Azure Machine Learning workspaces* (https://docs.microsoft.com/en-us/azure/machine-learning/how-to-manage-workspace?tabs=azure-portal#create-a-workspace)
- *Azure Machine Learning documentation* (https://docs.microsoft.com/en-us/azure/machine-learning/)
- *Microsoft Sentinel Notebook Ninja series* (https://techcommunity.microsoft.com/t5/azure-sentinel/becoming-an-azure-sentinel-notebooks-ninja-the-series/ba-p/2693491)

Section 4: Integration and Automation

In this section, you will learn how to create solutions that automate the responses required to handle security incidents and integrate with a ticketing system.

This section contains the following chapters:

- *Chapter 12, Creating Playbooks and Automation*
- *Chapter 13, ServiceNow Integration for Alerts and Case Management*

12
Creating Playbooks and Automation

In the previous chapters, you learned about the **Security Information and Event Management (SIEM)** side of Microsoft Sentinel. Now, it is time to learn about its **Security Orchestration, Automation, and Response (SOAR)** capabilities.

Microsoft Sentinel's SOAR features allow automated or semi-automated responses to be created regarding alerts and incidents. This allows you to develop workflows that can perform tasks such as blocking an IP address from getting through a firewall, blocking a suspicious username, or something simple such as sending an email to the security team, letting them know a new high-severity alert was generated. When you combine the automation capabilities offered by Microsoft Sentinel with the protection capabilities of the many other security products you deploy, the sky's the limit!

In this chapter, you will learn about Microsoft Sentinel playbooks, including how to write and edit them, configuring their workflow, and managing them. You will also learn about Microsoft Sentinel's Automation feature, which allows you to perform certain actions without the use of playbooks.

At the end of this chapter, we will walk through the process of creating a simple playbook. By the end of the chapter, you should feel comfortable writing playbooks.

We will cover the following topics in this chapter:

- Introduction to Microsoft Sentinel playbooks
- Introduction to Microsoft Sentinel Automation
- Adding a new Automation rule
- Playbook pricing
- Types of playbooks
- Overview of the Microsoft Sentinel connector
- Exploring the Playbooks tab
- Logic Apps settings page
- Creating a new playbook
- Using the Logic Apps Designer page
- Creating a simple Microsoft Sentinel playbook

Introduction to Microsoft Sentinel playbooks

Microsoft Sentinel uses Azure Logic Apps for its workflow automation. An Microsoft Sentinel playbook is a logic app that uses the Microsoft Sentinel connector to trigger the workflow. As we go through this chapter, many of the screenshots we will be looking at will be logic app pages, which reinforces this concept. The full extent of how to use Logic Apps is beyond the scope of this book, so we will just cover the Microsoft Sentinel connector, which contains logic app triggers and actions for Microsoft Sentinel.

> **Note**
> For this chapter, the terms *playbook* and *logic app* will be used interchangeably. For more information on Azure Logic Apps, go to `https://azure.microsoft.com/en-us/services/logic-apps/`.

Logic apps use *connectors* (not to be confused with Microsoft Sentinel data connectors) and *actions* to perform a workflow's activities. A logic app connector provides access to events and data. Actions will perform a specific task, such as sending an email, posting a message on Microsoft Teams, extracting **JavaScript Object Notation** (**JSON**) objects, and so much more.

By using Azure Logic Apps as the backend technology, Microsoft Sentinel playbooks already have a rich ecosystem of connectors and actions that they can call upon to perform their activities. Let's look at one of the ways to use them.

Introduction to Microsoft Sentinel Automation

When Microsoft Sentinel was first released, each playbook had to be assigned to each analytic rule individually and all actions required the use of a playbook. Microsoft Sentinel Automation was introduced to make using playbooks much easier, while, at the same time, allowing a user to perform actions, including changing an incident's severity, without needing to write a playbook.

> **Note**
> When this chapter was being written, the Automation features were in preview, so some features may have changed.

Let's start by looking at the **Automation** page. To access this page, select the **Automation** navigation menu entry from the Microsoft Sentinel navigation pane. The **Automation** screen will be displayed, as shown in the following screenshot:

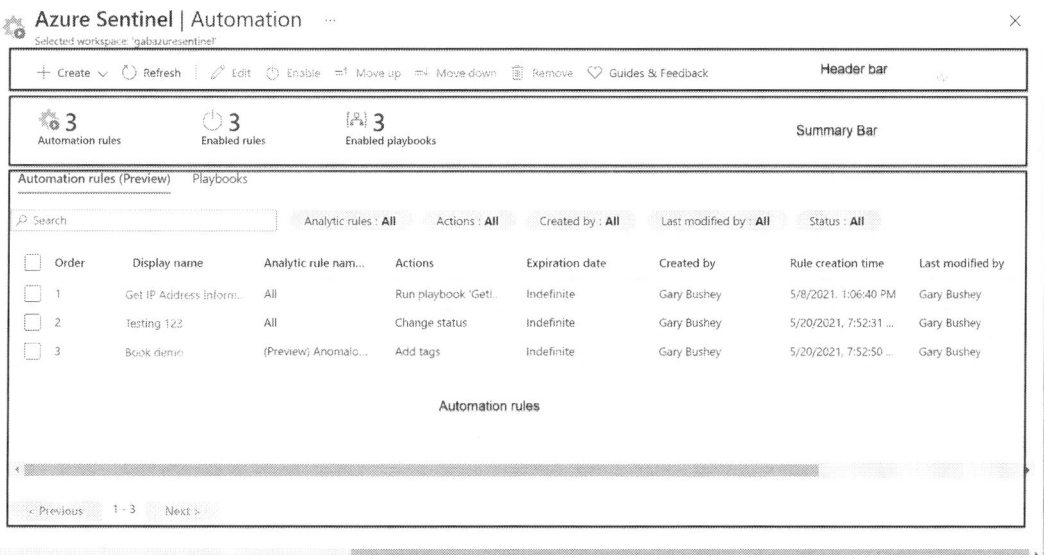

Figure 12.1 – Microsoft Sentinel Automation home screen

We shall look at each part of this page in the following sections.

The header bar

The header bar, as shown in the following screenshot, contains various buttons:

Figure 12.2 – The Microsoft Sentinel Automation page header bar

Let's discuss each field in detail:

- The **+Create** button allows you to add a new automation rule (called **Add new rule**) or a new playbook (which is described in the *Adding a new playbook* section).
- The **Refresh** button will refresh the display.
- The **Edit** button will allow you to edit an existing automation rule. Note that a single automation rule must be selected before this can be enabled.
- The **Enable** and **Disable** buttons are only available if one or more rules are selected and will either enable a disabled rule or disable an enabled rule.
- The **Move up** and **Move Down** buttons are only available if one or more rules are selected and will either move the automation rule higher or lower in the run order. Refer to the *Adding a new automation rule* section of this chapter for more details.
- The **Remove** button will delete the selected automation rule(s).
- The **Guides & Feedback** button will open a new pane and provide you with more information regarding Microsoft Sentinel Automation, as well as allow you to provide feedback to Microsoft.

The header bar can be used to create new automation rules and playbooks, as well as change the order, status, and give you more documentation on how to work with automation rules.

The summary bar

Under the header is the status bar, as shown in the following screenshot:

Figure 12.3 – The Microsoft Sentinel Automation page summary bar

All the information presented here shows how many automation rules and playbooks are available:

- On the left-hand side is the **Automation rules** number. This shows the total number of automation rules there are, and whether they are enabled or not.
- To the right of that is **Enabled rules**, which is the total number the automation rules that are enabled.
- After that is **Enabled playbooks**, which shows how many playbooks are available that can be used in the automation rules.

Let's look at the automation rules listing.

Automation rules listing

Under the summary bar is a list of all the automation rules, as shown in the following screenshot. Notice that there is a tab for **Automation rules (Preview)** and one for **Playbooks**. The **Playbooks** section will be covered in the *Exploring the Playbooks tab* section, later in this chapter:

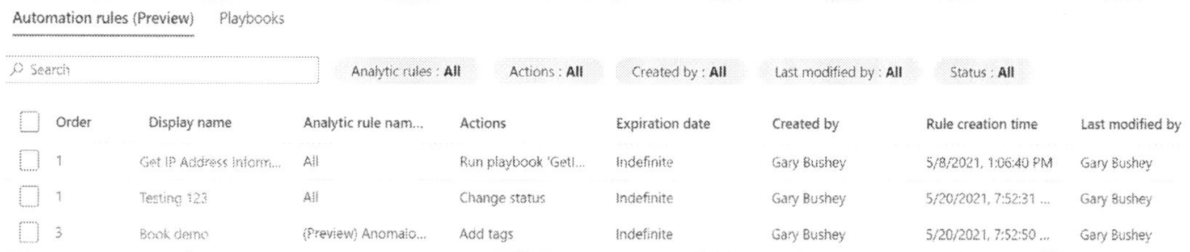

Figure 12.4 – Automation rules list

For each automation rule listed, there is a selection checkbox, followed by the following fields:

Field Name	Description
Order	This is the order in which the automation rule will be run. If there is more than one automation rule associated with a given analytic rule, then the rule with the lowest number will be run first.
Display Name	The name of the rule. Click on the rule to edit it.
Analytic rule names	This will show All if this rule is to be applied to every analytic rule or a listing of those individual analytic rules that this rule will be applied to.
Actions	Shows the action(s) that this rule will run when activated.
Expiration Date	Shows the date when this rule will expire. If it shows **Indefinite**, then the rule will not expire.
Created by	The name of the person that created the rule.
Rule creation time	The date and time that the rule was created.
Last modified by	The name of the person who last modified this rule.
Rule last modified	The date and time the rule was last modified (not shown in the preceding screenshot).
Status	Shows the rule's status, either **Enabled** or **Disabled** (not shown in the preceding screenshot).

Table 12.1

Now, we will learn how these rules can be created.

Adding a new automation rule

As we mentioned previously, to create a new automation rule, click on the **+Create** button in the header and select **Add new rule**.

This will open the **Create new automation rule** pane, as shown in the following screenshot:

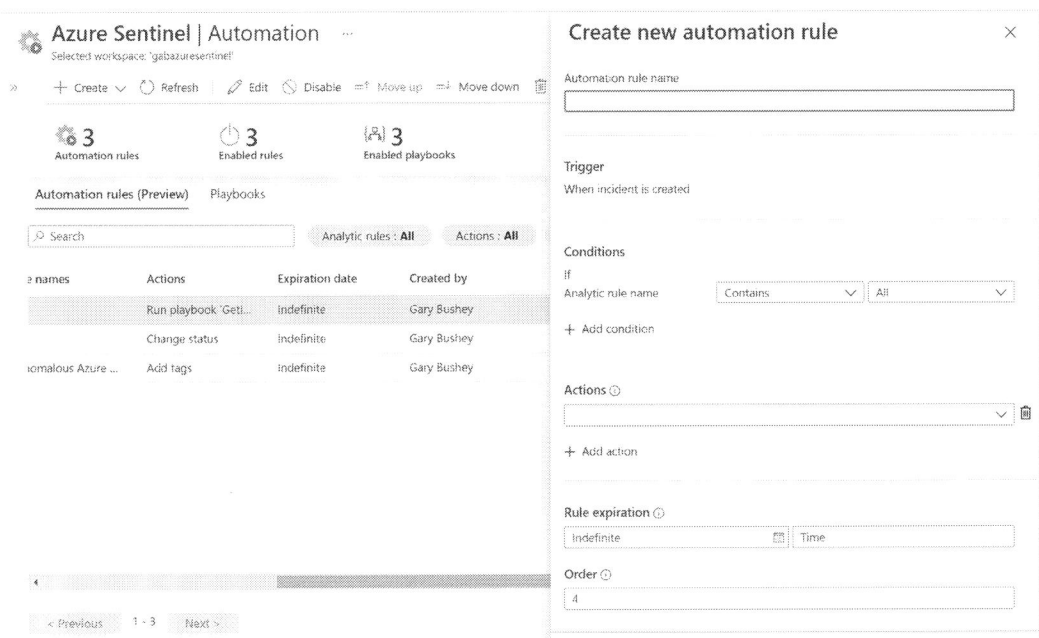

Figure 12.5 – Create new automation rule

Enter the rule's name in the **Automation rule name** text box. You will want to make this rule's name descriptive enough so that someone will understand what it will do by reading the title. For example, `Get IP Address information` tells the user that the rule will get some IP address information, while `Testing 123` doesn't tell the user anything, not that anyone would name their rule that.

Under the name, note that **Trigger** is automatically set to **When incident is created**. Refer to the *Types of playbooks* section in this chapter for more information on this.

The **Conditions** section is where you set what analytic rules will trigger this automation rule. By default, every analytic rule will trigger this automation rule but that can be changed. Clicking on the **All** dropdown will show a list of all the analytic rules that are in your environment, as shown in the following screenshot. You can select one or more of the rules by checking the checkbox that appears before their name(s):

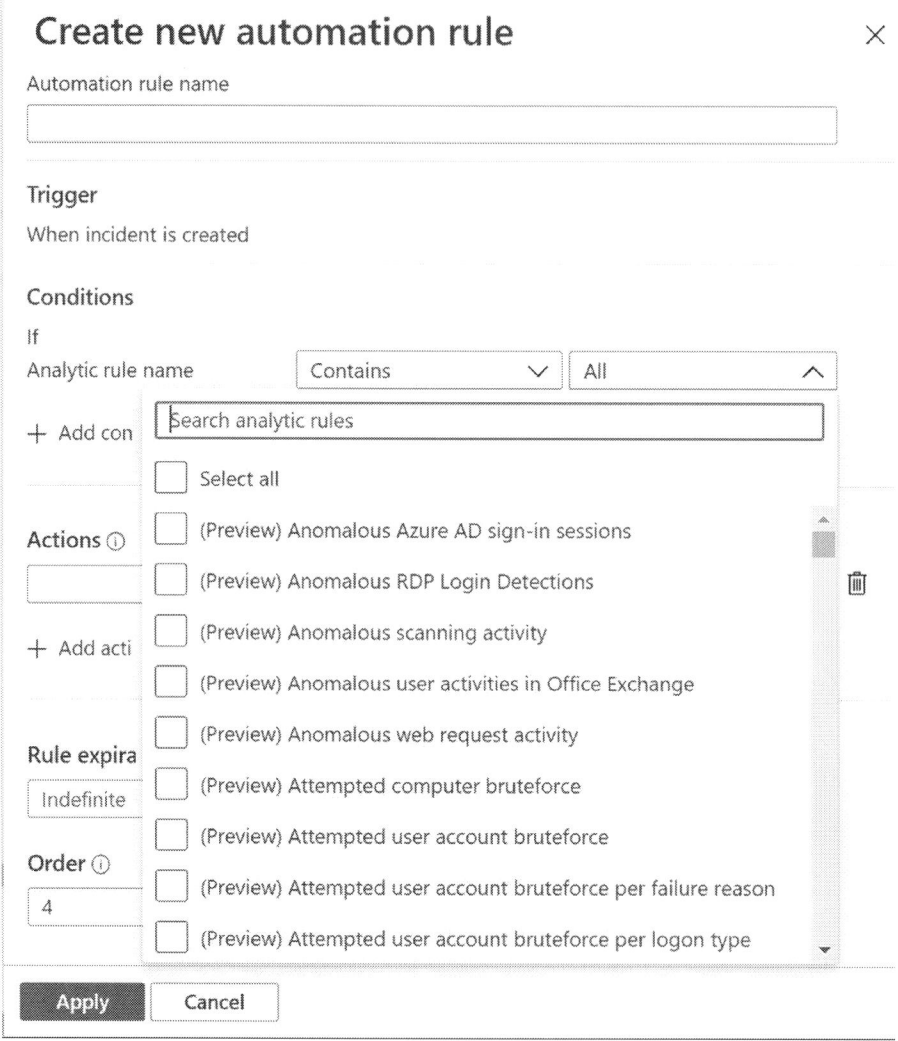

Figure 12.6 – Search analytic rules

If you refer to *Figure 12.5*, you will see that there is a dropdown that says **Contains**. This can be switched to **Does not contain** so that you can apply this automation rule to those analytic rules that do not contain the selected analytic rules.

If you click on the + **Add condition** link, you can add more filtering rules. Each time you click this link, another filter dropdown will appear, as shown in the following screenshot. This will allow you to add filters based on the properties of the incident, including **Title**, **Description**, **Severity**, **Status**, and others. In addition, other fields can be filtered on, including **Incident Provider**, **Azure Resource id**, **Host name**, and many more.

As shown in the following screenshot, you can also select the condition for the comparison and enter the string that will be used for the comparison. If you want to be able to filter on the multiple string values, click on the icon to the right of the string. This will add another text box that you can use to enter another string value. Note that in this case, it will be doing an **OR** search.

You can also click on the trash icon to delete either the entire rule or one of the additional text boxes as needed:

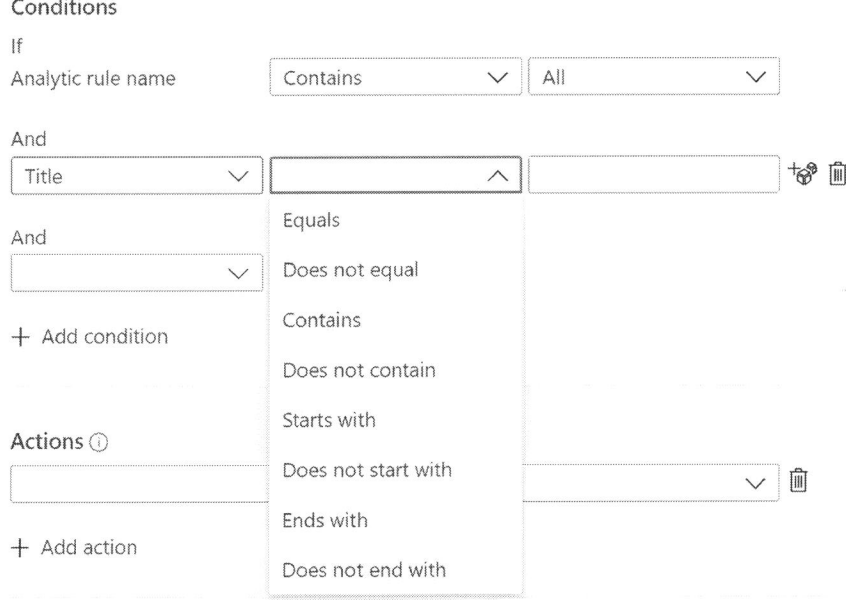

Figure 12.7 – Adding more conditions

Once you have determined which analytic rules will kick off this automation rule, you need to determine what this rule will do. This can be done by setting **Actions**.

As shown in the following screenshot, there are different actions that you can perform:

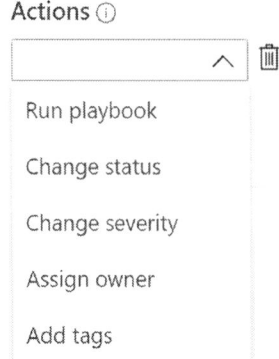

Figure 12.8 – Automation rule actions

Each of the available actions is described in the following table:

Action	Description
Run playbook	This will allow you to select which playbook you can run. Only those playbooks using the incident trigger will be shown. Refer to the *Types of playbooks* section in this chapter for more information.
Change status	This will automatically change the incident's status. If selected, another dropdown will be shown where you can choose its status.
Change severity	This will automatically change the incident's severity. If selected, another dropdown will be shown where you can choose its severity.
Assign owner	This will automatically change the incident's owner. If selected, another dropdown will be shown where you can choose the owner.
Add tags	This will automatically add the tag(s) to the incident. If selected, a new section where the tags can be entered will be shown.

Table 12.2

You can have multiple actions in the same rule. If there is more than one action, the first one will run, then the second one will be started after the first, and so on.

The **Rule expiration** field allows you to select how long this rule will be active. By default, it will be **Indefinite**, in which case the rule never stops being active. You can select a date and time when the rule will expire, in which case the rule will be deactivated when it reaches that date and time.

Order determines the order in which this rule will be applied. Looking back at *Figure 12.5*, you can see that the order for this rule has defaulted to 4 since there are already three other rules that are being run first, second, and third. You can change the number here to change the order that the rules will be run.

If there are two rules with the same order number, you will not be able to determine which one will be run first, so it is a good idea to make sure the rules have unique order numbers so that the order is always known if that matters. No matter the order, all the rules whose conditions match the new incident will be run.

Once all the fields have been filled in, click the **Apply** button to create the new rule.

Now, let's look at the pricing considerations when using playbooks.

Playbook pricing

As mentioned in *Chapter 1*, *Getting Started with Microsoft Sentinel*, running an Microsoft Sentinel playbook is not included in the ingestion costs of Microsoft Sentinel or Log Analytics. It has separate charges that, though they may be considered small, can add up quickly.

For example, in the East US region, each logic app action that is run (and this includes things such as looking up information, extracting JSON, and sending emails) will cost $0.000025 each time it is used. There is also an additional $0.000125 charge for each standard connector. Granted, this seems small, but if you write a logic app that has 100 actions with 1 connector that gets run every second of every day for a month, that one logic app would cost $3,564 each month!

> **Note**
>
> For more information on Azure Logic Apps pricing, go to `https://azure.microsoft.com/en-us/pricing/details/logic-apps/`.

Now, this is an extreme example, but it serves to remind you that when designing playbooks, you need to keep them as simple as needed and that you should not do a lot of extraneous work. Next, we will discuss the Microsoft Sentinel connector, which you will need to use in all Microsoft Sentinel playbooks.

Types of playbooks

Currently, there are two types of playbooks, those that use the **When a response to an Microsoft Sentinel alert is triggered** logic app trigger and those that use the **When Microsoft Sentinel incident creation rule was triggered** logic app trigger. Each has its uses, as described in the following section.

For those playbooks that use **When a response to an Microsoft Sentinel alert is triggered**, referred to as **Alert Playbooks** going forward, they only work against alerts. This can be useful since, at the time of writing, they are the only playbooks that can be run manually, meaning that when you are looking at the alerts in the incident's view full details page, these are the only ones that can be run by clicking on the playbooks link. However, to use these on analytic rules, they must be applied to each one.

Those playbooks that use **When Microsoft Sentinel incident creation rule was triggered**, referred to as **Incident playbooks** going forward, are the only ones that can be used with Automation rules. However, since they currently cannot be executed manually, they cannot be run against an incident other than through automation rules.

When should you use each? That depends on the use case.

As we mentioned previously, only the Alert playbooks can be executed manually, so they are good if you need to run them against alerts after they have been created. However, to use them on Analytic rules, you will need to go into each Analytic rule and state that this playbook will be used.

Incident playbooks are the only ones that can be used in Automation rules, so if you want to run the playbook when an incident is created, these are the ones to use. Just remember that they cannot be run manually.

Overall, you will probably have a mixture of these different types of playbooks to meet the different needs. Now, let's look at the logic app connector that's used to make the playbooks.

Overview of the Microsoft Sentinel connector

While there are many logic app connectors, and more are being added all the time, the one we are concerned with is the Microsoft Sentinel connector. It provides us with the triggers that can kick off our playbook. It also contains various actions that can perform tasks such as obtaining information about a specific incident, getting information about the entities associated with an alert, updating an incident, and more.

Overview of the Microsoft Sentinel connector   371

> **Note**
> At the time of writing, all the features of the Microsoft Sentinel connector were in preview, so they could have changed from what is shown and discussed here.

As discussed in the previous section, the connector currently has two triggers called **When a response to an Microsoft Sentinel alert is triggered** and **When Microsoft Sentinel incident creation rule was triggered**. This means that the trigger will fire whenever an alert or incident is created, depending on which one is selected.

It is worth noting that while the alert trigger returns a lot of information, it does not return the actual incident that gets created – if one gets created at all. To get the incident's information, you need to use one of the actions given in *Table 12.3*.

The following table lists all the current actions for the Microsoft Sentinel connector:

Name	Description
Add comment to incident	Adds a comment to the selected incident.
Add labels to incident (to be deprecated)	Adds a label to the selected incident. Note that it is recommended to use Update Incident going forward.
Change incident description (to be deprecated	Changes the description of the selected incident. Note that it is recommended to use Update Incident going forward.
Change incident severity (to be deprecated)	Changes the severity of the selected incident. Note that it is recommended to use Update Incident going forward.
Change incident status (to be deprecated)	Changes the status of the selected incident. Note that it is recommended to use Update Incident going forward.
Change incident title (to be deprecated)	Changes the title of the selected incident. Note that it is recommended to use Update Incident going forward.
Entities – Get Accounts	Gets a list of all the account entities.
Entities – Get FileHashes	Gets a list of all the filehash entities.
Entities – Get Hosts	Gets a list of all the host entities.
Entities – Get IPs	Gets a list of all the IP entities.
Entities – Get URLs	Gets a list of all the URL entities.
Alert – Get incident	Returns the incident associated with the selected alert.
Remove labels from incident (to be deprecated)	Removes the labels from the selected incident. Note that it is recommended to use Update Incident going forward.
Update incident	This allows you set various attributes of the incident, including tags, owner, severity, status, title, and description. It also allows you to remove tags.
Watchlists – Add a new watchlist item	Allows you to add a new entry to an existing watchlist or create a new one.
Watchlists – Update an existing watchlist item	Allows you to update an entry in an existing watchlist.

Table 12.3

As we mentioned previously, all Microsoft Sentinel playbooks will need to use this Microsoft Sentinel connector for the logic app to be considered a playbook. It also provides a lot of actions that you can use to get more information about, and update information in, incidents. You will be using this connector a lot and you should familiarize yourself with its actions. Next, we will start the journey of creating playbooks by looking at the **Playbooks** page.

Exploring the Playbooks tab

To access the list of playbooks, from the **Microsoft Sentinel Automation** page, select the **Playbooks** tab. This will show the Microsoft Sentinel **Playbooks** page.

This page will list all the logic apps in the subscription(s) you have selected to show in the Azure portal. You will need to look at the **Trigger kind** column to see whether the logic app can be used as a playbook. If it contains **Microsoft Sentinel**, you can use this logic app as a playbook:

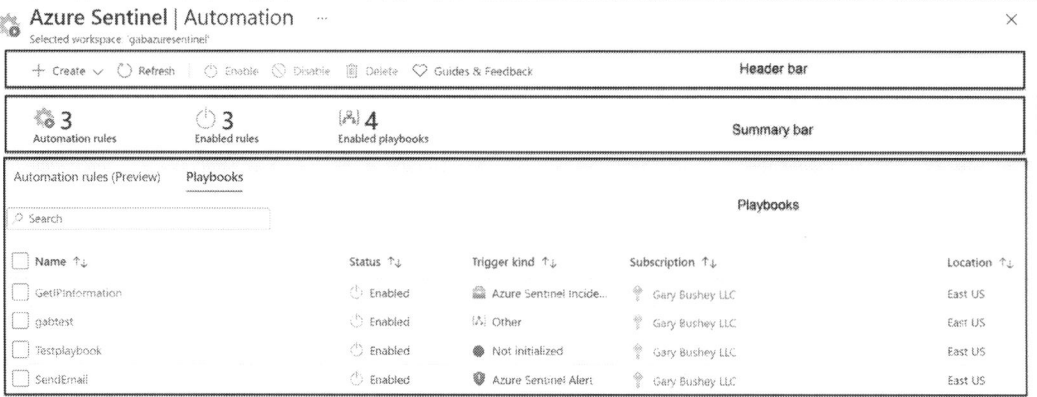

Figure 12.9 – The Microsoft Sentinel Playbooks page

> **Tip**
> You can also access your playbooks by going to the **Logic App** screen. However, it will not present the same amount of information as what's shown in the preceding screenshot.

Since the header and the summary bars are the same as what we discussed earlier when talking about the Automation rules, they will not be discussed here again. Refer to those sections for more information if needed.

Let's look at the logic app listing.

Logic app listing

Under the summary bar is the listing for all the logic apps, as shown in the following screenshot. For each logic app listed, there is a selection checkbox, followed by the following fields:

Field Name	Description
Name	The name of the rule. Click on the rule to be taken to the logic app page for it.
Status	Shows the logic app's status, either **Enabled** or **Disabled**.
Trigger kind	Shows which trigger is being used for this logic app. For this chapter, we are only concerned with those that contain Azure Sentinel.
Subscription	Shows the Azure subscription that this logic app belongs to.
Location	Show the location where this logic app resides.

Table 12.4

That is the makeup of the playbook overview page. Next, we will look at a specific playbook while using the logic app settings page.

Logic app settings page

You've just seen the overview section. But what if you want to look at a specific item? We'll discuss that now.

Clicking on the name of the logic app, shown in *Figure 11.9*, will bring you to the logic app settings page. This is where you can create, edit, or delete an individual logic app and see more information regarding your logic app, as well as see the history of your logic app's runs, as shown in the following screenshot:

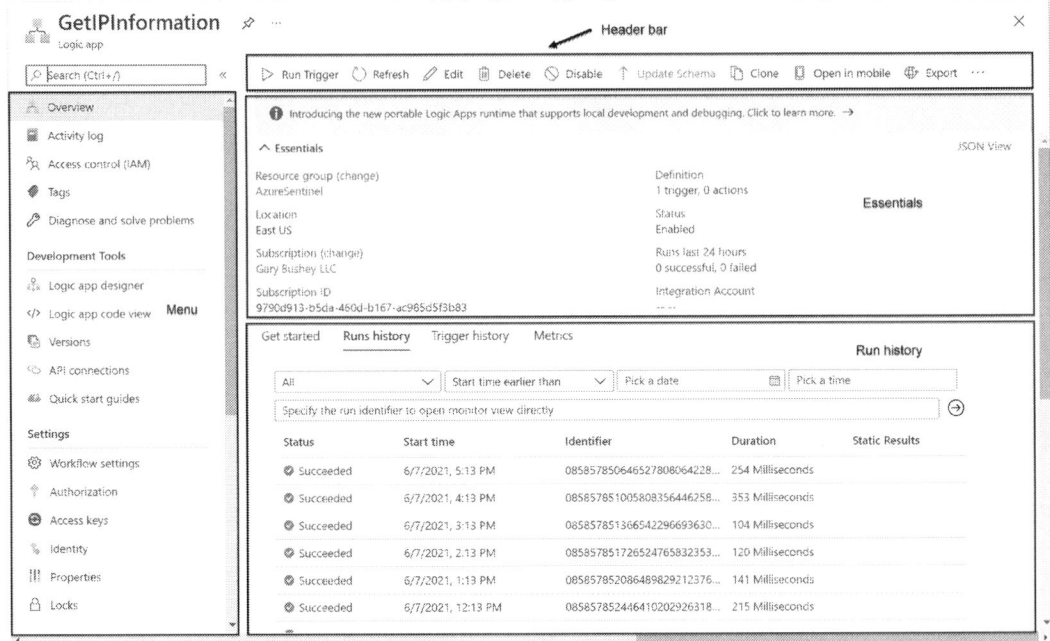

Figure 12.10 – Logic app overview page

Let's discuss each section in more detail.

The menu bar

This is where you perform more actions against this logic app. We will not discuss all the options available in the left-hand navigation menu as they are beyond the scope of this book. However, we encourage you to take some time to study the full capabilities of logic apps.

The header bar

The header bar contains the following buttons, which allow you to quickly manage the logic app:

Figure 12.11 – Logic app overview page header bar

Each field is as follows:

- The **Run Trigger** button will cause the logic app to run. This is not very useful with most playbooks as they will require an alert trigger's information to run.
- The **Refresh** button will refresh the page. This can be useful when you're running a playbook to tell you when it is finished running, as the results of the run will show up in the **Runs history** section.
- The **Edit** button will allow you to edit the logic app's workflow. Refer to the *Using the Logic Apps Designer page* section for more information.
- The **Delete** button will allow you to delete this logic app after confirming you want to do this.
- The **Disable** button will disable the logic app so that it will not run, even if the connector is triggered. If the logic app is disabled, then this button will be called **Enable**.
- The **Update Schema** button will only rarely be enabled and only if a change has been made to a logic app that requires you to update the underlying schema.
- The **Clone** button will allow you to make a copy of this logic app. This can be useful if you want to try out some changes without losing the original.
- The **Export** button will allow you to export the logic app to Power Automate and Power Apps. As playbooks cannot be exported, this feature will not be covered here.

Let's look at the next field.

The essentials section

This section shows the most essential information for the logic app. Most of the fields are shown with all other types of Azure resources and are self-explanatory, so they will not be covered, with two exceptions:

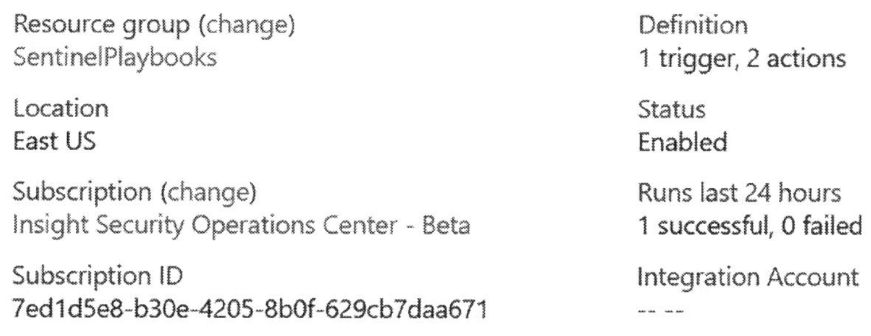

Resource group (change)
SentinelPlaybooks

Location
East US

Subscription (change)
Insight Security Operations Center - Beta

Subscription ID
7ed1d5e8-b30e-4205-8b0f-629cb7daa671

Definition
1 trigger, 2 actions

Status
Enabled

Runs last 24 hours
1 successful, 0 failed

Integration Account
-- --

Figure 12.12 – The logic app overview page's essentials section

Each field is as follows:

- The **Definition** field will show the number of triggers and actions that make up this logic app.

- The **Integration Account** field will show you the integration account you are using if you are using enterprise integrations.

> **Tip**
> For more information on using **Integration Account** with Logic Apps, go to `https://docs.microsoft.com/en-us/azure/logic-apps/logic-apps-enterprise-integration-create-integration-account?tabs=azure-portal`.

The Runs history section

This section will provide you with information on all the times this logic app has run:

Status	Start time	Identifier	Duration	Static Results
▷ Running	2/28/2020, 9:08 AM	08586187079601445097697406115...	--	
❶ Failed	2/28/2020, 9:05 AM	08586187081299801860970022871...	737 Milliseconds	
✓ Succeeded	2/26/2020, 2:12 PM	08586188625626606183880618787...	2.94 Seconds	
✓ Succeeded	2/25/2020, 2:53 PM	08586189464724709471560635203...	970 Milliseconds	

Figure 12.13 – The logic app overview page's Runs history section

Each field is as follows:

- The **Status** field will show whether this instance of the logic app is running, has failed, or has succeeded.

- The **Start time** field will show the date and time that the logic app instance started.

- The **Identifier** field will show a unique ID that represents this logic app. You may need to provide this if you are ever debugging a logic app issue with Microsoft.

- The **Duration** field will show how long it took this instance to run.

- The **Static Results** field will show any static results you have set up to test this logic app.

The main items on this page that we will focus on are the **Edit** button in the header, so that we can make changes to our playbook, and **Runs history** at the bottom of the page, which lets us know which instance of the logic app succeeded or failed, and if it failed, why.

> **Tip**
> For more information on debugging logic apps, go to `https://docs.microsoft.com/en-us/azure/logic-apps/logic-apps-diagnosing-failures`.

Now that you know how to look at existing playbooks, how do you go about adding one? The next section will cover adding a new playbook.

Creating a new playbook

You are going to want to create playbooks, so now is the time to learn how to do that.

On the Microsoft Sentinel **Automation** page (see *Figure 11.1*), click on the **Add Playbook** link in the header. This will open a new tab in your browser that will lead to the **Logic App** screen, as shown in the following screenshot:

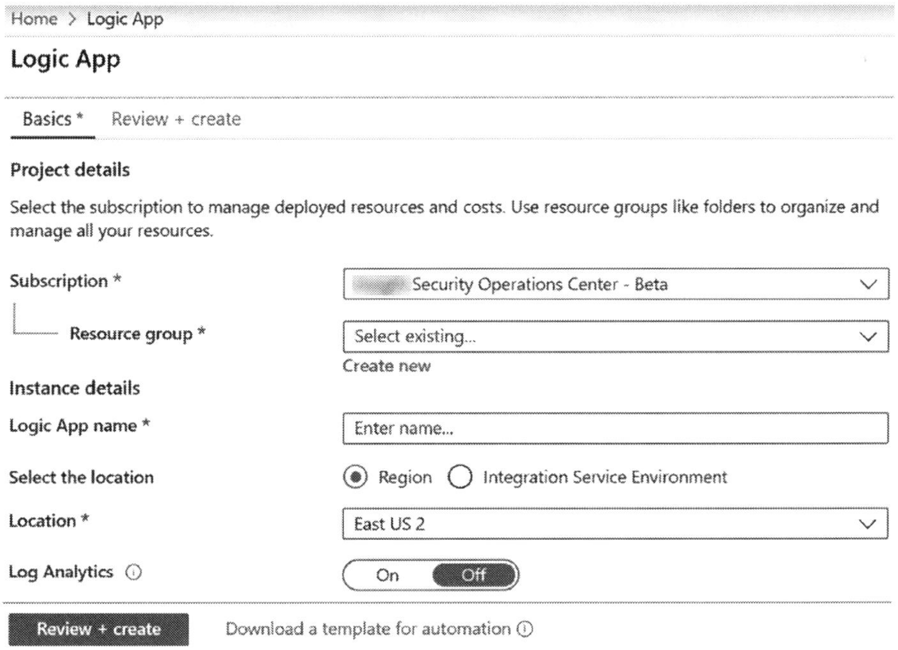

Figure 12.14 – Adding a new playbook

Let's discuss the different fields:

- In the **Logic App name** field, enter a descriptive name. No blanks are allowed but you can use underscores. Make the name descriptive enough so that other users will know what the playbook intends to do.
- From the **Subscription** dropdown, select the appropriate subscription. This should be the same subscription as where your Log Analytics (and Microsoft Sentinel) workspace is located.
- In the **Resource group** field, select an existing resource group or create a new one. It does not matter whether your playbooks are in the same resource group as your Log Analytics workspace. However, you should follow your organization's Azure architecture design policies if there are any.
- From the **Location** dropdown, select the appropriate location. This should be the same location as where your Log Analytics workspace is located to avoid egress charges.
- In the **Log Analytics** field, if you want information about this playbook's runtime events to be stored in Log Analytics, turn this option on. This will be useful if you need to allow another system, such as Microsoft Sentinel, to perform queries against this information.

Once this information has been filled in, click the **Review + create** button. This will validate that the information you have entered is correct and, if it is, will allow you to create the logic app. If not, it will inform you of what is wrong and allow you to go back to the main page to fix the issues.

It may take a little while for your logic app to be created. You will be taken back to the main playbook page while this happens.

That is how you create the basis for your playbook. As it stands right now, it does nothing as there are no workflow steps in it. Next, we will explore how to add the workflow components to make your playbook useful.

Using the Logic Apps Designer page

Once the playbook has been created, you will be taken to the **Logic Apps Designer** page. There are two different views for this page.

The first view, as shown in the following screenshot, will be shown if your workflow is empty. It provides a quick introduction video, some common triggers, and predefined templates that can be used to help you get started building your workflow. Note that the view shown in the following screenshot will only appear the first time you edit the workflow for a specific logic app. After that, if there is no workflow, you will be shown a listing of templates and the **Blank Logic App** button, which will allow you to create an empty workflow that you can add to:

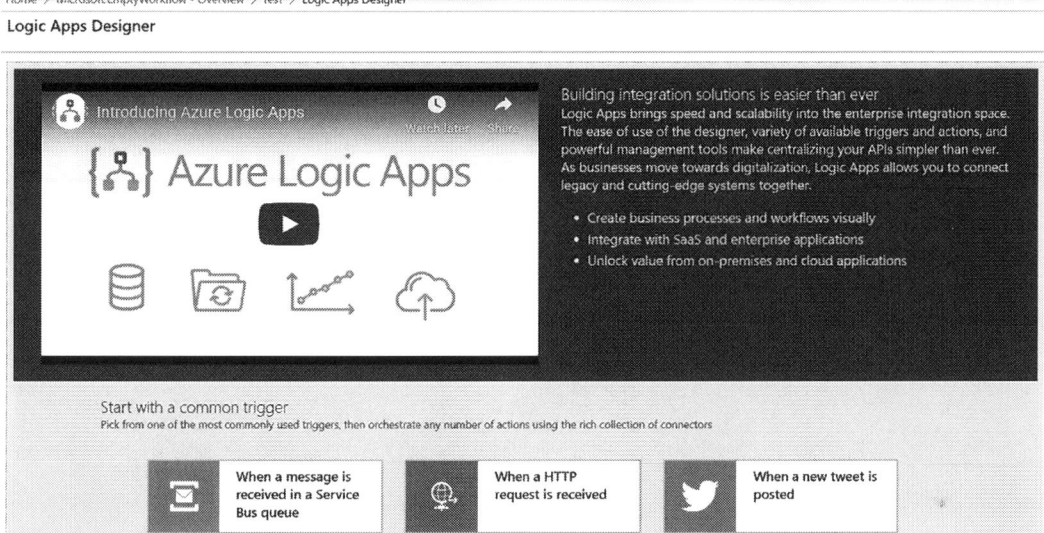

Figure 12.15 – Logic Apps Designer first view

> **Note**
> At the time of writing, there are no Microsoft Sentinel playbook templates on this page, but, hopefully, there will be soon.

Scroll down the page and then click on the **Blank Logic App** button to start building your playbook.

380   Creating Playbooks and Automation

Once you click on this button, the second view will be shown, which will look like what is shown in the following screenshot. Depending on what connectors and actions you have used recently, the listing under **Recent** in the workflow editor section will be different, or it could be empty:

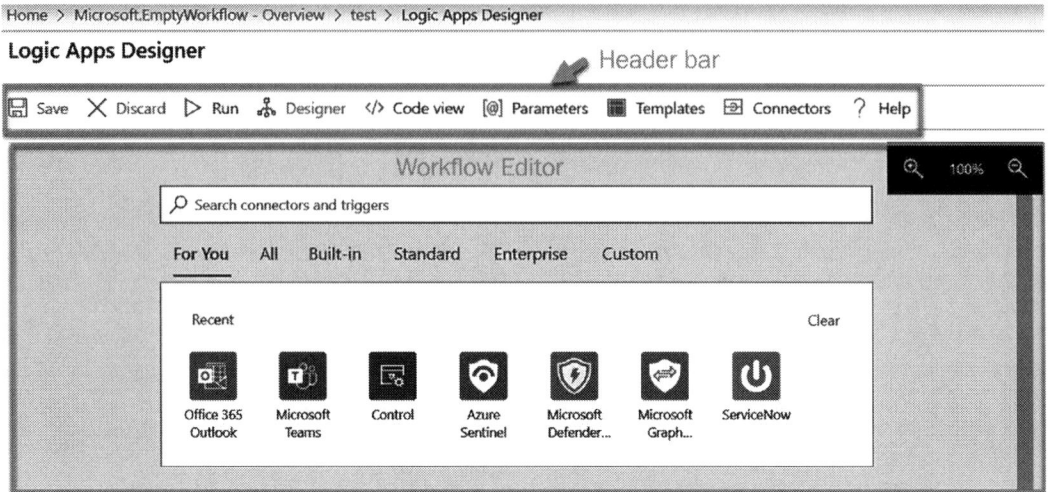

Figure 12.16 – Logic Apps Designer second view

Each section of this page will be described in more detail in the next section.

The Logic Apps Designer header bar

The header bar, as shown in the following screenshot, contains all the buttons for working with this workflow. Here, you can save or discard your changes, switch between the GUI and the code views, add parameters, and more:

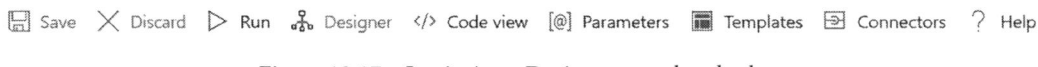

Figure 12.17 – Logic Apps Designer page header bar

Each button is as follows:

- The **Save** button will allow you to save your changes. It will only be active if you have made any changes to the workflow.
- The **Discard** button will discard all the changes you have made and revert the workflow to the last saved instance. It will only be active if you have made any changes to the workflow.

- The **Run** button will run the workflow you are currently viewing.
- The **Designer** and **Code view** buttons work together to either show you the designer view or the code view. If you press the **Code view** button, the JSON code that makes up this playbook will be shown. If you press the **Designer** button, you will be taken to the GUI view. You can work in either view; however, only one of the buttons will be active at a time. If you are in **Designer** mode, then the **Code view** button will be active. Likewise, if you are in **Code view** mode, then the **Designer** button will be active.
- The **Parameters** button will bring up the **Parameters** blade, which will allow you to add, edit, or delete the parameters of this playbook. Parameters are a way of passing information to your logic app, mainly during automated deployments.

> **Note**
> Go to `https://docs.microsoft.com/en-us/azure/logic-apps/logic-apps-azure-resource-manager-templates-overview` to find more information on using parameters in logic app deployments.

- **Templates** will bring up a list of pre-existing templates that you can use to base your playbook on. Note that when you click this button and select a template from the list, your existing playbook's design will be overwritten by the template.
- The **Connectors** button will open a new page that will discuss logic app connectors, as well as provide a list of existing, non-preview connectors and actions. This is a good place to start if you need information on your connector.

> **Note**
> Go to `https://docs.microsoft.com/en-us/connectors/connector-reference/` to see all the available connectors in the *Connector Reference* section.

Now, let's discuss the workflow editor section.

The Logic Apps Designer workflow editor section

The **Logic Apps Designer** page workflow editor section, as shown in the following screenshot, is where you will do most of the work when you're creating your workflow:

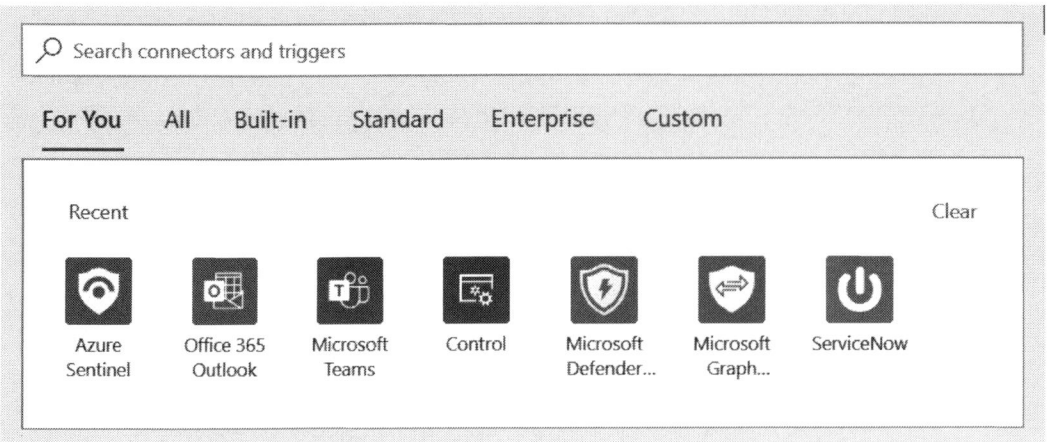

Figure 12.18 – The Logic Apps Designer page workflow editor section

This is where you will select the trigger that will start the workflow and then add the various actions that you need to use.

Now, you know how to create an Microsoft Sentinel playbook. While the process itself is simple, the workflows you can create can be as complex as you want. In the next section, we will take everything we have learned in this chapter and create a simple playbook.

Creating a simple Microsoft Sentinel playbook

This example will take you through the process of creating a new Microsoft Sentinel playbook. The scenario we are solving is notifying our security analysts, using Microsoft Teams that a new, high-severity incident has been created.

The first step is to create a new playbook that Microsoft Sentinel can use. Remember that for Microsoft Sentinel to be able to use a playbook, it must use the Microsoft Sentinel connector:

1. Go to the Microsoft Sentinel playbook screen and click the **Add Playbook** button in the header. Follow the *Creating a new playbook* section to add a new playbook. I am calling this playbook `BookDemo`. Select the appropriate resource group and location. For this example, you do not need to store information in Log Analytics.

2. Once your playbook has been created, click on the **Blank Logic App** button to create a new logic app that has nothing in it.

3. On the **Logic Apps Designer** page, find and select the Microsoft Sentinel connector. If you do not see this connector listed in the **Recent** connector listing, enter `Microsoft Sentinel` in the search box and select the connector when it appears.

4. Connect to Microsoft Sentinel if the connector requires it. As we mentioned previously, the trigger from the Microsoft Sentinel connector returns information about the alert and most of the actions work against an incident. So, how do you get the incident? Use the **Alert – Get incident** action. Click on the **New step** link, select the **Microsoft Sentinel** entry in the **Recent** section, or search for it if need be. The connector will be added again and this time it will show the actions, as shown in the following screenshot:

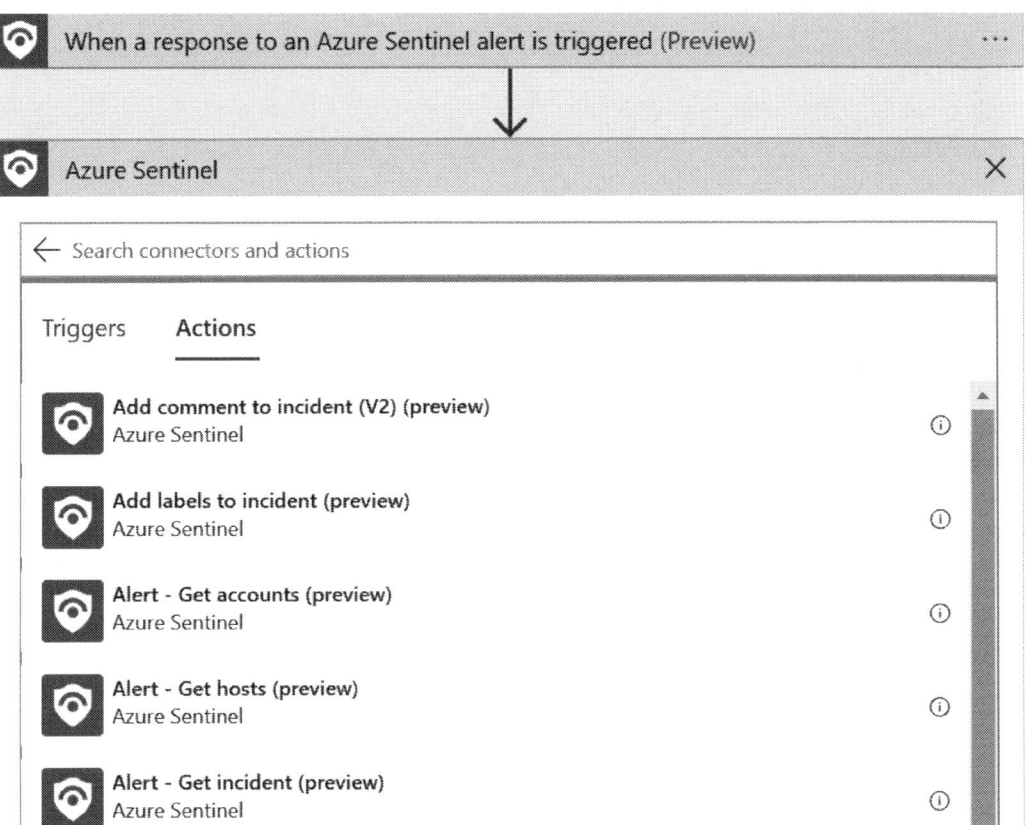

Figure 12.19 – Microsoft Sentinel connector actions

Note

There is a functionality in Microsoft Sentinel that allows you to create analytic rules that will raise alerts without generating incidents. For this example, we are assuming that the analytic rule(s) using this workflow will create an incident.

5. Scroll down until you find **Alert - Get incident (preview)** and select it.
6. Once this action has been added, the following fields need to be filled in:

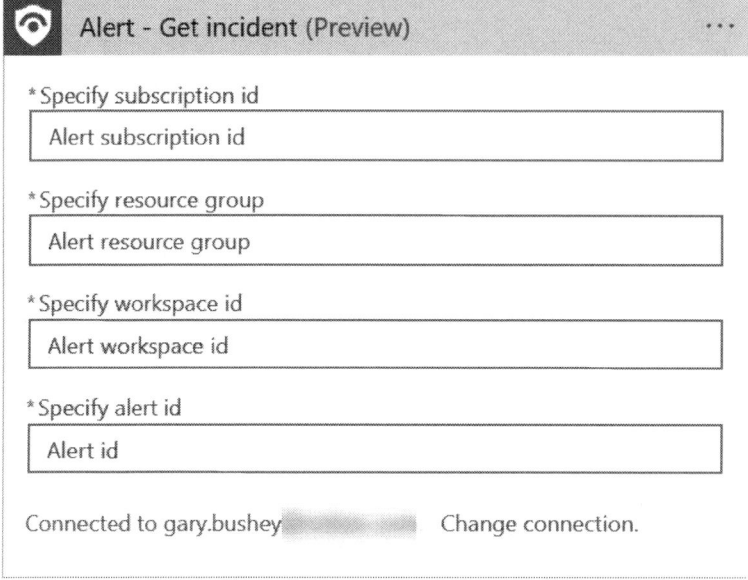

Figure 12.20 – Alert – Get incident fields

7. The great thing is that the Microsoft Sentinel trigger can provide all these fields for us via dynamic content. Click on the **Specify subscription id** field. A new window will appear that contains a list of all the fields that the trigger provides, as shown in the following screenshot:

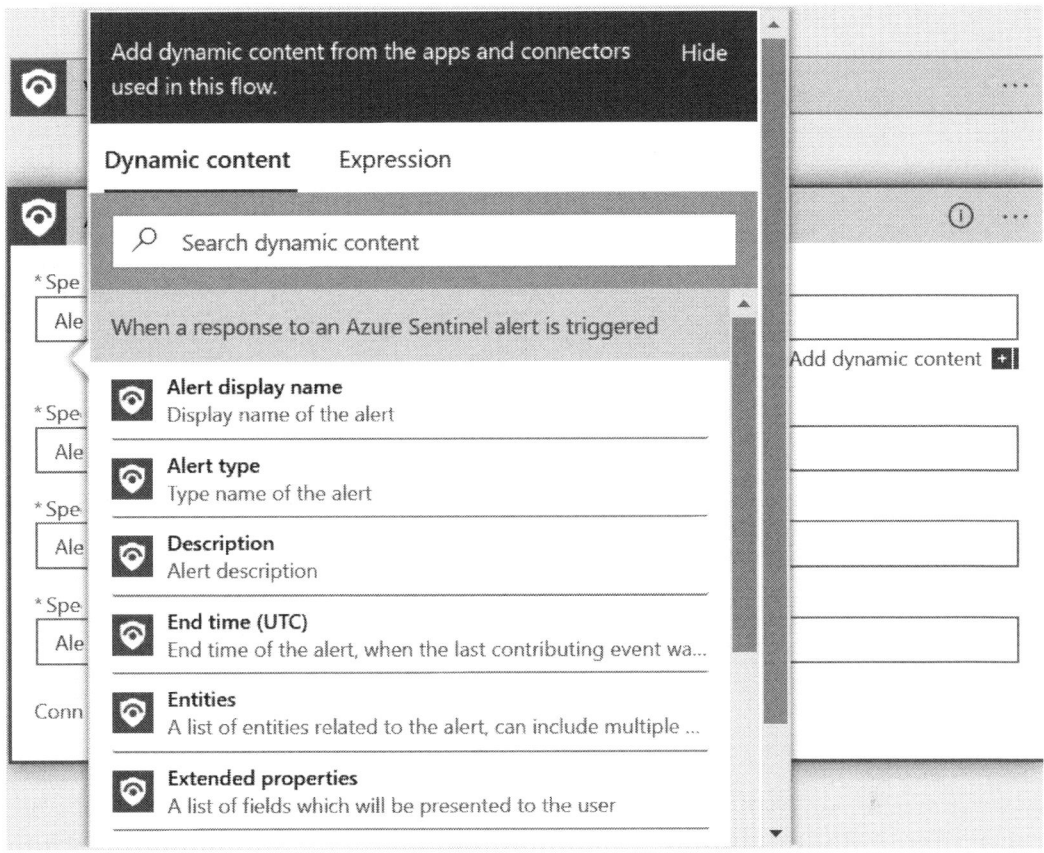

Figure 12.21 – Dynamic content

8. These fields are the dynamic content that comes from earlier steps. Here, the variable name will be replaced with the actual value when the playbook runs. Most triggers and alerts have dynamic content and as new steps are added, this list will grow.

9. Map the fields to the trigger values, as shown in the following table:

Action Name	Trigger Value
Specify subscription id	Subscription ID
Specify resource group	Resource group
Specify workspace id	Workspace ID
Specify alert id	System alert ID

Table 12.5

10. When you are done, your alert should look as follows:

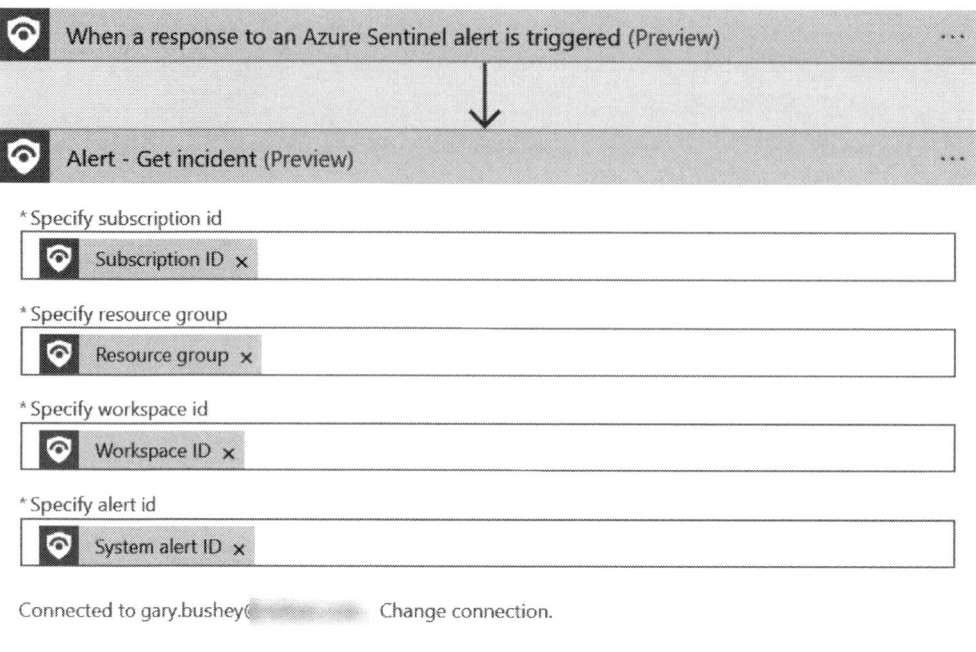

Figure 12.22 – Alert – Get incident completed

Now that we have the information from the incident, what do we do with it? The scenario states that we need to alert the analysts if a high-severity alert is raised. The **Alert – Get Incident** action returns all the incidents, so we need to filter for just the high-severity ones:

1. Click on the **New step** link and search for **Condition**.
2. Select the **Control** connector when it appears. We are going to be using an `If` statement, but all the control-type statements are bundled into that one connector.
3. Select the **Condition** action and the action will be added, as shown in the following screenshot. Notice that it has three parts: the top part is where the actual condition is entered, the lower-left part shows what to do if the test returns true, and the lower-right part shows what to do if the test returns false:

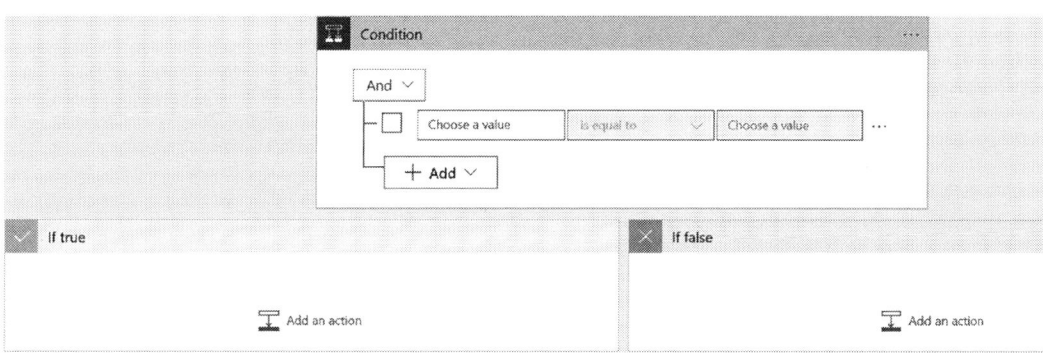

Figure 12.23 – Condition step options

4. Based on what you have learned in this section, set up the condition so that you are checking whether **Severity** is equal to **High**.

> **Hint**
> Both the Microsoft Sentinel connector's trigger and the **Alert – Get incident** action return the severity, so it does not matter which one you choose.

The following screenshot shows how it should look:

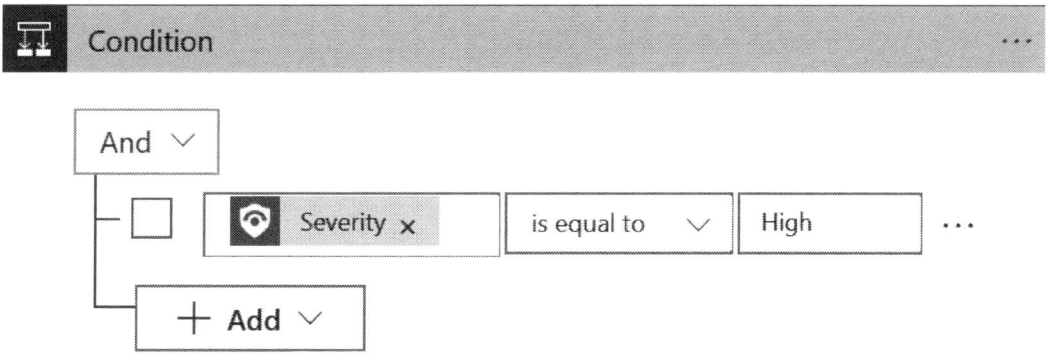

Figure 12.24 – Condition step options completed

You can easily add more conditions if you need to in the future.

Now, we need to post the message. To do this, follow these steps:

1. Click the **Add an action** link in the **If true** box.
2. Since we don't care about any incidents that do not have a high severity, we are going to ignore the **If false** box. Search for the **Microsoft Teams** connector and select it.
3. Select the **Post a message (V3) (Preview)** action and connect if prompted. The action will look as follows:

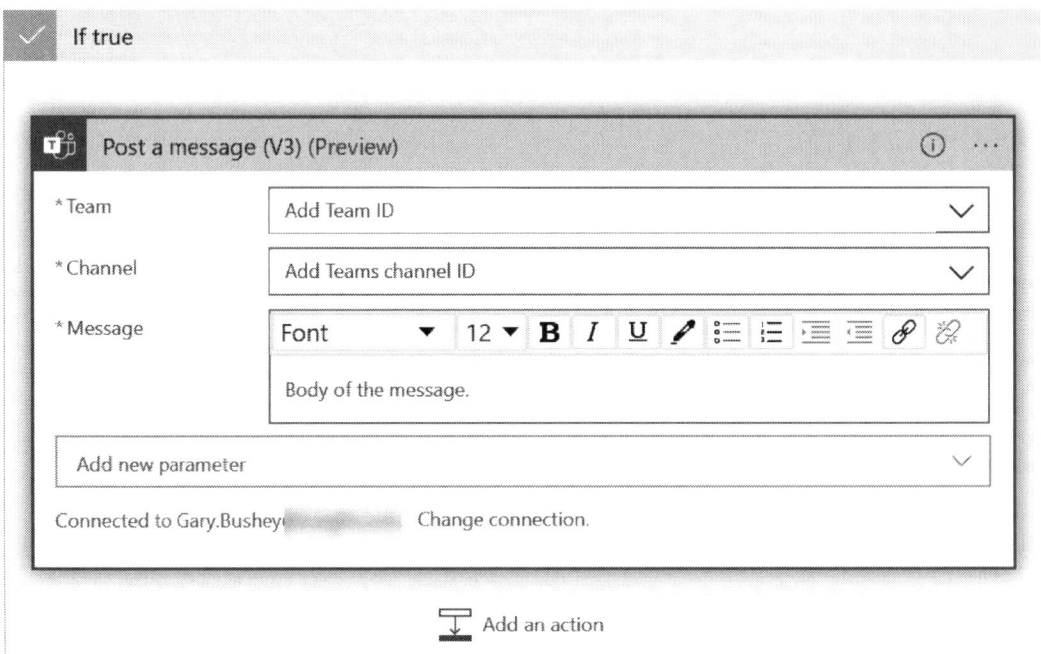

Figure 12.25 – Posting a message

4. One thing that is different in this action from the others is that both the **Team** and **Channel** fields are dropdowns. The **Team** field will be populated with all the teams you have access to and, once a team is selected, the **Channel** field will be populated with all the channels in that team.
5. Once you have those filled in, you can fill in the **Message** field. This can be anything that you want. In this case, we need to tell the analysts about a new, high-severity incident, so the message should be something like *A new high-severity incident has been generated. Its identification number is: …*, followed by the incident's ID number.

6. To do this, we are going to mix regular text and a dynamic content field. First, add the hardcoded text that was just listed. Then, using the dynamic content variable listing popup, select the **Number** variable. You may need to expand the **Alert – Get incident** listing in this popup to see all the available variables.

7. Once you are done, you should see the following:

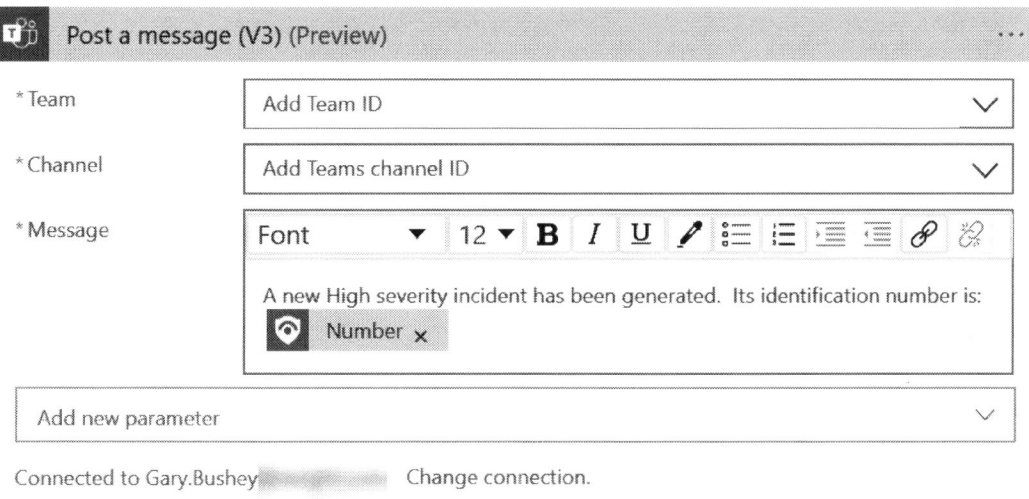

Figure 12.26 – Posting a message completed

8. Once you are all done, click on the **Save** button in the **Logic Apps Designer** page header to save this playbook. If there are any errors, you will be informed of them. If not, the playbook will be saved. You will notice that the **Save** button in the header is grayed out until new changes are made.

9. As a final step, you need to attach this playbook to an alert to verify that the code is working as designed. Refer to *Chapter 7, Creating Analytic Rules*, for instructions on how to do this.

There you have it! A fully functional and incredibly useful Microsoft Sentinel playbook with no coding required. You just needed to figure out which fields to use where. This was a very simple example but, hopefully, it has given you some idea of what to use playbooks for.

Summary

In this chapter, you learned how to create a playbook that you can use in your analytic query rules to perform SOAR actions. Playbooks are based on Azure Logic Apps, with the only difference being that the Microsoft Sentinel connector must be used for a Logic App to be a playbook.

With what you have learned, you can now create playbooks to automate a lot of actions that had to be performed manually previously. You read about one such example, but there is no limit to what you can do!

In the next chapter, we will use what we learned in this chapter to build a playbook that will create a new ServiceNow ticket and update the incident with the ticket number.

Questions

Answer these questions to test your knowledge of this chapter:

1. What needs to be done before a logic app can be used as an Microsoft Sentinel playbook?
2. How can I tell whether a specific playbook was successful the last time it ran?
3. In a playbook's workflow, how can I get information regarding an incident?
4. What is dynamic content?
5. Can I combine dynamic and static content in one field?

Further reading

Please refer to the following links for more information on the topics that were covered in this chapter:

- Logic Apps overview: `https://docs.microsoft.com/en-us/azure/logic-apps/logic-apps-overview`
- Connectors for Azure Logic Apps: `https://docs.microsoft.com/en-us/azure/connectors/apis-list`
- Sample Azure logic apps: `https://docs.microsoft.com/en-us/samples/browse/?products=azure-logic-apps`

- Sample Microsoft Sentinel playbooks: `https://github.com/Azure/Azure-Sentinel/tree/master/Playbooks`
- Testing logic apps with mock data but setting up static results: `https://docs.microsoft.com/en-us/azure/logic-apps/test-logic-apps-mock-data-static-results`

13
ServiceNow Integration for Alert and Case Management

Microsoft Sentinel is a powerful solution for gathering logs, enriching those logs with threat intelligence, and discovering threats across your environment. However, this is only part of the technology stack required to run a **Security Operations Center** (**SOC**). When a security alert is raised in Microsoft Sentinel, the SOC may need assistance from several other teams to investigate the issue, mitigate the threat, and remediate any impact caused. There also may be other security alert sources that do not flow through Sentinel and the SOC needs to correlate those alerts with Sentinel alerts before processing all the alerts in one location. Organizations require a solution to bridge these people and technologies together.

There are multiple solutions available for this bridging of SOC technologies and processes, with **JIRA**, **ZenDesk**, and **ServiceNow** being among the more commonly utilized solutions.

This chapter will cover the following main topics:

- A brief history of Microsoft Sentinel and ServiceNow integration
- Steps to integrate Microsoft Sentinel with ServiceNow

A brief history of Microsoft Sentinel and ServiceNow integration

The Microsoft Sentinel and ServiceNow integration capabilities have come a long way since the first release of our book. The evolution has been as follows:

1. Integrate Microsoft Sentinel with ServiceNow **IT Service Management** (**ITSM**) using Microsoft Sentinel Logic Apps.

   (This method was covered in our original release of this book.)

2. Integrate Azure security alert sources (not just Sentinel) with ServiceNow Security Incident Response via the Microsoft Graph Security API.

3. Integrate Microsoft Sentinel with ServiceNow Security Incident Response via an API directly to Microsoft Sentinel.

We'll discuss each of these methods in the following sections.

Integrating Microsoft Sentinel with ServiceNow ITSM using Microsoft Sentinel Logic Apps

We will not go into too much detail here since we covered this method in the first edition of this book. While this method achieved the integration step and was able to ingest alerts from Sentinel into ServiceNow, it fell short of meeting the SOC's requirements for the following reasons:

- SOCs are gravitating away from using ServiceNow ITSM to using Security Incident Response.

  We will cover key features of Security Incident Response later in this chapter, but in general, it is designed for security incidents, while ITSM is designed for IT incidents.

- The integration mapped a limited number of specific fields.
- The integration required more manual configurations.
- The integration required specialized skill sets; specifically, while using Azure Logic Apps.

Let's look at the next method.

Integrating Azure security alert sources (not just Sentinel) with ServiceNow Security Incident Response via the Microsoft Graph Security API

Since the release of the first edition of this book, Microsoft and ServiceNow have partnered to enable Microsoft Sentinel and ServiceNow Security Incident Response integration via the Microsoft Graph Security API.

The Microsoft Graph Security API is "*an intermediary service (or broker) that provides a single programmatic interface to connect multiple Microsoft Graph Security providers (also called security providers or providers). Requests to the Microsoft Graph Security API are federated to all applicable security providers. The results are aggregated and returned to the requesting application in a common schema.*" – `https://docs.microsoft.com/en-us/graph/security-concept-overview`

This method of integrating Microsoft Sentinel with ServiceNow has one key benefit: it does not require all your security alerts in Azure to flow through Sentinel. It does not even require you to utilize Sentinel. These are less common use cases, though. Most organizations do utilize Sentinel and do aggregate and correlate all their Azure security alerts using Sentinel.

Some of the limitations of integrating Microsoft Sentinel with ServiceNow using the Microsoft Graph Security API include the following:

- The Microsoft Graph Security API does not support sending data back to Sentinel from ServiceNow. For example, when a security incident in ServiceNow closes, organizations often want the corresponding alerts in Sentinel to automatically close.

- The integration plugin provided by ServiceNow for the Microsoft Graph Security API does not support complex conditions on aggregating multiple Sentinel alerts into the same ServiceNow security incident. For example, aggregation on two fields will require both fields to match; there is no option for one field OR another field to match.

> **Note**
> There are ways to work around this that require doubling the number of integration profiles created, adding a lot of complexity. But it can be done.

Overall, the integration capabilities provided by the Microsoft Graph Security API are streets ahead of the previously mentioned methods.

Integrating Microsoft Sentinel with ServiceNow Security Incident Response via an API directly to Microsoft Sentinel

The latest and most advanced method of integrating Microsoft Sentinel with ServiceNow is via a plugin provided by ServiceNow that taps into an API directly with Sentinel. Since most organizations aggregate all Azure security alerts into Sentinel, this is easily the most common and most recommended approach. Plus, this method adds new features not available in prior methods, such as the following:

- Aggregation, which uses more complex conditions such as an **OR** condition between two or more matching fields.
- Sending data back into Microsoft Sentinel, such as to close an alert in Sentinel when the corresponding security incident closes in ServiceNow.

There are many features of this method that we will cover in more detail in the next section, where we'll outline how to implement the integration and how to optimize its features. We'll also look at where to watch out for the known pitfalls.

Steps to integrate Microsoft Sentinel with ServiceNow

This section will outline how to integrate Microsoft Sentinel with ServiceNow Security Incident Response using the latest ServiceNow plugin, which taps directly into an API in Sentinel. ServiceNow provides *good documentation* on how to establish this integration. There is no need to fully reproduce these steps in this chapter. We will outline the steps and point out the common pitfalls, as well as the opportunities to optimize the integration.

Configuring the Microsoft Azure portal

This step is where you will configure Azure to allow ServiceNow to integrate with it. To do this, you will need to create an application in Azure. When you configure the ServiceNow Sentinel plugin later, the key variables you will need to collect are as follows:

- Tenant ID
- Client ID
- Client secret
- Subscription ID
- Resource Group name
- Workspace name

You will need these variables when you configure ServiceNow to authenticate to Microsoft Sentinel. Be sure to maintain the confidentiality of your client secret as it is the password for your application. If you are working with a third party to configure your ServiceNow instance, do not need to send the third party your client secret through an insecured channel such as email or chat. Instead, ask your third party to schedule a desktop sharing working session via your favorite video conferencing tool. Then, when they get to the step where they need the client secret, take control of their desktop and input it for them.

There are two ways that you can create a new application within Azure. The first is to go into **Azure Active Directory** inside the Azure portal, while the second is to go to the **App registrations** feature of Microsoft Sentinel. We will be taking the latter route here:

1. When you go to the **App registrations** page, it will look as follows. If you have created any app services already, they will also appear here. So, the following screenshot may not match your screen:

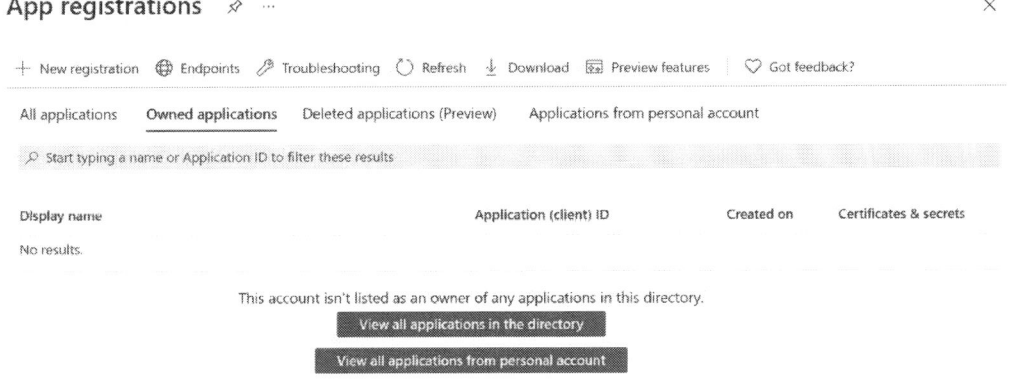

Figure 13.1 – App registrations

2. Click on the **New registration** button in the header to start the process of creating a new application registration. This will open a new window, as shown in the following screenshot:

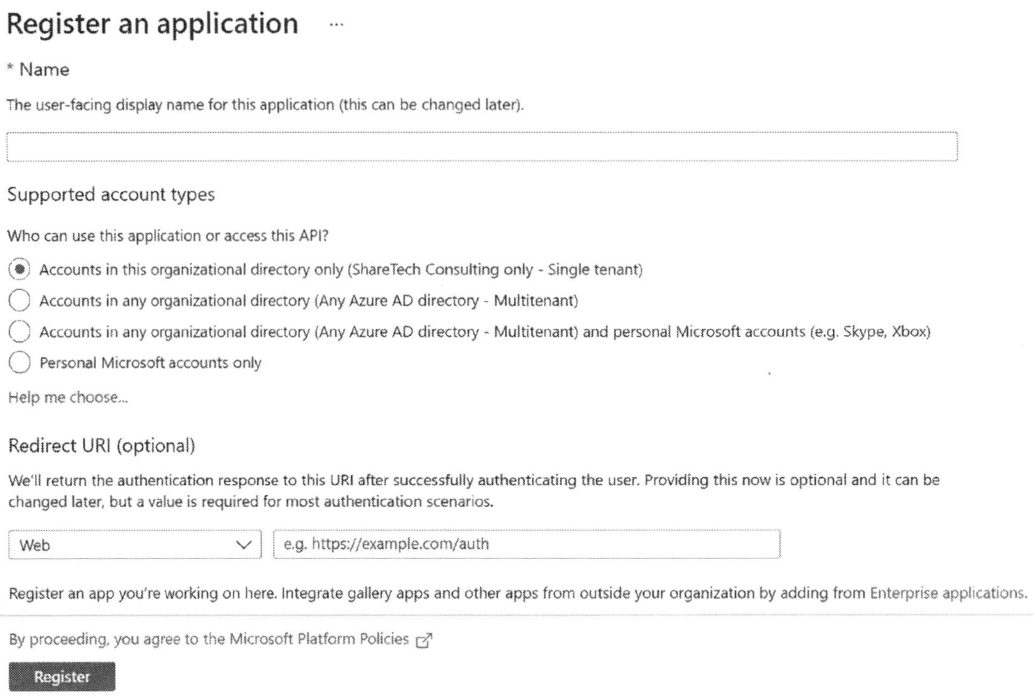

Register an application ...

* Name

The user-facing display name for this application (this can be changed later).

[   ]

Supported account types

Who can use this application or access this API?

(●) Accounts in this organizational directory only (ShareTech Consulting only - Single tenant)

( ) Accounts in any organizational directory (Any Azure AD directory - Multitenant)

( ) Accounts in any organizational directory (Any Azure AD directory - Multitenant) and personal Microsoft accounts (e.g. Skype, Xbox)

( ) Personal Microsoft accounts only

Help me choose...

Redirect URI (optional)

We'll return the authentication response to this URI after successfully authenticating the user. Providing this now is optional and it can be changed later, but a value is required for most authentication scenarios.

| Web ∨ | e.g. https://example.com/auth |

Register an app you're working on here. Integrate gallery apps and other apps from outside your organization by adding from Enterprise applications.

By proceeding, you agree to the Microsoft Platform Policies ↗

[Register]

Figure 13.2 – Register an application

You will need to fill in this form with the required values. For the application to work with the plugin, all you need to do here is fill in the **Name** field with a descriptive name and click on the **Register** button.

Once the application has been created, you will be taken to the application's **Overview** page, as shown in the following screenshot. You will notice that for this example, I chose to call my application **SentinelServiceNow**:

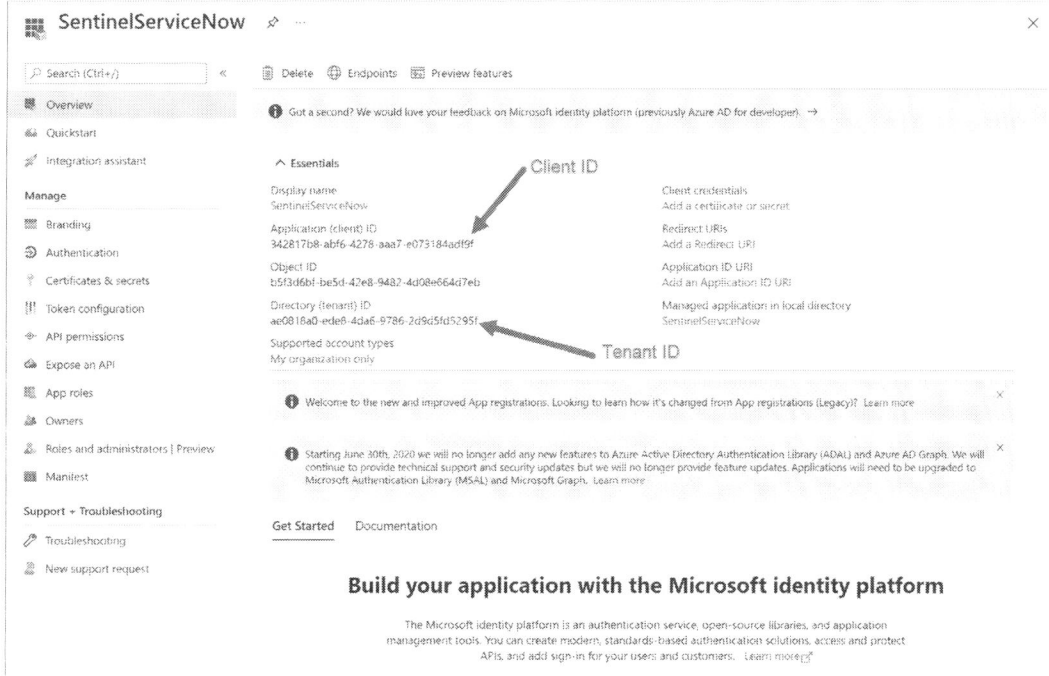

Figure 13.3 – Overview page

Notice that there are two pieces of information that you will need later, as indicated in the preceding screenshot: the Client ID and the Tenant ID. You will be able to mouse over each of those entries and select the **copy to clipboard** icon that appears to copy them.

3. Now, we need to create a new secret. Click on **Certificates & secrets** in the left-hand navigation menu. This will change the screen to the one shown here:

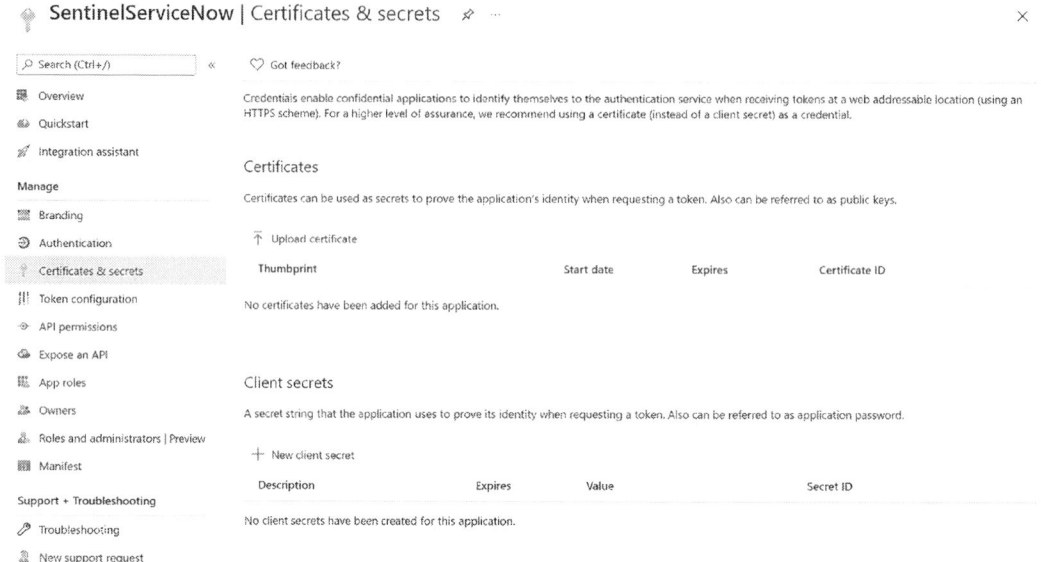

Figure 13.4 – Certificates & secrets

4. In the **Client secrets** section, click on the **New client secret** link to create a new secret. A new pane will open on the right-hand side of the screen, as shown in the following screenshot:

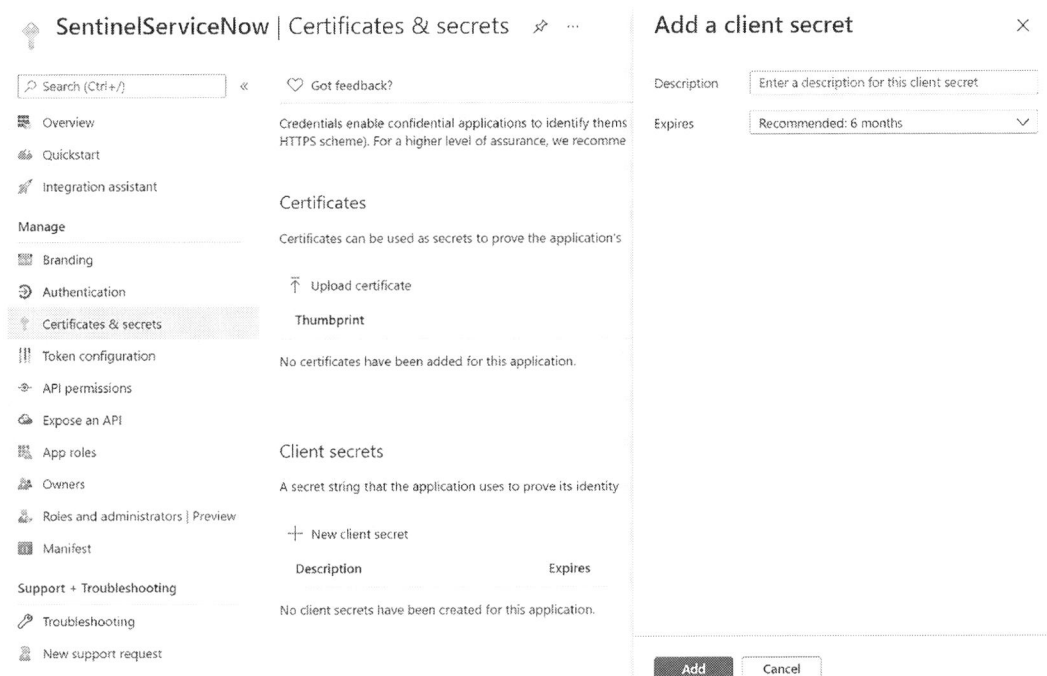

Figure 13.5 – Add a client secret pane

Enter the description for the secret and use the **Expires** dropdown to determine how long you want this secret to live. You need to balance how long you want the secret to live with to how often you will need to come in, create a new secret, and update the plugin with this new information.

5. Click the **Add** button to add the new secret. Once you've done this, the pane will close and you will be taken back to the **Certificates & secrets** page, as shown here:

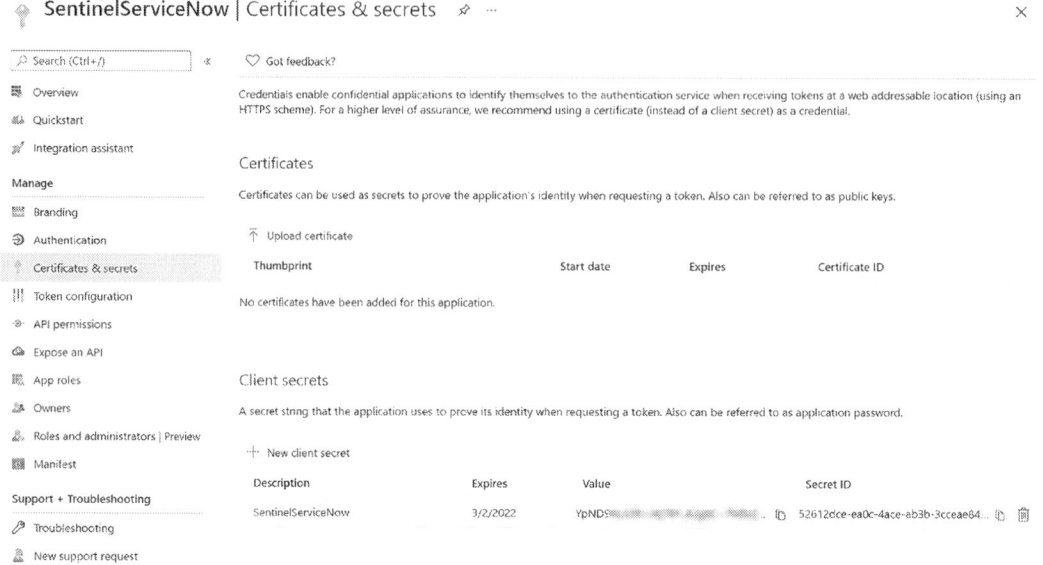

Figure 13.6 – New secret created

From this page, you will want to copy the secret's **Value** field. This is the **client secret key** that we will need to provide to the plugin. Again, keep this text confidential and consider storing it in a secure vault and programmatically retrieving and rotating the secrets. Treat it as you would a user's password.

We now have three out of the six pieces of information we need to provide to the plugin: the Client ID, Tenant ID, and client secret. To get the Subscription ID, the Resource Group name, and the Workspace name, we will need to go into Microsoft Sentinel.

6. In Microsoft Sentinel, click on the **Settings** link in the left-hand navigation menu and click on the **Workspace settings** link in the header. This will take you to the **Log Analytics workspace Overview** page, as shown in the following screenshot (this screenshot has been cropped to save space):

Figure 13.7 – Log Analytics workspace Overview page

As you can see, the remaining three pieces of information that are needed are shown here. You can mouse over each one and click on the copy to clipboard icon to the right of each to copy the text.

7. Also on this page, you will need to click on the **Access control (IAM)** link. You will need to grant the application you just created the **Microsoft Sentinel Responder** rights so that it can update the incidents as needed. Refer to the following link for more detailed instructions on how to do this:

```
https://docs.microsoft.com/en-us/azure/role-based-access-
control/role-assignments-portal?tabs=current
```

That is all the information that is needed from Azure to give to the Microsoft Sentinel integration plugin. Next, we will learn how to install the plugin and configure it using the values from this section.

Installing the Microsoft Sentinel integration plugin in ServiceNow

This plugin is available on the ServiceNow store. Be sure that you read the release notes to confirm you meet all the requirements, such as the ServiceNow instance version.

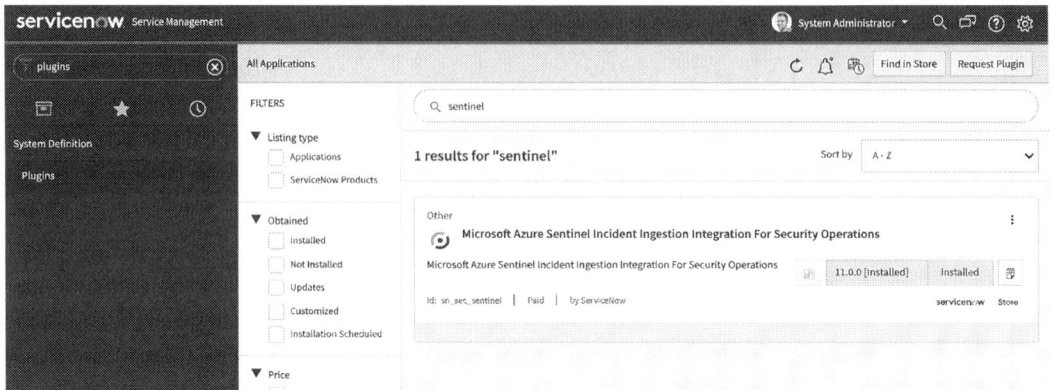

Figure 13.8 – ServiceNow Sentinel plugin

It is recommended to work with the latest version of the plugin when developing, as well as to always use the same version in production as the version that was used during development.

Configuring the ServiceNow Sentinel plugin to authenticate to Microsoft Sentinel

This step is where you will input the variables you collected in the *Configuring the Microsoft Azure portal* section. Remember to not provide a third-party service provider with your client secret. Instead, use a screen sharing and desktop control solution to input it yourself when they get to this step.

A gotcha of this step is that there is a slight delay after clicking submit and it will not tell you it was successful. It will, however, tell you if there is an error. If the window closes without error, then you have successfully authenticated your ServiceNow instance to your Microsoft Sentinel instance. If there is an error, it is typically caused by either missing a step in the *Configuring the Microsoft Azure portal* section or a typo in the data of the form (watch out for leading or trailing spaces if you're copying/pasting). Be patient – it takes 20 seconds or so to decide if it worked:

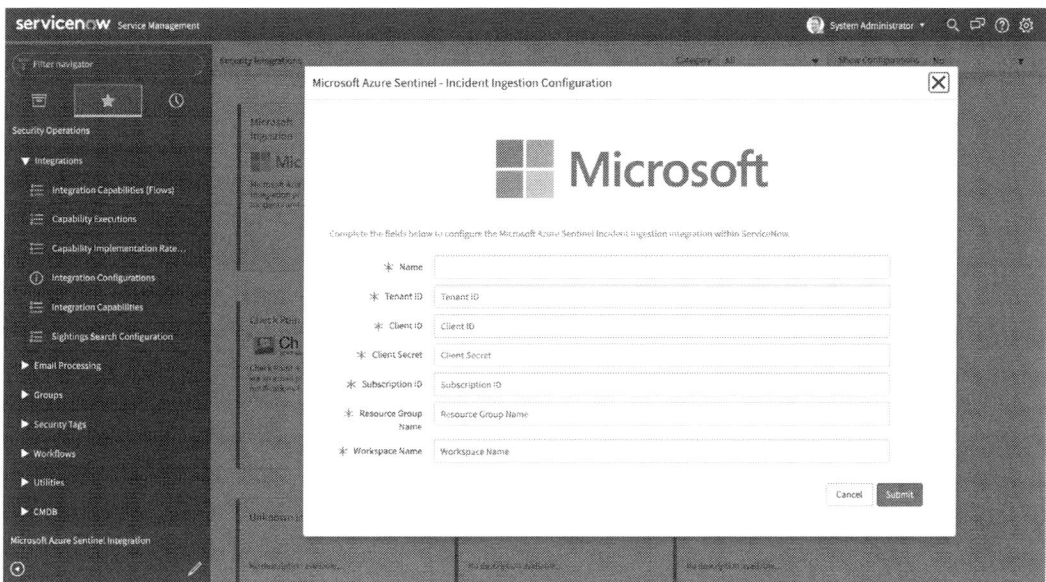

Figure 13.9 – Sentinel API credentials

Once this step is complete, all the new alerts from Sentinel will start to become visible in ServiceNow in the **Microsoft Sentinel Integration | Azure Sentinel Incident Import** path. This may not happen right away. Grab lunch and come back to it. Also, ServiceNow is not doing anything with these incidents yet.

Creating profiles in the ServiceNow Sentinel integration plugin

Profiles, which are called incident profiles, are what determine how ServiceNow processes the alerts from Sentinel. There are countless ways to configure these profiles. We will cover the most common and most advantageous, which is to create a profile for each product while reporting its logs and alerts to Sentinel. For example, you may have a profile for *Microsoft Defender ATP* and another profile for *O365 Advanced Threat Protection*. The key reason to separate the profiles by product is to optimize the field mappings that are unique to each product.

We will cover field mapping next but first, let's cover another gotcha. When configuring the profiles, there is a **Save and submit** button at the top of the form. There is also a **Continue** button at the bottom of the form that will progress through the different configurations in the profile. It is essential to use the **Continue** button because, on the last form, the **Continue** button turns into a **Finish** button. We have found that using the **Save and submit** button will result in the **Incomplete** status of the profile when it is enabled. However, using the **Continue** button and then clicking **Finish** at the end does not produce this issue.

Ordering profiles

The first page on the profile configuration requires a name, a description, an active or inactive checkbox, and an order. We will provide a brief explanation of the order field since it is impactful. The other fields should be self-explanatory.

The profile configuration page looks as follows:

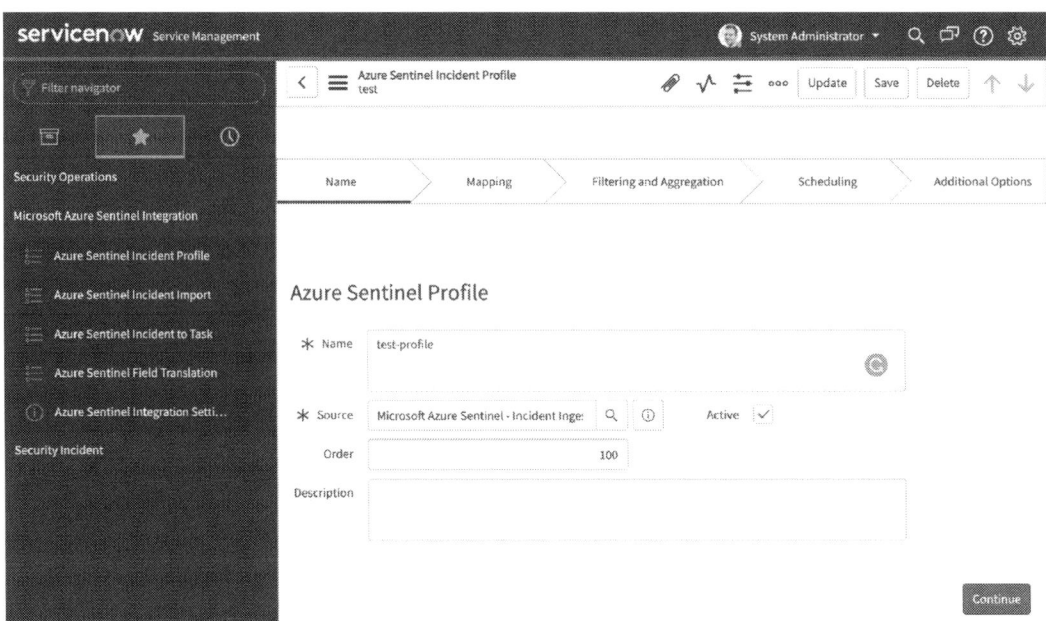

Figure 13.10 – Profile configuration name form

When there is more than one profile, the order field configures the profiles to work like firewall rules. This means that it tries each profile in order; then, once a profile's conditions have been matched, that profile is used, and the proceeding profiles are not checked. There is currently not an option to continue checking proceeding profiles, but that would be a nice option to have in a future release. There are some use cases where this would be valuable, and there are other areas of ServiceNow that have a similar feature. So, we would not be surprised if you see this feature in a later release of the plugin.

Field mapping

The next section of the profile configuration is for mapping fields from Sentinel into fields in the ServiceNow Security Incident table and form. There are common fields that apply to all types of alerts. Then, there are unique fields per product for reporting its logs and alerts in Sentinel, as stated in the opening paragraphs of the *Creating profiles in the ServiceNow Sentinel integration plugin* section.

The first step is to capture sample alerts from Sentinel. But first, we will take a quick sidestep to configure a property to optimize this capability.

Follow these steps to increase the number of sample alerts provided in field mappings:

1. Navigate to **Microsoft Azure Sentinel Integration | Azure Sentinel Integration Settings**.

    Here, you will find five different properties to set. We will cover the one that's relevant to field mapping. Then, we will revisit the other settings as needed for the other configurations. Do not change these settings unless you need to. Change the settings as per our recommendations. Their defaults are designed to work for most use cases.

The setting we recommend changing for the field mapping configuration is called **Enforce a limit on the number of sample incidents that can be fetched**. The default is **5**. Change this to 20, which is the maximum value it will take. Click **Save** and go back to the alert profile:

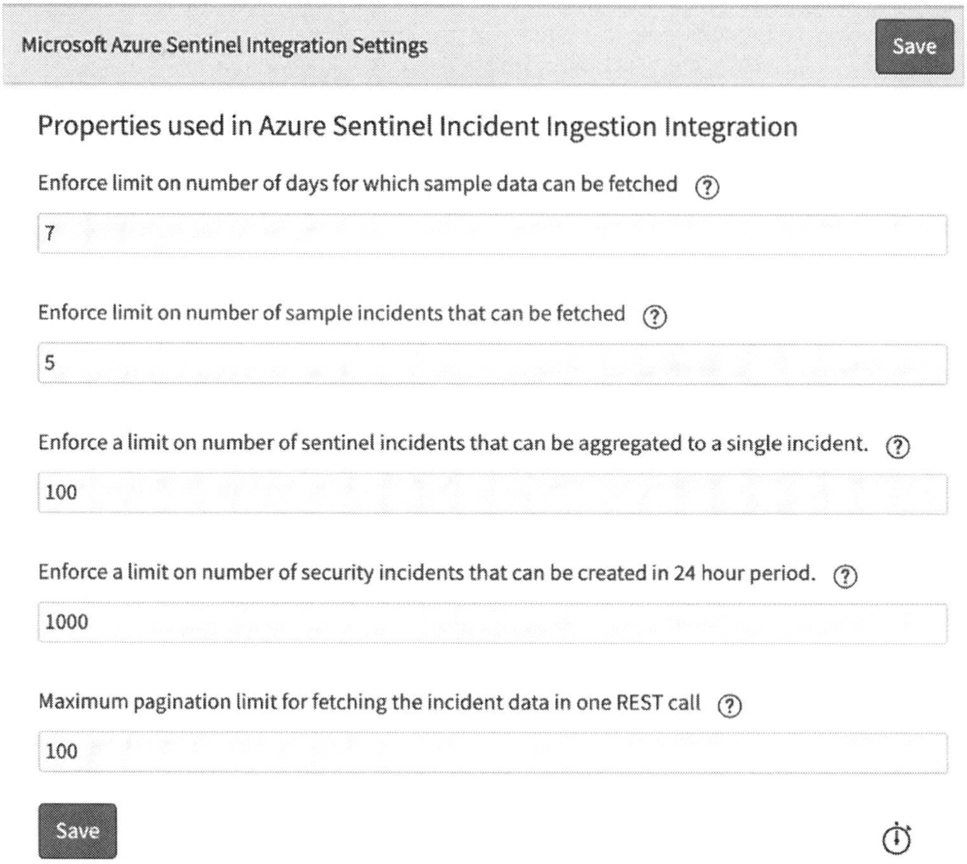

Microsoft Azure Sentinel Integration Settings   Save

Properties used in Azure Sentinel Incident Ingestion Integration

Enforce limit on number of days for which sample data can be fetched (?)

| 7 |

Enforce limit on number of sample incidents that can be fetched (?)

| 5 |

Enforce a limit on number of sentinel incidents that can be aggregated to a single incident. (?)

| 100 |

Enforce a limit on number of security incidents that can be created in 24 hour period. (?)

| 1000 |

Maximum pagination limit for fetching the incident data in one REST call (?)

| 100 |

Save

Figure 13.11 – Configuration settings

2. Back on the alert profile mapping configuration, click the drop-down for **Sample Ingestion Method**. The two options are as follows:

    - **All default incident and entity fields**: This will not bring over any fields that are unique to a certain product reporting its logs in Sentinel. It will also water down your options for field mapping.

- **Retrieve recent Microsoft Sentinel incidents**: This will bring over recent sample incidents from Sentinel. You should get 20 of them since you changed this setting previously. This depends on the Sentinel instance having incidents to work with:

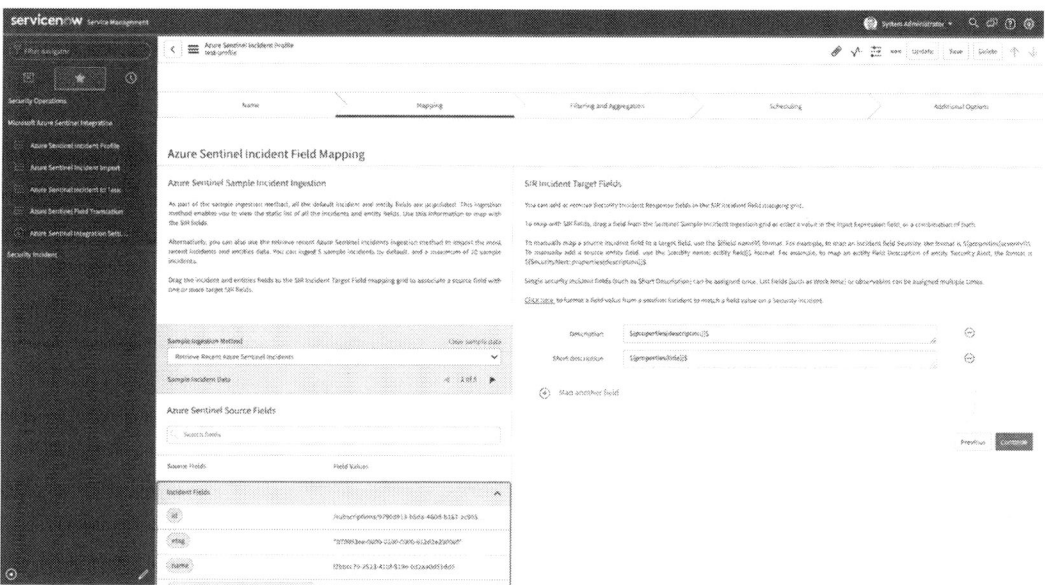

Figure 13.12 – Mapping form

After setting the drop-down to **Retrieve recent Microsoft Sentinel incidents**, click the **Import Sample Data** button. This will take a few minutes, as the message will indicate on the form. We have seen that it can take less than a minute, but we have also seen that it can take several minutes, up to the point that you may want to go get a coffee or take a walk and come back to it. Once the sample records appear, you can click through them to see the products they were produced by. We use the term *catching samples* here because you are trying to catch sample records of product types so that you can create a profile that's specific to that product type. Start with the product that is first represented in the samples. Then, continue working through the sample records until you cannot catch any new products. It may require several import attempts and specific timing to catch sample incidents for uncommon products.

When you catch a sample incident for the product you are creating the profile for, look through the available Sentinel fields to determine what fields you want to map into the Security Incident table and form in ServiceNow Security Incident Response. On the right-hand side of the form, you will see the default security incident fields to map to. You can remove these defaults or keep some or all of them, and there is a button beneath them to add more security incident fields to map into. Here is a list of common mappings:

*requires a transform or that you map to a custom field called Vendor Severity.

Sentinel Field	ServiceNow Field
Properties (additionalData(alertProductNames))	Short Description
Properties (Severity)	Severity*
Properties (firstActivityTimeUtc)	Start time
Properties (createdTimeUtc)	Detection time
Properties (description)	Description

You also have the option to append Sentinel fields to a ServiceNow string field such as **Description** or **Short Description**. For example, you could map both the properties (description) and all the fields from Sentinel representing a hostname or username or IP address into the **Description** field on the Security Incident table and form.

A gotcha on field mapping is where, when mapping into reference fields or choice list fields on the ServiceNow Security incident response table and form, the field values mapping into the reference and choice list fields must match an option in those destination fields on the Security Incident Response table and form. If there is no match, don't worry – it won't fail the integration. That specific field mapping will simply not do anything.

This integration also lets you script transforms. Some **transforms** are already built in, such as the configuration item field. Common transforms are for normalizing Sentinel field values to **Security Incident Response** field values. For example, a severity field from Sentinel uses high, medium, and low values, while Security Incident Response uses 1-Critical, 2-High, 3-Medium, and 4-Low.

Transforms can be complex and sometimes they are necessary, but sometimes, it is both easier and less complex to maintain if the target field is adjusted to accept the different forms of data. Alternatively, there is a feature in Security Incident Response called **security risk calculators** that allows for post-integration transforms using simple conditional rules. These are commonly used on the severity and other risk rating types of fields, such as priority and impact.

However, you can use them in other fields too. You also have the option of creating business rules in Security Incident Response to do post-integration transforms. Transforms is a complex topic, so we won't cover it here in detail. The key thing to remember is that using a transform in the integration plugin is not the only option and is often the most complex and costly of the options available.

A final key field mapping to do is to map Sentinel fields with URLs, email addresses, email subjects, IP addresses, user IDs, hostnames, and other IOCs in the observable fields. ServiceNow Security Incident Response provides a generic observable field or observable fields of specific types, such as one for a URL or one for the email address. Mapping to the specific type of observable field predefines the type of observable it is on the target table. This is helpful for reporting and during analysis when you're processing a lot of observables.

Filtering and aggregation

The next section of the profile configuration is for filtering and aggregation. These are two very different configurations, so we will address them separately. The following screenshot shows the **Filtering and Aggregation** configuration page:

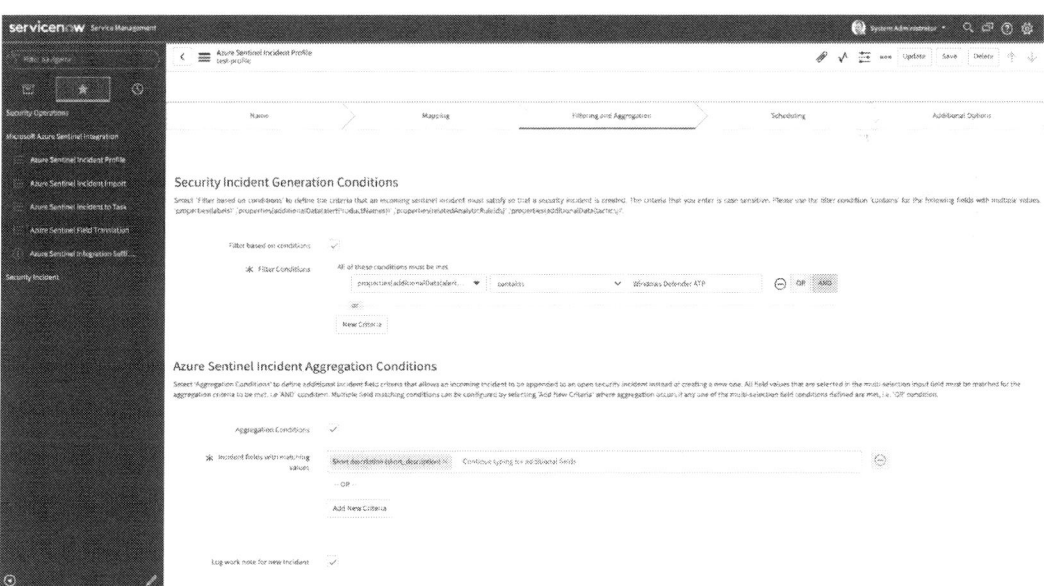

Figure 13.13 – Filtering and Aggregation

Let's discuss filtering and aggregation in detail.

Filtering

Filtering is just what the name suggests. These are the conditions you set to determine which alerts from Sentinel your profile will process. This is valuable when you're creating separate profiles for different products and sending their logs and alerts to Sentinel. It is also valuable for filtering out alerts that are commonly false positives or low risk.

Aggregation

Aggregation is also just as the name suggests. These are the conditions that determine which Sentinel alerts are combined into the same Security Incident record in ServiceNow. For example, if Sentinel reports five alerts from Microsoft Defender ATP, all for the same alert type and same hostname, you will likely want to aggregate those into the same security incident rather than create separate security incidents.

Aggregation has improved greatly in the Sentinel integration plugin compared to the Graph Security API plugin. We can now create **OR** conditions – this field OR that field must match. However, there are still two key features that are missing that we hope to see in a future release:

- **Time-based aggregation**: Currently, if a new alert from Sentinel matches the aggregation conditions on an existing security incident in ServiceNow that was opened long ago (we will say a year for dramatic purposes), it will aggregate. You will not want that and should prefer a separate security incident on that condition.

- **Empty field value aggregation**: Currently, if an existing security incident has an empty value in a field in the aggregation conditions and a new incident from Sentinel also has that field empty, it will aggregate. This is not something you would want to aggregate on. There is a way to work around this, but it doubles the number of profiles you will need and adds a lot of complexity and overhead.

Finally, you can check a box to record a work note when the aggregation occurs. You will almost certainly want to do this to have a visual aid for the aggregation while processing the security incident.

The last point on aggregation is another gotcha. The default setting only allows 100 Sentinel alerts to be aggregated into one ServiceNow Security Incident. In larger environments, this will not be enough. We recommend increasing this to 1,000. This setting is also in the **Microsoft Azure Sentinel Integration | Azure Sentinel Integration Settings** path, just like the other setting we recommended changing earlier.

Scheduling

The next section of the profile configuration is for scheduling the import. This is self-explanatory and there are no known gotchas. Check the **Ongoing incident ingestion** checkbox and move on to the next configuration, as shown in the following screenshot:

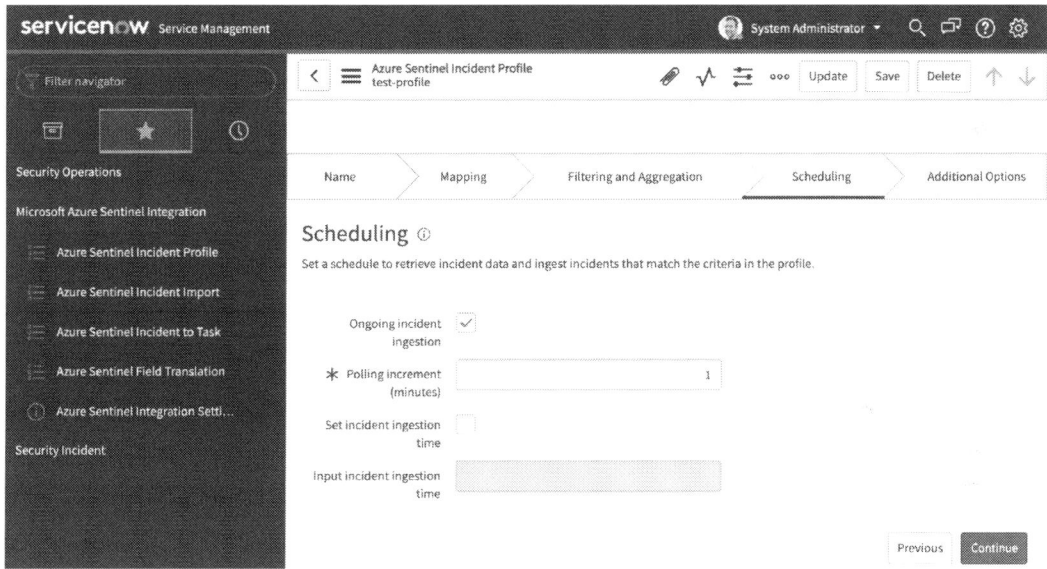

Figure 13.14 – Scheduling

Now, let's look at a few additional options.

Additional options

The final section of the profile configuration is for bi-directional field mapping between Sentinel and ServiceNow. For example, ServiceNow can tell Sentinel to close a Sentinel alert when the corresponding security incident in ServiceNow is closed. There are several options in this section, and they are rich in features. We recommend utilizing them. However, be careful not to turn them on if your ServiceNow is in a development environment and you are integrated with a production Sentinel environment. It will mess up your Sentinel production records with your lab activity:

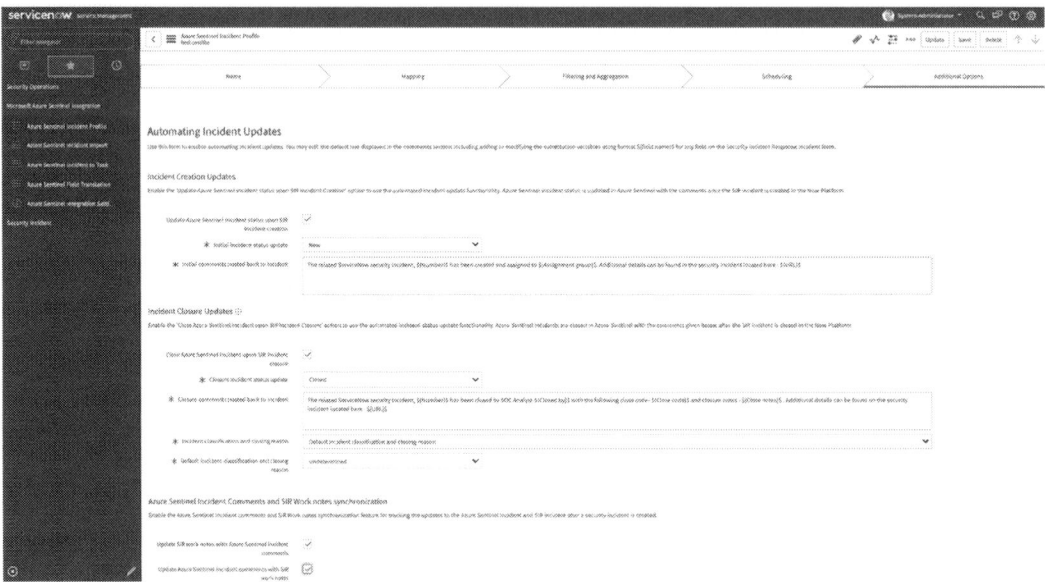

Figure 13.15 – Additional Options

Your Sentinel to ServiceNow integration (and possibly back if you enabled those options) is now configured. Navigate to the **Microsoft Azure Sentinel Integration | Azure Sentinel Incident to Task** path in ServiceNow and wait for the records to begin populating.

When you are in this area of ServiceNow, try grouping by the task column. This will show you where the aggregation is occurring. Any groups that have more than one record represent an aggregation.

You also can navigate to **Security Incident Records** (in the task column) to review the results of the field mappings you configured.

Summary

This chapter showed you how to create an integration with a solution – in our example, ServiceNow – to provide a single place to process security incidents. It does not matter what alert source the security incident started from or who needs to work on it. There are countless ways to achieve this outcome. We only covered a more common approach in this chapter.

Be creative and focus on simplicity and licensing reduction. For example, if Sentinel does not provide correlation for alerts coming from an alert source because that alert source has very high fidelity, then consider ingesting those alerts directly into ServiceNow and bypassing Sentinel to save on licensing costs and to reduce complexity in your architecture.

We also only scratched the surface of what can be done with a security incident once it is automatically created in ServiceNow Security Incident Response. ServiceNow is not just a workflow and case management solution with fancy forms and dashboards. ServiceNow Security Incident Response is an industry-leading **Security Orchestration, Automation and Response** (**SOAR**) platform capable of streamlining and automating much of the security incident detection and response process. In the next chapter, we will discuss some of the operational tasks we can perform to maintain peak operational efficiency in Microsoft Sentinel.

Section 5: Operational Guidance

In this section, you will learn how to ensure the system remains in peak operational efficiency and keep up to date with solution improvements.

This section contains the following chapters:

- *Chapter 14, Operational Tasks for Microsoft Sentinel*
- *Chapter 15, Constant Learning and Community Contribution*

14
Operational Tasks for Microsoft Sentinel

As with any service or solution, an ongoing maintenance routine is a critical process to ensure timely service improvements, maintain operational efficiency, control costs, and—most importantly—ensure the service remains highly effective in detecting and responding to security issues.

In general, **Security Operations Center** (**SOC**) operations are performed by two distinct roles: SOC engineers and SOC analysts. In a small organization, this may be a single person carrying out both roles; in larger organizations, these roles will span many teams and will be carried out by dedicated professionals. In this chapter, we will provide details of the daily, weekly, and monthly tasks required for each role, and any ad hoc tasks that should be carried out as required. You can use this list as a starting point for building your own tasks list to ensure optimal SOC operations.

The information in this chapter is meant to provide a starting point for your own planning and ongoing improvement, so you can carry out the necessary processes to produce a high-performing team and ensure a well-managed **Microsoft Sentinel** solution.

In this chapter, we will cover the following topics:

- Dividing SOC duties
- Operational tasks for SOC engineers
- Operational tasks for SOC analysts

Dividing SOC duties

A well-developed SOC will be made up of multiple roles to divide up responsibilities and ensure that everyone can focus on their specific tasks. Depending on the size of the team, there could be many roles and many layers of management, leadership, and expertise, or it could be a smaller team in which two or three individuals carry out all the roles between them.

At a high level, the operation of an SOC will require experts that know how to install and maintain the technology solutions required to run the SOC (that is, *SOC engineers*) and another set of experts that are able to use the solutions to hunt for threats and respond to security incidents (that is, *SOC analysts*). These two roles work together to provide constant feedback on what works well and where improvements are required.

Let's review the primary differences between these two roles to understand the type of operational tasks they carry out. For detailed role guidance and permissions, please see this article: https://docs.microsoft.com/en-us/azure/sentinel/roles.

SOC engineers

SOC engineers are responsible for the initial design and configuration of Microsoft Sentinel. Their role includes the connection of data sources, setting retention policies, and configuring any **threat intelligence** (**TI**) feeds. The SOC engineer is responsible for implementing and managing **role-based access controls** (**RBACs**) to secure access to the platform and the data it contains (review **Azure Active Directory** (**AD**) as an additional research topic).

Once the service is operational, SOC engineers are then responsible for ensuring that data connectors remain healthy, providing ongoing improvements, creating analytic rules for threat detection, and fine-tuning the service to ensure it remains operationally cost-effective and efficient.

The SOC engineers will implement new features made available by **Microsoft** and develop automation functionalities and other improvements based on feedback from the SOC analysts and recommendations from the wider security community.

SOC analysts

SOC analysts focus on using the tools and data available to respond to alerts and hunt for other threats that may not have been automatically detected.

This role relies on the continuous development of new detection methods, the advancement and integration of machine learning algorithms, and the automation of threat responses to ensure SOC analysts can react quickly to new alerts.

To ensure they can focus on threat detection, SOC analysts offload the tooling and rule configuration to SOC engineers, allowing the engineers to create and maintain their playbooks, and define their standard operating procedures for identifying and responding to suspicious events and behaviors.

Operational tasks for SOC engineers

In this section, we will provide an initial list of tasks that have been identified as *engineering tasks*. You can use this list as a starting point and then add your own tasks based on what works for your specific requirements. Each component that is added to the SOC architecture will have its own task requirements—for example, if you integrate a **cloud access security broker** (**CASB**) solution, you will need to carry out similar tasks within that platform to ensure it is well maintained and sending the appropriate information to Microsoft Sentinel.

Daily tasks

A list of daily tasks for SOC engineers is as follows:

- **Monitor the data connectors for two key performance indicators**:

    A. Ensure the data ingestion is consistent with the expected volume; if the volume drops below the average daily rate it could be caused by a configuration error on the source, preventing the data from being sent to Microsoft Sentinel. This should be investigated immediately to ensure no loss of security log data.

B. Ensure the total ingestion per day does not exceed the expected ingestion rates. There may be multiple reasons for an increased ingestion rate on a single day, such as a spike in the volume of threats or an increase in business activity, such as higher sales or increased remote work. However, if the volume continues to increase day by day, there will be an impact on the expected budget for the costs, and this will need to be reviewed with the management teams.

There is a workbook available to assist with this monitoring: `https://docs.microsoft.com/en-us/azure/sentinel/monitor-data-connector-health`.

- **Monitor the service health of all core components**:

    Monitor the service health of all core components, for example, the Azure platform, **Azure AD** for **Identity and Access Management** (**IAM**), and any data collection servers (syslog), ensuring dashboards are available and alerts are triggering as expected.

- **Review the planned maintenance, service health, and availability monitoring of the Microsoft Azure platform**:

    Do this using the following resources:

    A. Publicly viewable information: `https://status.azure.com/en-us/status`

    B. Signing in to your Azure portal and viewing specific details: `https://portal.azure.com/#blade/Microsoft_Azure_Health/AzureHealthBrowseBlade/serviceIssues`

Weekly tasks

A list of weekly tasks for SOC engineers is as follows:

- Review the data connectors to ensure each connector that is enabled is still functioning correctly. Check for any new or preview connectors, as well as updates to existing connectors. If a new connector can be used instead of a custom connector (or a syslog server), plan to replace this as soon as possible to benefit from the new capability and reduce the reliance on customizations and server-based solutions.

- Review the **Workbooks** page and the **News & Guides** page for new workbook templates, connector announcements, and any new updates. Ensure that existing workbooks are functioning correctly after the updates.

Monthly tasks

A list of monthly tasks for SOC engineers is as follows:

- Review the trends for data ingestion to carry out projected cost analysis; adjust the **pricing** tier to reflect the most cost-effective option (see the *Service pricing for Microsoft Sentinel* section in *Chapter 1, Getting Started with Microsoft Sentinel*, for more details).

- Validate the quality of the logs ingested and carry out noise-reduction tuning, especially after the introduction of new data sources.

- Validate the current retention period set for each data type and confirm it is suitable for investigation requirements and budgeting guidelines.

- Carry out a scenario-mapping exercise with the SOC analysts to identify additional detection and response requirements (see the *Scenario mapping* section in *Chapter 1, Getting Started with Microsoft Sentinel*, for more details). Transfer this knowledge to key stakeholders across the business and technology teams.

- Review the roles and access permissions granted, ensuring minimum permissions are assigned and only active team members retain roles as required.

Ad hoc tasks

A list of ad hoc tasks for SOC engineers is as follows:

- Review any changes made to the IT infrastructure; look for opportunities to integrate additional log data to gain key insights and configure automated responses based on attack scenarios.

- Review any new data resources that may be suitable to assist in threat hunting scenarios.

- Review announcements from Microsoft via their website, blogs, technical community, or events (such as Microsoft **Ignite** and Microsoft **Build**) for potential changes to the Microsoft Sentinel platform or changes to any integrated services and solutions. If you have non-Microsoft solutions deployed, also check the appropriate announcements for supported product updates.

- Update the Microsoft Sentinel architecture documentation to reflect any changes made.

- Engage with external services that offer advanced security practices to further test and train your SOC capabilities, including **penetration testing**, **social engineering**, and defining advanced SOC activities.

Operational tasks for SOC analysts

In this section, we will provide an initial list of tasks that have been identified as operational requirements for SOC analysts. These tasks focus on the work required to create, maintain, and organize Microsoft Sentinel components to ensure operational efficiency.

Daily tasks

A list of daily tasks for SOC analysts is as follows:

- Check the **Incidents** page to ensure any new incidents are assigned to an owner and all **open** or **in-progress** incidents are actively investigated to completion.
- Go to the **Hunting** page and select **Run all queries**:

    A. Review the results for each query that returns at least one result.

    B. If any queries return a result of N/A, then investigate why the results are not available (you should at least receive a return of 0 as a result).

- Review TI sources for current activities and new findings and apply any findings to your threat hunting procedures.

Weekly tasks

A list of weekly tasks for SOC analysts is as follows:

- Go to the **Hunting** page and review all bookmarks that have been created, ensuring they are still associated with an active incident. Aim to keep this list short by deleting those that are no longer relevant.
- Review TI feeds to ensure they are still active; look for any recommended new TI feeds relevant to your specific industry and region.
- Review all existing analytics queries; check those that are disabled and decide whether they should be removed or enabled. For all active queries, review the following:

    A. When possible, each analytic rule should be associated with an appropriate automated task to ensure notifications are sent, a case is raised in the ticketing system, or other runbooks are triggered to carry out remediation activities.

    B. Work with SOC engineers to implement any changes to further automate detection and response capabilities.

    C. Review tuning metrics to ensure analytic rules are not overly suppressed, which may cause important events to be missed. These metrics are as follows: rule period and frequency, rule threshold, and suppression.

Monthly tasks

A list of monthly tasks for SOC analysts is as follows:

- Carry out a scenario-mapping exercise with SOC engineers to identify additional detection and response requirements (see the *Scenario mapping* section in *Chapter 1, Getting Started with Microsoft Sentinel,* for more details). Transfer this knowledge to key stakeholders across the business and technology teams.
- Review all Microsoft Sentinel workbooks to ensure they are relevant and run correctly (execute them using test cases).
- Review the tag taxonomy. A good resource for more details on resource tagging can be found here: `https://docs.microsoft.com/en-us/azure/cloud-adoption-framework/decision-guides/resource-tagging/`.

Ad hoc tasks

A list of ad hoc tasks for SOC analysts is as follows:

- Check the naming conventions that are being used for various components that are created manually. Keeping strict governance over naming conventions and other standards ensures easier communication across the team when handing over incidents for review.
- Engage with external services that offer advanced security practices to further test and train your SOC capabilities, including penetration testing, social engineering, and **purple team** activities.

Summary

While this is one of the shorter chapters in this book, it has covered the importance of the ongoing maintenance that will ensure SOC teams remain vigilant with respect to ongoing changes in the threat landscape and will also keep Microsoft Sentinel tuned for efficient and effective security operations.

In the final chapter of this book, we will introduce some resources you can use to continue gaining the knowledge required to implement and operate Microsoft Sentinel and its related solutions.

Questions

Review the following questions to test your knowledge of this subject:

1. What are the two main types of roles within an SOC?
2. Which role carries out the scenario-mapping exercise?
3. How frequently should you check the log ingestion rate and pricing tier?
4. How often should an SOC analyst check the **Incidents** page?
5. If you, as an SOC engineer, are told that a new project using an Azure SQL instance is just starting, when should you start ingesting its logs?

15
Constant Learning and Community Contribution

Thank you for taking the time to read this book and gain a thorough understanding of this new solution. In this final chapter, we want to provide some useful resources that you can use to continue your learning journey and get involved with community-based efforts to share knowledge. You can also find resources to directly provide feedback to Microsoft, ensuring the continual improvement of this solution.

This chapter will explore the official resources from Microsoft, additional resources for **Security Operations Center** (**SOC**) operations, and other resources made available by GitHub.

In this chapter, we will cover the following topics:

- Official resources from Microsoft
- Resources for SOC operations
- Using GitHub
- Specific components and supporting technologies

Official resources from Microsoft

In this section, we will cover resources that are made available by Microsoft to support the design, implementation, and operation of Microsoft Sentinel as a core security platform. This will include links to official documentation, blogs and technical forums, feature requests, and groups on LinkedIn.

Official documentation

Microsoft Docs (https://docs.microsoft.com/en-us/) is a great resource for documentation on every Microsoft solution. The following list provides some specific links to relevant documents you should start with:

- There is a comprehensive section on Microsoft Sentinel that will provide the latest official release of information about products, and product-specific guidance for the design and implementation of solutions: https://docs.microsoft.com/en-us/azure/sentinel/.

- Azure Monitor, and Log Analytics specifically, has a separate section that can be used to further study information on what we covered in *Chapter 2*, *Azure Monitor – Introduction to Log Analytics*. Visit this site for more details: https://docs.microsoft.com/en-us/azure/azure-monitor/.

- Azure **Active Directory** (**AD**) is another key component that is worth studying in more depth to ensure you can properly secure access to the Microsoft Sentinel subscription and critical resources. Guidance for Azure AD can be found here: https://docs.microsoft.com/en-us/azure/active-directory/.

Tech community – blogs

Microsoft has built a tech community for many different areas of its solutions, each offering a blog to allow expert articles to be shared via specific, focused blog posts. The one dedicated to Microsoft Sentinel can be found here: https://techcommunity.microsoft.com/t5/azure-sentinel/bg-p/AzureSentinelBlog.

You can join this site to keep up to date on announcements and new product features, or to ask questions that will be answered by members of the community and experts from Microsoft. The Microsoft team provides links to future training and webinars, and to previously recorded sessions and their associated resources, such as presentation slides.

You may also want to subscribe to the **Really Simple Syndication** (**RSS**) feed to ensure the latest information is instantly available and easy to find.

Here are some additional blogs and related material available:

- Microsoft blog for **Chief Information Security Officers (CISOs)**: `https://www.microsoft.com/security/blog/ciso-series`.
- The Microsoft Security Response Center is a great resource for information on all the latest attacks that have been detected and analyzed: `https://msrc-blog.microsoft.com/tag/mstic/`.
- The Microsoft DART team (incident response experts) have their own space to provide the latest guidance; this should be high on your review list: `https://www.microsoft.com/security/blog/microsoft-detection-and-response-team-dart-blog-series/`.
- Blog for all Microsoft security initiatives: `https://www.microsoft.com/security/blog`.
- Microsoft Azure security blog: `https://azure.microsoft.com/en-us/blog/topics/security`.
- Microsoft Graph Security API blog: `https://docs.microsoft.com/en-us/graph/api/resources/security-api-overview?view=graph-rest-1.0`.
- Microsoft Sentinel questions on Reddit: `https://www.reddit.com/r/AzureSentinel/`.

Tech community – forums

As with blogs, there are many forums that cover Microsoft products. Forums allow you to read questions from other members, learn more about potential challenges and resolutions, then raise your own questions if you can't find answers elsewhere. Some of them are as follows:

- Forum for Microsoft Sentinel: `https://techcommunity.microsoft.com/t5/azure-sentinel/bd-p/AzureSentinel`
- Forum for Azure Log Analytics: `https://techcommunity.microsoft.com/t5/azure-loganalytics/bd-p/AzureLogAnalytics`
- Forum for the Azure Security community: `https://techcommunity.microsoft.com/t5/security-identity/bd-p/Azure-Security`

Feature requests

If you have a good idea to improve Microsoft Sentinel, or you find a gap in any of the Microsoft security solutions that needs to be addressed, you can provide your ideas via the feedback option within the Azure portal. The feedback option appears in the top right-hand corner of the screen and looks as in the following screenshot. You can select the smiley face to provide positive feedback, or the sad face to explain any issues you may have with the functionality, as shown in the following screenshot:

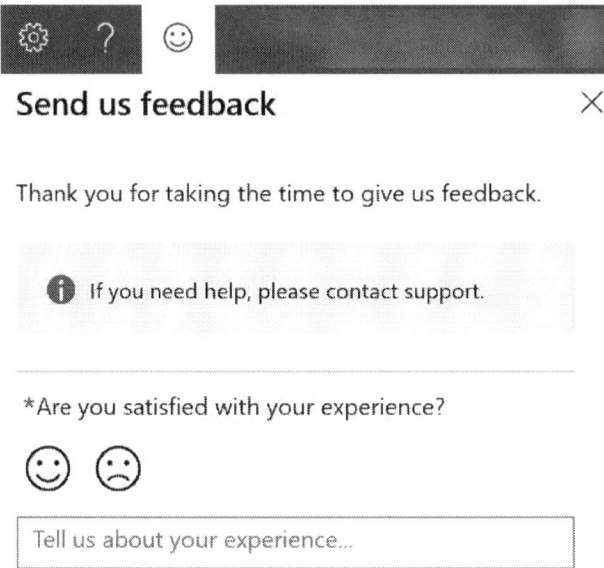

Figure 15.1 – Azure feedback options

While blogs and forums are a good resource for research and to ask questions, you should not rely on them for problems that are having an immediate effect and may need specific technical expertise to resolve. If you need immediate assistance with your implementation of Microsoft Sentinel, you should reach out to Microsoft Support, using one of the official channels.

If you do not have a support plan, you can sign up for one here: `https://azure.microsoft.com/en-us/support/plans`.

If you have a **Microsoft Premier Support** agreement, you will be provided with direct contact details for your dedicated support team.

In the Azure portal, navigate to the Microsoft Sentinel home page, then select the question mark icon from the menu at the top right of the screen, as shown in the following screenshot:

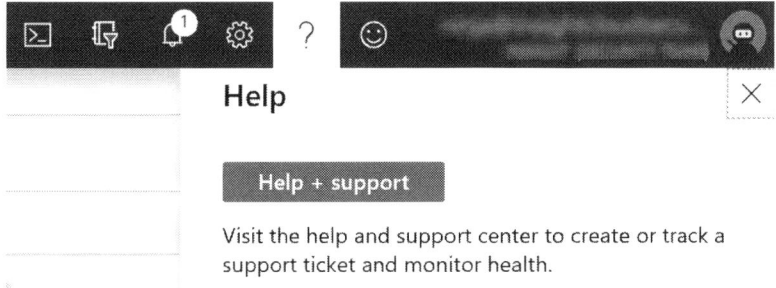

Figure 15.2 – Help and support

When the drop-down box appears, you can select the **Help + support** button, which will guide you through the instructions to create a new support request.

LinkedIn groups

LinkedIn can be used to build your professional network and gain access to other experts in your field. Groups are for general discussion on topics of interest and, usually, anyone can join. Microsoft moderates its own LinkedIn group dedicated to the security community.

To join, use the following link to get to the group, then ask to join: `https://aka.ms/AzureSentinelLinkedIn`.

Other resources

Microsoft also provides resources on their official Docs site, Facebook, and Twitter. The following links are shortcut links you can use to directly get to these resources:

- **Microsoft Sentinel newsletter**: Subscribe to emails here: `https://cda.ms/2jr`.
- **Microsoft Sentinel Ninja Training**: `https://aka.ms/sentinelninja`.
- **Microsoft learning paths**: `https://docs.microsoft.com/en-us/learn/paths/security-ops-sentinel/`.
- **Microsoft Certification SC-200**: `https://docs.microsoft.com/en-us/learn/certifications/exams/sc-200`.

- **Facebook**: https://aka.ms/AzureSentinelFacebook.
- **Twitter**: https://aka.ms/AzureSentinelTwitter.

Resources for SOC operations

The following study resources are available for improving SOC capabilities, such as advanced threat-hunting procedures, incident response tactics, and adopting a strategic *zero-trust* approach to implementing technology.

MITRE ATT&CK® framework

The MITRE **ATT&CK** framework stands for **Adversarial Tactics, Techniques, and Common Knowledge** (**ATT&CK**). The MITRE ATT&CK framework was developed to ensure documentation of these behaviors and that they are applicable to real environments. The framework provides a common taxonomy to promote comparison across different types of adversary groups using the same terminology.

The MITRE ATT&CK® framework contains four common use cases:

- Detection and Analytics
- Threat Intelligence
- Adversary Emulation and Red Teaming
- Assessment and Engineering

This framework has been embedded across Microsoft Sentinel to ensure ease of reference. To learn more about this framework, and to gain access to relevant resources, start by reading the guide to the MITRE ATT&CK® framework at https://attack.mitre.org/resources/getting-started.

National Institute of Standards for Technology (NIST)

NIST provides a rich source of materials that have been developed for the advancement of security across a range of industries, government, and critical infrastructure. If you are not based in the US, you can still use this information as a guide to secure your own operations and infrastructure.

One of the key articles to review is the **Cybersecurity Framework** (**CSF**), aimed primarily at private sector organizations to assess and improve their ability to prevent, detect, and respond to cyberattacks. You can view this here: https://www.nist.gov/cyberframework.

If you are working in government, or looking for the strongest guidance for security controls, we recommend reviewing the information provided by NIST specifically for risk management in government, NIST 800-53 – Security and Privacy Controls for Federal Information Systems and Organizations: `https://csrc.nist.gov/publications/detail/sp/800-53/rev-5/final`.

Using GitHub

GitHub is the largest, and one of the best, platforms for sharing content and securely storing your code. The platform is primarily used for software development version control, using a distributed version control system called **Git**. When you start to use GitHub, you create a new project. This contains the code repository and allows secure collaboration between different authors and contributors. The repository can be set to **Private**, ensuring only specific people can view the contents, or you can allow others to view and contribute by making it **Public**.

GitHub is available for free and offers plans for professional and enterprise accounts. To learn how to get started with GitHub, sign up for the tutorial. If you get stuck at any time, there is also a help site dedicated to getting the most out of this unique solution. You can choose between Learning Lab or the Help site, which can be accessed at the following links:

- GitHub Learning Lab: `https://lab.github.com`
- GitHub Help site: `https://help.github.com`

GitHub for Microsoft Sentinel

Microsoft created a specific GitHub repository for Microsoft Sentinel and maintains it. You can use this repository to find sample queries for Microsoft Sentinel hunting to aid in the development of techniques for threat hunting by leveraging logs from multiple sources. With these sample queries, you can get a head start in learning the **Kusto Query Language** (**KQL**) and understanding different data sources. To get started, simply paste a sample query into the user interface and run the query. To view Microsoft Sentinel hunting queries on GitHub, go to the following link: `https://github.com/Azure/Azure-Sentinel/tree/master/Hunting%20Queries`.

GitHub for community contribution

One of the great benefits of adopting Microsoft Sentinel as your SOC platform is access to a community of like-minded security professionals who want to help make the world a more secure place. If you have a great idea for a hunting, investigation, or detection query that can be shared with the Sentinel community, you can submit it to the repository, and it will be brought directly into the Microsoft Sentinel service for direct customer use. To learn how to do this, use one of the following resources:

- Microsoft Sentinel wiki pages: `https://github.com/Azure/Azure-Sentinel/wiki`.
- Send an email with questions or feedback to `AzureSentinel@microsoft.com`.

Specific components and supporting technologies

As we have covered in this book, Microsoft Sentinel is built upon the Log Analytics platform, as part of Azure Monitor, which uses KQL for queries, Jupyter Notebook, and Logic Apps, and has machine learning capabilities. Mastering Microsoft Sentinel requires growing your skills in each of these areas. The following are some of our top picks for resources available today. You may find many more by joining the communities or developing your own groups of special interests.

Kusto Query Language

In *Chapter 5*, *Using the Kusto Query Language*, we introduced KQL, and in *Chapter 6*, *Microsoft Sentinel Logs and Writing Queries*, we showed how to use it to query logs within Microsoft Sentinel. However, you will probably need to continue learning this technology to write more useful queries and use advanced techniques to fine-tune the results.

For the official KCL documentation, go to the following link: `https://docs.microsoft.com/en-us/azure/kusto/`.

Pluralsight (`https://pluralsight.com`) is another great resource for many types of training courses across the IT landscape. Specifically, we think the Pluralsight KQL course may be of interest to you: `https://www.pluralsight.com/courses/kusto-query-language-kql-from-scratch`.

Jupyter Notebook

Jupyter Notebook is an open-source application used to create and share documents that contain notes, visualizations, live code, and other resources you can share between SOC analysts to improve threat-hunting and response capabilities.

Find more resources for Jupyter Notebook at the following link: `https://jupyter.org/`.

Machine learning with Fusion

Microsoft uses machine learning algorithms to help Microsoft Sentinel detect multi-stage attacks, which is known as Microsoft Fusion. The technique works by combining two or more alert activities, such as anomalous behavior and suspicious activities that may have been low-level alerts. Microsoft Sentinel can then produce accurate, high-fidelity incidents, reducing false positives and detecting attacks that may otherwise have gone unseen. For this to be successful, you must ensure the appropriate data connectors are enabled and you have at least 30 days of historical data to train the machine learning algorithms.

This feature is enabled by default and currently supports multiple scenarios, including the following:

- Monitoring users that trigger impossible travel alerts, followed by anomalous Office 365 activity
- User sign-in activity for an unfamiliar location, which is then followed by anomalous Office 365 activity
- User sign-in activity from an infected device, which is then followed by anomalous Office 365 activity
- User sign-in activity from an anonymous IP address, which is then followed by anomalous Office 365 activity
- User sign-in activity from a user with leaked credentials, which is then followed by anomalous Office 365 activity

To learn more about this technology and keep up with the latest developments, visit the following site: `https://docs.microsoft.com/en-us/azure/sentinel/fusion`.

Azure Logic Apps

Azure Logic Apps can be used for a wide variety of automation tasks, including the following:

- **Schedule-based workflow**: Creating a task to automatically carry out actions on a frequent basis, such as gathering data, then comparing that value to the last time it was gathered and raising an alert if the value exceeds a threshold.

- **Approval-based workflow**: Creating a task to monitor for a given trigger, then sending an approval request (such as an email) and continuing the requested action once the approval is received.

- **Azure Functions**: This can be integrated with Azure Logic Apps to carry out additional tasks and integrations, such as the following:

    A. Running code based on HTTP requests

    B. Scheduling code to run at predefined times

    C. Processing new and modified Azure Cosmos DB documents

    D. Processing new and modified Azure Storage blobs

    E. Responding to Azure Storage queue messages

    F. Responding to Azure Event Grid events via subscriptions and filters

    G. Responding to high volumes of Azure Event Hubs events

    H. Connecting to other Azure, on-premises, or other cloud services by responding to a Service Bus queue or topic messages

- **Storage workflow**: Enables integration with Azure Storage to enable the automated collection and retrieval of data.

To enable this automation, Azure Logic Apps can use connectors to provide quick access to events, data, and actions across other apps, services, systems, protocols, and platforms. This integration works for on-premises workloads, Azure, and other cloud platforms. Learn more about connectors at the following link: `https://docs.microsoft.com/en-us/connectors/`.

We recommend studying these capabilities further, to ensure you can automatically trigger actions when alerts and incidents are raised in Microsoft Sentinel, at `https://docs.microsoft.com/en-us/azure/logic-apps/logic-apps-overview`.

Summary

As you can see, there are plenty of opportunities for extended learning and contributing your own expertise to benefit others. As Microsoft adds new features to Microsoft Sentinel, read about the improvements from their blogs and official documentation, then apply the most appropriate changes to your own implementation.

We encourage you to engage and pass on your experience and expertise to others. As we have learned from writing this book, it is only by sharing your knowledge and listening to others' feedback that you will truly master the topic and appreciate how much more there is to learn!

Assessments

Chapter 1

1. It is used to assist with the discovery and mapping of current security solutions, and plan for the future state.
2. The three main components are Azure Monitor, Microsoft Sentinel, and Logic Apps.
3. The main platforms include **Identity and Access Management (IAM)**, **Endpoint Detection and Response (EDR)**, **Cloud Access Security Broker (CASB)**, **Cloud Workload Protection Platform (CWPP)**, and **Next Generation Firewall (NGFW)**.
4. Third-party solution providers include AWS, Cisco, Palo Alto Networks, Fortinet, and Symantec.
5. There are seven steps in the scenario mapping exercise.

Chapter 2

1. The name of the query language is **Kusto Query Language (KQL)**.
2. Azure Lighthouse enables the central management of multiple Azure tenants, usually deployed by managed service providers, but can also be used in complex environments.
3. Some of the ways that data is protected in Log Analytics include Microsoft-managed incident management processes, data retention and deletion policies, per data source type, and data segregation and isolation with geographic sovereignty.
4. Log Analytics workspaces can be created via the web portal, PowerShell, and the command-line interface.
5. Engineers should be provided the roles of Microsoft Sentinel Contributor and Log Analytics Reader.

Chapter 3

1. The seven Vs of big data are volume, velocity, variety, variability, veracity, visualization, and value.

2. The four types of connectors are native, direct, API, and agent-based.

3. The Syslog server acts as a central collector for logs that support Syslog or CEF data types, and forwards data to the SIEM solution.

4. Microsoft Sentinel will store data for 90 days as part of the service. If longer retention is required, a charge will be applied based on the volume of data retained and the length of time it is to be retained for (which can be up to 2 years).

5. Alternative storage options include Azure Data Explorer and Azure Blob storage.

Chapter 4

1. Threat indicators include IP addresses, URLs, and specific files.

2. **ATT&CK** stands for **Adversarial Tactics, Techniques, and Common Knowledge**.

3. The following Microsoft Sentinel components can utilize threat intelligence feeds:

    - Analytics
    - Workbooks
    - Hunting queries
    - Notebooks

4. STIX and TAXII were developed as a community effort, sponsored by the US Department of Homeland Security in partnership with the MITRE Corporation.

Chapter 5

1. You need to filter the StormEvents table by all the states that are set to California (remember the case-sensitive versus non-case-sensitive filters) and then get a count of those rows. You could cheat and look at the output of the first two lines of the code in the following snippet in Azure Data Explorer but that isn't really the best way to get the answer, which is 898:

```
StormEvents
| where State =~ "California"
| summarize count()
```

2. This entails looking at the `StormEvents` table and getting just one instance of each state. Use the `distinct` operator for this:

   ```
   StormEvents
   | distinct State
   ```

3. You will need to look at the `DamageProperty` field in the `StormEvents` table and make sure that the field is greater than 10,000 and less than 15,000:

   ```
   StormEvents
   | where DamageProperty >10000 and DamageProperty <15000
   ```

4. You have three out of the four columns needed in the `StormEvents` table already. The fourth column, the one for the total amount of damage, can be created by adding the `DamageProperty` column and the `DamageCrop` property. In the following answer, it is called `TotalDamage` but it really does not matter what you call it as long as you use the same name in the `extend` and `project` commands. Bonus points if you combined `extend` and `project` into one. While this is perfectly legal in KQL, if you want to use the variable again then `extend` will be needed as `project` just outputs the results:

   ```
   StormEvents
   | extend TotalDamage = DamageCrops + DamageProperty
   | project State, DamageProperty, DamageCrops, TotalDamage
   ```

Chapter 6

1. You can see pre-made queries by using the sample queries and the query explorer.
2. Use the filter icon at the top of the **Result** pane to show specific computes without changing the query.
3. To see a preview of the log entries, go to the **Tables** pane, mouse over the desired log, and click on the eye icon.
4. To change the number of results on a page when viewing all results page, go to the page settings, and change the **Set # of rows per page** dropdown to **200**.
5. To change the number of results on a page when viewing a single results page, go to the results footer and change the **Items per page** dropdown to **200**.

Chapter 7

1. The six different rule types are Scheduled, Fusion, Microsoft Security, Machine Learning Behavior Analytics, Fusion, and Anomaly.
2. To run a rule on a set interval, use the Scheduled rule type.
3. Yes, you can have alerts from other Azure security systems create incidents in Microsoft Sentinel.
4. When creating/editing a scheduled analytic rule, select a playbook from the **Automated response** page's **Alert automation** section.
5. To delete a rule that's no longer required, you can hover your mouse over the rule and select **Delete** from the context menu, or select the rule and click **Delete** in the header.

Chapter 8

1. To create a new workbook, you either use a template or create one from scratch.
2. To show user instructions on how to use the workbook, use the **Text** step type.
3. To change how far back in time a query in a workbook will search, create a time parameter and change all the query steps to use the new parameter.
4. Yes, you can have a workbook step only show when certain conditions are met. Enable **Make this item conditionally visible** in the step's advanced settings and then add a condition.
5. To show two steps side by side, go to each step's advanced settings and under the **Style** tab, enable **Make this item a custom width** and set each step's width to **50%**.

Chapter 9

1. To change the incident's view to show **In Progress** only, go to the **Search and Filtering** section and under the **Status** dropdown, select **In Progress**.
2. An incident's severity can be viewed in two ways: the first way is by looking at the colored strip at the top of the page and the second is by looking at the **Severity** dropdown.
3. In the **Incident Detail** pane, if the **Investigate** button is grayed out, this indicates this incident has no **entities**.

Assessments   443

4. To get the full details of an alert, follow these steps:
5. Find the incident in the incident list.
6. Click on the **View full details** link.
7. In the **Alerts** tab, click on the alert's ID.
8. Look at the incident's detail pane and under the Analytics rule entry will be a link to the analytic rule that created this incident. Click that link to be taken into the analytic rule's configuration.

Chapter 10

1. The three types of entities that can be viewed in Entity behavior are accounts, hosts, and IP addresses.
2. The three types of information that can be presented in the entity's timeline are alerts, bookmarks, and activities.
3. Use the **Timeline** content filter and set it to show only **Activities**.
4. A custom activity can be created in the following ways:

   - Click the **Add activity** link on the **Entity settings** page.
   - Or, select an out-of-the-box template and click on the **Create activity** button in the details pane.

5. The two entity types that can be used to create a custom activity are hosts and account.

Chapter 11

1. To run a single hunting query, select the query, and in the **details** pane click the **Run Query** button.
2. To run all hunting queries, click the **Run all queries** button in the hunting page's header.
3. To view the results of a single hunting query, select the query and in the **details** pane, click the **View query results** link.
4. To create a new bookmark, run the query on the **Logs** page, select the results to add to the bookmark, and then click the **Add bookmark** button.

5. To associate a bookmark with an incident, you can use one of two methods:
   - Create a new incident from a bookmark.
   - Or, add a bookmark to an existing incident.

Chapter 12

1. To use a logic app as an Microsoft Sentinel playbook, it must use the **Microsoft Sentinel connector**.
2. To tell whether a playbook ran successfully, select the playbook from the **Playbooks** page and then look at the **Run History** section.
3. When using a playbook's workflow to get information about an incident, use the **Alert | Get Incident** action and pass in the necessary parameters.
4. Dynamic content is information provided by either a connector or an action that can change for each instance of the playbook – for example, the **System Alert ID** field that was used to get the incident in the *Creating a simple Microsoft Sentinel playbook* section.
5. Yes, you can combine dynamic and static content in one field.

Chapter 14

1. The two roles are SOC engineer and SOC analyst.
2. Both roles need to be involved in carrying out the scenario mapping exercise.
3. The log ingestion rate and pricing tier should be checked at least once per month by the SOC engineer.
4. The SOC analyst should check the **Incidents** page every day.
5. You should look at ingesting logs the first moment the instance is created. This will provide maximum visibility of security events.

Packt.com

Subscribe to our online digital library for full access to over 7,000 books and videos, as well as industry leading tools to help you plan your personal development and advance your career. For more information, please visit our website.

Why subscribe?

- Spend less time learning and more time coding with practical eBooks and Videos from over 4,000 industry professionals

- Improve your learning with Skill Plans built especially for you

- Get a free eBook or video every month

- Fully searchable for easy access to vital information

- Copy and paste, print, and bookmark content

Did you know that Packt offers eBook versions of every book published, with PDF and ePub files available? You can upgrade to the eBook version at packt.com and as a print book customer, you are entitled to a discount on the eBook copy. Get in touch with us at customercare@packtpub.com for more details.

At www.packt.com, you can also read a collection of free technical articles, sign up for a range of free newsletters, and receive exclusive discounts and offers on Packt books and eBooks.

Other Books You May Enjoy

If you enjoyed this book, you may be interested in these other books by Packt:

Microsoft Azure Security Technologies Certification and Beyond

David Okeyode

ISBN: 9781800562653

- Manage users, groups, service principals, and roles effectively in Azure AD
- Explore Azure AD identity security and governance capabilities
- Understand how platform perimeter protection secures Azure workloads
- Implement network security best practices for IaaS and PaaS
- Discover various options to protect against DDoS attacks
- Secure hosts and containers against evolving security threats
- Configure platform governance with cloud-native tools
- Monitor security operations with Azure Security Center and Azure Sentinel

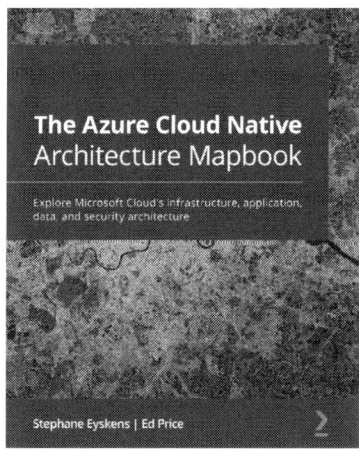

The Azure Cloud Native Architecture Mapbook

Stéphane Eyskens, Ed Price

ISBN: 9781800562325

- Gain overarching architectural knowledge of the Microsoft Azure cloud platform
- Explore the possibilities of building a full Azure solution by considering different architectural perspectives
- Implement best practices for architecting and deploying Azure infrastructure
- Review different patterns for building a distributed application with ecosystem frameworks and solutions
- Get to grips with cloud-native concepts using containerized workloads

Work with AKS (Azure Kubernetes Service) and use it with service mesh technologies to design a microservices hosting platform

Packt is searching for authors like you

If you're interested in becoming an author for Packt, please visit `authors.packtpub.com` and apply today. We have worked with thousands of developers and tech professionals, just like you, to help them share their insight with the global tech community. You can make a general application, apply for a specific hot topic that we are recruiting an author for, or submit your own idea.

Share Your Thoughts

Now you've finished *Microsoft Sentinel in Action*, we'd love to hear your thoughts! Scan the QR code below to go straight to the Amazon review page for this book and share your feedback or leave a review on the site that you purchased it from.

`https://packt.link/r/1801815534`

Your review is important to us and the tech community and will help us make sure we're delivering excellent quality content.

Index

Symbols

.NET 42

A

access control lists (ACLs) 17
Active Directory (AD) 96
Adversarial Tactics, Techniques, and
    Common Knowledge (ATT&CK) 93
agent-based connectors 75
aggregate functions
  reference link 126
aggregation 412
aggregation, features
  empty field value aggregation 412
  time-based aggregation 412
ago( ) function 140
alert definition 92
Alert playbooks 370
alert trigger 284
alternative storage options
  reviewing 88
Amazon Web Services
    (AWS) 13, 17, 74, 224

analytic rules
  creating 197
  creating, from rule template 197
  creating, with wizard 198
  managing 218, 219
analytic rules, types
  about 186
  anomaly 187, 188
  Fusion 187
  machine learning, behavioral
      analytics 187
  Microsoft Security 186, 187
  scheduled 186
Anomali ThreatStream 93
anomaly detection 187
API connections 75
approval-based workflow 436
Artificial Intelligence (AI) 14
Attack Surface Reduction (ASR) 13
automation rule
  about 363, 364
  adding 364-368
Azure Active Directory (Azure AD)
  about 74, 228, 420-422
  reference link 428

450　Index

Azure Active Directory identifier 202
Azure Automation 88
Azure Blob Storage 88
Azure CLI
　reference link 44
Azure Data Explorer (ADX)
　about 21, 23, 72, 88, 118
　cons 23
　pros 23
　reference link 118
Azure Functions 436
Azure Lighthouse 33
Azure Logic Apps
　about 436
　reference link 360
　reference link, for pricing 369
Azure Monitor
　about 23, 32
　cons 23
　pros 23
　reference link 48, 428
Azure Monitor agent
　about 75
　reference link 75
Azure Monitor Logs data security
　reference link 35
Azure Monitor PowerShell samples
　reference link 88
Azure naming best practices
　reference link 36
Azure portal
　used, for creating Log Analytics
　　workspace 37, 38
Azure pricing calculator
　using 86
Azure Resource Management template
　creating 39-41

Azure security alert sources
　integrating, with ServiceNow Security
　　Incident Response via Microsoft
　　Graph Security API 395, 396
Azure Security Center 74
Azure Sentinel
　about 394
　enabling 49-51
　integrating, with ServiceNow 396
　integrating, with ServiceNow ITSM
　　using Azure Sentinel Logic Apps 394
　integrating, with ServiceNow Security
　　Incident Response via API
　　directly to Azure Sentinel 396
　reference link 428
　security solution integrations 15, 16
　ServiceNow Sentinel plugin, configuring
　　to authenticate 404, 405
　service pricing 20-24
Azure Sentinel Agents
　configuration 60, 61
　management 59
Azure Sentinel Analytics 185
Azure Sentinel Analytics, home page
　details pane 191-197
　header bar 189
　navigating through 188
　parts 189
　rule and template listings 189-191
Azure Sentinel Automation
　about 361
　automation rule 363, 364
　header bar 362
　summary bar 363
Azure Sentinel connector
　configuring 77-82
　overview 370-372

Index

Azure Sentinel Entity behavior
  about 298
  enabling 298, 299
Azure Sentinel Hunting page
  about 320
  header bar 321-323
  hunting queries list 323, 324
  query details pane, hunting 324-327
  summary bar 323
Azure Sentinel hunting queries
  analytics rule, creating 330
  livestream, adding 330
  query, adding 328
  query, cloning 329, 330
  query, deleting 330
  query, editing 329
  working with 327
Azure Sentinel Incidents page
  Actions button, using 279, 280
  filtering section 269-271
  header bar 268, 269
  incident details pane 273-279
  incident listing 271, 272
  search section 269-271
  summary bar 269
  using 268
Azure Sentinel integration plugin
  installing, in ServiceNow 404
Azure Sentinel Logic Apps
  used, for integrating Azure Sentinel
    with ServiceNow ITSM 394
Azure Sentinel Logs page 144
Azure Sentinel notebooks
  details pane 344-347
  header bar 342, 343
  list 343, 344
  summary bar 343
  using 342

Azure Sentinel Overview page
  Data source anomalies section 53
  Democratize ML for your
    SecOps section 53
  Events and alerts over time section 53
  exploring 52
  header bar 52
  Potential malicious events section 53
  Recent incidents section 53
  summary bar 53
Azure Sentinel playbook
  about 360
  creating 382-389
Azure Sentinel tools, optional features
  analytics 95
  hunting 95
  notebooks 95
  workbooks 95
Azure Sentinel wiki pages
  reference link 434
Azure virtual machines
  information, obtaining from 54-57

B

big data
  seven Vs 71
billable data
  ingesting 177
blogs, Microsoft
  references 429
bookmarks
  associating, with incident 339-341
  creating 333-335
  viewing 335-338
  working with 332

C

Chart tab 173-175
Chief Information Officer (CIO) 352
Chief Information Security
    Officer (CISO) 352
CLI
  used, for creating Log Analytics
      workspace 43-45
client secret key 402
Cloud Access Security Broker
    (CASB) 6, 70, 421
cloud platform integrations
  about 16
  with Amazon Web Services (AWS) 17
  with Google Cloud Platform (GCP) 17
  with Microsoft Azure 18, 19
cloud security
  architecture requirement 4
Cloud Security Posture Management
    (CSPM) 8, 13
cloud security reference framework 5
  Client Endpoint Management 6
  Cloud Access Security Broker (CASB) 6
  Cloud Workload Protection Platform 8
  Identity and Access Management 6
  Industrial Control Systems (ICSes) 7
  Information Security 8
  Information Technology (IT/OT) 7
  Perimeter Network 6
  Private Cloud Infrastructure 7
  Privileged Access Management (PAM) 8
  Productivity Services 6
  Public Cloud Infrastructure 7
  Security Operations Center (SOC) 5
Common Event Format (CEF) 76

computer groups
  adding, from query 63-65
connectors
  about 73
  reference link 436
connectors, types
  agent based 75
  API connections 75
  direct connections 74
  native connections 74
cost
  calculating, of data ingestion 85-87
  calculating, of retention 85-87
count command 125
Cybersecurity Framework (CSF) 432

D

data
  selecting 70, 71
data source
  connecting 54
data sources, key considerations
  validity 10
  value/veracity 10
  variety 10
  velocity 10
  visualization 11
  volatility 10
  volume 10
  vulnerability 11
Department of Homeland
    Security (DHS) 94
direct connections 74
distinct command 131, 132
Distributed Denial of Service
    (DDoS) attack 18

E

empty field value aggregation 412
Endpoint Detection and
    Response (EDR) 6, 70
End User Behavior Analytics (EUBA) 15
Entity behavior. *See* Azure
    Sentinel Entity behavior
Entity behavior details page
  information, identifying 303, 304
  Insights section 307
  notable events 304, 305
  overview 303
Entity behavior page
  Activities list 309
  Activity configuration 312, 313
  Activity details pane 310
  activity queries, creating 307
  Activity query 313, 314
  Activity templates tab 309
  Activity wizard 315-317
  entities with alerts 302
  General tab 311, 312
  header bar 301, 308
  main screen 300
  new activity, adding 311
  overview 300
  search section 301
  settings page 308
essentials section 375, 376
exploration queries 290
extend command 127-129

F

field
  mapping 407-411
filtering 412

Filter pane 160-163
Flighting mode 188
full details page
  Alerts tab 283, 284
  Bookmarks tab 284
  Comments tab 286
  Entities tab 285, 286
  exploring 281
  Timeline tab 282
Functions pane 159, 160
Fusion
  about 187
  reference link 187

G

Git 433
GitHub
  for Azure Sentinel 433
  for community contribution 434
  using 433
  reference link, for Help 433
  reference link, for Learning Lab 433
Google Cloud Platform (GCP) 17
Grafana 175
graphical user interface (GUI) 237
Greenwich Mean Time (GMT) 152

H

header bar 362, 374, 375

I

Identity and Access Management 6
incident
  Entities button 292, 293
  Help button 293

Info button 292
Insights button 293
investigating 287, 288
   Related alerts actions, showing 288-291
   Timeline button 291
Incident playbooks 370
incident trigger 284
Indicators of Compromise (IoCs) 92
Industrial Control Systems (ICS) 4, 7
Information Security 8
Information Technology/Operational Technology (IT/OT) 7
Infrastructure-as-a-Service (IaaS) 7
Integrated Cyber Defense Exchange (ICDx) 75
intel feeds
   selecting 95
Intellisense 164
Internet of Things (IoT) 4, 77

J

JavaScript Object Notation (JSON) 172, 360
join command 134
Jupyter Notebook 175, 435
Just In Time (JIT) 13

K

KCL documentation
   reference link 434
kill chain 25
KQL code window
   about 164
   advantages 164
   Export 167
   Format query 168
   header 165
   New alert rule 167
   Pin to dashboard 168
   Run 165
   Save 166
   Share link 167
   Time range 166
KQL commands
   about 120
   reference link 122
KQL queries
   running 118-120
Kusto Query Language (KQL) 32, 88, 326, 433, 434

L

let statement 139
livestream
   working with 330-332
Log Analytics
   about 32, 144
   advanced settings 58
   data, managing 35
   reference link, for pricing 36
   storage options, configuring 83-85
Log Analytics workspace
   about 33, 34
   creating, with Azure portal 37, 38
   creating, with CLI 43-45
   creating, with PowerShell 42, 43
   overview page, exploring 46, 47
   planning 36
   using 35
Logic App listing 373
Logic Apps debugging
   reference link 377

Index 455

Logic Apps Designer page
  header bar 380, 381
  using 378-380
  workflow editor section 382
Logic Apps, integration account
  reference link 376
Logic Apps settings page
  about 373, 374
  essentials section 375, 376
  header bar 374, 375
  menu bar 374
  Runs history section 376, 377
logins
  map view 178
Logs page
  Filter pane 160-163
  Functions pane 159, 160
  KGL code window 164
  Learn more section 176
  navigating 144, 145
  page header 145
  Queries pane 159
  results window 168
  Tables pane 155-159

M

machine learning
  behavioral analytics 187
Malware Information Sharing
    Project (MISP)
  about 92, 93
  reference link 92
menu bar 374
Microsoft Azure 18
Microsoft Azure Machine
    Learning (AML) 342

Microsoft Azure portal
  configuring 397-403
Microsoft Defender 74
Microsoft Defender 365 74
Microsoft Docs
  reference link 428
Microsoft Fusion
  machine learning 435
  reference link 435
Microsoft Graph Security API 395
Microsoft Graph Security tiIndicator 95
Microsoft incident rule
  creating 213-217
Microsoft, official resources
  about 428
  feature requests 430
  LinkedIn groups 431
  official documentation 428
  tech community, blogs 428, 429
  tech community, forums 429
Microsoft Premier Support agreement 430
Microsoft Security rules 186, 187
MineMeld TI feed
  Azure Sentinel connector,
      configuring 106-113
  configuring 104
  installing 104
  Microsoft Graph Security API
      extension, installing 105, 106
  VM, building 104
MineMeld TI sharing 93
MITRE ATT&CK® framework
  about 190, 194, 432
  reference link 432
  use cases 432
Mobile Application Management
    (MAM) 6
Mobile Device Management (MDM) 6

N

National Institute of Standards for Technology (NIST) 432
native connections 74
Network Security Groups (NSGs) 74
Next-Generation Firewall (NGFW) 70
notable events, Entity behavior details page
  about 304, 305
  alerts and activities timeline subsection 307
  events and alerts over time subsection 306
  search and filter subsection 306
Notepad 164
Notepad++ 164

O

Office 365 74
Open-Source Intelligence (OSINT) 94

P

page header
  about 145
  feedback 146
  help 154
  queries 146-148
  Query explorer 148-151
  settings 152, 153
Palo Alto Networks MineMeld 93
Pay as You Go (PAYG) 21
penetration testing 423
Perimeter Network 6
Platform-as-a-Service (PaaS) 7, 87
playbook pricing 369

playbooks
  Alert playbooks 370
  creating 377, 378
  Incident playbooks 370
  types 370
playbooks tab
  exploring 372, 373
  Logic App listing 373
Pluralsight
  reference link 434
PowerShell
  about 42
  using, to create Log Analytics workspace 42
print command 122
Private Cloud Infrastructure 7
private infrastructure integrations 20
Privileged Access Management (PAM) 8
Production mode 188
Productivity Services 6
profile configuration
  additional options 414
  aggregation 411
  filtering 411
profiles
  creating, in ServiceNow Sentinel integration plugin 405, 406
  ordering 406, 407
project command 129, 130

Q

quality data management 70
Queries pane 159
query
  computer groups, adding from 63-65
  running 168
  writing 176

Index 457

query statements
  about 139
  let statement 139

R

Really Simple Syndication (RSS) feed 428
related entities 290
render command 136-138
resources, Microsoft
  references 431
results footer 172, 173
results tab 169-172
Results window 168
Results window header 169
role-based access controls (RBACs) 420
rule template
  rule, creating from 197
Runs history section 376

S

scalar functions
  about 140
  ago( ) function 140
scenario mapping
  about 24
  actions, defining by analyst 27, 28
  actions, performing 27
  detection, performing 26
  kill chain stage 25
  methods, defining 24, 25
  purpose, defining 25
  severity and output 27
schedule-based workflow 436
scheduled analytic rules 186
scheduled query rule
  creating 198-212

scheduling 413
search command 122, 123
Security Incident Response 410
Security Information and Event
  Management (SIEM) 186
Security Operations Center (SOC) 5
Security Orchestration and Automated
  Response (SOAR) 5
security risk calculators 410
ServiceNow
  Azure Sentinel integration
    plugin, installing 404
  used, for integrating Azure Sentinel 396
ServiceNow integration 394
ServiceNow Sentinel integration plugin
  configuring, for Azure Sentinel
    authentication 404, 405
  profiles, creating in 405, 406
SIEM solution
  Cloud Access Security Broker
    (CASB) 12, 13
  Cloud Workload Protection
    Platform (CWPP) 13
  Endpoint Detection and
    Response (EDR) 12
  Extended Detection and Response
    platforms (XDR) 12
  Identity and Access
    Management (IAM) 11
  Next-Generation Firewall (NGFW) 13
SigninLogs table 179
SOC analysts 421
SOC analysts, operational tasks
  about 424
  ad hoc tasks 425
  daily tasks 424
  monthly tasks 425
  weekly tasks 424

SOC architecture
    data sources 10, 11
    log management 10, 11
    mapping 10
    mapping summary 14, 15
    operations platforms 11
    threat hunting 14
    threat intelligence 14
SOC duties 420
SOC engineers 420
    ad hoc tasks 423
    monthly tasks 423
    weekly tasks 422
SOC engineers, operational tasks
    about 421
    daily tasks 421, 422
social engineering 423
SOC operations
    resources 432
SOC platform component
    about 8
    Azure Monitor 9
    Azure Sentinel 9
    Logic Apps 9
Software-as-a-Service (SaaS) 7, 87
sort/order command 132-134
STIX standard
    reference link 94
storage options
    about 23
    cons 23
    pros 23
storage workflow 436
string operators
    about 140, 141
    reference link 141
Structured Threat Information
        eXpression (STIX) 93, 94

summarize command 125, 126
summary bar 363
Syslog connector
    reference link 76
Syslog data sources
    reference link 61
Syslog server
    about 76
    with CEF 76, 77

T

Tables pane 155-158
tabular operator
    about 122
    count command 125
    distinct command 131, 132
    extend command 127-129
    join command 134
    print command 122
    project command 129, 130
    render command 136-138
    search command 122, 123
    sort/order command 132-134
    summarize command 125-127
    take/limit command 124
    union command 135, 136
    where command 124
TAXII protocol
    reference link 94
ThreatConnect 93
threat hunting
    data, determining 350, 351
    improving 353
    investigation, executing 352
    monitoring 352
    performing 349
    planning 351

premise, developing 350
responding 352
threat indicators 92
Threat Intelligence (TI) 92, 93
TI connectors
  app, registering in Azure AD 98-104
  data, confirming by Azure
    Sentinel 113-115
  data connector, enabling 96-98
  implementing 96
  MineMeld TI feed, configuring 104
tiIndicator API 93
time-based aggregation 412
Trusted Automated eXchange of Indicator
    Information (TAXII) 93, 94

U

union command 135, 136
Universal Time Coordinated (UTC) 152
Usage table 179
User and Entity Behavior
    Analytics (UEBA) 298

V

virtual machine (VM) 104
Virtual Private Cloud (VPC) 17
VS Code 164

W

Web Application Firewall (WAF) 6
where command 124
Windows Server Update
    Service (WSUS) 58

wizard
  rule, creating with 198
workbook
  advanced editing 237, 238
  creating 230
  creating, from scratch 232, 233
  creating, with template 231
  editing 234-236
  managing 239-241
  walk through 228-230
workbooks page
  detail view 225
  overview 222
  required data types, missing 225, 226
  saved template buttons 226, 227
  template view 224
  workbook header 223
workbook step types
  about 241, 242
  advanced settings 260-263
  group 258, 259
  group tab, adding 259, 260
  link, adding 256, 257
  link/tab 254-256
  metric 247
  parameter 248-250
  parameter, adding 250, 251
  parameter types 252, 253
  preview section 254
  query 243-247
  style 264, 265
  text 242
workspace
  creating 348, 349
  permissions, managing for 47, 48

Printed in Great Britain
by Amazon

85041701R00271